I0131076

Descendants of Johann Jacob Lantz

1721-1789

IMMIGRANT SETTLER OF ALBANY TOWNSHIP, BERKS COUNTY, PENNSYLVANIA

Compiled and Edited by
Raymond C. Lantz

HERITAGE BOOKS
2013

HERITAGE BOOKS
AN IMPRINT OF HERITAGE BOOKS, INC.

Books, CDs, and more—Worldwide

For our listing of thousands of titles see our website
at
www.HeritageBooks.com

Published 2013 by
HERITAGE BOOKS, INC.
Publishing Division
5810 Ruatan Street
Berwyn Heights, Md. 20740

Copyright © 2013 Raymond C. Lantz

Heritage Books by the author:

Descendants of Johann Jacob Lantz, 1721–1789,
Immigrant Settler of Albany Township, Berks County, Pennsylvania

Lantz-Crossley: An Experience in Genealogy

Lantz-Crossley: An Experience in Genealogy, Volume I, A–E, Second Edition

Lantz-Crossley: An Experience in Genealogy, Volume II, F–J, Second Edition

Lantz-Crossley: An Experience in Genealogy, Volume III, K–O, Second Edition

Lantz-Crossley: An Experience in Genealogy, Volume IV, P–Z, Second Edition

Lantz-Crossley: An Experience in Genealogy, Supplement I to Volumes I–IV, Second Edition

Ottawa and Chippewa Indians of Michigan, 1855–1868

Ottawa and Chippewa Indians of Michigan, 1870–1909

Potawatomi Indians of Michigan, 1843–1904
Including Some Ottawa and Chippewa, 1843–1866
and Potawatomi of Indiana, 1869 and 1885

Seminole Indians of Florida: 1850–1874

Seminole Indians of Florida: 1875–1879

All rights reserved. No part of this book may be reproduced or transmitted in any form or by any means, electronic or mechanical, including photocopying, recording or by any information storage and retrieval system without written permission from the author, except for the inclusion of brief quotations in a review.

International Standard Book Numbers
Paperbound: 978-0-7884-5490-5
Clothbound: 978-0-7884-6864-3

Dedication

This book is dedicated to my loving and patient wife, Dianna, who has endured the more than twenty nine years of research necessary to make this version of this book a reality and to my son, Nelson, with the hope that he may someday continue this work when I am unable to pursue it any longer. To my new granddaughter, Jocelyn, born on her grandfather's birthday, with the hope she will someday be the motivation for her father to continue my lifelong efforts.

JOCELYN ROSE LANTZ

Acknowledgment

I wish to extend my thanks and eternal gratitude to all the fellow researchers and cousins who willingly shared and exchanged information throughout the many years regarding our common ancestors. A special thanks to John Charles and Sarah Mae (Huss) Lantz, of Lincolnton, NC, for his Y-DNA testing participation and her significant data content contributions resulting from her Lantz family research. Without our mutual efforts and convictions this work would never have transpired to the level it has. I look forward to much more progress in the years to come.

Table of Contents

This book is the result of the author's twenty seven years of research of the ancestry of Raymond Clyde Lantz. Should any descendants who read this book have any additional information, corrections, photographs, etc. that the author may use to include in future reprinted versions of this book, any such items or information may be sent to the author at 8939 Abbington Drive, Pensacola, FL 32534-5347. It is the author's intention to compile additional revisions to this book if and when sufficient additional information can be accumulated to warrant the printing of such a revision.

All information contained in this book has been kept as accurate as humanly possible. Due to the sometimes conflicting information often contained in various sources the author has utilized his judgment in use of the data which is believed by him to be the most correct. The dates of birth in some cases throughout the book were based on the age of individuals as they are listed in a census or their age as given at the time of their death or that of a baptismal date and in the case of some death dates a burial date was used. No attempt has been made to identify which dates are calculated and which dates are not or those that are baptismal. In such cases the author did not believe it would have a significant effect on the accuracy of the information as presented.

The book is broken down into chapters comprised of the immigrant and one each for the immigrants known children and their descendants. Each direct descendant is given a unique identifier based upon their descent from a child of the immigrant. Each child of the immigrant has been assigned a letter, their children a number 0 through 9 and a letter A through Z if more than 9 children. A number or letter as applicable is added to the parent's identified for each new generation.

In most cases a listing of reference numbers is given at the end of each family section pertaining to that descendant's family information. These reference numbers correspond to the references found listed in the reference section of this book. The author has included wherever possible the copies of wills, other estate records, land records and photographs. These documents and/or photographs that will follow immediately after the family section they apply to, if applicable will also include any record transcriptions.

CHAPTER I

I JOHANN JACOB LANTZ

JOHANN JACOB LANTZ was born in 1721 in Germany and died on 16 Dec 1789 in Albany Twp., Berks Co., PA. He married ANNA, maiden name is yet unknown. She was born in 1720 in Germany and died before 1763 in Albany Twp., Berks Co., PA. It is not certain if he married in Germany or sometime after having immigrated to Philadelphia aboard the ship "Snow Betsey" on 27 Aug 1739. He appears in the tax list 1767–1768 and 1779–1785 in Albany Twp., Berks Co., PA. He left a will dated 16 Jun 1789 in Albany Twp., Berks Co., PA and was probated on 07 Dec 1789 in Berks Co., PA.

"It was on the Snow Betsy, that Jacob Lantz came to this country, landing in Philadelphia, PA on August 27, 1739. He settled in Albany Twp., Berks Co., PA where he bought 150 acres of land. Later he bought an adjoining 100 acres. His will probated in 1789 mentions the oldest son JACOB, and two other sons, GEORGE (who received the large family Bible) and HENRY; and two daughters, SUSANNA and MAGDALINA."

"By the mid-1700's, the Colony of Pennsylvania was the most populous of the thirteen English colonies in America. Settled mostly by Germans, expansion within the colony spread from east to west like a gigantic wave, until most of the land between the Atlantic Ocean and the formidable Allegheny Mountains was bought up. The land that was left was exorbitantly priced. The settlers then turned their attention southward where land was plentiful and the climate was warm."

"The route these settlers followed to the Southern colonies was called the Great Philadelphia Wagon Road. It began in York, just west of Philadelphia and crossed the colony through Gettysburg, where it veered south, across the tip of Maryland and the Potomac River. Here, it entered western Virginia, following the valleys of the Shenandoah, through Winchester and Roanoke. Across the Dan River and into the foothills, the Wagon Road entered NC just above present-day Winston-Salem, where the Moravians had established the villages of Bethabara and Salem."

"In this area, the ancestors of most NC Germans made their homes. But some continued farther south, following the Yadkin and Catawba Rivers, into the foothills of the Blue Ridge Mountains."

"The German migration to the "back country" of NC was no trickle. In fact, in 1766, Governor Dobbs wrote of the influx, "I am of opinion that the province is settling faster than any on the continent, last autumn and winter, upwards of one thousand wagons passed through Salisbury with families from the northward, to settle in this province chiefly."

"Another writer stated in 1768, "There is scarce any history, either ancient of modern, which affords an account of such a rapid and sudden increase of inhabitants in a back frontier country as that of NC." One historian has noted that the estimated German population in the south-central counties in 1771 was nearly 15,000."

"...JOHANN GEORGE LANTZ, son of pioneer JACOB LANTZ, and his family were among the thousands of settlers that flooded into the foothills of NC, following the Great Wagon Road from Pennsylvania south, where promises of land and freedom awaited these hardy Europeans. HANS GEORGE, son of JACOB, emigrates to Lincoln Co., NC..."

"JACOB LANTZ came to America with his brother CONRAD, who was only a young boy then, aboard the 'Snow Betsy'. They landed in Philadelphia, Aug. 27, 1739. CONRAD settled in North Whitehall Twp., in what is now Lehigh Co., PA. CONRAD spelled his name LENTZ and became known as a farmer and stone mason near Unionville. He was buried in the old church graveyard there. (History of Lehigh Co., PA. pgs. 811-812)

"JACOB LANTZ settled in Albany Twp., near the Greenwich Twp., line. His first land was on a warrant issued by the state on 23 Feb. 1744 for 115 acres 93 perches. The state survey of 15 Aug. 1806 shows this land had neighbors HENRY FREY, PETER WAGEMAN, JOHN PRICKER, and MICHAEL ONANGST. Later Jacob filed another land Warrant application No. 3299 dated 16 May 1768 for 136 3/4 acres. Part of this land was in Albany Twp., and part was in Greenwich Twp. Neighbors of this land were FRANCIS ARNOLD, GEORGE HERRING, and GEORGE OLT. (Warrant Surveys, State of PA, PA State Archives)"

"According to JACOB's will, he names five children...The will states that Jacob is the name of the oldest son. The birth date for JOHANN GEORGE 21 Aug.1751. HENRY is the third son and was executor of the will. There were two daughters, SUSANNA and MAGDALENA...copy of the will...also in the Courthouse of Reading, Pa. He wrote his will 16 June 1789. It was witnessed by CARL UHL and MICHAEL IHRIG who were both active in the Bethel Evangelical Church of Greenwich Twp. JACOB and his family were active in this church during the period of 1775-1795."

"No mention of a wife is made in the will of JACOB. Since it was written in 1789, his wife must have been dead. Her name was ANNA because ANNA and JACOB were listed as sponsors in the baptisms of grandchildren in 1776 and 1782."

"In the inventory of his estate on 12 Dec 1789, the sum of 547 pounds was entered. On this inventory persons mentioned as owing on notes were: JACOB LANTZ Jr., HENRY LANTZ, GEORGE LANTZ, (all three of these are sons), NICKOLAS MEYER, GEORGE HERRING, PETER HAYMAN, and ADAM DIETRICH. (Inventory of Estate of JACOB LANTZ on file in Reading Pa. Courthouse)"

"In the accounting statement filed by Henry Lantz, executor of the estate, on Oct 1796, the following names appear. HENRY VANDERSLICE, MICHAEL CROLL, MICHAEL IHRIG, BENEDICT NIEDLINGER, WILLIAM LEIBY, MAGDALENA HALL, CHARLES UHL, HENRY FREY, Rev. PARSON HERTZEL and, NICKOLAS MEYER. (Inventory of Estate...)"

Also, from the inventory, the year 1782 was a time when Jacob Sr. loaned each of his sons money. Maybe this was the time at which he turned the farm over to Jacob, Jr.

At the present time sic (2001), I cannot find any references to Jacob and Anna for the years 1739-1744. I don't know when they were married or where they went to church. Jacob appeared to be a deeply religious man. Where he lived during those years and where he went to church are mysteries. Most references say the children were born near New Tripoli which is now in Lehigh Co.

"JACOB LANTZ, the founder of the LANTZ family of Albany Twp., Berks Co., Penna., was born in Germany. He came to the United States in 1739, landed in Philadelphia and settled in Albany Twp., where he bought 150 acres of land. Later, he bought an adjoining 100 acres. He will probated in 1789 mentions the oldest son, JACOB, and two other sons, GEORGE, (who received the large family Bible), and HENRY, and two daughters, SUSANNA, married BURNT KROMER, and MAGDALINA. Miss WILLIE AUGUSTA LANTZ, of Catawba College, N. Car., has an old prayer book on the fly leaf of which is written in German?

Johann Jacob Lantz
of the Weyler, Year 1739.

This prayer book was probably a farewell present to JACOB LANTZ when he started upon his trip to the new world."

Some known land transactions were:

23 Feb 1744 – warrant #78 100 acres Albany Twp., Philadelphia (now Berks) Co., PA

16 May 1768 – application #3299 136 acres Albany & Greenwich Twps., Berks Co., PA

15 Aug 1806 – survey D53-97 136 acres Albany & Greenwich Twps., Berks Co., PA

24 Nov 1873 – survey D63-268 115 acres Albany Twp., Berks Co., PA

24 Nov 1873 – survey C128-229 55 acres Maxatawny Twp., Berks Co., PA

22 Oct 1946 – survey D-98-58 113 acres Albany & Greenwich Twps., Berks Co., PA

Children of JOHANN JACOB LANTZ and ANNA are:

1. JOHANN JACOB LANTZ (A)
2. SUSANNA CATHARINA LANTZ (B)
3. HENRY LANTZ (C)
4. JOHANN GEORGE LANTZ (D)
5. MAGDALENA LANTZ (E)

References: 5, 19, 37, 6-Sarah Mae (Huss) Lantz, 6-Bill Lantz, 6- Elein Lantz Whitehead

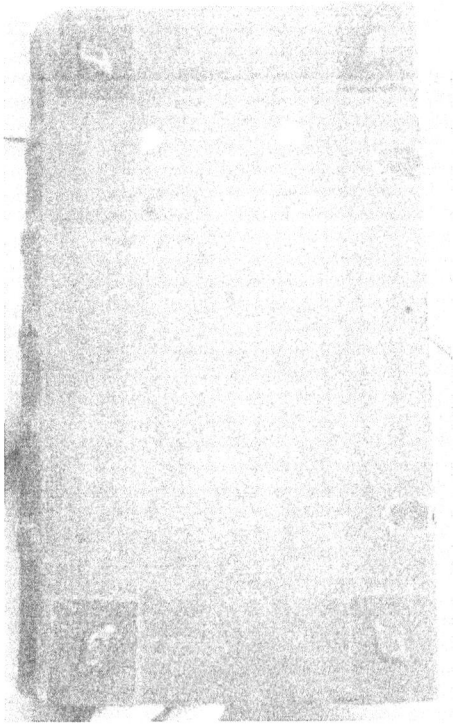

JOHANN JACOB LANTZ Bible

JOHANN JACOB LANTZ Prayer Book Flyleaf

16 May 1768
Jacob Lantz
Alb.

Jacob Lantz, 40 Acres adjoining Land of George Arnold and George
May 16. 1768. Herring, Albany Township, Berks Conty

Jacob Lantz

EAST SIDE APPLICATIONS

DATE	NO.	APPLICANT	ACRES	COPIED SURVEY WHERE COPIED	DESCRIPTION	SURVEY CALLS FOR
1768						
May 13th	3298	John Clauser Retd & May 16th 1870 to Jacob Schaffer etal. on WI to accept	300	C221	153 joing Fette Powell & Jacob Hoffman over the first blue Mountain Berks County	Brunswick Schuylkill
16th	3299	Jacob Lantz 62.145.68 Pat. Mar. 4. 1947 to Calvin George Bachman H-80-38	40	D 53	97 joing George Arnold & George Herring in Albany Tp. Berks Coty	Greenwich Berks

Pennsylvania, ss

By the Proprietaries.

WHEREAS [illegible] of the County of [illegible] hath requested that we would grant [illegible] to take up [illegible] Acres of Land [illegible]

[illegible] in the [illegible] County of [illegible] for which [illegible] agrees to pay to our Use [illegible] Hundred Acres *Fifteen Pounds Ten Shillings*, current Money of this Province, for [illegible] and the yearly Quit-Rent of *One Halfpenny Sterling* for every Acre thereof.

These are therefore to authorize and require you to survey or cause to be survey'd unto the said [illegible] at the Place aforesaid, according to the Method of Townships appointed, the said Quantity of [illegible] Acres, if not already survey'd, and make Return thereof into the Secretaries Office, in Order for further Confirmation, for which this shall be your sufficient Warrant; which Survey, in Case the said [illegible] fulfil the above Agreement within [illegible] Months from the Date hereof, shall be valid, otherwise void. GIVEN under my Hand and Seal of the Land-Office, by Virtue of certain Powers from the said Proprietaries, at *Philadelphia*, this [illegible] Day of [illegible] *Anno Dom.* 174[illegible]

[illegible]

To *William Parsons*, Surveyor General.

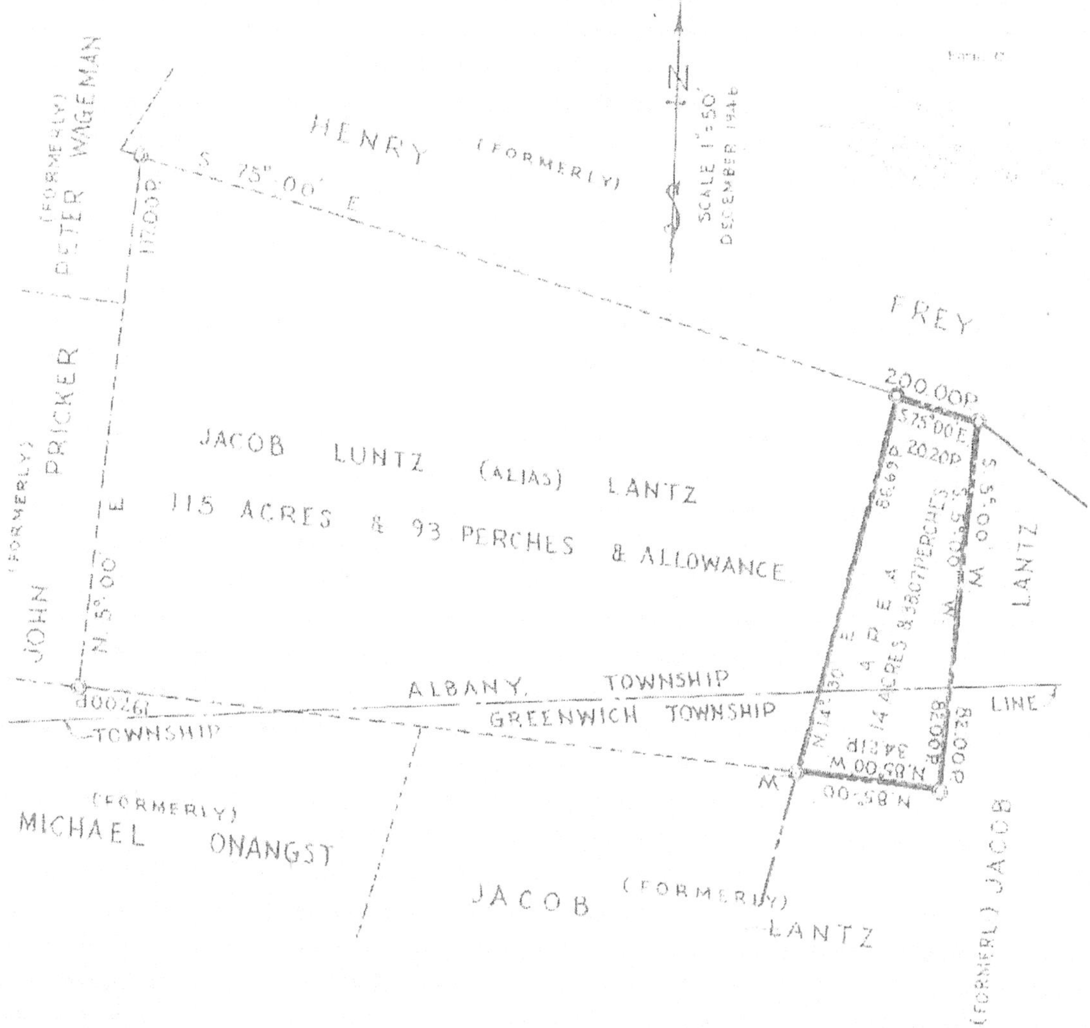

A DRAFT of a tract of land situate partly in the Township of Albany and partly in the Township of Greenwich and County of Berks, containing fourteen acres thirty-eight and seven one-hundredths perches strict measure ~~and allowance of six per cent, for roads, etc.~~ Surveyed for William Michael the Twenty-second day of October 1946 it being part of a larger tract containing one hundred fifteen acres, and ninety-three perches and allowance, originally surveyed in pursuance of a warrant granted to Jacob Luntz alias Lantz dated the twenty-third day of February, 1744.

EARLE M. FRANKHOUSER, Registered Professional Engineer, Reading, Penna.

To Hon. William S. Livengood Jr.
Secretary of Internal Affairs.

Engineer SEAL or Surveyor

Lawson G. Dietrich
County Surveyor

Approved by:

NOTE. When this form is used the County Surveyor should indicate by dotted lines the remainder of the original survey in order to show the location of the part returned and its relation to the whole tract.

übrigen Vermögen [illegible] meine gemelte [illegible]

[illegible] magdalena [illegible]

[illegible] meiner ältesten Tochter [illegible]

[illegible] von meinem Vermögen [illegible]

[illegible]

[illegible]

[illegible]

[illegible] meine gemelte Tochter [illegible]

[illegible]

[illegible] meine gemelte Tochter [illegible]

[illegible]

[illegible]

[illegible] meine Tochter [illegible]

[illegible]

[illegible]

[illegible]

[illegible]

[illegible]

[illegible] Testament [illegible]

[illegible] Testament [illegible]

[illegible]

[illegible]

[illegible]

Carl [illegible]

Michel [illegible]

Jacob [illegible]

Reading in the County of Berks the [illegible] Day of [illegible] Anno Domini [illegible] Then personally affirmed Carl Wohl and Michael Stirech the subscribers to the within writing as [illegible] thereof [illegible] and upon their solemn affirmation according to Law respectively did declare and say that they were present and saw and heard [illegible] the Testator therein named [illegible] pronounce, publish and declare the same writing to be his last Will and Testament and that at the time of doing thereof he the said Testator was of sound mind memory and understanding as they verily believe, And further that they [illegible] Carl Wohl and Michael Stirech [illegible] subscribed [illegible] proper hand writing of the said affirmants [illegible] their names [illegible] in the presence of each other at the request and in the presence of the said Testator —

Coram me

[illegible] Register

Translation

In the Name of the Holy Trinity God the Father, Son and Holy Ghost Amen. I Jacob Lantz the Elder of Albany Township Berks County and State of Pennsylvania, being now old, though not by [illegible] Memory and Understanding God be thanked, I thank my most Holy Creator and Keeper of all things in Jesus Christ through the Assistance of the Holy Ghost for the [illegible] of the Frailty of my Body, well knowing that it is appointed all People once to dye to make and ordain this my last Will and Testament that is to say Principally and first of all I give and recommend my Soul in the Hands of the Almighty who gave it, and my Body I recommend to be Buried in the earth in a Christianlike and decent Burial, not doubting I shall receive the same again at the general resurrection through the mighty Power of God [illegible] touching my Worldly Estate wherewith it hath pleased God to bless me with in this life I give and bequeath the same in following manner and form, viz. Whereas for some years since I have given and sold my Plantation in the aforesaid Township and County unto my Eldest Son Jacob Lantz upon which a Conveyance in regard of the afore mentioned Plantation the Bills and Payments which he has already received that he have his Inheritance in full for himself and his Heirs therefore my said Son Jacob nor his Heirs shall have or make no claim whatever of or to my other Estate. My Son George shall have my large Bible [illegible] to him and his Heirs. Then he shall with my Sons Henry, Stephanus and Magdalena distribute my remaining Effects among them, my Executor my son Henry Lantz shall be the my Executor of this my last Will and Testament [illegible] it with my Remaining Effects to wit that my Effects be distributed in equal shares amongst my said Children Henry, George, Stephanus & Magdalena one like the other, further I order that my Eldest Daughter Stephanus's Inheritance, which comes to her of my Estate shall not be given to her Husband Bernt [illegible] and

she

she shall have nothing thereof in Hand, unless it be that Bernt Ruemer should dye before my Daughter then she shall have full right to receive her Inheritance but should it happen that my said Daughter Susanna should dye then her Children shall have full right to receive her Inheritance and distribute it amongst them in equal Shares & I ordain and make my Son Henry Lentz as Executor & guardian of the my said Daughter her Children and Estate to look my Daughters Share out Honestly, and after the said Bernt Ruemer's Death my Daughter Susanna shall have full right to receive her Inheritance &c. but should she dye before her Husband then her Children shall have a right to receive the said Inheritance and distribute it in equal Shares. Lastly I nominate my Son Henry Lentz the only Executor or Guardian of this my last Will and Testament and so hereby declare Null and Void and make all Testaments Wills or Legacies by me hitherto made I also confirm this and no other to be my Last Will whereof I have hereunto set my Hand and Seal in the year of our Lord one thousand seven hundred and eighty nine the 11th June

Jacob Lentz (Seal)

Test

Michael King

Translation Will
Jacob Lentz

A True & Perfect Inventory of All & Singular the Goods & Chattels Rights & Credits which were of Jacob Lenty Late of Albany Township County of Berks & Commonwealth of Pensylvania Deceased, Appraised the 12th Day of December 1789 by us the Subscribers to wit

	£	s	d
To His wearing Apparel	6	13	3
To his Bed & Bedding	5	1	"
To his Linning & Sundery House hold Goods	3	6	"
A Bond from Jacob Lenty Due 27 May 1782	20	"	"
Interest Due	9	1	"
One Ditto from Jacob Lenty Due 27 May 1783	20	"	"
Interest	7	17	"
One Ditto from Jacob Lenty Due 27 May 1784	10	"	10
Interest	3	6	6
One Ditto from Jacob Lenty Due 27 May 1785	20	"	"
Interest	5	9	"
One Ditto from Jacob Lenty Due 27 May 1786	20	"	"
Interest	4	5	"
One Ditto from Jacob Lenty Due 27 May 1787	20	"	"
Interest	3	1	"
One Ditto from Jacob Lenty Due 27 May 1788	20	"	"
Interest	1	17	"
One Ditto from Jacob Lenty Due 27 May 1789	20	"	"
Interest	"	13	"
One Ditto from Jacob Lenty Pabl 27 May 1790	20	"	"
One Ditto from Jacob Lenty Pabl 27 May 1791	20	"	"
One Ditto from Jacob Lenty Pabl 27 May 1792	20	"	"
One Ditto from Jacob Lenty Pabl 27 May 1793	20	"	"
One Ditto from Jacob Lenty Pabl 27 May 1794	20	"	"
	£303	9	7

	£	s	d
One Note from Jacob Lanif [illegible] 27 Day November 1782	4	12	"
Interest	1	17	9
One Ditto from Henry Lanif [illegible] 27 November 1782	30	15	"
Interest	12	13	6
One Ditto from Leonhard [illegible] 27 Novr 1782	23	14	"
Interest	9	15	1
One Ditto from George Lanif [illegible] 27 Novr 1782	17	16	9
Interest	7	10	2
One Ditto from Michael Mayer [illegible] 26 March 1787 [illegible] with Interest	2	1	1
One Ditto from Michael Mayer [illegible] 26 March 1787	9	"	"
Interest	1	8	8
One Ditto from Georg [illegible] 27 Novr 1788	2	15	"
Interest	"	2	8
Peter Hagman to a Book Debt	5	6	"
One Bond from Adam Detrich [illegible] 27 May 1790	10	"	"
One Ditto from Adam Detrich [illegible] 27 May 1791	10	"	"
One Ditto from Adam Detrich [illegible] 27 May 1792	10	"	"
One Ditto from Adam Detrich [illegible] 27 May 1793	10	"	"
One Ditto from Adam Detrich [illegible] 27 May 1794	10	"	"
One Ditto from Adam Detrich [illegible] 27 May 1795	10	"	"
One Ditto from Adam Detrich [illegible] 27 May 1796	10	"	"
One Half from Adam Detrich [illegible] 27 May 1797	1	2	6
To Cash — Cash	40	4	9
	£232	4	10½

We the Subscribers [illegible] appraised the [illegible] [illegible] to the amount of [illegible] [illegible] [illegible] Shillings [illegible] [illegible] Half penny [illegible] [illegible] [illegible] Ditto [illegible]

[illegible]

Michael [illegible]

[illegible]

[illegible]	347	6	6	1764	[illegible]		
[illegible]	26	15	–		[illegible]		
					[illegible]	1	5 7
					[illegible]	–	10 –
					[illegible]	–	15 –
					[illegible]	–	7 6
					[illegible]	–	15 –
					[illegible]	–	5 –
					[illegible]	–	13 2
					[illegible]	–	11 9
					[illegible]	1	2 6
					[illegible]	–	10 –
					[illegible]	–	11 3
					[illegible]	–	5 –
					[illegible]	–	15 –
					[illegible]	–	9 –
					[illegible]	–	11 3
					[illegible]	–	16 9
						10	9 1
					[illegible]	24	6 7½
					[illegible]	536	7 4½

FORM No. 1. 229

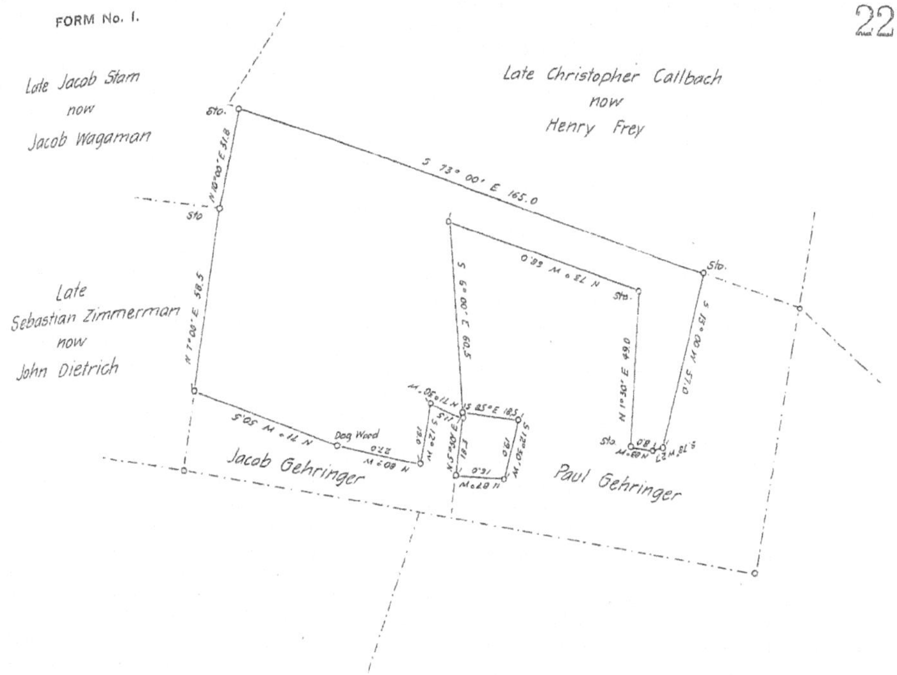

Draft of a tract of land situate in the Township of Albany in the County of Berks, containing Fifty five acres One hundred and eight perches and the allowance of six per. cent. for roads, &c. surveyed for Augustus Gehringer and John Deitrich the twelfth day of November 1873 being part of a large tract of One hundred and fifteen acres Ninety three perches and allowance originally surveyed in pursuance of a Warrant granted to Jacob Lantz dated the 23rd day of February 1744.

Daniel S. Zacharias
County Surveyor

To Hon Robert B. Beath
Surveyor General

IN TESTIMONY that the above is a copy of the original remaining on file in the Department of Internal Affairs of Pennsylvania, made conformably to an Act of Assembly approved the 16th day of February, 1833, I have hereunto set my Hand and caused the Seal of said Department to be affixed at Harrisburg, this fifteenth day of November 1905

Secretary of Internal Affairs.

FORM No. 1.

Situate in Albany Township Berks County Cont g. A^s 115:93^p & the allowance of six ℔ Cent &c^a. Resurveyed the 15. August 1806 to Jacob Luntz by virtue of a warrant dated the 23^d February 1744.

To Samuel Cochran Esqr. Surveyor General.

Henry M. Richards D.S.

IN TESTIMONY that the above is a copy of the original remaining on file in the Department of Internal Affairs of Pennsylvania, made conformably to an Act of Assembly approved the 16th day of February, 1833, I have hereunto set my Hand and caused the Seal of said Department to be affixed at Harrisburg, this Seventh day of April 1909.

Henry Houck

Secretary of Internal Affairs.

FORM No 1.

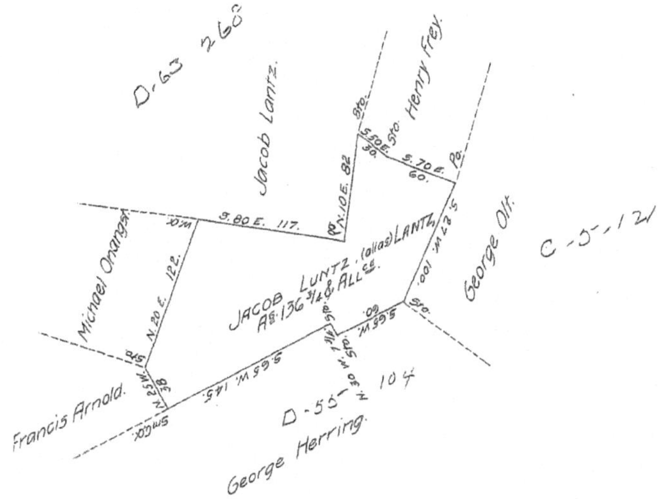

Situate in Albany & Greenwich Township, Berks County, Containing As. 136 3/4 & the allowance of six ⅌ Cent &ca. Resurveyed the 15 August, 1806, to Jacob Luntz by Virtue of an Application No. 3299, dated 16th May, 1768.

Henry M. Richards, D.S.

To Samuel Cochran, Esqr., Surveyor General.

IN TESTIMONY that the above is a copy of the original remaining on file in the Department of Internal Affairs of Pennsylvania, made conformably to an Act of Assembly approved the 16th day of February, 1833, I have hereunto set my Hand and caused the Seal of said Department to be affixed at Harrisburg, this twenty-seventh *day of* May *1908.*

Henry Houck

Secretary of Internal Affairs.

CHAPTER II

A JOHN JACOB LANTZ I

JOHN JACOB LANTZ, Jr. was born 1744 in Albany Twp., Berks Co., PA and died after 1800 in Albany Twp., Berks Co., PA. He married MAGDALENA in Berks Co., PA. She died after 1800 in Albany Twp., Berks Co., PA. Berks Co., PA wills do not list a will for either and it is assumed they both died intestate without a will.

"We find JACOB, Jr. and his wife MAGDALENA's name associated with Friedens White Church at Sony Run, REV. DANIEL SCHUMAKER's Baptism Records, and Bethel Zion Lutheran and Reformed Church of Greenwich Twp., Berks Co., Pa...between the years 1761 and 1795. From baptism records of Friedens White Church...SUSANNA born 19 Aug. 1775 baptized 10 Sept. 1775; ANNA MARIA born 7 Sept. 1777 baptized 12 Oct. 1777; MARGARETHA born 18 May 1782 baptized 30 July 1782. The last baptism was recorded at Bethel Zion Church of Greenwich Twp."

According to the *Lantz Family Record* by J. W. LANTZ says that JACOB Jr. "went south and settled in Maryland." At first glance this seems to be confirmed by the 1790 census for Washington Co., MD listing a JACOB LANTZ enumerated 1 male 16 & up, 4 males to 16 and 3 females. This book only lists three of JACOB Jr's children consisting of 3 sons. Based on the 1790 census it appears he had an additional son and at least 2 daughters or 3 if his wife was deceased by 1790. However, this has been disproven through FTDNA Y-DNA test results of member BRAD LANTZ number 26063.

In addition the author has found many claims that those of the name LANTZ found in Jefferson Co., PA in the 1800s are also descendants of JOHN JACOB LANTZ, Jr. However, these claims have also been disproven through FTDNA Y-DNA test results of member EDWARD PAUL LANTZ number 10746.

Y-DNA testing for proof of descent of JOHN JACOB LANTZ, Sr., the immigrant, can be found at the FTDNA LENTZ Surname DNA Project (Includes: Lentz Lance Lantz Lenz Lents etc.) http://freepages.genealogy.rootsweb.ancestry.com/~gbonner/lentzdna/ Comparisons should be made to the author descendant C1256111 RAYMOND CLYDE LANTZ number 68362 and descendant D38454 JOHN CHARLES LANTZ number 22930.

Based on the previously stated evidence and existing census information it is highly unlikely that JOHN JACOB LANTZ, Jr. moved to MD after the death of his father as the *Lantz Family Record* by J. W. LANTZ claims. The census information also disputes that there were three sons and confirms there were in fact only three daughters.

After the death of his father and according to his father's wishes as stated in his will. JOHN JACOB LANTZ, Jr. and family took physical possession of the Albany Twp. property. This property remained in his family's possession until his and his wife's death. Search of the Warrant, Patent and Deed records for Berks Co., PA indicate that neither, JOHN JACOB LANTZ, Jr. or his father, was ever patented the Albany Twp. land which the father originally obtained through applications and warrants. All the land is later found patented by others reflected by PA Patent and Survey Records.

The 1790 Federal Census for Albany Twp., Berks Co., PA, enumerated a JACOB BANZ with 1 male 16 & up and 4 females. This confirms that his family consisted of him, his wife and three daughters. In the 1793 Septennial Census lists a JACOB LANTZ in Albany Twp., Berks Co., PA. He next appears in the 1798 US Direct Tax List as JACOB LONTZ and the 1800 Septennial Census as JACOB LANTZ. Finally the 1800 Federal Census for Albany Twp., Berks Co., PA, enumerated as JACOB LANTZ with 1 male 45 & up, 1 female 10-16 and 1 female 45 & up., indicating two of the daughters had either died or married. No one of the name LANTZ can be found in Albany Twp., Berks Co., PA after 1800.

To date the author has been unable to positively locate marriage records for any of the three known daughters. In addition likewise no credible evidence has surfaced to identify the maiden name of JACOB's wife MAGDALENA. There are many researchers that have confused this JACOB LANTZ with the well documented Amish Mennonite JACOB LANTZ who did marry a MAGDALENA KURTZ was the son of JOHANNES LANTZ, another immigrant of Berks Co., PA. I think it is more than safe to assume that JACOB LANTZ, Jr.'s, wife was not a KURTZ unless credible evidence can be found to support that claim. The Amish Mennonites do not believe in baptism at birth for their children.

Children of JOHN LANTZ and MARIA KURTZ are:

1. SUSANNA LANTZ, born on 19 Aug 1775 in Albany Twp., Berks Co., PA.
2. ANNA MARIA LANTZ, born 07 Sep 1777 in Albany Twp., Berks Co., PA.
3. MARGARETHA LANTZ, born 18 May 1782 in Albany Twp., Berks Co., PA.

References: 5, 6-Sarah Mae (Huss) Lantz, 6-Bill Lantz, 6-Edward Paul Lantz, 38-Albany Twp Berks Co PA, 20-Albany Twp Berks Co PA, 6-Brad Lantz, 39--Albany Twp Berks Co PA, 37, 19

1

Names of Heads of Families	Free White Males of 16 Years and upwards including Heads of Families	Free White Males under Sixteen Years	Free White Females including Heads of Families	All other Free Persons	Slaves
Albany				270	
Geo Poh	2	1	4		
Geo Stump	2	1	4		
Jno Engelhaupt	1	—	3		
Henry Klick	1	—	3		
Jacob Keller	1	2	2		
John Greenewalt	1	2	5		
Danl Klick	1	4	2		
Peter Klick	1	1	2		
John Folk	1	—	2		
Ferdinand High	1	1	1		
Phil Beckindorn	1	—	1		
Thos Mason	2	3	2		
Danl Boutcher	4	—	3		
Adam Kiehl	2	3	1		
John Shoeman	1	4	1		
Peter Broucher	1	—	—		
Jacob Younrich	1	—	1		
Jacob Shoemaker	1	—	4		
Jacob Stapleton	2	—	3		
Saml [illegible]man	2	2	3		
Christn Henry	1	—	1		
Jno Henry	1	3	4		
Jno Berk	1	1	6		
Jno Reinhart	1	—	1		
Jno Smith	1	—	3		
Joseph Steinberger	1	3	3		
Fredk Leiby	1	—	2		
Nichs Leiby	2	—	3		
Jacob Bang	1	—	4		
Card Over	39	31	74		

1790 Federal Census

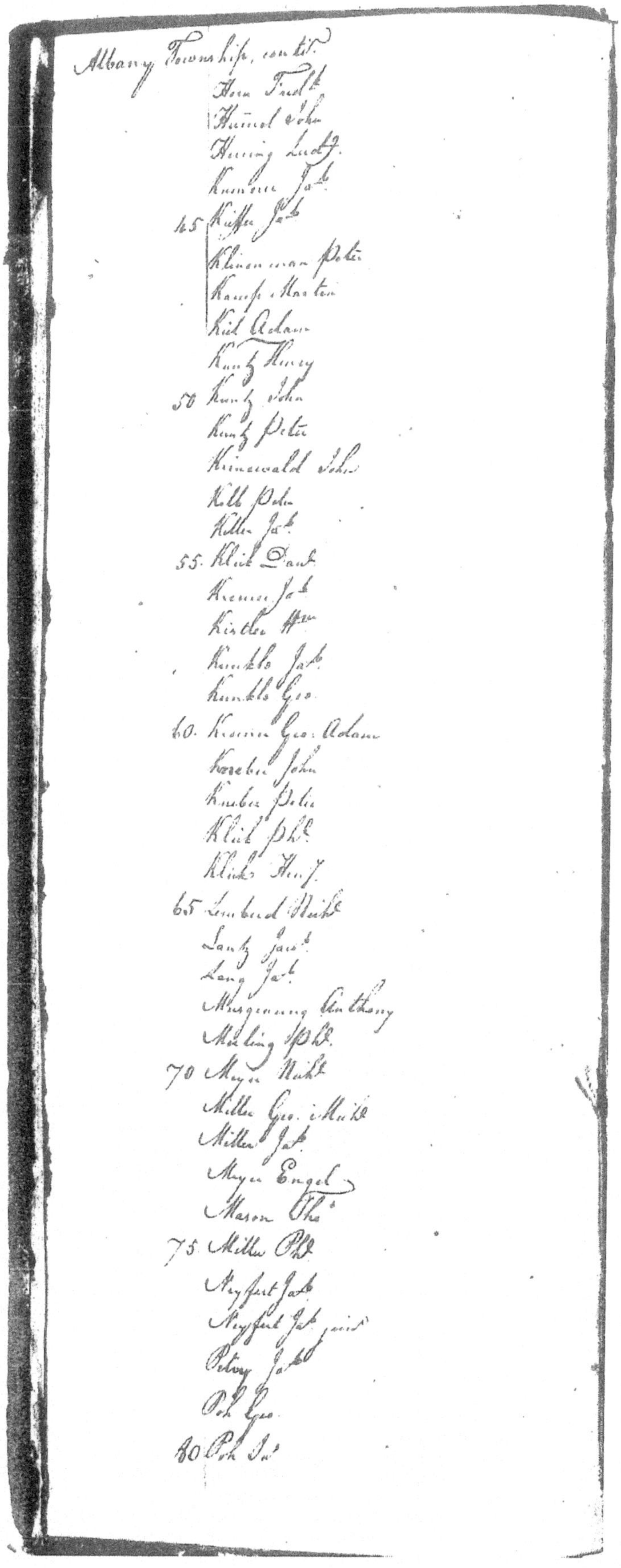
Albany Township, contd.
Horn Fredk.
Hummel John
Henning Ludwig
Kummerer Jacob
45 Kiefer Jacob
Klineman Peter
Kampf Martin
Kiel Adam
Kuntz Henry
50 Kuntz John
Kuntz Peter
Kinewald John
Kell Peter
Keller Jacob
55. Klick Danl.
Kremer Jacob
Kistler Wm.
Kunkle Jacob
Kunkle Geo.
60. Kessner Geo. Adam
Korsber John
Kreber Peter
Klick Phil.
Klicks Henry
65 Lambert Michl.
Lantz Jacob
Lang Jacob
Mergenning Anthony
Mosling Phil.
70 Meyer Michl.
Miller Geo. Michl.
Miller Jacob
Meyer Engel
Mason Thos.
75 Miller Phil.
Neyfert Jacob
Neyfert Jacob junr.
Petrey Jacob
Pok Geo.
80 Pok Jno.

1793 Septennial Census

Albany Township

	Occupants	Owners	Value of Land, Dwelling Houses, &c.	Rate of Assessment in Cents	Assessment D.	Cts.	Mills
46		Hall John	2000	do	3	80	—
47		Herbster Frederick	800	—	1	52	—
48	K	Kramer Jacob	360	—	—	68	4
49		Klingeman Peter	1816	—	3	44	6
50		Keal Adam	500	—	—	95	—
51		Kuntz Henry	500	—	—	95	—
52		Kreseman John	5000	—	9	50	—
53		Knapper John	912	—	1	73	3
54		Knapper Peter	912	—	1	73	3
55		Kemp Martin	1040	—	1	97	6
56		Kronewald	2000	—	3	80	
57		Keaser Jacob	2150	—	4	8	5
58		Kolp Jacob	832	—	1	58	1
59		Kronewald George	1880	—	3	57	2
60		Kunkel George	2480	—	4	71	2
61		Kistler William	200	—	—	38	—
62		Kumerer Jacob	80	—	—	15	2
63	L	Lontz Jacob	2730	—	5	18	7
64	M	Miller Geo. Michael	1800	—	3	42	—
65		Masono Thomas	2380	—	4	52	2
66	N	Neufard Jacob	1000	—	1	90	—
67	O	Opp Conrad	550	—	1	4	5
68	P	Petory Valentine	1210	—	2	29	9
69		Poh Jacob	160	—	—	30	4
70		Petory Jacob	1200	—	2	28	—
71		Poh Fardenand	100	—	—	19	—

Albany	\	Geringer Andrew	Farmer
		Herman John	Wheelwright
		Hagebuch Michael	Farmer
		Hagebuch Christian	—
		Heninger John	Labourer
		Horn Frederick	do.
		Hall John	Farmer
		Heninger George	Farmer
		Heninger Frederick	do.
		Hall Henry	B Smith
		Herbster Frederick	Farmer
		Hechler Ann Maria	do.
		Henry John	do.
		Heyman Peter	Joiner
		Heyn John	Farmer
		Hommel John	do.
		Herbster George	B Smith
		Janzer Jacob	Cordwainer
		Kneper Peter	Farmer
		Kneper John	do.
		Kamp Martin	do.
		Klick Daniel	do.
		Kremer Jacob	do.
		Klose Jacob	do.
		Kistler William	Weaver
		Kieffer Jacob	Farmer
		Kuntz Henry	Potter
		Kummerer Jacob	Bluedier
		Kunckel George	B Smith
		Kunckel John	Taylor
		Kiel Adam	Cordwainer
		Kiel Jacob	do.
		Klick Henry	Farmer
		Koll Jacob	do.
		Lantz Jacob	do.

549

131

Albany	Jacob Klose	2	1		1		3	2	2	1		
	Adam Keel	1	1	1		1	2		1		1	
	Jacob Lantz					1		1			1	
	George Miller					1					1	
	Jacob Miller	2	1		1		1			1		
	Thomas Mason	1		3		1		1			1	
	Conrad Miller	1		1					1			
	Conrad Miller				1				1			
	George Miller			1					1			
	Jacob Seifert					1			1			
	Jacob Pilry	2	1		2		1		1	1		
	Ferdinant Poh	1	1		1					1		
	Jacob Poh Jr.	1	1		1					1		
	Jacob Ritter	2		1	1		2	1		2		
	John Reichelsdorfer	2	2	1		1	1	3			1	
	Henry Reichelsdorfer		1	1	1		2		1		1	
	Michael Reichelsdorfer	1	1			1	1	2	2		1	
	Ferdinant Ritter Jr.			1					1			
	George Brener			1	1	1			1		1	
	Daniel Rausch			1			1		1			
	Frederick Schlick	1			1				1			
	Jacob Poh					1					1	
	Ferdinant Ritter			1		1		2			1	
	Conrad Stump	1	1	1	1	1	2	2		1	1	
	George Stein	2		1		1	3	1	1		1	
	John Stableton			1		1	2				1	
	Robert Stableton		1	1		1		2	1		1	
	Henry Shoemaker				1		2			1		
	George Strafer				1		1		1			
	Jacob Sitler	2	2	1		1	3	1			1	
	George Sweeny		2	1		1				1	1	
	John Shuman	3	1	1		1				1		
	Jacob Shoemaker	2			1		2			1		2
	George Stump				1			1				
	Nicholas Smaltz				1		2	2		1		

1800 Federal Census

CHAPTER III

B SUSANNA CATHARINA LANTZ I

SUSANNA CATHERINA LANTZ was born 1745 in Albany Twp., Berks Co, PA and died after 30 Mar 1820 in Schuylkill Co., PA. She married BERNHART KRAMER. He died before 19 Jan 1819 in Manheim Twp, Schuylkill Co., PA. His estate was filed on 26 Oct 1819 in Schuylkill Co., PA.

'In the history of Friedens Lutheran Church in Berks Co, PA, on the occasion of the first 200th anniversary from 1790 to 1990 one of the 19 signers on the founding group was BERNARD KRAMER. Also a JORG ADAM KRAMER was listed."

Children of SUSANNA LANTZ and BERNHART KRAMER are:

1. JACOB KRAMER, born 1761 in Albany Twp, Berks Co., PA; died young.
2. ANNA ELIZABETH KRAMER, born 08 Jun 1763 in Albany Twp, Berks Co., PA.
3. MARIA MAGDALENA KRAMER, born 16 Mar 1766 in Albany Twp, Berks Co., PA.
4. JOHANN JACOB KRAMER (B4)
5. JOHANN JÜRG ADAM KRAMER born Apr 1770 in Albany Twp, Berks Co., PA.
6. JOHANN HENRICH KRAMER (B6)
7. SUSANNA CATHERINA KRAMER, born 25 Jan 1774 in Albany Twp, Berks Co., PA.
8. MARIA BARBARA KRAMER, born 09 Nov 1775 in Albany Twp, Berks Co., PA.
9. JOHANNES KRAMER (B9)

References: 6-Sarah Mae (Huss) Lantz, 6-Bill Lantz, 19, 53

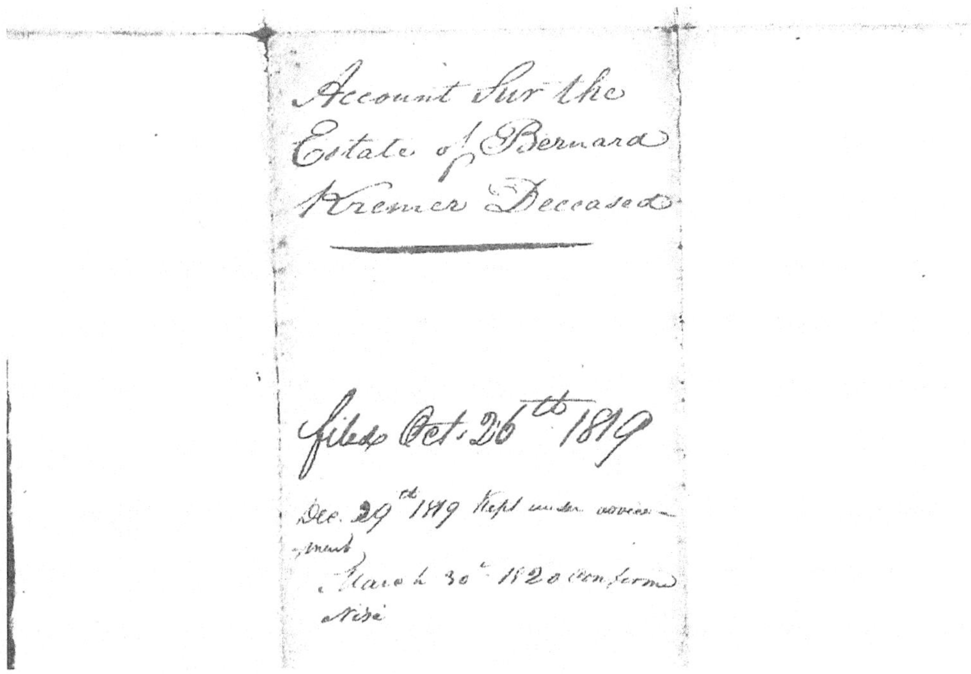
Account Sur the Estate of Bernard Kremer Deceased

filed Oct. 26th 1819

Dec. 29th 1819 Kept under advise-ment

March 30th 1820 Confirmed Nisi

A true and Perfect Inventory and Conscionable Appraisement of all and singular the Goods and Cattle Rights and Credits which were of Bernt Kreamer of Manheim Township Schuylkill County as follows to wit

To weaving Loom	$ 6..00
To Lot of weaving gears	8..00
Spooling weel & spools	1..00
half Barrel	0..67
To a Bead and Bead Stead	7..00
To a Table	0..40
To 2 iron pots and frying pan	1..80
	2..00
To a Chest	0..25
To dough trough	0..40
To 2 Baskets	
To a Pucking tub & 2 small tubs	1..50
To a Spinning wheel	1..25
To 3 Earthen Pots Broom & Slate	0..25
To a Steelyard	2..00
To 2 Drawers or small boxes	0..25
To a Prayer Book & old Bible	1..00
To an Axe	1..00
To 2½ yards of flaxen Linnen	1..25
Book account from the following person to wit: William Becker	1..00
George Kimmel Jr.	6..61
	43 63

Taken and appraised by us the subscribers this 17 Day of December A.D. 1818

34 52

Inventory
of the Estate of
Bernard Kreme decd
filed 19 Jany 1819

Schuylkill County ss

On the 19 day of January AD 1819 personally appeared before Philip Frailey Register for the Probate of Wills and granting Letters of Administration in & for the County of Schuylkill Henry Stager Esqr & George Heebner and being duly sworn according to law on oath do say that the foregoing Instrument of writing contains a just and true Appraisement & Valuation of the Goods & Chattels Rights & Credits which were of Bernard Kreme late of Manheim Township deceased so far as they came to their Knowledge

Henry Stager
George Heebner

Sworn & subscribed
before
Phil Frailey

The account of Susanna Catharine Kremer by her agent John Kremer Administratrix of all Credits which were of Bernards Kremer late of Ma

The acct. charges himself with amt. of Inventary	...	43	63
Balance due accountant	...	10	34
		53	97

Exhibited into the Registers office at Orwigsburg the 26th October 1816 which account I have examined do allow of and pass the administrators being first duly sworn there to. ——

Jacob Dreibelbis Regr.

and singular the goods and chattles right and
heim Township dec^d —

The accountants craves credit for
the following disbursment

By cash ℘ George Heebner ℘ receipt	"	41
By " " Nicholas Border "	1	00
By " " Conrad Berger "	"	75
By " " Philip Fraily "	3	00
By " " Benjn Nehf "	7	09
By " " Henry Kremer "	11	33
By " " do do "	10	66
By " " Henry Hager "	"	30
By " " do do "	1	00
By " " Henry Kremer "	5	00
~~By " " George Heebner "~~	~~1~~	~~41~~
By decrease in Sales	6	23
By commision on receiving 37.40 } at 10 ℘ ct	6	80
By do " paying 32.61 }		
	53	97
Balance due the accountant	$10	34

October 26th 1819
Errors excepted
Johannes Bumgartner

B4 JOHANN JACOB KRAMER B

JOHANN JACOB KRAMER was born 07 Feb 1768 in Albany Twp, Berks Co., PA. He married MARIA. He was baptized on 27 Mar 1768 at Jerusalem Lutheran and Reformed Church in Albany Twp., Berks Co., PA.

Child of JACOB KRAMER and MARIA is:

1. CATHARINE KRAMER, born 15 Apr 1804; baptized on 13 May 1804 in Berks Co., PA Friedens New Alemangel-White Church Lutheran, Wesnersville, Berks Co., PA

References: 62

B6 JOHANN HENRICH KRAMER B

JOHANN HENRICH B. KRAMER was born 04 Mar 1772 in Albany Twp, Berks Co., PA and died before 20 Aug 1851 in West Brunswick Twp, Schuylkill Co., PA. He married twice. He is buried along with his 2nd wife at Saint Paul Church in Summer Hill in Wayne Twp, Schuylkill County, PA. He lived 1810-30 in Manheim Twp., Schuylkill (formerly Berks) Co., PA and 1840-50 in West Brunswick Twp, Schuylkill Co., PA. His will is recorded in Will Book 2 Page 231, Schuylkill Co., PA.

Children of HENRICH KRAMER and are:

1. FRANKLIN KRAMER (B61)
2. JOHN KRAMER (B62)
3. PETER KRAMER (B63)
4. SAMUEL KRAMER (B64)
5. HENRY KRAMER, born in 1812 in Manheim Twp, Schuylkill Co, PA; died before 1851.
6. JOHANN GEORGE KRAMER, born in 20 Mar 1815 in Manheim Twp, Schuylkill Co, PA; died 20 Nov 1894 in Henderson Twp, Jefferson Co, PA; married SARAH. No children.
7. JACOB KRAMER, born in 1817 in Manheim Twp, Schuylkill Co, PA.
8. WILLIAM KRAMER
9. CHARLES B. KRAMER (B69)
10. EDWARD "EDWIN" KRAMER (B6A)
11. REBECCA CATHARINE KRAMER (B6B)
12. BENJAMIN KRAMER (B6C)
13. KARL KRAMER, born on 19 Nov 1819 in Manheim Twp, Schuylkill Co, PA.
14. WILHELM, born on 27 Nov 1808 in Manheim Twp, Schuylkill Co, PA.

References: 24-West Brunswick Twp Schuylkill Co PA H280, 48

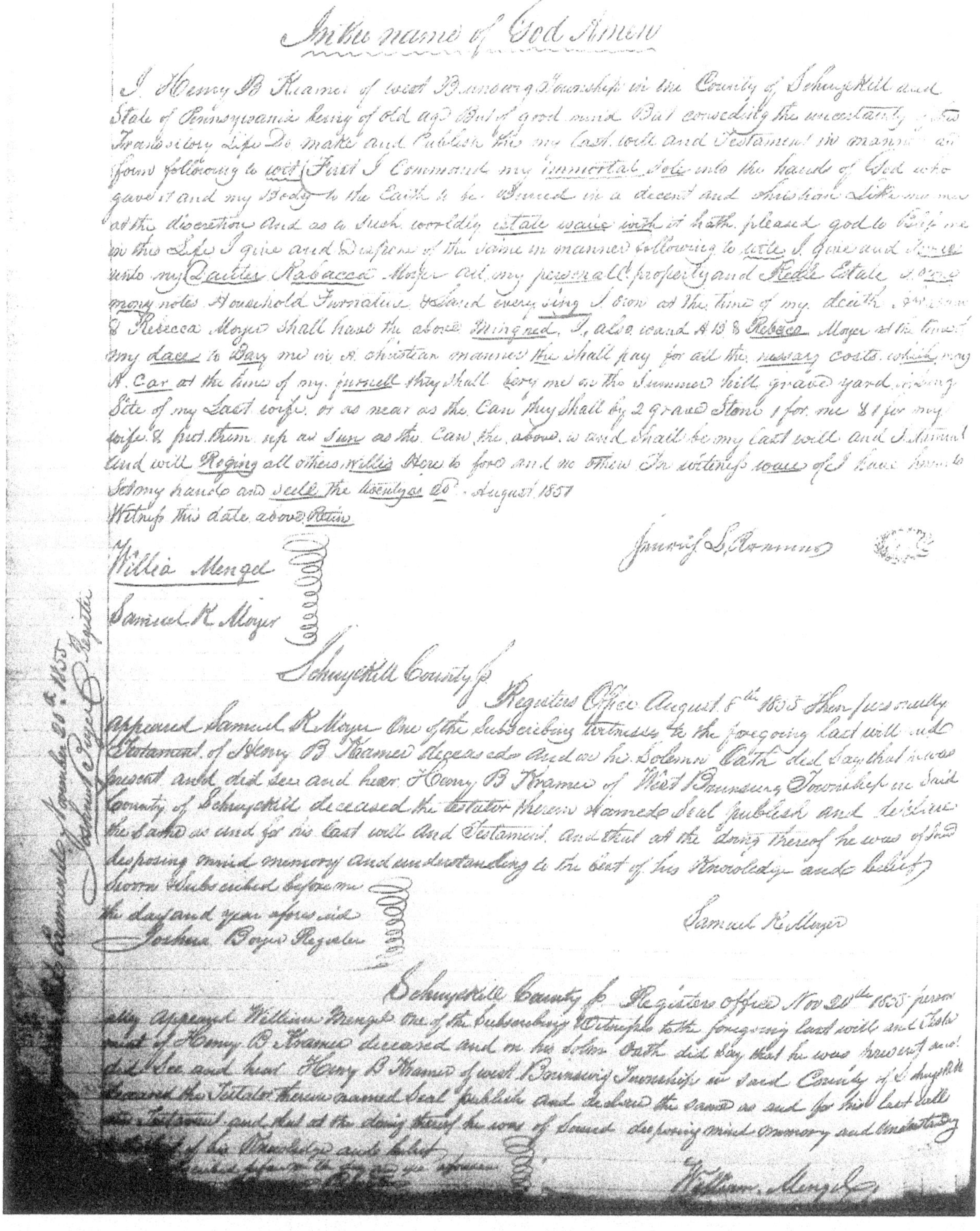
In the name of God Amen

I Henry B Kramer of west Brunswig Township in the County of Schuylkill and State of Pennsylvania being of old age But of good mind But considering the uncertainty of this Transitory Life Do make and Publish this my last will and Testament in manner and form following to wit First I Commend my immortal Sole into the hands of God who gave it and my Body to the Earth to be Buried in a decent and Christian Like manner at the discretion And as to such worldly estate wair with it hath pleased god to Bless me in this Life I give and Dispose of the same in manner following to wite I give and Devise unto my Daughter Rabacca Moyer all my personall property and Reale Estate & money notes Household Furniture & Land every sing I own at the time of my death ... & Rebecca Moyer shall have the above Mingned. I, also wand A B & Rebecca Moyer at the time of my daceas to Bury me in A christian manner the shall pay for all the nesary costs which may A. Car at the time of my funerall they shall bery me in the Summer hill grave yard ... Site of my Last wife. or as near as the Can they shall by 2 grave Stone 1 for me & 1 for my wife & put them up as Sun as the Can the above ward shall be my Last will and Testament And will Reging all others willis Here to fore and no other In witness wair of I have hereunto Set my hands and seale the twentyas 20th August 1851

Witness this date above Rittin

Henry B Kramer

William Mengel

Samuel K Moyer

Schuylkill County ss

Registers Office August 8th 1855 Then personally appeared Samuel K Moyer One of the Subscribing witnesses to the foregoing last will and Testament of Henry B Kramer deceased And on his Solemn Oath did say that he was present and did see and hear Henry B Kramer of West Brunswig Township in Said County of Schuylkill deceased the testator therein Named Seal publish and declare the same as and for his last will And Testament. And that at the doing thereof he was of Sound disposing mind memory and understanding to the best of his Knowledge and belief

Sworn & Subscribed before me the day and year aforesaid

Joshua Boyer Register

Samuel K Moyer

Schuylkill County ss Registers Office Nov 20th 1855 personally Appeared William Mengel One of the Subscribing Witnesses to the foregoing last will and Testament of Henry B Kramer deceased and on his Solm Oath did Say that he was present and did See and hear Henry B Kramer of west Brunswig Township in Said County of Schuylkill deceased the Testator therein named Seal publish and declare the same as and for his last will and Testament and that at the doing thereof he was of Sound disposing mind memory and understanding to the best of his Knowledge and belief

Sworn & subscribed before me the day and year aforesaid

William Mengel

Commenced November 20th 1855 Joshua Boyer Register

B9 JOHANNES KRAMER B

JOHANNES KRAMER was born on 11 Sep 1777 in Albany Twp, Berks Co., PA and died 1866 in Berks Co., PA. He married CATHARINE RUHL was born on 29 Mar 1780 in PA and died 1848 in Berks Co., PA. Both are buried in Epler's Church Cemetery, Bern Twp., Berks Co., PA. Letters of Administration issued Dec 1866 and distribution of his estate filed Aug 1867 Berks Co., PA

Children of JOHANNES KRAMER and CATHARINE RUHL are:

1. ELIZABETH KRAMER (B91)
2. ANNA MARIA KRAMER (B92)
3. CATHARINE KRAMER (B93)
4. JOHN R. KRAMER (B94)
5. MARGARET KRAMER; married (?) HERLACH died before 1867.
6. DANIEL RUHL KRAMER (B96)
7. SUSANNA KRAMER (B97)
8. JACOB KRAMER (B98)
9. SARAH KRAMER (B99)
10. REBECCA KRAMER (B9A)

References: 45, 49

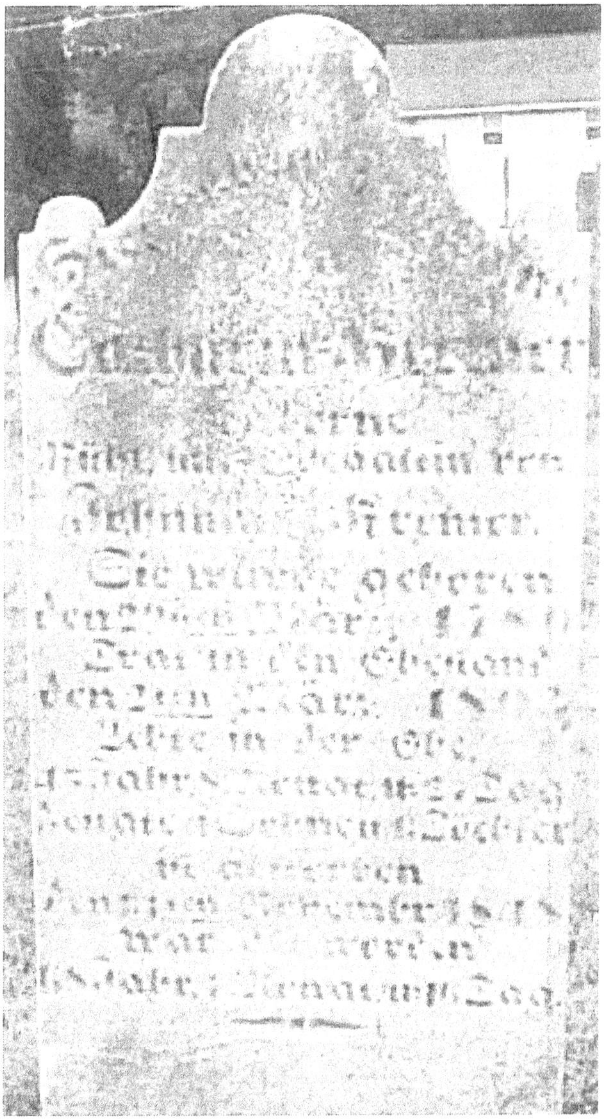

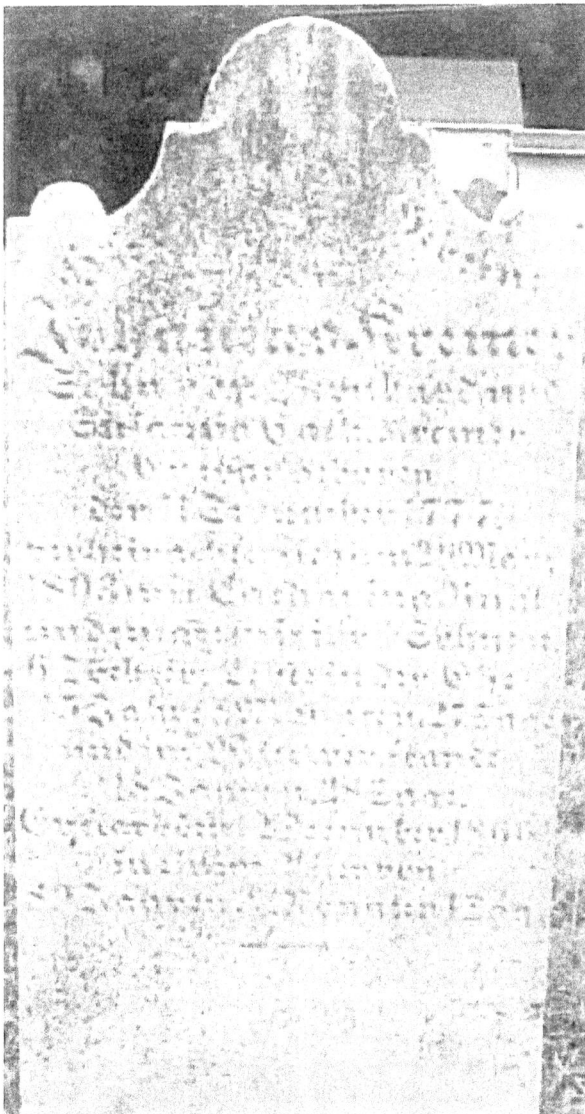

The account of Daniel R. Kraemer and John Kraemer, Administrators of all and singular the goods and chattels, rights and credits, which were of John Kraemer late of the Township of Bern, in the County of Berks, deceased.

Dr.

		$	cts.
1847.	The said accountants charge themselves with all and singular, the goods and chattels, rights and credits, which of the said deceased, agreeably to an inventory and appraisement thereof, filed in the Register's Office in Reading, amounting to	2091	75
	To increase on sale of Personal property ..	12	25
	" Interest on Ben. Bitner's note	1	[illegible]
	" " Ben. B. Bieber's note	1	57
	" " Henry Shell's note		40
	" Franklin G. Harin note	10	00
	" " Jacob Kraemer note	5	42
	" " John B. Himmer "		74
	" " Christian Rothe "	1	12
	" " Henry Rothe "	13	17
		$2140	64

Reading August 1847.

Daniel R. Kraemer

John Kraemer

1846. Cr.

The said accountants claim credit and allowance for the following disbursements viz.

				$	cts	$	cts
Dec	4	Paid C. A. Leinbach	Rio		30		
	12	" do	"	9	45		
	"	" Wm. Thomas	"	1	92		
	"	" B. J. Taylor	"	2	92		
	20	" Abraham & Tobias	Lumber	1	00		
	24	" Ritter & Co	Adm. Rect. Book	3	00		
	"	" J. Lawrence Getz	"	2	50		
	"	" M. S. Rheinoehler	Letters	5	67		
	26	" John Mells	Coffin	30	00		
	"	" Samuel Stein	appraising	1	10		
	"	" John George	"	1	10		
1847	"	" Wm. G. Prunee	clerking	1	50		
Jany.	23	" Henry Rapp	[illegible]	4	50		
Feby	4	" [illegible] W. Deppen	[illegible]	8	75		
	25	" [illegible] G. [illegible]	[illegible]	4	10		
Mar	15	" Jonathan [illegible]	[illegible]	3	40		
	22	" Henry Schell	[illegible]		50		
April	13	" [illegible] Ritner	"		20		
	29	" John Kaemmerer	[illegible]	2	42	88	66

Above payments made by Daniel.

				$	cts	$	cts
1846.							
Dec	24	Paid Ritter & Co	Receipt Book		50		
1847 Jany	22	" do	Publishing &c	1	25		
	"	" M. S. Rheinoehler	Filing &c		40		
Feby	9	" [illegible] Binkley	copying &c	2	00		
	"	" John Heinz	clerking	1	00		
Mar	22	" Rebecca Starbuck	Boarding	5	28		
Ap.	27	" Daniel R. Kaemmerer	Inv.	14	48		
Aug	9	" John Heinz	Tombstone	25	75		
		" J. D. Kaemmerer	Filing [illegible] papers		50	51	16
		By note of Henry Bernhard [illegible] uncollected		24	54		
		Register, preparing & filing accounts		9	00	33	54
						$ 173	36
		" Funeral Expenses		116	13		
		" Book Account of Jacob Kaemmerer [illegible]		70	00		
		" Cash paid Jacob [illegible] for collecting note of Catharine [illegible]		39	25		

" Cash paid Catharine Kramer for services	100	00		
" " Daniel Kramer for boarding	66	67		
" Jacob S. Livingood attorney	50	00		
By Accountants Compensation	100	00	472	15
			645	41
Balance in favor of Estate			1495	23
			$ 2141	64

Distribution

1	John Kramer share	1/9	166	13 2/3
2	Daniel S. Kramer	"	166	13 2/3
3	Jacob Kramer	"	166	13 2/3
4	Elizabeth Roth wife of Christian Roth	"	166	13 2/3
5	Anna Maria Robinson Widow		166	13 2/3
6	Catharine Hiester wife of John B. Hiester		166	13 2/3
7	Margaret Gerlach Widow		166	13 2/3
8	Sarah Batty wife of John Batty		166	13 2/3
9	Children of Susanna Hiester dec'd			
	1 Adam Hiester share	1/4	41	53 5/12
	2 John Hiester	"	41	53 5/12
	3 Lydia Hiester wife of Meyer	"	41	53 5/12
	4 Catharine Hiester	"	41	53 5/12
			$ 1495	23

B61 FRANKLIN KRAMER B6

FRANKLIN KRAMER was born in 1796. He married ANGALINE was born in 1800 in PA.

Child of FRANKLIN KRAMER and ANGALINE is:

1. JACKSON KRAMER, born 1835 in Schuylkill Co., PA.

References: 24-South Manheim Twp Schuylkill Co PA H54

B62 JOHN KRAMER B6

JOHN KRAMER was born in 1808 in Schuylkill Co, PA. He married REBECCA. She was born in 1810 in PA. He was a master blacksmith by occupation.

Children of JOHN KRAMER and REBECCA are.

1. ADAM KRAMER (B621)
2. HENRY KRAMER, born before 1844 in PA.
3. GEORGE KRAMER (twin), born 1844 in Auburn Twp., Schuylkill Co., PA; ; died ca 08 Sep 1865 killed in Civil War within days of his twin brother. Filed joint will recorded Will Book 3 Page 176 Schuylkill Co., PA.
4. SAMUEL KRAMER (twin), born 1844 in Auburn Twp., Schuylkill Co., PA; died ca 08 Sep 1865 killed in Civil War within days of his twin brother. Filed joint will recorded Will Book 3 Page 176 Schuylkill Co., PA.
5. ESTHER KRAMER, born 1849 in Schuylkill Co., PA.

References: 25-Auburn Schuylkill Co PA H65

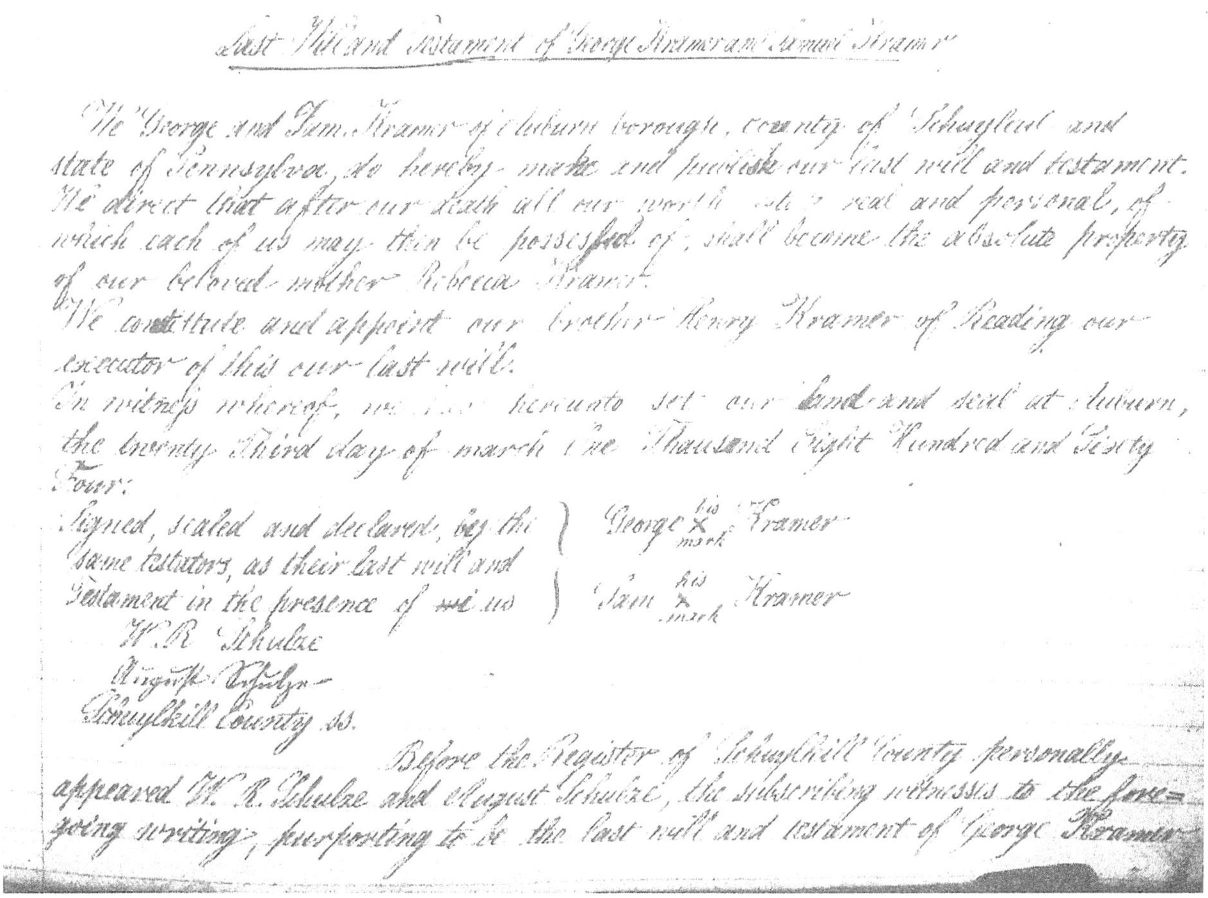

Last Will and Testament of George Kramer and Samuel Kramer

We George and Sam. Kramer of Auburn borough, county of Schuylkill and state of Pennsylvania, do hereby make and publish our last will and testament.
We direct that after our death all our worth etc. real and personal, of which each of us may then be possessed of, shall become the absolute property of our beloved mother Rebecca Kramer.
We constitute and appoint our brother Henry Kramer of Reading our executor of this our last will.
In witness whereof, we have hereunto set our hand and seal at Auburn, the twenty Third day of march One Thousand Eight Hundred and Sixty Four.

Signed, sealed and declared, by the same testators, as their last will and Testament in the presence of us

George his X mark Kramer
Sam his X mark Kramer

W. R. Schulze
August Schulze

Schuylkill County ss.

Before the Register of Schuylkill County personally appeared W. R. Schulze and August Schulze, the subscribing witnesses to the foregoing writing, purporting to be the last will and testament of George Kramer

176

and Samuel Kramer, late of the borough of Auburn, in said county, deceased, who being duly sworn, do depose and say, that they were present and did see the said George and Samuel Kramer sign the foregoing writing, and heard them pronounce and declare the same as and for their last will and testament, and that at the time of so doing, they were of sound mind, memory and understanding.

Sworn and subscribed before me, Sept. 8th/1863 A. Lehrmann, Register. | W. F. Schultz Augustus Schultz | 5 cts. Int. Rev. stamp

B63 PETER KRAMER B6

PETER KRAMER was born in 1810 in Manheim Twp, Schuylkill Co, PA. He married CORINDA was born in 1820 in PA.

Children of PETER KRAMER and CORINDA are:

1. RUBEN KRAMER, born 1846 in Schuylkill Co., PA.
2. LOUISIANNA KRAMER, born 1849 in Schuylkill Co., PA.

References: 24-West Brunswick Twp Schuylkill Co PA H281

B64 SAMUEL KRAMER B6

SAMUEL KRAMER was born on 30 Oct 1810 in Manheim Twp, Schuylkill Co, PA and died 11 Oct 1886 in Auburn, Schuylkill Co., PA. He married ESTHER was born in1813 in PA and died 30 Dec 1873 in Schuylkill Co., PA. His will is recorded in Will Book 6 Page 538, Schuylkill Co., PA. Both are buried in Auburn Cemetery, Auburn, Schuylkill Co., PA.

Children of SAMUEL KRAMER and ESTHER are:

1. FRANKLIN KRAMER (B641)
2. ANGALINA KRAMER, born 1832 in Schuylkill Co., PA; died before 08 Jan 1886 in Schuylkill Co., PA.

References: 24-South Manheim Twp Schuylkill Co PA H53, 48, 45

338

Last Will & Testament of Samuel Kreamer Decd

I Samuel Kreamer of the Boro of Auburn County of Schuylkill State of Pa being of sound mind and good judgement make this my last will and testament hereby revoking any other wills that may have been made and is as follows to wit:

First I commit my soul and body into the hands of Almighty God who gave it and through whose mercy I hope for eternal life.

I give and bequeath to my grand daughter Sarah Kreamer now Sarah Miller and daughter of Franklin Kreamer deceased the house I now live in for her [illegible] & for the consideration that it shall be in payment for her attention of me while I live & leave my executor to give her a deed for the same it being the brick house & lot adjoining estate of Abraham Moyer deceased I also give and bequeath the said Sarah Miller all the furniture contained in said house. The [illegible] that is built against the house bequeathed to the said Sarah Miller I desire my executors to sell to the best advantage and the lot [illegible] all property both real and personal that I may own to [illegible] pay all debts and with the proceeds of all my property not herein mentioned shall divide share and share alike between the following persons Emma Kreamer wife of Franklin Kreamer deceased. Sarah Miller, Jackson Kreamer, George Kreamer Wellington Kreamer Abraham Kreamer "Dolly" or Carrie Kreamer and Lucian Kreamer my grand children share and share alike, I desire that that my executor shall see that my body is decently buried attend to the funeral expenses Have a tomb stone placed at my grave and at the grave of my deceased wife Esther Kreamer

And I hereby appoint Chas C. [illegible] executor of this my last will and testament. In witness hereunto I have caused my signature to be made this 8th day of January AD 1886.

(Witnesses at signing mark)
Erastus Focht (Seal)
Isaac Moyer (Seal)

Samuel his + mark Kreamer

State of Pennsylvania } ss.
County of Schuylkill }

Before me George W. Johnson Register for the Probate of Wills and Granting Letters of Administration, &c and for Schuylkill County personally appeared Erastus Focht and Isaac Moyer subscribing witnesses to the above and foregoing instrument of writing purporting to be the last will and testament of Samuel Kreamer late of the Borough of Auburn in said County deceased who being by me duly sworn according to law did depose and say that they were present and did see the testator Samuel Kreamer now deceased sign seal and heard him publish pronounce and declare the above and foregoing instrument of writing as and for his last will and testament and at the time of the doing thereof the said Samuel Kreamer was of sound mind memory and understanding to the best of their knowledge & belief

Sworn & subscribed before me this 18th day of October AD 1886.
Geo W. Johnson Register

Erastus Focht
Isaac Moyer

State of Pennsylvania } ss
Schuylkill County }

You do swear that as Executor of Samuel Kreamer deceased you will well and truly administer the goods and chattels rights and credits of the decedent according to law and diligently and faithfully regard and well and truly comply with the provisions of the law relating to collateral inheritances

Sworn & subscribed before me this 18th day of Oct. 1886.
Geo. W. Johnson
Register
} Charles E. Quail.

Filed 18 Oct. 1886.

Reg. & Ex. Dec. 15- 1887.

B69 CHARLES B. KRAMER B6

CHARLES B KRAMER was born on 19 Nov 1819 in Manheim Twp, Schuylkill Co, PA and died 13 Jun 1897 in Lisbon, Linn Co, IA. He married (1) LYDIA GREENWALT the daughter of MOLLY. She was born in 1825 in PA and died before 1856. She is listed in the census as lame in 1850. He married (2) ANNIE TOBIN was born in 1837 in NY and died in Apr 1875. He and his 2nd and 3rd wives are buried in Lot 59 Lisbon Cemetery, Lisbon, IA. He married (3) LOVINA FITZPATRICK. She was born 1833 in PA and died 02 Apr 1903 in Lisbon, Linn Co., IA.

Child of CHARLES B. KRAMER and LYDIA GREENWALT is:

1. FRANCIS KRAMER, born in 1846 in PA.

Children of CHARLES KRAMER and ANNIE TOBIN are:

2. CLARA AGNES KRAMER (B692)
3. LYDIA ANN KRAMER (B693)
4. EMMA REBECCA KRAMER (B694)
5. SARAH JANE KRAMER (B695)
6. CHARLES HENRY KRAMER, born in 1863 in PA; married ELIZABETH BOYD on 09 Aug 1883 Cedar Co., IA.
7. ANNETTA LOUISA KRAMER, born in 1865 in Clearfield Co., PA; married LEWIS FILLOON 20 Jan 1887 Cedar Co., IA; born 21 Nov 1864 in KY; died 12 Aug 1938 in IA. No children.
8. GEORGE E. KRAMER, born in 1867 in PA.
9. WILLIAM E. KRAMER, born in 1869 in PA; Resided 1914 Des Moines, IA.
10. NELSON ROBERT KRAMER (B69A)
11. JESSE A. KRAMER, born in 1873 in Linn Co., IA; died in infancy.
12. INFANT KRAMER (twin of JESSE), born in 1873 in Linn Co., IA.
13. MARY "MATE" CATHARINE KRAMER (B69D)

References: 27-Lisbon Franklin Twp Linn Co IA H205, 25-Brady Twp Clearfield Co PA H2679

B6A EDWARD KRAMER B6

EDWARD "EDWIN" "EDGAR" KRAMER was born in Oct 1826 in Manheim Twp, Schuylkill Co, PA. He married SARAH in Schuylkill Co, PA. She was born in Apr 1826 in PA.

Children of EDWARD KRAMER and SARAH are:

1. SAMUEL KRAMER (B6A1)
2. CYRUS KRAMER (B6A2)
3. HENRY KRAMER (B6A3)
4. GEORGE E. KRAMER (B6A4)

References: 27-Huntington Twp Huntington Co IN H119, 29-Huntington Twp Huntington Co IN H531

B6B REBECCA CATHARINE KRAMER B6

REBECCA CATHARINE KRAMER was born on 30 Oct 1824 in Manheim Twp, Schuylkill Co, PA and died 05 Nov 1878 in Schuylkill Co, PA. She married ABRAHAM MOYER was born on 05 Dec 1821 in PA and died 22 Feb 1882 in Schuylkill Co, PA. He was a RR Fireman by occupation. Both are buried in Auburn Cemetery, Auburn, Schuylkill Co, PA. His will is recorded in Will Book 5, Page 391 Schuylkill Co., PA.

Children of REBECCA KRAMER and ABRAHAM MOYER are:

1. JACKSON MOYER (B6B1)
2. MATILDA MOYER (B6B2)
3. GEORGE H. MOYER (B6B3)
4. MORGAN WALTER MOYER (B6B4)
5. MARY CECELIA MOYER (B6B5)
6. JOHN MOYER
7. HENRY Z. MOYER, born 13 Apr 1860, died 26 Jan 1878. He is buried in Auburn Cemetery, Auburn, Schuylkill Co, PA.
8. CARRIE MOYER, born 1864 Schuylkill Co, PA.

References: 24-West Brunswick Twp Schuylkill Co PA H280, 45, 25-West Brunswick Twp Schuylkill Co PA H248, 26-West Brunswick Twp Schuylkill Co PA H60, 26-Auburn Twp Schuylkill Co PA H60

Last Will &c of Abraham Moyer, dec'd

In the name of God Amen I Abraham Moyer of the Borough of Auburn Schuylkill Co Pa being of sound mind make this my last Will & Testament & by it revoking all former Wills that may have been made, and this being my Will & Testament of my own free will as follows to wit,

And first I commit my soul & body to Almighty God who gave it & trust Him for his mercy.

I desire that all my just debts be paid & if possible none of my property to be sold for that purpose untill a given time hereinafter specified has Elapsed.

I give and bequeath unto my daughter Tillie Westerfield all my right title & interest in the House at Reading Pa she now lives in the Deed being now in my possession, I desire my Executor or Executors to give her a Deed subject to a mortgage that is on it. and that my interest being $400, Four Hundred Dollars is to be a part of her inheritance that she would have to get after my Estate is settled up. the said $400. to be deducted from the share she would have to get.

I give & bequeath to my Son Jackson Moyer the use of the 8 acres of land situated between land of Dr Chas E Zuail and the Phil & R.R.R. for his sole use, to make out of the products from the same all he can, untill my estate is settled up, when the proceeds from the sale of said land shall be divided share & share alike, among all my children Jackson Moyer, George Moyer, Tillie Westerfield, Carrie Moyer, and Cecelia Luckinbill, and that my Son Jackson Moyer is to have the use of the said piece of land & for it he to Keep my daughter Carrie & board and Clothes untill the Estate is settled up.

I give & bequeath to my son Jackson Moyer the butcher shop that is built on my property for his use &c he is to be permitted to take it away if he desires.

It is my Will that when my Estate is to be settled all my Children are to have share & share alike.

It is my Will that Executor or Executors shall have four years time to settle up the Estate and to sell the same to the best advantage, and I hereby appoint my son Jackson Moyer and Chas. E Zuail my Executors.

In witness of the above Will & Testament I have hereunto set my hand & seal this Eleventh day of February A.D. 1882

Witness at signing { J.M. Diefenderfer
John O. Moyer.

Abram Moyer (Seal)

Schuylkill County, ss:

This day before me J. C. Purcell, Register for the probate of Wills &c. in and for said County, personally came J. M. Diefenderfer and John O. Moyer the subscribing witnesses to the above will and who being duly sworn according to law do depose and say that they were present and did Abraham Moyer, the testator therein named sign, seal, publish and declare the same as and for his last will and testament and that at the doing thereof he was of sound disposing mind, memory and understanding to the best of their knowledge and belief.

Sworn and subscribed before me this 6th day of March A.D. 1882.
J. C. Purcell
Register.

J. M. Diefenderfer
John O. Moyer.

Schuylkill County, ss:

Register's Office Pottsville March 6. 1882.

We Jackson Moyer and Chas. E. Quail do swear that as the Executors of the foregoing last will of Abram Moyer, deceased, we will well and truly administer the goods, Chattels and Credits of said deceased, agreeably to law-

Jackson Moyer
Chas. E. Quail

Sworn and subscribed before me the day and year aforesaid, and letters testamentary issued to Jackson Moyer and Chas. E. Quail.

J. C. Purcell.
Register.

Reg. & Ex. 6 March 1882.

B6C BENJAMIN KRAMER B6

BENJAMIN KRAMER was born in 1822 in Manheim Twp, Schuylkill Co, PA and died 05 Nov 1859 South Manheim Twp., Schuylkill Co., PA of typhoid fever. He married HANNAH MENGEL. She was born in 1817 in PA and died 24 Aug 1890 Auburn, Schuylkill Co., PA. Her will is recorded in Will Book 7 Page 593 in Schuylkill Co., PA. Both are buried in St. John's Church Cemetery, Auburn, Schuylkill Co., PA.

Children of BENJAMIN KRAMER and HANNAH are:

1. WILLIAM KRAMER was born in 1844 in Schuylkill Co., PA and died before 1888 in Schuylkill Co., PA. He married SARAH in Schuylkill Co., PA.
2. DANIEL KRAMER (B6C2)
3. REBECCA KRAMER (B6C3)
4. BENJAMIN KRAMER (B6C4)
5. CHARLES M. KRAMER, born in 1852 in Schuylkill Co., PA; died 1939 in Schuylkill Co., PA; married SUSANA E. in Schuylkill Co., PA; born 1856 in PA; died 1928 in Schuylkill Co., PA. Both are buried in St. John's Church Cemetery, Auburn, Schuylkill Co., PA.
6. JOHN KRAMER, born in 1854 in Schuylkill Co., PA
7. HENRY KRAMER, born on 21 Jun 1856 in Schuylkill Co., PA; died 02 Feb 1920 in Schuylkill Co., PA; buried in St. John's Church Cemetery, Auburn, Schuylkill Co., PA.
8. LEWIS T. KRAMER (B6C8)

References: 24-South Manheim Twp Schuylkill Co PA H69, 25-Auburn Schuylkill Co., PA, 41-1860 South Manheim Twp Schuylkill Co PA H2, 45, 29-Auburn Schuylkill Co PA H46, 45

Last Will &c. of Hannah Kramer, dec'd.

I Hannah Kramer widow, of the Borough of Auburn Schuylkill County State of Pennsylvania being of sound mind, memory and understanding, do make this my last Will and Testament hereby revoking all other Wills & Testaments I may have made, and is the following to wit,—

And first I committ my soul & body into the hands of Almighty God, I desire that after my death my body be given a decent burial, at no great expence & desire the grave walled out, with Bricks,—

I give & bequeath to Sarah Kramer wife of William Kramer my son my German Bible.

I desire that as soon as it can be legaly done that my hereinafter Executor sell all of my estate both real & personal and after paying the just expences divide the same share and share alike among the following named persons, all being my Children who I desire to have equal shares of the proceeds of my whole estate, including my houshold furniture, pictures, carpets, bedding &c. and who are William Kramer, Daniel Kramer Rebecca Tallman, Benjamin Kramer, Charles Kramer, and Lewis Kramer and Henry Kramer, share and share alike.

I hereby appoint my son Lewis S. Kramer my Executor of this my last Will & Testament and have hereunto set my hand and seal this 22nd day of November, A.D. One thousand Eight Hundred and Eighty Eight

Hannah her X mark Kramer (Seal)

Witnesses at making (mark)
Chas G. Quail.
H. C. Diefenderfer.

State of Pennsylvania, }
County of Schuylkill. } ss:

Before me, Samuel Beard, Register for the Probate of Wills, and granting Letters of administration, in and for Schuylkill County, personally appeared, Chas. G. Quail and H. C. Diefenderfer, subscribing

594

witnesses to the above and foregoing instrument of writing purporting to be the last will and testament of Hannah Kramer, late of the Borough of Auburn, in said County, deceased, who being by me duly affirmed according to law, did depose and say, that they were present, and did see the testatrix, Hannah Kramer, now deceased, sign, seal and heard her publish, pronounce and declare, the above and foregoing instrument of writing as and for her last will and testament, and at the time of the doing thereof, the said Hannah Kramer, was of sound mind, memory, and understanding, to the best of their knowledge and belief.

Affirmed and subscribed before me, this 28th. day of August, A. D. 1890.
Samuel Beard,
Register of Wills.

Chas. W. Snaill M. D.
H. W. Diefenderfer.

Estate of Hannah Kramer, Deceased.
State of Pennsylvania, } ss:
County of Schuylkill. }

You do swear that as Executor of Hannah Kramer, deceased, you will well and truly administer the goods and chattels, rights and credits of the decedent according to law, and diligently and faithfully regard and well and truly comply with the provisions of the law relating to collateral inheritances.

Sworn and subscribed before me, this 28th day of August, A. D. 1890.
Samuel Beard,
Register of Wills.

Lewis S. Kramer. [Seal]

Filed 28 Aug. 1890.
Reg. + Exam. 28 Aug. 1890.

B91 ELIZABETH KRAMER B9

ELIZABETH KRAMER was born on 02 Jan 1803 and died in 1891. She married CHRISTIAN ROTH was born in 1804 in PA.

Child of ELIZABETH KRAMER and CHRISTIAN ROTH is:

1. JOHN ROTH, born1834 in PA.

References: 25-Bern Twp Berks Co PA H619

B92 ANNA MARIA KRAMER B9

ANNA MARIA KRAMER was born 17 Dec 1804 and died 1881. She married JAMES RICHARDSON. He died before 1867 in Berks Co., PA.

Child of ANNA KRAMER and JAMES RICHARDSON is:

1. REUBEN RICHARDSON (B921)

References: 27-Marion Twp Berks Co PA H3

B93 CATHARINE KRAMER B9

CATHARINE KRAMER was born on 28 Mar 1806 and died 03 Oct 1888. She married JOHN CRISTIAN HIESTER, son of JOSEPH HIESTER. He was born on 18 Sep 1798 and died 07 Nov 1867 in Berks Co., PA. He "was a man of ample fortune owning two farms near the well-known Bern Church, and he was noted both for his fine personal appearance and for his good judgment and foresight." Both are buried in Bern UCC Churchyard, Bern Twp., Berks Co., PA.

Children of CATHARINE KRAMER and JOHN HIESTER are:

1. BENNEVILLE HIESTER (B931)
2. JARED HIESTER
3. HARRISON K. HIESTER (B933)
4. WASHINGTON HIESTER, born in 1832 in Berks Co, PA.
5. MARIA HIESTER (B935)

References: 49, 24-Bern Twp Berks Co PA H105

B94 JOHN R. KRAMER B9

JOHN R. KRAMER was born on 20 Nov 1807 and died 22 Aug 1901 in Berks Co., PA. He married CATHARINE "KATE" BOHN. She was born on 30 Apr. 30 1815 and died 06 May 6 1857 in Berks Co., PA. Both are buried in Bern UCC Churchyard, Bern Twp., Berks Co., PA.

Children of JOHN KRAMER and CATHARINE BOHN are:

1. HARRISON, born 1836 in Berks Co., PA.
2. CATHARINE LYDIA KRAMER, born 1837 in Berks Co., PA.
3. CAROLINE KRAMER (B943)
4. JACOB KRAMER was born 1844 in Bern Twp., Berks Co., PA.
5. JARED KRAMER (B945)
6. MARY KRAMER, born 1851 in Berks Co., PA.
7. SARAH "SALLIE" KRAMER, born 1854 in Berks Co., PA.

References: 49, 24-Bern Twp Berks Co PA H217, 25-Bern Twp Berks Co PA H557, 26-Bern Twp Berks Co PA H353, 27-Bern Twp Berks Co PA H3, 29-Bern Twp Berks Co PA H82

B96 DANIEL RUHL KRAMER B9

DANIEL RUHL KRAMER was born on 27 Oct 1813 Bern Twp., Berks Co., PA and died 21 Jun 1886 in Berks Co., PA. He married CATHERINE FISHER in Berks Co., PA, daughter of JOHN FISHER. She was born on 07 Apr 1816 and died 21 Feb 1887 in Berks Co., PA. "By trade he was stonemason and this trade he followed all his life in connection with farming a small tract of land in Bern Township. For twenty-five years he was assessor and tax collector, and he gave good service to the public, faithfully and conscientiously performing the duties of his respective offices. He was a deacon and elder in the Bern Church, and in his political faith he was a Democrat." He is buried in Bern UCC Churchyard, Bern Twp., Berks Co., PA.

Children of DANIEL KRAMER and CATHERINE FISHER are:

1. SON KRAMER, born in Bern Twp., Berks Co., PA; died in infancy.
2. JOHN F. KRAMER (B962)
3. DANIEL F. KRAMER (B963)
4. BENNEVILLE F. KRAMER, born 25 Apr 1841 in Bern Twp., Berks Co., PA; died in 23 Mar 1902; married REBECCA LERCH. None of their children are living. He is buried in Epler's Church Cemetery, Leesport, Berks Co., PA.
5. ALBERT F. KRAMER (B965)
6. CATHARINE F. KRAMER (B966)
7. ELIZA KRAMER, born on 01 Jan 1848 in Bern Twp., Berks Co., PA; unmarried and lived in the same house where she was born.
8. LOUISA KRAMER, born on 08 Aug 1850 in Bern Twp. Berks Co., PA; married (1) FRANKLIN WINTER; died before 1909; married (2) DAVID SHIFFERT; died before 1909; married (3) DANIEL LINDEMUTH.
9. GEORGE F. KRAMER (B969)
10. HENRY F. KRAMER (B96A)
11. EDWARD F. KRAMER (B96B)

References: 49, 24-Bern Twp Berks Co PA H202, 45

B97 SUSANNA KRAMER B9

SUSANNA KRAMER was born on 25 Jul 1816 and died 14 Oct 1858 in Berks Co., PA; married JACOB HIESTER on 29 Oct 1837 in Berks Co., PA. He was born on 01 Jul 1801 and died 13 Mar 1873 in Berks Co., PA. Both are buried in Bern UCC Churchyard, Bern Twp., Berks Co., PA. "In politics he was a Democrat, but he held no office except that of school director, a position he filled for six years. He and his family were members of the Bern Church, of which he was one of the leading elders. For many years he served as lieutenant in the State militia, and he made a fine appearance, as he was a man of commanding presence."

Children of SUSANNA KRAMER and JACOB HIESTER are:

1. ADAM HIESTER (B971)
2. LYDIA HIESTER (B972)
3. GABRIEL HIESTER, died young.
4. JOHN K. HIESTER (B974)
5. CATHARINE HIESTER, born Berks Co., PA; died unmarried in Berks Co., PA.

References: 45, 49, 24-Bern Twp Berks Co PA H168, 27-Bern Twp Berks Co PA H148, 26-Bern Twp Berks Co PA H289

B98 JACOB KRAMER B9

JACOB KRAMER was born on 11 Dec 1819 and died 01 Oct 1895 in Berks Co., PA. He married MARY KRICK in Berks Co., PA. She was born on 04 Jul 1824 and died 21 Sep 1906 in Berks Co., PA. Both are buried in Bern UCC Churchyard, Bern Twp., Berks Co., PA.

Children of JACOB KRAMER and MARY KRICK are:

1. JOHN KRAMER, born in 1844 in Berks Co., PA.
2. JACOB KRAMER, born in 1846 in Berks Co., PA.
3. ADAM KRAMER, born in 1847 in Berks Co., PA.
4. RUBEN KRAMER, born in 1849 in Berks Co., PA.
5. WILLIAM KRAMER, born in 1853 in Berks Co., PA.
6. FRANKLIN KRAMER, born in 1857 in Berks Co., PA.
7. SARAH KRAMER, born in 1858 in Berks Co., PA.

References: 49, 24-Bern Twp Berks Co PA H205, 45, 25-Bern Twp Berks Co PA H613, 26-Bern Twp Berks Co PA H321

B99 SARAH KRAMER B9

SARAH "SALLIE" KRAMER was born in Apr 1811 and died in 1904. She married JACOB BODY. He was born in 1811 in PA and died before 1900 in Berks Co., PA. He was listed as a carpenter in 1870.

Children of SARAH KRAMER and JACOB BODY are:

1. CHARLES BODY, born 1837 in PA.
2. EMMA M. BODY, born 1839 in PA.
3. CAROLINE BODY, born 1843 in PA.
4. ANNA BODY, born 1845 in PA.
5. WILLIAM BODY, born 1848 in PA.
6. JOHN KRAMER BODY (B996)

References: 29-Reading Berks Co PA H112, 26-Ward 7 Reading Berks Co PA H289, 24-Norristown Lower Ward Montgomery Co PA H677, 49

B9A REBECCA KRAMER B9

REBECCA KRAMER was born 12 Jan 1809 and died in 1891. She married PETER HARBACH.

Child of REBECCA KRAMER and PETER HARBACH is:

1. PETER S. HARBACH, born 1843 in PA.

References: 26-Bern Twp Berks Co PA H352

B621 ADAM KRAMER B62

ADAM KRAMER was born in 1837 in PA. He married MARGARET. She was born in 1840 in MD.

Children of ADAM KRAMER and MARGARET are:

1. TEMPERANCE KRAMER, born in 1864 in Berks Co., PA.
2. ADELAIDE KRAMER, born in 1866 in Berks Co., PA.
3. AMBROSE KRAMER, born in 1867 in Berks Co., PA.

References: 27-Cranberry Twp Schuylkill Co PA H291

B641 FRANKLIN KRAMER B64

FRANKLIN KRAMER was born in 1830 in Schuylkill Co., PA and died before 08 Jan 1886 in Schuylkill Co., PA. He married LAONIA in 1826 in PA. His occupation was boatman in 1870.

Children of FRANKLIN KRAMER and LAONIA are:

1. SARAH KRAMER, born in 1855 in Schuylkill Co., PA; married (?) MILLER.
2. JACKSON KRAMER (B6412), born in 1850 in Schuylkill Co., PA
3. GEORGE KRAMER, born in 1852 in Schuylkill Co., PA
4. WELLINGTON KRAMER, born in 1860 in Schuylkill Co., PA.
5. ABRAHAM KRAMER, born in 1861 in Schuylkill Co., PA.
6. CARRIE "DOLLY" KRAMER
7. LUCIAN KRAMER, born in 1866 in Schuylkill Co., PA.
8. CLARA KRAMER, born in 1868 in Schuylkill Co., PA.

References: Father's Will, 24-South Manheim Twp Schuylkill Co PA H53, 26-Auburn Schuylkill Co PA H66, 25-Auburn Schuylkill Co PA H41, 27-Auburn Twp Schuylkill Co PA H25

B692 CLARA AGNES KRAMER B69

CLARA AGNES KRAMER was born in 17 Sep 1856 in Auburn, Schuylkill Co., PA and died 11 Dec 1914 Lisbon, Linn Co., IA. She married GEORGE STINE MCCLELLAND on 27 Nov 1878 Lisbon, Linn Co., IA. He was born in 1856 in IA and died before 1900 in Linn Co., IA. Both are buried in Lot 46 Lisbon Cemetery, Lisbon, IA.

Child of CLARA KRAMER and GEORGE MCCLELLAND is:

1. JEAN E. MCCLELLAND, born in Sep 1879 in Linn Co., IA.
2. JOHN EMERY MCCLELLAND, born in Mar 1885 in Linn Co., IA.
3. LOU G. MCCLELLAND (f), born in Jun 1889 in Linn Co., IA.
4. THREE CHILDREN, born 1880-1900 and died by 1900 in Linn Co., IA

References: 27-Mt Vernon Linn Co IA H79, 29-Franklin Linn Co IA H28, 45

B693 LYDIA ANN KRAMER B69

LYDIA ANN KRAMER was born in 1859 in PA. She married HENRY FRUCHEY on 20 Oct 1881 Linn Co., IA. He was born in 1858 in PA.

Children of LYDIA KRAMER and HENRY FRUCHEY are:

1. GEORGE FRUCHEY, born in 1882 in Linn Co., IA.
2. LEWIS FRUCHEY, born in 1884 in Linn Co., IA.
3. CLAUDE FRUCHEY, born in 1893 in Linn Co., IA.
4. LEONARD FRUCHEY, born in 1896 in Linn Co., IA.

References: 30-Cedar Rapids Linn Co IA H515, 10-Cedar Rapids Linn Co IA H163

B694 EMMA REBECCA KRAMER B69

EMMA REBECCA KRAMER was born in Sep 1860 in Clearfield Co., PA. She married ROBERT E. MORFORD on 23 Apr 1891 Linn Co., IA; born 1861. He died 1914 Mt. Vernon, Linn Co., IA. They are buried at Mt. Vernon, Linn Co., IA.

Child of EMMA KRAMER and ROBERT MORFORD is:

1. UNKNOWN MORFORD, born 1891-1900 and died by 1900 in Linn Co., IA.

References: 29-Franklin Linn Co IA H351

B695 SARAH JANE KRAMER B69

SARAH "AUNT SADIE" JANE KRAMER was born in Nov 1862 in Clearfield Co., PA. She married PLINY A. HANDLEY on 27 Feb 1883 Linn Co., IA. He was born in May 1856 in IL.

Children of SARAH KRAMER and PLINY HANDLEY are:

1. OTHO N. HANDLEY, born in Nov 1884 in Linn Co., IA.
2. GLADYS M. HANDLEY, born in Sep 1891 in Linn Co., IA.
3. MAYNARD A. HANDLEY, born in Mar 1898 in Linn Co., IA.

References: 29-Franklin Linn Co IA H89

B69A NELSON ROBERT KRAMER B69

NELSON ROBERT KRAMER was born in 1871 in Linn Co., IA. He married MARGARET. She was born in 1885 in NY.

Children of NELSON KRAMER and MARGARET are:

1. ALICE KRAMER, born in 1905 in MT.

2. ROBERT KRAMER, born in 1907 in MT.
3. HURBERT KRAMER, born in 1908 in MT.
4. GLADYS KRAMER, born in 1910 in MT.
5. LAURA KRAMER, born in 1915 in MT.
6. LEROY KRAMER, born in 1916 in MT.
7. JACK B. KRAMER, born in 1920 in MT.

References: 10-Eureka Lincoln Co MT H196, 31-Kalispell Flathead Co MT H327

B69D MARY CATHARINE KRAMER B69

MARY "MATE" CATHARINE KRAMER was born in 09 Mar 1875 in Linn Co., IA and died 16 Mar 1958 in Cedar Rapids, Linn Co., IA. She married OTTIS LEROY ELLISON on 07 Oct 1903 Lisbon, Linn Co., IA. He was born 13 Aug 1878 near Mt. Vernon, Linn Co., IA and died18 Oct 1955 Solon, Johnson Co., IA. She was a seamstress by occupation and a homemaker. Both are buried in Mt. Vernon Cemetery, Franklin Twp., Linn Co., IA.

Children of MARY KRAMER and OTTIS ELLISON are:

1. MYRON L. ELLISON, born in 1906 in Linn Co., IA.
2. FLORENCE M. ELLISON, born in 1908 in Linn Co., IA.
3. GORDON W. ELLISON, born in 1910 in Linn Co., IA.
4. HARLAN E. ELLISON, born in 1912 in Linn Co., IA.
5. DORIS A. ELLISON, born in 1915 in Linn Co., IA.
6. MARY K. ELLISON, born in 1917 in Linn Co., IA.
7. ARLO C. ELLISON, born in 1923 in Linn Co., IA.

References: 30-Linn Twp Linn Co IA H184, 10-Linn Twp Linn Co IA H70, 31-Linn Twp Linn Co IA H35

B6A1 SAMUEL T. KRAMER B6A

SAMUEL T. KRAMER was born on 05 May 1855 in Huntington Co., IN and died 19 Sep 1932 in Huntington Co., IN. He married KATHERINE in Huntington Co., IN. She was born in 28 Nov 1858 in OH and died 10 Dec 1936 in Huntington Co., IN. Both are buried in Pilgrims Rest Cemetery, Huntington Twp., Huntington Co., IN.

Children of SAMUEL KRAMER and KATHERINE are:

1. ALFRED KRAMER, born in 1876 in Huntington Co., IN.
2. GEORGE KRAMER, born in Feb 1878 in Huntington Co., IN.

References: 27-Huntington Twp Huntington Co IN H120, 45, 29-Dist 0080 Huntington Twp Huntington Co IN H116

B6A2 CYRUS KRAMER B6A

CYRUS KRAMER was born in 1857 in Huntington Co., IN and died 1933 in Huntington Co., IN. He married (1) LOTTIE in IN. She was born in 1865 in OH. He divorced his 1st wife and married (2) EVETTA in IN. She was born in Oct 1878 in OH and died before 1910 in IN. He is buried in Mount Hope Cemetery, Huntington Twp., Huntington Co., IN.

Child of CYRUS KRAMER and LOTTIE is:

1. FRANK R. KRAMER, born in 1886 in IN.

Children of CYRUS KRAMER and EVETTA are:

2. WILLIAM KRAMER, born in Oct 1896 in IN.
3. PAUL F. KRAMER, born in May 1899 in IN.

References: 29-Noble Wabash Co IN H291, 30-Huntington Twp Ward 4 Huntington Co IN H17, 45

B6A3 HENRY KRAMER B6A3

HENRY KRAMER was born in 1861 in Huntington Co., IN. He married LENORA in Huntington Co., IN. She was born in Oct 1864 in OH.

Children of HENRY KRAMER and LENORA are:

1. CHESTER A. KRAMER, born in Feb 1882 in Huntington Co., IN.
2. MAMIE KRAMER, born in Apr 1886 in Huntington Co., IN.
3. HENRY L. KRAMER, born in Sep 1891 in Huntington Co., IN.
4. NINA KRAMER, born in Aug 1894 in Huntington Co., IN.
5. OTHEL D. KRAMER, born in Jun 1897 in Huntington Co., IN.
6. ERWIN O. KRAMER, born in 1902 in Huntington Co., IN.
7. HELEN L. KRAMER, born in 1908 in Huntington Co., IN.

References: 29-Huntington Twp Huntington Co IN H208, 30-Huntington Twp Ward 4 Huntington Co IN H240

B6A4 GEORGE E. KRAMER B6A

GEORGE E. KRAMER was born in May 1867 in Huntington Co., IN. He married MARY E. in Huntingdon Co., IN. She was born in Nov 1874 in IN.

Children of GEORGE KRAMER and MARY are:

1. LEROY KRAMER, born in Feb 1893 in Huntington Co., IN.
2. MARY KRAMER, born in Mar 1896 in Huntington Co., IN.
3. HAZEL KRAMER, born in Mar 1899 in Huntington Co., IN.

References: 29- Huntington Twp Huntington Co IN H531

B6B1 JACKSON MOYER B6B

JACKSON MOYER was born 1846 in Schuylkill Co., PA. He married Mary born in 1843 in PA.

1. ISAAC MOYER, born in 1866 in Auburn, Schuylkill Co., PA.
2. LOTTA MOYER, born in 1868 in Auburn, Schuylkill Co., PA.
3. MASUR A. MOYER, born in 1869 in Auburn, Schuylkill Co., PA.

References: 26-Auburn Schuylkill Co PA H79

B6B2 MATILDA MOYER B6B

MATILDA MOYER was born in 1849 in Schuylkill Co., PA. She married CHARLES WESTERFIELD in Schuylkill Co., PA. He was born in 1839 in NJ. He was a carpenter by occupation.

Children of MATILDA MOYER and CHARLES WESTERFIELD are:

1. HARRY M. WESTERFIELD, born in 1870 in Schuylkill Co., PA.
2. LORTON WESTERFIELD, born in 1870 in Schuylkill Co., PA.

References: 27-Reading Berks Co PA H921

B6B3 GEORGE H. MOYER B6B

GEORGE H. MOYER was born in 1853 Schuylkill Co, PA. He married KATE in Schuylkill Co., PA. She was born in 1854 in PA.

Children of GEORGE MOYER and KATE are:

1. VALEY MOYER (f), born in 1874 in Schuylkill Co., PA.
2. JESTER MOYER, born in 1877 in Schuylkill Co., PA.

References: 27-Pine Grove Borough Schuylkill Co PA H132, 29-Pine Grove Borough Schuylkill Co PA H235

B6B4 MORGAN WALTER MOYER B6B

MORGAN WALTER MOYER was born on 09 Feb 1855 in Schuylkill Co, PA and died 29 Nov 1857 in Schuylkill Co, PA. He married ELIZABETH "LIZZIE" in Schuylkill Co., PA. She was born in May 1850 in PA. He is buried in Auburn Cemetery, Auburn, Schuylkill Co, PA.

Children of MORGAN MOYER and ELIZABETH are:

1. ROSA MOYER (B6B41)
2. LILLIE MOYER, born in 1873 in Schuylkill Co, PA and died before 1910.

References: 27-Auburn Twp Schuylkill Co PA H62, 29-Auburn Twp Schuylkill Co PA H51, 30-Camden Ward 4 Camden Co NJ H247

B6B5 MARY CECELIA MOYER B6B

MARY CECELIA MOYER was born in Jan 1855 in Schuylkill Co, PA. She married HENRY LUCKINBILL in Schuylkill Co, PA. He was born in Oct 1853 in PA.

Children of MARY MOYER and HENRY LUCKINBILL are:

1. SARAH LUCKINBILL, born in 1874 in Schuylkill Co, PA.
2. KATE LUCKINBILL, born in 1876 in Schuylkill Co, PA.
3. WILLIAM LUCKINBILL, born in 1878 in Schuylkill Co, PA.
4. JOHN E. LUCKINBILL, born in May 1880 in Schuylkill Co, PA.
5. HENRY LUCKINBILL, born in Aug 1882 in Schuylkill Co, PA.
6. ROBERT N. LUCKINBILL, born in Oct 1885 in Schuylkill Co, PA.
7. EMMA V. LUCKINBILL, born in Nov 1888 in Schuylkill Co, PA.
8. MARTHA A. LUCKINBILL, born in Feb 1890 in Schuylkill Co, PA.
9. THOMAS J. LUCKINBILL, born in Apr 1894 in Schuylkill Co, PA.

References: 27-Auburn Twp Schuylkill Co PA H28, 29-South Manheim Twp Schuylkill Co PA H307

B6C2 DANIEL KRAMER B6C

DANIEL KRAMER was born on 10 Apr 1848 in Schuylkill Co., PA and died 12 Oct 1938 in Schuylkill Co., PA. He married LYDIA S. "ELIZABETH" BERGER on 17 May 1868 in Auburn, Schuylkill Co., PA. She was born on 21 Oct 1845 in PA and died 12 Feb 1898 in Schuylkill Co., PA. He served in the civil war in the Union Army Co. F, 116th PA Infantry from 01 Feb 1864 to 14 Jul 1865 as a musician and was wounded in the Battle of the Wilderness. Both are buried in the St. John's Church Cemetery, Auburn, Schuylkill Co., PA.

Children of DANIEL KRAMER and LYDIA BERGER are:

1. EDWARD KRAMER, born in 1869 in Auburn, Schuylkill Co., PA.
2. MARY ANN L. KRAMER, born in Jul 1874 in PA.
3. SUSAN D. KRAMER, born in Aug 1876 in PA.
4. WINFIELD SCOTT KRAMER, born in Jul 1878 in PA.
5. JAMES A. G. KRAMER, born in Aug 1880 in PA.
6. IDA M. KRAMER, born in Jan 1883 in PA.
7. JESSE J. KRAMER, born in Oct 1884 in PA.

References: 45, 26-Auburn Schuylkill Co PA H72, 27-Reading Berks Co PA H39, 29-Reading Ward 13 Berks Co PA H1004

B6C3 REBECCA KRAMER B6C

REBECCA KRAMER was born 1850 in Schuylkill Co., PA and died 01 Mar 1939. She married CHARLES TALLMAN. He was born on 17 May 1840 in NJ.

Children of REBECCA KRAMER and CHARLES TALLMAN are:

1. HENRY TALLMAN, born in 1870 in PA.
2. SADIE TALLMAN, born in 1871 in NJ.
3. HANNAH TALLMAN, born in 1873 in NJ.
4. BENJAMIN TALLMAN, born in Apr 1879 in PA.
5. LEWIS TALLMAN, born in Sep 1882 in NJ.
6. ISAAC TALLMAN, born in Apr 1883 in NJ.
7. HOWARD TALLMAN, born in Mar 1886 in NJ.

References: 27-Reading Berks Co PA H128, 29-Pequannock Twp Morris Co NJ H418

B6C4 BENJAMIN KRAMER B6C

BENJAMIN KRAMER was born Sep 1850 in Schuylkill Co., PA and died 14 Nov 1899 in PA. He married CATHARINE "KATE" RACER on 18 May 1872 in Schuylkill Co., PA. She was born in Oct 1846 and died 09 Feb 1884 in Schuylkill Co., PA. Both are buried in the St. John's Church Cemetery, Auburn, Schuylkill Co., PA.

Children of BENJAMIN KRAMER and KATE RACER are:

1. HENRY KRAMER, born in 1872 in Schuylkill Co., PA.
2. IRENE KRAMER, born in 1877 in Schuylkill Co., PA.
3. ELLEN KRAMER, born in 1879 in Schuylkill Co., PA.

References: 27-Palo Alto Schuylkill Co., PA H91

B6C8 LEWIS T. KRAMER B6C

LEWIS T. KRAMER was born in Jun 1860 in Schuylkill Co., PA and died 11 Jun 1930 in Schuylkill Co., PA. He married ALICE H. REBER on 25 Dec 1884 in Schuylkill Co., PA. She was born in 1861 and died 04 Jul 1950 in Schuylkill Co., PA. Both are buried in the St. John's Church Cemetery, Auburn, Schuylkill Co., PA.

Children of LEWIS KRAMER and ALICE REBER are:

1. HERMAN R. KRAMER, born in Sep 1886 in Schuylkill Co., PA.
2. LUTHER R. KRAMER, born in Oct 1887 in Schuylkill Co., PA.
3. ANNETTA R. KRAMER, born in Jun 1893 in Schuylkill Co., PA.
4. ESTELLA R. KRAMER, born in Jul 1896 in Schuylkill Co., PA.

References: 45, 29-South Manheim Twp Schuylkill Co PA H253, 30-South Manheim Twp Schuylkill Co PA H72

B921 REUBEN RICHARDSON B92

REUBEN RICHARDSON was born in 1825 in Berks Co., PA. He married SARAH. She was born in 1832 in PA.

Children of REUBEN RICHARDSON and SARAH are:

1. MARY RICHARDSON, born in 1855 in Berks Co., PA.
2. KATE RICHARDSON, born in 1855 in Berks Co., PA.

References: 27-Marion Twp Berks Co PA, 26-Heidelberg Twp Berks Co PA H163, 25-Marion Twp Berks Co PA H106

B931 BENNEVILLE HIESTER B93

BENNEVILLE HIESTER was born in 1829 in Berks Co., PA. He married ANNIE E. She was born in 1831 in PA.

Children of BENNEVILLE HIESTER and ANNIE are:

1. EMMA HIESTER, born in 1855 in Berks Co., PA.
2. ISAAC HIESTER, born in 1862 in Berks Co., PA.
3. MARY K. HIESTER, born in 1865 in Berks Co., PA.

References: 26-Bern Twp Berks Co PA H291

B933 HARRISON K. HIESTER B93

HARRISON K. HIESTER was born on 06 Aug 1832 in Bern Twp., Berks Co, PA. He married ROSABELLA KISCHNER. She was born on 16 Sep 1834 and died 24 Feb 1878 in Bern Twp., berks Co., PA. "He was the owner of the old homestead, consisting of 134 acres, and later he bought an adjoining farm of 107 acres from his brother BENNEVILLE, the transaction taking place in 1876. He was an enterprising farmer and a man of progress in his community. At the time of his death he was serving as school director. In politics he was a Democrat. He was a liberal supporter of the Reformed faith and of the Bern Church."

Children of HARRISON HIESTER are:

1. KATIE HIESTER, born in 1858 in Berks Co., PA, married AARON BOHN. Resided in Mt. Pleasant, Berks Co., PA.
2. ELLEN HIESTER, born in 1859 in Berks Co., PA, married J. F. YEAGER.
3. THOMAS K. HIESTER, born in 1861 in Berks Co., PA, born on 16 Dec 1861 in Bern Twp., Berks Co., PA.
4. MARY HIESTER, born in 1863 in Berks Co., PA, married JONATHAN OHLINGER.
5. ROSA HIESTER, born in 1865 in Berks Co., PA, married ADAM GUBER.
6. SALLIE HIESTER, born in 1867 in Berks Co., PA; died before 1909 Berks Co., PA; married CYRUS BOHN.
7. ANNIE HIESTER, born in 1869 in Berks Co., PA; married HENRY STAMM.
8. JEMIMA HIESTER
9. EDWARD K. HIESTER (B9339)
10. HARRY K. HIESTER (B933A)
11. LIZZIE HIESTER, married GRANT HARTMAN.

References: 49, 26-Bern Twp Berks Co PA H290

B935 MARIA HIESTER B93

MARIA HIESTER was born in 1826 in Berks Co, PA; married JOHN EYRICH. He was born in 1826 in PA.

Child of MARIA HIESTER and JOHN EYRICH is:

1. WELLINGTON EYRICH, born in 1857 in Berks Co., PA.

References: 25-Bern Twp Berks Co., PA

B943 CAROLINE KRAMER B94

CAROLINE KRAMER was born 1840 in Berks Co., PA. She married WILLIAM B. BLATT in Berks Co., PA, son of JOHN BLATT. He was born in 1838 in PA.

Children of CAROLINE KRAMER and WILLIAM BLATT are:

1. JOHN BLATT, born in 1864 in Centre Twp., Berks Co., PA.
2. CLARA BLATT, born in 1866 in Centre Twp., Berks Co., PA.
3. EMMA BLATT, born in 1867 in Centre Twp., Berks Co., PA.
4. RICHARD BLATT, born in 1869 in Centre Twp., Berks Co., PA.
5. JAMES BLATT, born in 1871 in Centre Twp., Berks Co., PA.
6. MILTON BLATT, born in 1873 in Centre Twp., Berks Co., PA.
7. AARON BLATT, born in Oct 1874 in Centre Twp., Berks Co., PA.
8. WILLIAM B. BLATT, born in Oct 1874 in Centre Twp., Berks Co., PA; married ANNA L. AULENBACH on 17 Oct 1903 in Reading, Berks Co., PA, daughter of ALLEN D. AULENBACH and KATHRYN R.

References: 26-Centre Twp Berks Co PA H69, 27-Centre Twp Berks Co PA H54, 31-Muhlenberg Twp Berks Co PA H4

B945 JARED KRAMER B94

JARED KRAMER was born 1846 in Bern Twp., Berks Co., PA. He married AMELIA in Berks Co., PA. She was born in 1856 in PA and died before 1900 in Berks Co., PA.

Children of JARED KRAMER and AMELIA are:

1. ALLISON F. KRAMER (B9451)
2. MAMIE KRAMER, born in Jul 1881 in Bern Twp., Berks Co., PA.
3. LUANN A. KRAMER, born in Oct 1887 in Bern Twp., Berks Co., PA.

References: 27-Bern Twp Berks Co PA H3, 29-Bern Twp Berks Co PA H82

B962 JOHN F. KRAMER B96

JOHN F. KRAMER was born on 24 May 1837 in Bern Twp., Berks Co., PA. He married CATHARINE KOENIG in WI. He served in the Civil war from 1861 until the close of the struggle and afterward he settled in WI.

Children of JOHN KRAMER and CATHARINE KOENIG are:

1. DAVID KRAMER
2. CHARLES KRAMER
3. LIZZIE KRAMER, died before 1903.
4. LAWRENCE KRAMER

References: 49

B963 DANIEL F. KRAMER B96

DANIEL F. KRAMER was born 1838 in Bern Twp., Berks Co., PA. He married (1) LOVINA LASH, daughter of JOHN LASH and SUSANNA RICHARD. She died 19 Jan 1877. He married (2) ELIZABETH R. HARTMAN, daughter of the late SAMUEL HARTMAN and HANNAH RAPP. "He attended public school until he was twenty years of age, when he went to Perry County and assisted in building the county barn. This was in 1860, and at the end of six months he returned to Berks County, where for sixteen years he had a good force of men working for him all over the county, building houses and barns. He then engaged in farming, having a tract of twenty-two acres. He has served as assessor in his township for a period of nineteen years, the court of the county having first appointed him to that position upon the death of his father. In politics he is a Democrat, and has served the county for nine years as prison inspector. He is a member of the Lutheran congregation at Epler's Church, and has been deacon and elder."

Children of DANIEL KRAMER and LOVINA LASH are:

1. MARIA KRAMER, married ABRAHAM BARR
2. MILTON KRAMER, born 14 May 1864 died in 26 Aug 1865. He is buried in Epler's Church Cemetery, Leesport, Berks Co., PA.
3. ELLEN KRAMER, died in 1875, aged ten years
4. ADAM KRAMER (B9634)
5. CLARA KRAMER, died in 1876, aged two years.

Children of DANIEL KRAMER and ELIZABETH HARTMAN are:

6. GEORGE WILLIAM KRAMER, died age three years.
7. CARRIE KRAMER, married SAMUEL STOUT. Resided in Reading, Berks Co., PA.

References: 49

B965 ALBERT F. KRAMER B96

ALBERT F. KRAMER was born on 27 Sep 1843 in Bern Twp., Berks Co., PA. He married ANNA M. DE TURK in Berks Co., PA. She was born in Dec 1845 in PA

Children of ALBERT KRAMER and ANNA DE TURK are:

1. HARVEY DE TURK KRAMER, born in Apr 1875 in Berks Co., PA.
2. EDITH M. KRAMER, born in Aug 1878 in Berks Co., PA.
3. ESTHER C. KRAMER, born in Nov 1879 in Berks Co., PA.
4. UNKNOWN CHILD KRAMER, died before 1909 in Reading, Berks Co., PA.

References: 49, 29-Dist 0052 Ward 3 Reading Berks Co PA H67

B966 CATHARINE F. KRAMER B96

CATHARINE "KATE" F. KRAMER was born on 17 May 1845 in Bern Twp., Berks Co., PA. She married JACOB B. SNYDER in Berks Co., PA. He was born in May 1841 in PA.

Children of CATHARINE KRAMER and JACOB SNYDER are:

1. CLARA K. SNYDER (B9661)
2. IDA K. SNYDER (B9662)
3. EVA ANN SNYDER (B9663)
4. HOWARD C. SNYDER (B9664)
5. IRVIN J. SNYDER (B9665)
6. ALLEN SNYDER (B9666)

References: 49, 26-Penn Twp Berks Co PA H151, 27-Penn Twp Berks Co PA 035 H78, 29-Dist 0031 Lower Heidelberg Twp Berks Co PA H215

B96A HENRY F. KRAMER B96

HENRY F. KRAMER was born in 24 Mar 1856 in Bern Twp, Berks Co., PA. He married to EMMA H. DUNKELBERGER in Berks Co., PA. She was born in Jan 1862 in PA.

Children of HENRY KRAMER and EMMA DUNKELBERGER are:

1. BERTHA K. KRAMER (B96A1)
2. MACIE KRAMER, born and died before 1909 in Berks Co., PA.
3. JOHN D. KRAMER, born in Jun 1891 in Berks Co., PA.

References: 49, 29-Dist 0037 Muhlenberg Berks Co PA H60, 29-Dist 0037 Muhlenberg Berks Co PA H57

B96B EDWARD F. KRAMER B96

EDWARD F. KRAMER was born on 09 Jan 1860 in Bern Twp, Berks Co., PA. He married EMMA C. LIEB on 07 Apr 1884 in Berks Co., PA. She was born in Mar 1859 in PA.

Children of EDWARD KRAMER and EMMA LIEB are:

1. HARRY LIEB KRAMER, born in Dec 1885 in Berks Co., PA.
2. FLORENCE MAY KRAMER, born in Jul 1887 in Berks Co., PA.

3. DANIEL JOSHUA KRAMER, born in Jan 1893 in Berks Co., PA.

References: 49, 29-Dist 0071 Ward 8 Reading Berks Co PA H84

B969 GEORGE F. KRAMER B96

GEORGE F. KRAMER was born on 01 Mar 1853 in Bern Twp. Berks Co., PA and died 27 Mar 1909 Berks Co., PA. He married (1) LOUISA SUENDERS on 19 May 1875, daughter of GEORGE SUENDERS and CATHARINE EISENHARD. She was born on 24 Nov 1852 and died 02 Jun 1887 Berks Co., PA. He (2) SUSAN E. LERCH, daughter of JACOB LERCH and REBECCA ROTH. She was born on 04 Aug 1859 and died 08 Dec 1951 Berks Co., PA. "He was a truck farmer and tax collector of his township. He was reared to farming, and when eighteen years of age learned the trade of stone-mason from his brother Daniel F. This he followed until 1895, working at different places. He was foreman for Howard E. Ahrens, a contractor of Reading for a number of years, for whom he worked in Steelton, Newport (Perry county), Reading and elsewhere, having under him all the time from twenty to thirty men. He was also in the employ of JOSEPH P. O'REILY, a contractor of Reading, for whom he worked at the Schuylkill avenue bridge at Reading and also at the Cross Key Bridge. Since 1895 he has lived at the old home farm, having about twenty acres of good truck land, keeps two cows and an average of 125 chickens (besides what he uses for his family), and during 1908 sold five hundred and sixty-three pounds of butter from the two cows, the price ranging from thirty to thirty-four cents a pound, and ten hundred and seventy-one dozens of eggs, the price ranging from sixteen to forty cents a dozen. He attends the Reading market. He is a Democrat in politics, and his first public office was that of precinct inspector. Then he became judge of election, and in 1903 was appointed by the court, tax collector of Bern Township, and three years later was elected to the same office. He is a Lutheran member of Bern Church, while his wife belongs to the Reformed Congregation. He has served as deacon and elder."

Children of GEORGE KRAMER and LOUISA SUENDERS are:

1. CHARLES MILTON KRAMER (B9691)
2. JENNIE B. KRAMER (B9692)

Children of GEORGE KRAMER and SUSAN LERCH are:

3. ANNIE R. KRAMER, born in 1895 in Berks Co., PA
4. MARY C. KRAMER, born in 1903 in Berks Co., PA.

References: 49, 45

B971 ADAM HIESTER B97

ADAM HIESTER was born on 05 Sep 1838 in Berks Co., PA and died 26 May 1923 in Berks Co., PA. He married REBECCA GRING. She was born on 29 Oct 1833 in PA and died 22 Oct 1913 in Berks Co., PA. Both are buried in Bern Cemetery, Bernville, Berks Co., PA.

Children of ADAM HIESTER and REBECCA GRING are:

1. REBECCA G. HIESTER (B9711)
2. GABRIAL JACOB HIESTER, born in 11 Oct 1862 in Berks Co., PA; died 01 Mar 1887 in Berks Co., PA; buried in Bern Cemetery, Bernville, Berks Co., PA.

References: 26-Bern Twp Berks Co PA H289, 45, 27-Bern Twp Berks Co PA H157

B972 LYDIA HIESTER B97

LYDIA M. HIESTER was born in 1840 in Berks Co., PA. She married JONATHAN MOYER. He was born in 1838 in PA.

Children of LYDIA HIESTER and JONATHAN MOYER are:

1. ALMA A. MOYER, born 1865 in Berks Co., PA.
2. ALICE MOYER, born 1869 in Berks Co., PA.

3. VIELLA MOYER, born 1875 in Berks Co., PA.

References: 26-Spring Twp Berks Co PA H158, 27-Bern Twp Berks Co PA H148

B974 JOHN K. HIESTER B97

JOHN K. HIESTER was born on 02 Nov 1848 in Berks Co., PA. He married HETTIE A. DEISHER on 30 Oct 1890 in Berks Co., PA, daughter of WILLIAM DEISHER and SARAH STAYER. She was born on Oct. 30, 1857 in Berks Co., PA. "His education was obtained in the township schools, at a Reading academy, and at the Keystone State Normal School, at Kutztown. In the fall of 1866 he began teaching at HIESTER's school in Bern township, and during the winter of 1868-69 he taught in Maiden-creek township; later taught one year in Bern township; three terms in Ruscombmanor township; three terms in Exeter township; one term in Jefferson; one term in Ontelaunee; two terms in Birdsboro; three terms in Cumru; two terms in Robeson, and then thirteen terms in Bern township, in all thirty-two terms, his services being given all over the county, with fifteen terms in his native township. He thus became widely known, and is held in high esteem, and he constantly meets his former pupils, many of whom never received other instruction than that he gave them. During the summer months, until 1890, Mr. HIESTER worked upon the farm in his native township, but in that year he came to Reading and in the following year he purchased his comfortable home at No. 314 South Thirteenth street, where he has resided ever since. After establishing his home at Reading he continued to follow his profession during the winter months until 1898-1899, when he taught for the last time. For five summer seasons he was in the employ of Alderman Griesemer and subsequently worked as labor boss and shipping clerk in the Johnson Foundry & Machine Company, where he continued for seven years; when that firm went out of business he went to the American Iron & Steel Company, where he has remained until the present...Mr. HIESTER has spent almost all of his life in Berks county, but in January, 1869, he went to Lee county, Iowa, where he worked on a farm until his return to Berks county in the following October. Politically he is a Democrat. He is a member of Bern Union Church and the Reformed denomination. His wife worships in Grace Lutheran Church."

Children of JOHN HIESTER and HETTIE DEISHER are:

1. S. ADELLA HIESTER, born on 21 Feb 1892 in Berks Co., PA.
2. MORRIS W. HIESTER, born in Aug 1893; died in Oct 1893 in Berks Co., PA.
3. WILLIAM L. HIESTER, born on 17 Jun 1895 in Berks Co., PA.

References: 49

B996 JOHN KRAMER BODY B99

JOHN KRAMER BODY was born in Dec 1850 in PA. He married ANNIE. She was born in Sep 1867 in PA.

Child of JOHN BODY and ANNIE is:

1. MAUDE E. BODY, born in Jan 1888 in Berks Co., PA.

References: 29-Reading Berks Co PA H112

B6412 JACKSON KRAMER B641

JACKSON KRAMER was born in 1850 in Schuylkill Co., PA and died 1940 Schuylkill Co., PA. He married JOANNA FEGLEY. She was born in 1848 in PA and died 1936 Schuylkill Co., PA. Both are buried in Saint John's Church Cemetery, Auburn, Schuylkill Co., PA.

Child of JACKSON KRAMER and JOANNA is:

1. BERTHA KRAMER, born in 1877 in Auburn, Schuylkill Co., PA.

References: 27-Auburn Schuylkill Co PA H95, 45

B6B41 ROSA MOYER B6B4

ROSA MOYER was born in Jan 1871 in Schuylkill Co, PA. She married MILTON M. DIEBERT in Schuylkill Co, PA. He was born in May 1870 in PA.

Child of ROSA MOYER and MILTON DIEBERT is:

1. ROBERT DIEBERT, born in 1890 in Schuylkill Co, PA.

Reference: 29-Auburn Twp Schuylkill Co PA H51, 30-Camden Ward 4 Camden Co NJ H247

B9339 EDWARD K. HIESTER B933

EDWARD K. HIESTER was born on 01 May 1871 in Bern Twp., Berks Co., PA and died 23 Feb 1951 in Berks Co., PA. He married SALLIE ANN SCHWOYER in 1892 in Berks Co., PA, daughter of CORNELIUS SCHWOYER and SARAH LOOSER. She was born 17 Sep 1867 in PA and died 31 Oct 1948 in Berks Co., PA. "He attended the public schools of his native township and during 1888-89 was a student for two sessions at the Kutztown State Normal School, after which he worked for his father on the farm. In 1898 he began to farm for himself and bought one of the HIESTER homesteads. It is valuable land, and Mr. HIESTER has improved it by erecting fine buildings and modernizing his residence to a large degree, putting in a system of water pressure. His land adjoins the Bern Church property. Politically Mr. HIESTER is a Democrat, and he has served as township assessor. He is serving in his third term in this office and is a popular public official. For two years he served as a deacon of the Bern Reformed Church." Both are buried in Bern Cemetery, Bernville, Berks Co., PA.

Children of EDWARD HIESTER and SALLIE SCHWOYER are:

1. ABNER S. HIESTER (B93391)
2. HARRY EDWARD HIESTER, born in 22 Aug 1894 in Berks Co., PA; died 21 Sep 1955 in Berks Co., PA; buried in Bern Cemetery, Bernville, Berks Co., PA.
3. EARL SWOYER HIESTER (B93393)

4. BERTHA EDNA HIESTER, born in 11 Feb 1898 in Berks Co., PA; died 12 Oct 1972 in Berks Co., PA; buried in Bern Cemetery, Bernville, Berks Co., PA.
5. EDWARD LEROY HIESTER, born in 28 Jul 1900 in Berks Co., PA; died 02 Dec 1974 in Berks Co., PA; buried in Bern Cemetery, Bernville, Berks Co., PA.
6. JOHN E. HIESTER (B93396)

References: 49, 45, 29-Dist 0005 Bern Twp Berks Co PA H154, 30-Bern Twp Berks Co PA 0005 H43

B933A HARRY K. HIESTER B933

HARRY K. HIESTER was born on 27 Jul 1874 in Bern Twp., Berks Co., PA and died 26 Mar 1947 in Berks Co., PA. He married KATE ELLEN MENGEL in 1895 in Berks Co., PA, daughter of WILLIAM MENGEL and ANNA E. KEIM. She was born on 02 Feb 1871 in PA and died 02 Feb 1936 in Berks Co., PA. He "received his early education in the schools of Bern Township and later pursued his studies at the Keystone State Normal School, at Kutztown, Berks County. Remaining at home with his father until he was nineteen years old, he made his home with his sister, Mrs. Kate Bohn, for the next four years, at the end of that time commencing farming on his own account. He first lived on JOSEPH REBER's farm in Bern Township, for one year, and then moved to the WILLIAM DUNDORE farm, in the same township, for three years, after which he was on JAMES T. REBER's farm, in Lower Heidelberg Township, for two years. In October, 1904, he bought a place in Penn Township from his father's estate, and there he has ever resided, carrying on general agricultural pursuits. He has 118 acres of fine land, upon which he is continually making improvements, and he attends the reading market once a week, having a steady demand for his products. Mr. HIESTER is a member of Bern Reformed Church and, in fraternal connection, of the K. G. E. at Leesport. He is a Democrat in political opinion."

Children of HARRY HIESTER and KATE MENGEL are:

1. MINERVA HIESTER, born in Jun 1892 in Berks Co., PA.
2. LESTER W. HIESTER, born in Nov 1896 in Berks Co., PA.
3. CHARLES W. HIESTER, born in 1904 in Berks Co., PA.
4. CARRIE A. HIESTER, born in 1907 in Berks Co., PA.

References: 49, 45, 29-Dist 0004 Bern Twp Berks Co PA H30, 30-Penn Twp Berks Co PA 0044 H113, 10-Dist 8 Penn Twp Berks Co PA H86

B9451 ALLISON F. KRAMER B945

ALLISON F. KRAMER was born in Dec 1877 in Bern Twp., Berks Co., PA. He married (1) (?) in Berks Co., PA. She died before 1900 in Berks Co., PA. He married (2) ARABELLA Y. in Berks Co., PA. She was born in 1878 in PA.

Child of ALLISON KRAMER and (?) is:

1. KATIE M. KRAMER, born in May 1894 in Bern Twp., Berks Co., PA.

Child of ALLISON KRAMER and ARABELLA is:

2. JOHN L. KRAMER, born in 1900 in Bern Twp., Berks Co., PA.

References: 30-Bern Twp Berks Co PA H163, 29- Bern Twp Berks Co PA H82

B9634 ADAM KRAMER B963

ADAM KRAMER married (1) GERTRUDE STAMM. She died leaving two daughters. He married (2) MARY ROTHENBERGER.

Children of ADAM KRAMER and GERTRUDE STAMM are:

1. STELLA KRAMER
2. ELLEN KRAMER

References: 49

B9661 CLARA K. SNYDER B966

CLARA K. SNYDER was born in Mar 1867 in Berks Co., PA. She married JONATHAN S. REBER in Berks Co., PA. He was born in Jul 1863 in PA.

Children of CLARA SNYDER and JONATHAN REBER are:

1. WILLIAM A. REBER (B96611)
2. ADAM S. REBER (B96612)
3. LEWIS F. REBER (B96613)
4. HOWARD S. REBER (B96614)
5. JONATHAN S. REBER (B96615)
6. KATIE S. REBER, born in Jul 1892 in Berks Co., PA.
7. EDNA S. REBER, born in Aug 1894 in Berks Co., PA.
8. ALICE S. REBER, born in Oct 1897 in Berks Co., PA.
9. CLAYTON D. REBER (B96619)
10. IRVIN J. REBER, born in 1903 in Berks Co., PA.
11. RAYMOND R. REBER (B9661B)
12. NORMAN F. REBER, born in 1909 in Berks Co., PA.

References: 29-Dist 0010 Centre Twp Berks Co PA H134, 30-Centre Twp Berks Co PA 0012 H81

B9662 IDA K. SNYDER B966

IDA K. SNYDER was born in 01 Dec 1868 in Berks Co., PA and died 23 May 1948 in Berks Co., PA. She married JACOB C. KIRKHOFF in Berks Co., PA. He was born in 04 Mar 1866 in PA and died 30 Sep 1927 in Berks Co., PA. Both are buried in Bern Cemetery, Bernville, Berks Co., PA.

Children of IDA SNYDER and JACOB KIRKHOFF are:

1. ALBERT S. KIRKHOFF (B96621)
2. HARVEY S. KIRKHOFF (B96622)
3. JAMES J. KIRKHOFF (B96623)

References: 45, 29-Dist 0042 Penn Twp Berks Co PA H271

B9663 EVA ANN SNYDER B966

EVA ANN SNYDER was born on 06 Oct 1870 in Berks Co., PA and died 20 Jan 1956 in Berks Co., PA. She married WALLACE R. SPATZ in Berks Co., PA. He was born on 10 Apr 1863 in PA and died 17 Jun 1948 in Berks Co., PA. All are buried in Bern Cemetery, Bernville, Berks Co., PA.

Child of EVA SNYDER and WALLACE SPATZ is:

1. JENNIE D. SPATZ, born on 20 Feb 1895 in Berks Co., PA; died 23 Nov 1966 in Berks Co., PA.

References: 45, 29-Dist 0042 Penn Twp Berks Co PA H286, 30-Bern Twp Berks Co PA 0004 H23

SPATZ
JENNIE D.
1895 — 1966
WALLACE R.
1863 — 1948
EVA ANN
1870 — 1956

B9664 HOWARD C. SNYDER B966

HOWARD C. SNYDER was born in 1873 in Berks Co., PA. He married EMMA V. MOGEL in Berks Co., PA, daughter of ALBERT F. MOGEL and ALICE H. She was born in 1888 in PA. He was principal and teacher West Leesport High School.

Children of HOWARD SNYDER and EMMA MOGEL are:

1. RUTH NAOMI SNYDER, born in 1908 in Berks Co., PA.
2. LUKE MATTHEW SNYDER, born in 1919 in Berks Co., PA.

References: 10-Dist 49 Ontelaunee Berks Co PA H201, 31-Dist 128 Ontelaunee Berks Co PA H48, 40-Ontelaunee Berks Co PA 6-70 H212

B9665 IRWIN J. SNYDER B966

IRWIN J. SNYDER was born in 1878 in Berks Co., PA. He married JENNIE E. WEITZEL in Berks Co., PA. She was born in 1881 in PA.

Children of IRWIN SNYDER and JENNIE are:

1. LEROY M. SNYDER, born in 1901 in Berks Co., PA.
2. EDITH H. SNYDER, born in 1908 in Berks Co., PA.
3. EMMA K. SNYDER, born in 1911 in Berks Co., PA.
4. ESTHER H. SNYDER, born in 1912 in Berks Co., PA.

References: 30-Lower Heidelberg Twp Berks Co PA 0031 H1, 10-Dist 37 Lower Heidelberg Twp Berks Co PA H102, 31-Dist 158 West Lawn Berks Co PA H65

B9666 ALLEN H. SNYDER B966

ALLEN H. SNYDER was born in 23 Jul 1884 in Berks Co., PA and died 29 Nov 1966 in Berks Co., PA. He married LILLIAN in Berks Co., PA. She was born in 1885 in PA. He is buried in Memorial Mausoleum, Wyomissing Hills, Berks Co., PA. He was the superintendant of public school in New Jersey.

Child of ALLEN SNYDER and LILLIAN is:

1. THOMAS SNYDER, born in 1905 in Berks Co., PA.

References: 45, 31-Dist 44 Paterson Twp Passaic Co NJ H75

B9691 CHARLES MILTON KRAMER B969

CHARLES MILTON KRAMER was born on 28 Nov 1878 Berks Co., PA and died 1957. He married ANNIE REBECCA POTTEIGER. She is born on 12 Nov 1879 and died 14 Aug 1948 in Berks Co., PA. Both are buried in Bern UCC Churchyard, Bern Twp., Berks Co., PA.

Children of CHARLES KRAMER and ANNIE POTTEIGER are:

1. LUELLA M. KRAMER
2. EDNA L. KRAMER
3. INFANT DAUGHTER KRAMER, died in infancy Berks Co., PA.

References: 49, 45

B9692 JENNIE B. KRAMER B969

JENNIE B. KRAMER was born in 1883 and died 1959. She married CHARLES GIBSON. Both are buried in Bern UCC Churchyard, Bern Twp., Berks Co., PA.

Children of JENNIE KRAMER and CHARLES GIBSON are:

1. IRA M. GIBSON
2. C. ELWOOD GIBSON

References: 49, 45

B96A1 BERTHA K. SNYDER B96A

BERTHA K. KRAMER was born in May 1880 in Berks Co., PA. She married FRANKLIN ROTHERMEL. He was born in Jul 1875 in PA.

Child of BERTHA KRAMER and FRANKLIN ROTHERMEL is:

1. HAROLD K. ROTHERMEL, born in 1901 in Berks Co., PA.

References: 30-Ward 15 Reading Berks Co PA 0104 H125

B9711 REBECCA G. HIESTER B971

REBECCA G. HIESTER was born on 06 Sep 1859 in Berks Co., PA and died 28 Feb 1944 in Berks Co., PA. She married 1st _______ ADAMS in Berks Co., PA. She married 2nd DAVILLA H. BLATT in Berks Co., PA. He was born on 11 Aug 1851 in PA and died 12 Dec 1918 in Berks Co., PA. She and 2nd husband are buried in Bern Cemetery, Bernville, Berks Co., PA.

Children of REBECCA G. HIESTER and ________ ADAMS are:

1. SALLIE ADAMS, born in Feb 1878 in Berks Co., PA; married HARVEY J. ALBRIGHT in Berks Co., PA; born in Sep 1878 in PA.
2. CALVIN ADAMS, born in Apr 1884 in Berks Co., PA

Child of REBECCA HIESTER and DAVILLA BLATT is:

3. STELLA H. BLATT, born 1895 and died 1955 in Berks Co., PA; buried in

References: 45, 29-Ward 13 Reading Berks Co PA H318, 30-Spring Twp Berks Co PA 0118 H179

B93391 ABNER S. HIESTER B9339

ABNER S. HIESTER was born in 17 Feb 1893 in Berks Co., PA and died 11 Sep 1977 in Berks Co., PA. He married LILLIE M. DIETRICH in Berks Co., PA. She was born in 13 Aug 1893 in PA and died 10 Nov 1979 in Berks Co., PA. Both are buried in Bern Cemetery, Bernville, Berks Co., PA.

Children of ABNER HIESTER and LILLIE DIETRICH are:

1. ELSIE HIESTER, born in 1912 in Berks Co., PA.
2. MARIAN IRENE HIESTER, born in 09 Aug 1915 in Berks Co., PA; died 17 Sep 2006 in Berks Co., PA; married _____ Kutz. She is buried in Bern Cemetery, Bernville, Berks Co., PA.
3. EARL H. HIESTER, born in 1919 in Berks Co., PA.
4. ELIZABETH "BETTY" E. HIESTER, born in 1923 in Berks Co., PA.

References: 45, 10-Dist 7 Bern Twp Berks Co PA H54, 31-Dist 51 Reading Berks Co PA H51, 40-Reading Berks Co PA 70-69 H50

B93393 EARL SWOYER HIESTER B9339

EARL SWOYER HIESTER, born in 01 Jan 1896 in Berks Co., PA and died 18 Jul 1970 in Berks Co., PA. He married ESTHER J. STUMP in Berks Co., PA. She was born in 21 Mar 1908 in PA and died 30 May 1992 in Berks Co., PA. Both are buried in Bern Cemetery, Bernville, Berks Co., PA.

Child of EARL HIESTER and ESTHER is:

1. LOUISE HIESTER, born in 1931 in Berks Co., PA.

References: 45, 40-Penn Twp Berks Co PA 6-71 H4

B93396 JOHN ELMER HIESTER B9339

JOHN ELMER HIESTER, born in 17 Aug 1903 in Berks Co., PA and died 29 Oct 1999 in Berks Co., PA. He married HELEN GRACE MOYER in Berks Co., PA. She was born in 07 Aug 1909 in PA and died 03 Nov 1996 in Berks Co., PA. Both are buried in Bern Cemetery, Bernville, Berks Co., PA.

Child of JOHN HIESTER and HELEN MOYER are:

1. DORIS A. HIESTER, born in 1931 in Berks Co., PA.
2. CARLA A. HIESTER, born in 1936 in Berks Co., PA.

References: 45, 31-Dist 18 Reading Berks Co PA H300, 40-Reading Berks Co PA 70-23 H321

B96611 WILLIAM A. REBER B9661

WILLIAM A. REBER was born in Oct 1882 in Berks Co., PA. He married STELLA E. in Berks Co., PA. She was born 1887 in PA.

Children of WILLIAM REBER and STELLA are:

1. FLORENCE REBER, born in 1908 in Berks Co., PA.
2. EDNA REBER, born in 1910 in Berks Co., PA.
3. PAUL REBER, born in 1916 in Berks Co., PA.
4. RUTH A. REBER, born in 1926 in Berks Co., PA.

References: 10-Dist 37 Lower Heidelberg Twp Berks Co PA H141, 31-Dist 111 Lower Heidelberg Twp Berks Co PA H156, 40-Lower Heidelberg Twp Berks Co PA 6-50 H239

B96612 ADAM S. REBER B9661

ADAM S. REBER was born in 1884 in Berks Co., PA and died 1964 in Berks Co., PA. He married EDNA L. ALTHOUSE in Berks Co., PA. She was born in 1886 in PA and died 1960 in Berks Co., PA. Both are buried in Salem-Berne Methodist Church Cemetery, Berks Co., PA.

Children of ADAM REBER and EDNA are:

1. WAYNE A. REBER, born in 1910 in Berks Co., PA.
2. CATHERINA E. REBER, born in 1912 in Berks Co., PA; died in 1979 in Berks Co., PA; married GEORGE GOODMAN in Berks Co., PA; born in 1886 in PA; died in 1960 in Berks Co., PA. Both are buried in Salem-Berne Methodist Church Cemetery, Berks Co., PA.
3. PAUL J. REBER, born in 1915 in Berks Co., PA.
4. MARK D. REBER, born in 1919 in Berks Co., PA.
5. DOROTHY C. REBER, born in 1921 in Berks Co., PA.

References: 45, 10-Dist 15 Centerport Berks Co PA H4, 31-Dist 87 Centre Twp Berks Co PA H19, 40-Centerport Berks Co PA 6-19 H20

B96613 LEWIS F. REBER B9661

LEWIS F. REBER was born in 1888 in Berks Co., PA. He married KATIE R. in Berks Co., PA. She was born in 1893 in PA.

References: 45, 31-Dist 18 Reading Berks Co PA H300, 40-Reading Berks Co PA 70-23 H321

B96611 WILLIAM A. REBER B9661

WILLIAM A. REBER was born in Oct 1882 in Berks Co., PA. He married STELLA E. in Berks Co., PA. She was born 1887 in PA.

Children of WILLIAM REBER and STELLA are:

1. FLORENCE REBER, born in 1908 in Berks Co., PA.
2. EDNA REBER, born in 1910 in Berks Co., PA.
3. PAUL REBER, born in 1916 in Berks Co., PA.
4. RUTH A. REBER, born in 1926 in Berks Co., PA.

References: 10-Dist 37 Lower Heidelberg Twp Berks Co PA H141, 31-Dist 111 Lower Heidelberg Twp Berks Co PA H156, 40-Lower Heidelberg Twp Berks Co PA 6-50 H239

B96612 ADAM S. REBER B9661

ADAM S. REBER was born in 1884 in Berks Co., PA and died 1964 in Berks Co., PA. He married EDNA L. ALTHOUSE in Berks Co., PA. She was born in 1886 in PA and died 1960 in Berks Co., PA. Both are buried in Salem-Berne Methodist Church Cemetery, Berks Co., PA.

Children of ADAM REBER and EDNA are:

1. WAYNE A. REBER, born in 1910 in Berks Co., PA.
2. CATHERINA E. REBER, born in 1912 in Berks Co., PA; died in 1979 in Berks Co., PA; married GEORGE GOODMAN in Berks Co., PA; born in 1886 in PA; died in 1960 in Berks Co., PA. Both are buried in Salem-Berne Methodist Church Cemetery, Berks Co., PA.
3. PAUL J. REBER, born in 1915 in Berks Co., PA.
4. MARK D. REBER, born in 1919 in Berks Co., PA.
5. DOROTHY C. REBER, born in 1921 in Berks Co., PA.

References: 45, 10-Dist 15 Centerport Berks Co PA H4, 31-Dist 87 Centre Twp Berks Co PA H19, 40-Centerport Berks Co PA 6-19 H20

B96613 LEWIS F. REBER B9661

LEWIS F. REBER was born in 1888 in Berks Co., PA. He married KATIE R. in Berks Co., PA. She was born in 1893 in PA.

1. EARNESTINE V. E. REBER, born in 1926 in Berks Co., PA.
2. CLARENCE A. REBER, born in 1928 in Berks Co., PA.
3. LEE K. REBER, born in 1930 in Berks Co., PA.
4. SHIRLEY P. REBER, born in 1935 in Berks Co., PA.

References: 31-Dist 86 Centre Twp Berks Co PA H56, 40-Centre Twp Berks Co PA 6-18 H198

B9661B RAYMOND R. REBER B9661

RAYMOND R. REBER was born in 1905 in Berks Co., PA. He married MABEL S. in Berks Co., PA. She was born in 1911 in PA.

Child of RAYMOND REBER and MABEL is:

1. STANLEY I. REBER, born in 1928 in Berks Co., PA.
2. GERALD REBER, born in 1936 in Berks Co., PA.
3. JANICE REBER, born in 1939 in Berks Co., PA.

References: 31-Dist 87 Centre Twp Berks Co PA H25, 40-Centerport Berks Co PA 6-19 H17

B96621 ALBERT S. KIRKHOFF B9662

ALBERT S. KIRKHOFF was born in Jun 1887 in Berks Co., PA. He married MARGARET D. in Berks Co., PA. She was born in 1891 in PA.

Children of ALBERT KIRKHOFF and MARGARET are:

1. ELLEN J. KIRKHOFF, born in 1912 in Berks Co., PA.
2. LEWIS J. KIRKHOFF, born in 1914 in Berks Co., PA.
3. JOHN A. KIRKHOFF, born in 1915 in Berks Co., PA.
4. RICHARD D. KIRKHOFF, born in 1917 in Berks Co., PA.
5. LEON G. KIRKHOFF, born in 1919 in Berks Co., PA.
6. MILES W. KIRKHOFF, born in 1921 in Berks Co., PA.
7. MARGARET M. KIRKHOFF (B966217)
8. ELWOOD P. KIRKHOFF, born in 1925 in Berks Co., PA.
9. WILFORD L. KIRKHOFF, born in 1928 in Berks Co., PA.

References: 10-Dist 8 Penn Twp Berks Co PA H73, 31-Dist 86 Centre Twp Berks Co PA H182

B96622 HARVEY S. KIRKHOFF B9662

HARVEY S. KIRKHOFF was born on 23 Jul 1889 in Berks Co., PA and died 24 Apr 1932 in Berks Co., PA. He married ROSA M. WAGNER in Berks Co., PA. She was born on 19 Apr 1888 in PA and died 02 Jan 1966 in Berks Co., PA. Both are buried in Haags Cemetery, Bernville, Berks Co., PA.

Children of HARVEY KIRKHOFF and ROSA M. are:

1. EDITH I. KIRKHOFF, born in 1912 in Berks Co., PA.
2. ESTHER D. KIRKHOFF (B966222)
3. IRVIN J. KIRKHOFF (B966223)

References: 45, 31-Dist 78 Penn Twp Berks Co., PA H84, 40-Bernville Berks Co PA 6-7 H30

B96623 JAMES J. KIRKHOFF B9662

JAMES J. KIRKHOFF was born on 15 Apr 1894 in Berks Co., PA and died 28 Feb 1958. He married MINNIE S. HIMMELBERGER in Berks Co., PA, daughter of JOEL HIMMELBERGER and EMMA. She was born in 02 May 1892 in PA and died 15 Sep 1967 in Berks Co., PA. Both are buried in Bellsman's Church Cemetery, Mohrsville, Berks Co., PA.

Children of JAMES KIRKHOFF and MINNIE HIMMELBERGER are:

1. CATHERINE M. KIRKHOFF, born in 1916 in Berks Co., PA.
2. ELSIE I. KIRKHOFF, born in 1918 in Berks Co., PA.
3. MILDRED E. KIRKHOFF, born in 1920 in Berks Co., PA.
4. WILLIAM J. KIRKHOFF, born in 1924 in Berks Co., PA.
5. HELEN J. KIRKHOFF, born in 1926 in Berks Co., PA.
6. ARLENE KIRKHOFF, born in 1929 in Berks Co., PA.

References: 45, 10-Dist 8 Penn Twp Berks Co PA H73, 31-Dist 86 Center Twp Berks Co PA H203, 31-Dist 86 Center Twp Berks Co PA H81

B966131 GRANT R. REBER B96613

GRANT R. REBER was born in 1913 in Berks Co., PA. He married ANNA B. in Berks Co., PA. She was born in 1917 in PA.

Children of GRANT REBER and ANNA are:

1. LARUE J. REBER, born in 1934 in Berks Co., PA.
2. KENNETH L. REBER, born in 1938 in Berks Co., PA.

References: 40-Centre Twp Berks Co PA 6-18 H195

B966217 MARGARET M. KIRKHOFF B96621

MARGARET M. KIRKHOFF was born on 04 Jan 1922 in Berks Co., PA and died 28 Nov 2008 in Berks Co., PA. She married NORMAN J. BAER in Berks Co., PA. He was born on 08 Jan 1917 in PA and died 16 Jun 2009 in Berks Co., PA. Both are buried in Saint Lukes Cemetery,
Shoemakersville, Berks Co., PA.

References: 45

B966222 ESTHER D. KIRKHOFF B96622

ESTHER D. KIRKHOFF was born on 12 Sep 1913 in Berks Co., PA and died 24 Apr 2003 in Berks Co., PA. She married CARL F. WILHELM in Berks Co., PA. He was born on 21 Feb 1912 in PA and died 04 Dec 1995 in Berks Co., PA. Both are buried in Saint Thomas Cemetery, Bernville, Berks Co., PA.

Child of ESTHER KIRKHOFF and CARL WILHELM is:

1. C. FREDERICK WILHELM, born in 1939 in Bernville, Berks Co., PA.

References: 40-Bernville Berks Co PA 6-7 H30, 45

B966223 IRVIN J. KIRKHOFF B96622

IRVIN J. KIRKHOFF was born in 1915 in Berks Co., PA and died in 2008 in Berks Co., PA. He married ISABEL M. in Berks Co., PA. She was born in 1916 in PA and died in 1991 in Berks Co., PA. Both are buried in the Haags Cemetery, Bernville, Berks Co., PA.

Child of IRVIN KIRKHOFF and ISABEL is:

1. BRENDA M. KIRKHOFF, born in 1939 in Berks Co., PA.

References: 40-Penn Twp Berks Co PA 6-71 H84, 45

CHAPTER IV

C HENRY LANTZ I

HENRY LANTZ was born in 1746 in Philadelphia (now Berks) Co., PA. He died on 14 Sep 1802 in Northumberland Co., PA. He married MARGARETHA SIEGFRIED in 1775 in Berks Co., PA, daughter of JOHANNES SIEGFRIED and CATHARINA FETTERHOFF. She was born in 1758 in Berks Co., PA. She died on 23 Sep 1823 in Northumberland Co., PA. Both are buried in Sunbury, Northumberland Co., PA (Lantz's Emmanuel Cemetery).

'HENRY's name shows up in the baptism records of Rev. DANIEL SCHUMAKER. In the years before his own children were born, he witnessed baptisms of his sister SUSANNA KRAMER's children and others in Friedens White Church at Stony Run.'

'Some of his children were baptized at Friedens, some at New Bethel Zion of Greenwich Twp., and one by Rev. HELFRIG in Maxatawney Twp. His name also appears as a deacon in the Greenwich Church mentioned above."

"Apparently he was over in Maxatawny Twp. and associated with Rev. HELFRIG there. A birth certificate for a SAMUEL LANTZ was issued in 1783 naming HENRY and MARGARETHA (SIEGFRIED) LANTZ as parents."

"Around 1792 he and his family moved to Northumberland Co., PA. He settled on Shamokin Creek and apparently did well. He set most of his daughters up with farms of their own. It seems strange that he left no will but maybe he died kind of sudden. We know that he died intestate because the petition to the court for partition of the estate was filed by his son JACOB and his mother. This petition was dated Nov. 6, 1804. This means that the date of death for HENRY as Sept. 14, 1802 is probably correct. It also stated that MARGARETHA had married again. Her husband was LEONARD STINE."

Children of HENRY LANTZ and MARGARETHA SIEGFRIED are:

1. JOHANN JACOB LANTZ (C1)
2. JOHANNES LANTZ, born 27 Aug 1778, Berks Co., PA; died 1802, Northumberland Co., PA.
3. DANIEL LANTZ (C3)
4. MARY LANTZ (C4)
5. SAMUEL LANTZ (C5)
6. JONATHAN LANTZ, born 01 May 1785, Berks Co., PA.
7. SARAH LANTZ, born 01 May 1785, in Berks Co., PA.
8. HENRY LANTZ (C8)
9. ELIZABETH LANTZ (C9)
10. MARGARETHA LANTZ (CA)

References: 19, 20-Augusta Twp Northumberland Co PA, 5, 36, 37, 43, 44, 6-Sarah Mae (Huss) Lantz, 53, 55

The Condition of Vendue held here this day by the undersigned Administrators of the late Henry Lantz Dec^d as follows

1 The highest Bidder to be the Buyer —

2 Any person whose purchases does not amount to Ten Shillings to pay the Cash before the articles are taken away —

Fil# 39

3 Any person whose purchase Amount to Ten Shillings and under Three pounds, to have a Credit of Three months from this day, provided such purchaser gives his Note with approved Security, before the Goods are Removed

4 Any person whose purchase Amount to Three pounds & upwards to have a Credit of Six Months from this day, provided such purchaser gives his Note with approved Security, before the Goods are Removed —

Augusta Township Octr 28 1802

Margaret Lantz
Jacob Lantz &
Henry Lantz } Adm^rs

+	Daniel Boger	1 Pick Ax		4	3	10
+	Daniel Boger	1 Cleaver		4	2	7
+	Daniel Boger	Saw plates		4	3	10
#	John Snyder	6 Iron Rings	H		4	0
#	George Spies	1 Cut Saw	H		16	9
#	John Snyder	Adze &c	H		2	11
.	Daniel Lantz	1 Scythe			1	2
N	Adam Lang	Hames &c			2	[illegible]
N.	Adam Lang	Old Scythe				[illegible]
#	Jacob Yoner p^r J. Lantz	1 Hatchet	H		2	[illegible]
#	George Spies	Oats Cradle & Scythe	H		6	8
#	Jacob Weitner	1 do do	H		1	6
.	Henry Lantz	Lot of old Iron			7	6
#	Jacob Weitner	1 Auger			1	[illegible]
#	Jacob Weitner	1 do	H		[illegible]	[illegible]
			£2	2	18	[illegible]

				£	s	d
		Brought Over		2	18	2
4	John Snyder	1 Auger	#		2	6
	Jacob Lantz	Drawing Knife		"	3	0
#	Jacob Weitner	Old Sickles	#	"	2	3
	Daniel Lantz	Sickle			3	10
	Samuel Lantz	Rings		"	7	7
	Jacob Lantz	Auger			5	
	Jacob Lantz	Chizzels			5	
	Jacob Lantz	Compass			1	6
	Jacob Lantz	Chizzels			2	6
+	Daniel Boger	Hammer & Trowel	+	"	2	7
	Henry Lantz	Anvil & Hammer			3	1
	Henry Lantz	Clevis		"	1	8
+	Daniel Boger	1 Scythe	#	"	4	6
	Henry Lantz	1 Saw & Square			12	8
N	Conrad Rickert	Bell & Lauth		"	2	6
	Daniel Lantz	1 Saddle		1	11	0
	Henry Lantz	Saddle Bag		"	15	0
	Jacob Lantz	1 Steel yard		"	12	2
N#	Christian Miller	1 Steel yard	#	1	7	0
N	Daniel Mason	2 old Saws			[illegible]	4
+	Henry Renner	1 Bee hive		+	"	8
#	John Snyder	4 Bee hives	#	"	4	6
	Daniel Lantz	1 Deer Skin			3	1
	Daniel Lantz	1 do. dressed			8	7
	Henry Lantz	4 Saws		"	18	
+	John Conrad	1 Reel	#	"	1	[illegible]
#	Joseph Lorentz	Stove plate	#	"	[illegible]	[illegible]
N	Conrad Rickert	1 Rifle		4	[illegible]	[illegible]
4	Jno. Wecht	Harrow	#	1	[illegible]	[illegible]
#	Jacob Zimmerman	1 Log Chain	#		[illegible]	[illegible]
	Henry Lantz	Table [illegible]			[illegible]	[illegible]
				£		

				£	s	d
	Henry Lantz	Breast Chain			1	7
					1	5
N	George Lang	1 do	8			
N	Christian Miller	1 Waggon Screw	11		12	6
N	Daniel Boyer	1 Plough				
N	George Lang	[illegible]				
H	Jacob Shepman	[illegible]				
	[illegible] Bacon	1 Waggon				
N	Chr. Kreeger	1 Cow				
N	Valentine Miller	1 do				
N	Valentine Bellman	1 do				
H	James Alexander	1 Bull				
N	Ezekiel Bacon	2 Calves				
	Henry Lantz	1 Oxen				
	Jacob Lantz	Heifer				
	Henry Lantz	1 Cow				
	Henry Lantz	1 Plow				
N	Walter Brady	1 Horse				
H	George Spies	1 Still with 12 hogsheads				
N	Christian Shepman	1 Sheep				
N	Adam Long	1 do				
N	Christian Shepman	1 do				
N	Robert Roach	6 ditto				
	Jacob Lantz	1 do			19	6
N	Henry Yorkman	1 do		1	3	
N	Henry Rinehart	10 Bushels Buckwheat	3/2	1	11	8
N	William Baker	10 B. do	3/1½	1	11	3
N	Robert Roach	10 B. do	3/3	1	12	6
N	Timothy Harris	10 B. do	3/1	1	10	10
N	William Becker	10 B. do	3/	1	10	
N	Adam Long	10 B. do	3/	1	10	
N	Adam Long	10 B. do	3/	1	10	
		Amt. [illegible]		[illegible]	[illegible]	[illegible]

		10 B. Buckwheat	3	1	10	
N	Daniel Bacon	10 Baskets Buckwheat	3/	1	10	[illegible]
+	Henry Renner					
	Jacob Lantz	10 B. Indian Corn	4/1	2	0	[illegible]
	Henry Lantz	5 B. Indian Corn	4/	1	0	0
N	Henry Vanderbilt	5 B. do do	3/11		19	[illegible]
N	Henry Vanderbilt	8 B. do do	3/10	1	10	8
N	Christian Shisler	10 B. Rye	4/2	2	1	[illegible]
#	Christopher Kinsman	20 B. do	# 4/2	4	3	4
#	Christopher Kinsman	20 B. do	# 4/3	4	5	[illegible]
N.	Henry Yocum	20 B. do	4/2	4	3	4
#	Christopher Kinsman	20 B. do	# 4/2½	4	4	2
N.	Christian Shisler	20 B. do	4/3	4	3	[illegible]
N	Adam Long	20 B. Wheat	5/11	5	18	4
N.	Adam Long	40 B. Wheat	5/11	11	16	8
#	Christopher Kinsman	40 B. do	5/8	11	6	[illegible]
#	Christopher Kinsman	40 B. do	5/8	11	6	[illegible]
		20 B. do	5/7½	5	12	6
N	Jacob Deerst	10 B. do	5/9	2	17	6
	Jacob Lantz	10 B. do	5/8	2	16	8
N	David Mertz	1 Stack of Hay		5	3	[illegible]
#	George Bright	1 Stack do		3	1	[illegible]
	Daniel Lantz					
	~~[illegible]~~	1 Wheelbarrow	#		3	[illegible]
N	~~[illegible] Hopper~~ Tom Hopper	1 Barrel	#		6	[illegible]
#	William Shipman	1 do do	#		5	[illegible]
#	William Shipman	1 Blind Bridle	#		2	[illegible]
#	Leonard Stein	1 do do	#		3	[illegible]
#	Leonard Stein	Collar			2	[illegible]
N	John Reed	2 Cruppers	#		6	
#	Henry Walker	1 Collar	#		3	
#	Conrad Recker (pd J Lantz)	1 Flax Brake	#		6	
N	George Long	Quilter		1	2	[illegible]
	Henry Lantz	2 Collars			2	
	Henry Lantz	Harness & Traces	#		16	
N	Ezekiel Bacon					
				95	11	

N	John Reed	Gero		7	7
N	John Reed	Thaw		2	7
N	Leonard Stein	1 Sleigh	3	0	0
29th	Henry Lantz	1 keg		1	0
+	Henry Renner	1 do		3	10
	Jacob Lantz	1 Tub		1	11
	Jacob Lantz	1 drawing knife		2	0
	Jacob Lantz	1 Stone Sledge		1	10½
	Jacob Lantz	1 Small do			11
	Margaret Lantz	1 Kitchen Cupboard with &c	2	12	6
	Henry Lantz	1 Chair		2	—
	Henry Lantz	3 do		8	1
	Margaret Lantz	2 Windsor Chairs		7	—
	Henry Lantz	2 do do		8	6
	Henry Lantz	1 large Walnut Table	[illegible]	[illegible]	[illegible]
+	Henry Renner	2 old Chairs	[illegible]	[illegible]	[illegible]
	Henry Lantz	1 Clock & Case	7	10	[illegible]
	Margaret Lantz	1 ten plate Stove & Pipe	3	[illegible]	[illegible]
	Henry Lantz	1 Shovel & Tongs		2	[illegible]
	Margaret Lantz	1 Case of Drawers &c	4	[illegible]	[illegible]
	Margaret Lantz	1 Bed Curtains &c	2	[illegible]	[illegible]
	Mary Lantz	1 do Bed	1	[illegible]	[illegible]
	Daniel Lantz	1 Gun	3	[illegible]	[illegible]
	Jacob Lantz	1 ten plate Stove & Pipe	4	[illegible]	[illegible]
	Jacob Lantz	29 Iron Rings	[illegible]	[illegible]	[illegible]
	Jacob Lantz	1 German Family Bible	[illegible]	[illegible]	[illegible]
	Margaret Lantz	6 Books diff^t sorts	[illegible]	[illegible]	[illegible]
4ff	George Spies	1 Gallon Brandy	[illegible]	[illegible]	[illegible]
4ff	George Spies	1 Tin Lamp	[illegible]	[illegible]	[illegible]
4ff	George Spies	1 half Gallon Brandy	[illegible]	[illegible]	[illegible]

			£	s	d
	Margaret Lantz —	1 Flat Iron — —	.	1	[illegible]
N	Christian Miller —	1 Chair	..	1	0
	Margaret Lantz —	1 Frying Pan		2	6
	Margaret Lantz —	Quantity Earthen potts —	...	1	[illegible]
N	Christian Miller —	1 + Crop Ax	..	7	0
#	Jno Greninger p D Lantz	1 Bell	..	1	2
#	Samuel Bloom p D	1 Paring knife		.	11
	Margaret Lantz	1 doz Brass Spoons	.	2	1
N	Christian Miller —	1 Bell	..	1	0
	Henry Lantz — —	1 Sheep Shears	..	2	3
N-	James McCune —	1 Hog	.	10	7
##	George Spees	1 piece Stoveplate #	..	4	1
	Henry Lantz —	4 Halter Chains	1	0	0
#	George Spees	1 Beewith Hive #	.	19	5½
	Daniel Lantz	1 do do	1	3	6
	Henry Lantz	5 Cow Chains	1	0	1
	Samuel Lantz	1 Slate	0	8	0
			~~5~~	~~16~~	~~5½~~
		£	5	18	3½
		Amount of Vendue List £	182	17	3

#26 #37

Supplementary Account of Margaret [illegible] [illegible] and [illegible] the Goods and Chattels Rights and [illegible] in the County of Northumberland Deceased, who died [illegible] Rights and Credits of the said Deceased, which have [illegible] of their payments and Disbursements thereout [illegible]

The Accountants charge themselves with the Balance remaining in their hands on settlement of former Administration account amounting to	123. 14 3
Jacob Lantz charges himself with £22. 10. 0 rec^d from the Estate of [illegible] [illegible]	22. 10. 0
Jacob Lantz also rec^d from [illegible] [illegible] £8. 2. 8 omitted from former account	8. 2. 8
Jacob charges also with the following Grain not in Inventory as follows	
26½ Bushels of Wheat, [illegible] sold for [illegible] [illegible] [illegible] for 7/6 pr Bushel	9. 19. 3
Seventy six and an half Bushels of Rye for 5/. pr B.	19. 2 6
Henry Lantz charges with a [illegible] worth 7/6.	0. 7. 6
D^o with Plough [illegible] [illegible]	0. 5. 0
Jacob further charges with a Flax [illegible]	0. 5. 0
Jacob Lantz also further charges himself with the Rent of the Saw Mill for the year 1804.	15. 10. 0
Henry Lantz also further charges himself with [illegible] & a [illegible] from Notes and judgments	[illegible] 5 . 0

Exhibited unto the Register Office the 9th Day of September A.D. 1808 which Acct. then Examined and as allowing and pass'd the Administrators being Duly Sworn thereto.

Before me
Robt. Craig
Depy. Regr.

Margaret Steinfeld late Lantz
Jacob Lantz
Henry Lantz

Balance this side of Acct. ... 43. 17. 6½

£ 264. 17. 8½

[illegible] Lintz) [illegible] Lintz and Henry Lintz Administrators [illegible] Chattels which were of Henry Lintz Senior late of Augusta County Intestate. as were of all and singular the goods and Chattels [illegible] to the Hands possession or knowledge of the said accountants [illegible] to wit. —

Item — The said Accountants pray an allowance [illegible] of their Payments and Disbursements [illegible] out of the same as follows, to wit.

No. 1. For £ 9. 1. 8 paid [illegible] a Bal. of Principle & Interest on Intestates Bond &c.	}	9. 1. 8
2. For £ 40. 5. 3 pd. [illegible] Bal. of pl. & Interest on Intestates Bond &c.	}	40. 5. 3
3. For £ 24. 6. 7 pd. [illegible] on Intestates Bond &c.	}	24. 6. 7
4. For £ 0. 5. 0 pd. [illegible] on his [illegible] &c.	}	0. 5. 0
5. For £ 0. 7. 6 pd. [illegible] for [illegible] &c.	}	0. 7. 6
6. For £ 0. 1. 0 pd. [illegible] for [illegible] &c.	}	0. 1. 0
7. For £ 1. 2. 6 pd. [illegible] for surveying Intestates Land &c.	}	1. 2. 6
8. For £ 3. 4. 1 retained by Henry Lintz for expences done to [illegible] the Year [illegible] the Term of Agreement) as [illegible] &c.	}	3. 4. 1
9. For £ 2. 12. 6 retained by [illegible] Henry Lintz for expences 8 Days to [illegible] County [illegible]	}	2. 12. 6
10. For £ 10. 14. 0 [illegible] Henry Lintz [illegible]	}	10. 14. 0
11. For £ 1. 17. 6 retained [illegible] Lintz for [illegible] after Intestates [illegible]	}	1. 17. 6
12. For £ 0. 10. 8 retained [illegible] Lintz for [illegible] Days [illegible]	}	0. 10. 8
13. For £ 0. 3. 7 pd. [illegible] for expences &c.	}	0. 3. 7
14. For £ 0. 3. 10 pd. [illegible] for expences &c.	}	0. 3. 10
15. For £ 13. 9. 5 pd. [illegible] of [illegible] for [illegible] part of partition &c.	}	13. 9. 5

[illegible]

16.	For £0.13.3½ retained [illegible] expences & Journey to [illegible] p Acct.	0. 13. 3½
17.	For £1.5.9 p [illegible] Register [illegible] examining passing, Recording Record &c.	1. 5. 9
18.	For £0.3.9 to [illegible] p Clk of Orphans Court on Confirming Acct.	0. 3. 9
19.	For £0.15.0 p [illegible] Atty to this [illegible] Confirmd	0. 15. 0
20.	For £1.10.0 p [illegible] on first Account (being [illegible])	1. 10. 0
21.	For £25.2.1 p [illegible] as p [illegible] Acct of George [illegible] as p Acct	25. 2. 1
22.	Allowance for Acct for the trouble and Expences Leaving to go to Reading [illegible] the Estate three times	[illegible]
23	For £106.0.0 p Henry [illegible] the Estate of John Harrison Decd for a Bond and [illegible] as p Receipt	106. 0. 0
24.	For £0.15.9 p Martin [illegible] for [illegible] for a Judgment and Costs on [illegible] as p Acct and Rect	0. 15. 9
26	For £0.15.0 p Jno Simpson for Stating the Supp Acct	0. 15. 0
	£	254. 14. 8½

The Above Acct has been Adjusted as the Law directs on the 9th Day of Sept 1808

Robt [illegible]
Depy Reg

HENRY LANTZ

C1 JOHANN JACOB LANTZ C

JOHANN JACOB LANTZ was baptized 03 Nov 1776 at New Allemangel Lutheran or Friedens Church, Albany Twp., Berks Co., PA and died 1848 in Blair Co., PA. He married ELIZABETH MARTZ about 1807 in Northumberland Co., PA. She was born 10 Dec 1784 in Huntingdon Twp., Huntingdon Co., PA, and died before 1850 in Blair Co., PA. His occupation was listed as carpenter in 1820. He appears in the 1846, tax list for North Woodbury Twp., Blair Co., PA. He died intestate without a will and letters of administration issued to John S. Kyles.

JOHANN JACOB LANTZ was previously identified for more than 27 years as the son of JACOB LANTZ (1755-1816) and MAGDALENA KURTZ. Very recent Y-DNA test results for ERIC LANTZ member of the Family Tree LENTZ DNA Project has now proven this to be in error. ERIC E. P. LANTZ is a proven descendant of an uncle of JACOB LANTZ (1755-1816) and his Y-DNA does not match the authors Y-DNA. This has therefore based on additional research by the author guided by the Y-DNA match with JOHN CHARLES LANTZ, also member of the LENTZ DNA Project has led to the new parentage and as listed above and corrected generations 1, 2, and 3. Also there now is no evidence to suggest as previously thought that the immigrants who settled in Berks Co., PA, JOHANNES LANTZ in Bern Township and JOHANN JACOB LANTZ in Albany Township were related in any manner.

Children of JOHANN JACOB LANTZ and ELIZABETH MARTZ are:

1. LENA LANTZ (C11)
2. JOHN LANTZ (C12)
3. WILLIAM LANTZ (C13)
4. JONATHAN LANTZ, born 1820, Huntingdon Co., PA; died 05 Apr 1860, of Typhoid Fever, Altoona, Blair Co., PA; married SALLY LONG.

References: 3, 5, 31, 21-Allegheny Twp Huntingdon Co PA, 11, 8-1981, 22-Allegheny Twp Huntingdon Co PA, 20-Huntingdon Twp Huntingdon Co PA, 34, 35, 20-Augusta Twp Northumberland Co PA, 23-Allegheny Twp Huntingdon Co PA, 43, 44

C3 DANIEL LANTZ C

DANIEL LANTZ was born on 10 Feb 1782 in Berks Co., PA, and died 10 Aug 1847 in Northumberland Co., PA. He married CHRISTINA FOLLMER, Northumberland Co., PA. She was born on 26 Jan 1786 in Northumberland Co., PA, and died 17 Dec 1863 in Northumberland Co., PA. He was a farmer and they resided in Paradise, PA. Both are buried in the Follmer Church Cemetery, Turbot Twp., Northumberland Co., PA.

Children of DANIEL LANTZ and CHRISTINA FOLLMER are:

1. ELIZABETH LANTZ (C31)
2. MARY LANTZ, born on 04 Jan 1807; died in 1892 in Northumberland Co., PA; married HENRY LUDWIG; born in 1795 in PA; died 1881 Northumberland Co., PA. His will recorded in Will Book 7 Page 179 Northumberland Co., PA.
3. HENRY LANTZ (C33)
4. SARAH LANTZ (C34)

5. MARGARET LANTZ (C35)
6. DANIEL LANTZ (C36)
7. SAMUEL LANTZ, born 11 Jun 1818; died 01 Apr 1823 in Northumberland Co., PA.
8. ANNA LANTZ (C38)
9. CHRISTIANA LANTZ (C39)
10. SUSAN LANTZ, born 17 Apr 1825; died 1837, killed by lightning Northumberland Co., PA.
11. SAMUEL LANTZ, born 30 Apr 1828; died 1837, killed by lightning Northumberland Co., PA.

References: 5, 24-Turbot Twp Northumberland Co PA H88, 61, 67

DANIEL LANTZ Birth and Baptismal Certificate (Geburts und Taufschein Fraktur)

Transcription:

Diese beide Ehegatten als Henrich Lantz \ und seine Leiblige Haußfrau Margaretha eine \ Geborne Sigfriedin Reformirte Religion ist einen \ Sohn zur Welt geboren als Daniel ist Geboren \ im Jahr Unsers HERRN Jesu Christi 1782 den 10 February \ um 11 Uhr Abends in Maxitani Taunschip Bercks Caunti \ im Staat Pensilvanie und wurde darauf den [added in pencil:] (Starb Agust 10 1847) zur \ Heilige Tauffe gebragt, und vor Herrn Helffrig Diener \ des Gottligen Worts getauffet. Die dazu gebetene Tauff \ zeugen waren Daniel Levan und seine Hauß \ Frau

Magdalena und haben \ ihn den Namen beigelegt als \ Daniel

[in heart]

Gedenke an deinen Schöpfer \ in deiner Jugend ehedann die \ böse tage kom?en und die Jahre \ herzu treten dann du \ wirst sagen sie ge= \ fallen mir \ nicht

Translation:

To these two married people, namely Henrich Lantz and his bodily wife Margaretha, a born Sigfriedin, Reformed religion, a son was born into the world, named Daniel, was born in the year of our Lord Jesus Christ 1782, the 10 February at 11 o'clock in the evening in Maxatawny Township, Berks County, in the state of Pennsylvania, and was subsequently [added in pencil:] (died August 10 1847) brought to the holy baptism, and baptized before Mister Helffrig, servant of God's Word. The requested sponsors were Daniel Levan and his wife Magdalena and gave him the name Daniel.

[in heart]

Remember your Creator in your youth, before the evil days arrive and the years go by, then you will say, "I don't like them."

C4 MARY LANTZ C

MARY LANTZ was born 17 Nov 1783 in Berks Co., PA and died 25 Oct 1874 in Northumberland Co., PA. She married JACOB GASS in PA. He was born on 29 Sep 1782 in PA and died 29 May 1845 in Northumberland Co., PA. He died intestate without a will.

Child of MARY LANTZ and JACOB GASS is:

1. MARTIN GASS (C41)
2. HENRY L. GASS (C42)
3. JOSEPH GASS (C43)
4. WILLIAM GASS (C44)
5. MARY GASS, she married WILLIAM KUEBLER
6. SARAH GASS, she married REEDER CAMPBELL
7. ELIZA GASS, she married JACOB THOMPSON
8. SUSAN GASS, she married WESTLEY BASTIAN
9. LYDIA GASS (C49)

References: 24-Upper Augusta Twp Northumberland Co PA H7, 26-Shamokin Twp Northumberland Co PA H131, 67

C5 SAMUEL LANTZ C

SAMUEL LANTZ was born on 25 Nov 1783 in Berks Co., PA and died 16 Feb 1863 in Northumberland Co., PA. He married MAGDALENA MARTZ\MERTZ in 1805 in Northumberland Co., PA. She was born on 10 Oct 1782 in Magunschy Twp., Northampton Co., PA and died in 11 May 1859 in Rockefeller Twp., Northumberland Co., PA. His will is recorded in Will Book 5, Page 175 Northumberland Co., PA.

Children of SAMUEL LANTZ and MAGDALENA MARTZ are:

1. REBECCA LANTZ (C51)
2. HANNAH LANTZ, died at age of four in Northumberland Co., PA.
3. SARAH ANN LANTZ (C53)
4. MAGDALINE LANTZ (C54)
5. SUSANNAH LANTZ (C55)
6. GERTRUDE "CHARITY" LANTZ (C56)
7. HENRY LANTZ (C57)
8. CATHERINE LANTZ (C58)
9. SARAH LANTZ (C59)
10. SAMUEL LANTZ (C5A)

References: 5, 25-Lower Augusta Twp Northumberland Co PA H935, 67

C8 HENRY LANTZ C

HENRY LANTZ was born on 30 Apr 1780 in Berks Co., PA, and died 1850 in Northumberland Co., PA. He married CHRISTINA FOLLMER in 1804 in Northumberland Co., PA. She was born on 28 Nov 1782 in Northumberland Co., PA, and died 29 May 1872 in Northumberland Co., PA. Both are buried in the St. John's Church Cemetery, Delaware Twp., Northumberland Co., PA. His will is recorded in Will Book 4, Page 195 Northumberland Co., PA.

Children of HENRY LANTZ and CHRISTINA FOLLMER are:

1. MARY LANTZ married CHARLES BROWN, resided in OH, no children.
2. CHRISTIANA A. LANTZ (C82)
3. JOHN LANTZ (C83)
4. JONATHAN LANTZ (C84)
5. SIMON LANTZ (C85)
6. LAVINA LANTZ (C86)
7. ROSANNAH LANTZ (C87)
8. SALOME LANTZ (C88)

References: 5, 36

Henry Lantz Will

In the name of God Amen. I Henry Lantz of Delaware Township in the County of Northumberland and State of Pennsylvania, Farmer being weak in body but sound in mind and memory blessed be God for the same and being also mindful of my mortality do make this my last Will and testament in manner following to wit: My body I commit to the earth at the discretion of my Executor hereinafter named. — Item 1st. It is my will and I do order and direct that my beloved wife Christian shall have and occupy the frame house now occupied by my Daughter Solome for and during her natural life. I also give to my wife such of the household and Kitchen furniture as she may want also an uninterupted privilege in the spring house near the said dwelling. I also do direct my hereinafter named executor to place three thousand Dollars at Interest the Interest to go towards the maintainance of my said wife during her natural life and if that is not sufficient then take from the principal. — Item 2d. I give and devise to the Children of my son John of lower Sandusky County in the State of Ohio the farm he now lives on containing eighty acres be the same more or less with the appertenances thereunto belonging In trust however that they pay to him the yearly profits thereof and allow him to reside on the same during the period of his natural life if he was so desired in such a way however that no part of the same either of the land or the yearly income thereof shall be liable to the debts of the said John and that his receipt alone shall be a discharge to them from the above yearly profits required to be paid. — Item 3d. I give and devise unto my Daughter Solome Wagner the lot of ground on which I now live on containing seventeen acres and one hundred perches with an allowance of six per cent for roads &c together with the appertenances thereunto belonging to her and her heirs forever and for which she and her heirs are to be charged seventy five Dollars per acre but she and her heirs are to have twelve hundred Dollars allowed them as part of their legacy of my estate with Interest on the same from the first of April 1848 so long as I live and they are to pay me thirty six Dollars per year for their maintainance so long as I live from the first of April 1848. — Item 4. I give and devise to my Daughter Mary who intermarried with Charles Brown now of the State of Ohio and to their heirs the sum of seventy two Dollars. — Item 5. As respects the lot of ground I own adjoining lands which I sold to my son Simon. Wilson Hutchison Philip McWilliams and Seases land containing thirty eight acres and twenty perches and allowance I order and direct that the same be sold by my Executor as soon after my decease as practicable and my said Executor is hereby authorized and empowered to make execute and deliver a good Deed of Conveyance for the same but should my son Simon be willing and desirous to have said lot I do hereby give and devise the same to him upon his accounting to my estate for the sum of fifteen hundred and twenty five Dollars in three equal annual payments with interest, untill paid. — Item 6. I order and direct that all the residue of my estate of whatsoever kind be equally divided between all my said heirs share and share alike to my son John Children one share to my Daughter Salome Wagner and her heirs one share to my Daughter Mary Brown and her heirs one share to my Son Jonathan and his heirs one share to my son Simon and his heirs one share to my Daughter Lavina Hutchison and her heirs one share to my Daughter Rosanna Camp and her heirs one share to my Daughter Christiana Hoy and her heirs one share share and share alike except my son John Children to whom I advanced the sum of four hundred Dollars which said sum is to be divided deducted out of their share together with interest from the first of April 1848. — Item 7th It is my will and I do order and direct that as soon after my decease as convenient my executor is to take an inventory of all the personal estate that I may be seized of at the time of my decease and not chosen or taken by my said wife as directed in my first Item and sale thereof to be made for the equal benefit of all my said heirs and their heirs share and share alike It is further my will and I order and direct that at the death of my said wife (should she survive me) all the personal property retained by her out of my estate be sold as soon after her decease as practicable and the proceeds thereof equally divided amongst all my said heirs share and share alike and lastly I nominate constitute and appoint my son Simon to be the executor of this my last will and Testament. In witness whereof I have hereunto set my hand and seal this fifth day of January in the year of our Lord one thousand eight hundred & fifty

Sealed signed and declared to be the last will and testament of the testator in presence of us who at his request signed the same as witnesses thereto

Jacob Brown — Samuel Brown

Henry Lantz (Seal)

Northumberland County ss

Be it remembered that on the 2d day of April A.D. 1850 personally came before me John P. Purcel Register of Wills & granting Letters of Administration in and for said county, Jacob Brown and Samuel Brown the subscribing witnesses to the foregoing instruments of writing purporting to be the Last Will & Testament of Henry Lantz, late of Delaware Township deceased, who on their solemn oaths declare & say that they were personally present & did see and hear the Testator sign seal, publish & pronounce the said Instrument of writing as and for his last will & Testament and that at the time of so doing he was of sound mind & disposing memory, that they witnessed the same in his presence and at his request & in the presence of each other and further saith not.

Sworn & Subscribed
Before me
Jno. P. Purcel Reg.

Jacob Brown
Samuel Brown

Be it remembered that on the 2d day of April A.D. 1850 — was proved and approved the last will & testament of Henry Lantz late of Delaware Township dec'd of which the foregoing is a true copy, & that Letters Testamentary with the will annexed were granted to Simon Lantz, Executor in said will named

Witness my hand. Jno. P. Purcel Reg.

C9 ELIZABETH LANTZ C

ELIZABETH LANTZ was born in 1790 in Berks Co., PA and died in 1868 in Delaware Co., OH. She married JACOB SIEGFRIED, son of JACOB SIEGFRIED and DOROTHY LEVAN. He was born on 11 Nov 1788 in Berks Co., PA and died 31 Oct 1846 in Delaware Co., OH. He is buried in the Oak Grove Cemetery, Delaware Twp., Delaware Co., OH and she is buried in the Delaware Grove Cemetery, Delaware Twp., Delaware Co., OH. His will is recorded in Will Book 2 Page 336 and her will was recorded in Will Book 4 Page 390, Delaware Co., OH.

Children of ELIZABETH LANTZ and JACOB SIEGFRIED are:

1. SARAH "SALLY" SIEGFRIED, born in 1817 in Berks Co., PA. She was blind.
2. ANGELINA SIEGFRIED (C92)
3. WILLIAM SIEGFRIED (C93)
4. MARGARET REBECCA SIEGFRIED, born in 1826 in Berks Co., PA. She was deaf.
5. ISAAC SIEGFRIED, born in 1829 in OH. He was blind.
6. BENJAMIN SIEGFRIED (C96)
7. CATHARINE SIEGFRIED (C97)
8. SAMUEL SIEGFRIED, born in 1824 in PA.

References: 45, 24-Delaware Delaware Co OH H1326, 25-Delaware Delaware Co OH H111

Jacob Seigfried's Will

Proceedings at a Special Court for the County of Delaware before the Honorable William G. Norris Marshal S. Griffin and Almon Stark esquires Associate Judges of the Court of Common pleas for said County on the fifteenth day of January AD One thousand eight hundred and forty Seven

The Last Will and testament of Jacob Seigfried was this day brought before the Court and proven by the oaths of Nicholas Jones and Thomas Pettibone the subscribing Witnesses thereto. whose examinations were reduced to writing. And it appearing to the satisfaction of the Court that said Jacob Seigfried at the time of executing said Will was of sound mind and memory and under no restraint

It is thereupon Ordered that said Will and the testimony So reduced to writing be recorded.

Jacob Siegfrieds Will

And thereupon On motion of J E Brick Counsel for David High and William Siegfried the Executors in said Will named. It is Ordered that Letters Testamentary be granted them on their entering into bond in the sum of Two thousand Dollars with Nicholas Jones and David Robbins their Sureties Conditioned according to Law

It is further Ordered that Jesse Halloran Samuel Walker and John Graham appraise the personal Estate of said deceased

In the name of the benevolent Father of all. I Jacob Siegfried of the County of Delaware and State of Ohio. do make and publish this my last Will & testament. First- It is my will that my funeral expenses and just debts be paid. And secondly that all my personal and real Estate remain under the Control of my wife until my youngest son Samuel arrives at the age of twenty one years if she so long lives, and if she shall die or marry before that time then my son William is to have management of the same until Samuel is twenty one years of age. the following articles will be left in their care for the use of the house and farm, to wit, Eleven beds and bedding as they now stand, three stoves, two Clocks, three fall leaf tables, all the stands, all the Chairs all the kitchen furniture, fire tongs and shovels. One Bureau two Chests and five trunks, and all the articles of the Bar now in use for the Tavern. Two horses and harness for the same two, two horse waggons. one Cart two plows first Choice. one harrow, two log chains, two grain cradles, all the mowing Scythes, all the iron and wooden hay forks. four milk cows sixteen head of sheep. twenty five head of hogs first Choice, all the above described personal property is to be appraised at my death, and all other property of a personal nature not above specified is to be sold, and all the proceeds of said house and farm together with the personal property left with them, and the property not enumerated which will be sold is to be applied for the payment of debts and the support of the family until Samuel becomes of age, and said Samuel is to have good Schooling in the time of his minority And if my wife should want to rent out the house and farm while under her care as above She shall give my Son William

Jacob Seigfried's Will

the refusal of the same in preference to any other person

All the personal property set off with the house and farm and appraised or the value thereof is to be accounted for when my Son Samuel becomes of age, together with all the proceeds of said house and farm not necessarily expended for the payment of debts, the support of the family or necessary improvements on the farm, and at the same time that Samuel becomes of age all my real estate with the improvements thereon shall be appraised and the value thereof together with all the above specified personal property proceeds &c shall be equally divided among my children - the real estate after being appraised shall be divided in the following manner (to wit) the lane now running through the farm on which the house stands to be the line except that the (Barn) and stabling on the north side of said lane shall be included with the Tavern house on the south side of said lane And my son Samuel shall have his choice of said real Estate when so divided and my son William the other part And the said Saml and William after they have made the division as above shall be accountable and pay to the rest of the Children all over and above their equal share contained in said real estate so divided. the one having the land with the Tavern buildings on it is to pay to the other heirs Three hundred Dollars annually until he pays up all over and above his equal share, said real estate is worth, and the One ~~that gets~~ the other half of the above divided land is to pay to the other heirs Two hundred Dollars annually until he pays up all that his part of real estate is worth more than his equal share And there is six or seven acres of land not included in the above that lies north of the Stone Mill and East of the Sandusky Turnpike which I give to my son Benjamin, And if said land should not be appraised to as much as one equal share of all my property then the ballance to make it equal is to be paid by Saml and William as before stated - And the said William and Benjamin is to have the privilege of building them a house on their land before my son Saml becomes of age if they wish and others shall have the privilege of Timber, Stone, Lime &c of the farm to build the same

At the time that my son Samuel arrives at Age and the property is divided I want my wife to have her

Continued

Choice of any room in the house we now live in for herself and also the privilege of the Kitchen to cook for herself. my three children towit Sarah Rebecca and Isaac will have the privilege of living with any of their relations they please, and the person or persons taking care of them shall have what remains of their share of property, if any, at their death, if they use them well.

Third and last I do hereby nominate and appoint David High and my son William Executors of this my last Will and testament hereby authorizing and empowering them to compromise, adjust and release and discharge, in such manner as they may deem proper the debts and claims due me, I also authorize and empower them to superintend and carry out the requisitions of this my last Will and Testament

In Testimony whereof I have hereunto set my hand and seal this 10 Day of Septr 1816 — Jacob Seigfried (seal)

Signed and acknowledged by said Jacob Seigfried as his last Will and testament in our presence and signed by us in his presence (Signed) Nicholas Jones Thos Pettibone

The State of Ohio Delaware county ss Court of Common Pleas Special Term Jany 15th 1817

Personally appeared in open Court Thomas Pettibone and Nicholas Jones who being duly sworn depose and say, that the paper before them purporting to be the last will and Testament of Jacob Seigfried now deceased was by the said decedent acknowledged published and declared to be his last Will and Testament in the presence of these deponents; that the said deceased was of lawful age, that he was of sound and disposing mind and memory and under no restraint, as they verily believe that they subscribed their names as witnesses in the presence and at the request of Testator and in the presence of each other

Thos Pettibone

Sworn to and subscribed in open Nicht Jones

Court this 15th Day of January A D 1817

Geo W Sohnes Deputy Clk

Recorded January 18th 1817

Record of the last Will of Elizabeth Sigfried. decd

Proceedings had before Thomas W. Powell Judge of the Probate Court within and for the County of Delaware and State of Ohio at his office in the town of Delaware on the 16th day of March AD 1868

This day the last will and testament and the codicil thereto were presented to the court for probate and record. Thereupon William D. Heim, and H. M. Stephen, witnesses to the same came into court and were duly sworn and examined, and their testimony reduced to writing and filed with the will and codicil, and it appearing to the court that the said will and codicil were duly executed and attested, and that the said testatrix at the time of executing the same was of full age, and of sound mind and memory, and not under any restraint. Therefore the court upon consideration orders that the said will be admitted to probate as duly proved as the last will and testament of the said Elizabeth Sigfried deceased, and ordered to be recorded as such. Thereupon letters testamentary were granted to Ephriam Willey the Executor named in the will who gave bonds in the sum of $3000, with Abraham Worline and Jonathan Troutman his sureties

T. W. Powell, Probate Judge

(Copy of the Will)

"Be it known that Elizabeth Sigfried of Delaware County, Ohio, in view of the uncertainty of life, and certainty of death, and being of sound mind and memory do now make and publish this my last will and testament in manner following.

1st. It is my will that at my death that my Executor hereinafter appointed out of my Estate shall pay [illegible] and liabilities.

2d. I give and devise unto my son in law Ephriam Willey in trust for the uses and purposes hereinafter named Twenty one acres of land with my residence, which land I bought of Benjamin Ely, being immediately west of the woolen mill in Delaware Tp Delaware County Ohio, and all my personal and real Estate, to be by him possessed, used, contracted and sold if in his judgement it may be advisable. And the use rents and profits proceeds of sale and all income to be derived from the same to be appropriated and used in the maintainance of my three children, Susan Sigfried who is blind Margaret Sigfried who is deaf and Isaac Seigfried who is blind.

It is will and I so direct my said son in law Ephriam Willey that he is to see that my said children shall be supported and maintained, and indulged in small sums of spending money in all respects as near as may be practicable, as they have been maintained & indulged by me, and for the purpose of enabling said trustee to carry out my wishes & desire to give him the most ample power and discretion. At the same time it is my wish that he shall not sell the real estate unless the same may be reinvested to the advantage of said children or absolutely necessary for their support. And in case of the death of any one of my said children then the ballance of said property Real and Personal goes to the benefit of the survivor or survivors, and is to remain in trust until the death of the three. It is not anticipated that either of them will ever marry, if so I then leave it to the descrition of my said son-in-law to determine how much aid it is proper to extend to such one, or whether in his judgement a marriage shall not place such one in a condition of ~~having~~ forfeited their claim to his aid and protection, and I particularly desire and so direct if any marriage shall take place without his consent, that then and that case the one so marrying shall forfeit all claim to maintainance under this will unless it shall be a matter of indulgence from said trustee. It is my wish that my widowed daughter Mrs Angelina High shall remain with and take care of my said Children during her widowhood, and that my said Trustee shall make a liberal allowance to her for such services. And at the death of said three children, it is my will that whatever of Property that may then be unexpended after placing appropriate Toombstones at the Graves of said three children, shall be equally divided between my two daughters Angelina High and Katherine Stilley wife of Ephriam Stilley, or their Heirs. Lastly I hereby constitute and appoint Ephriam Stilley my son-in-law the Executor of this my last will and testament and also Testamentary guardian of my Three Children who are the principal beneficiaries under this will, to wit Sarah Seigfried, Margaret Seigfried and Isaac Seigfried, And I have so much confidence in the honesty and integrity of said Ephriam Stilley that I do not desire that he shall give any Bonds either as Executor or Testamentary Guardian under this will. Hereby revoking all former wills by me made and declaring this to be my last will and testament and I have called upon my friends Charles Switzer and Emery Moore to witness this my last will and testament to which I have this 24th day of October 1855 subscribed my name and affixed my seal.

her
Elizabeth X Seigfried
mark

Signed sealed acknowledged published and declared in our presence as witnesses the day and year above written
Charles Switzer
E Moore,

Record of the last will of Elizabeth Seigfried, dec'd

(Copy of the Codicil)

Whereas I Elizabeth Seigfried of Delaware County Ohio having made and duly executed the within writing, as my last will and testament bearing date the 24th October 1855. Now I do hereby declare this present writing to be a Codicil to my said will and direct the same to be annexed thereto and taken as part thereof. And I do hereby bequeath to my daughter Rebecca the sum of $350.00 and to my son Isaac the sum of $200.00 to be given them by Ephraim Welley their Trustee, to be used by them in such manner as they may desire.

In testimony whereof I the said Elizabeth Seigfried have to this codicil set my hand and seal this 7th day of November AD 1863

Elizabeth her X mark Seigfried (Seal)

Signed sealed and published by the said Elizabeth Seigfried as and for a Codicil to be added to and considered as a part of her last will and testament in the presence of us, who at her request have subscribed our names in her presence as witnesses

W. D. Heim.
H. M. Stephen

U S Stamp $2.50.

(Copy of Testimony & Record thereof)

The State of Ohio.
Delaware County, ss. } In the Probate Court.

In the matter of the will and testament of Elizabeth Seigfried Dec

Wm D Heim being duly sworn in open court this 16th day of March AD 1868 depose and say that the last will and testament of Elizabeth Seigfried hereto annexed, dated October 24th 1855 was exhibited by her as her last will at the time and place of the execution of the Codicil thereto annexed to wit November 7th 1863, and claimed by her to be her last will and testament and witnessed as such by Charles Switzer and E Moore i.e. Emery Moore. That this affiant now says that he is well acquainted with the handwriting of the said witnesses to the said will, to wit; Charles Switzer and Emery Moore and say that the said signature as witnesses to the said will is unquestionably theirs, and now further says that said Switzer and Moore are both dead, and further say not.

W. D. Heim.

Sworn to &c before me April 16th 1868

T. N. Powell, Probate Judge

The State of Ohio.
Delaware County, ss. }

In the matter of the Codicil to the last will and testament of Elizabeth Seigfried deceased.

We Wm D Heim and H. M. Stephen being

Record of the last Will of Elizabeth Seigfried deceased 393

duly sworn in open court this 16th day of March AD 1868, depose and say that we were present at the execution of the codicil to the last will and testament of Elizabeth Seigfried of Delaware County hereto annexed: that we saw said testator subscribe said Codicil and heard her publish and declare the same to be the codicil to the last will and testament; and that the said testator at the time of executing the same was of full age and of sound mind and memory, and not under any restraint; and that we signed the same as witnesses at her request and in her presence and in the presence of each other.

Wm D. Kain
G. M. Stephen

Sworn to and subscribed before me in the Probate Court this 16th day of March AD 1868

T. W. Powell Probate Judge

CA MARGARETHA LANTZ C

MARGARETHA LANTZ was born on 02 Apr 1796 in Berks Co., PA and died 09 Jul 1858 in Northumberland Co., PA. She married ABRAHAM FOLLMER, son of GEORGE FOLLMER and EVA BARBARA MOYER. He was born on 09 Nov 1796 in PA and died before 1850 in Turbot Twp., Northumberland Co., PA. Both are buried in the Follmer Lutheran Cemetery, Milton, Northumberland Co., PA. He died intestate without a will and her will is recorded in Will Book 4, Page 618 Northumberland Co., PA.

Children of MARGARETHA LANTZ and ABRAHAM FOLLMER are:

1. MARGARET ELIZABETH FOLLMER, born in Northumberland Co., PA.
2. CHARLES FOLLMER (CA2)
3. SARAH FOLLMER (CA3) see (C33)
4. GEORGE FOLLMER, born in Northumberland Co., PA.
5. JOHN FOLLMER, born on 05 Aug 1817 and died 02 Nov 1841 in Northumberland Co., PA.
6. HENRY FOLLMER, born on 18 Aug 1822 and died 27 Sep 1852 in Northumberland Co., PA.

References: 24-Delaware Twp Northumberland Co PA H207, 5, 55, 45, 67

Margaret Follmer's Will.

In the name of God Amen I Margaret Follmer widow of Abraham
Follmer dec'd late of the Township of Turbut in the County of Northumberland
and State of Pennsylvania being week in body, and of sound disposing
mind memory and understanding and considering the uncertainty
of this transitory life, knowing and feeling that mortal man must
die; therefore do make this my last Will and Testament, in
manner and form following to wit. First I recommend my soul
into the hands of that God who gave it and my body to the earth to
be buried in a Christian like manner. Item – I give and bequeath
unto my daughter Margaret Elizabeth (for services rendered me one age)
the Sum of forty dollars Cash to be paid to her out of my estate by my Executors
hereinafter named; also fifty bushels of Corn, twelve bushels of wheat, twenty
Bushels of oats; buggy and harness; one cow and one heiffer out of my stock

also three beds and bedding of her choosing, and the whole of my household furniture of every description and name, all extra bed clothes, two hogs of her choosing and hay for one horse, Corn Stocks for two head of cattle Side saddle and riding Bridle. Item. The remaining three beds and bedding and all my other property of every name and description which I have not herein before bequeathed to my daughter Margaret Elizabeth shall be distributed as hereinafter directed. Item. I do order and direct that all my just debts be duly paid and satisfied by my executors as soon as conveniently can be after my decease. Item. As touching all the rest residue and remainder of my estate of what kind or value soever the same may be, I give and bequeath, share and share a like, to be divided equally among my three children, namely one third part to my son Charles; one third part to my daughter Sarah (wife of Henry Lantz) and one third part to my daughter Margaret Elizabeth. Item. I do hereby grant and give full authority and power, to my three Children aforesaid to choose either of the following modes of distribution of the property to be divided among them: first they may divide among themselves; second; they may make public sale; third or they may divide by mutually choosing three disinterested neighbors to make apportionment for them. Item. It is my will and desire that my estate may amicably and peaceably settled, N.B. The hay and corn fodder referred to on the other page is to be for one season. And lastly, I nominate, constitute and appoint my son Charles and my son in law Henry Lantz to be the Executors of this my Will hereby revoking all other wills legacies and bequests, by me heretofore made, and declaring this and no other to be my last Will and testament. Interlining and erasing was done before signing. In witness whereof I have expressly directed Chas. Hollenstein for me to write hereunto my hand and seal this twenty seventh day of March A.D. one thousand eight hundred and fifty eight

Margaret Follmer [seal]

Ordered expressly, to be signed and sealed for her by the said Chas. Hollenstein and declared by the said Testatrix as her last Will and Testament in the presence of us
Chas. Hollenstein
Samuel Long

Northumberland County ss.

Be it remembered that on the thirteenth day of September A.D. 1858 before me C. Boyd. Pursel, Register of Wills &c. in and for said County personally came Chas. Hollenstein and Samuel Lantz, the subscribing witnesses to the foregoing instrument of writing, purporting to be the last will of Margaret Follmer dec'd. who being duly sworn according to law do depose and say that they were present and heard the Testatrix Margaret Follmer request her name to be signed to the said instrument of writing, and publish, pronounce and declare the said instrument of writing as and for her last will and testament — and at the time of so doing she was of sound mind memory and understanding to the best of their knowledge and belief

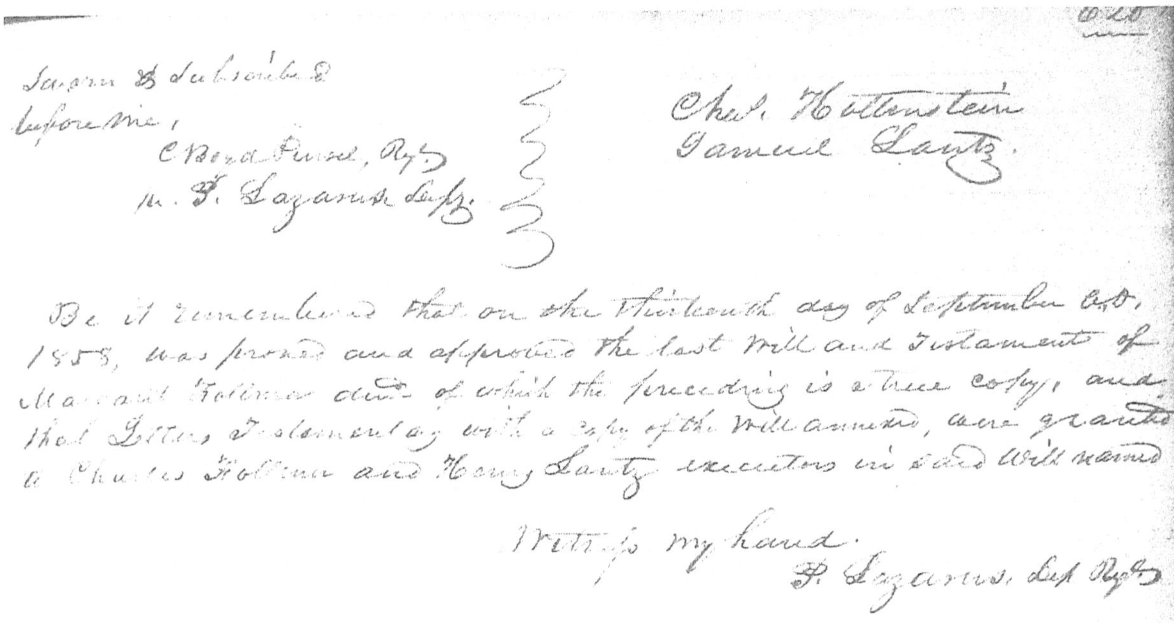

Sworn & subscribed
before me,
C Bird Pinel, Regr
M. F. Lazarus Depy.

Chas. Hettenstein
Samuel Lantz.

Be it remembered that on the thirteenth day of September A.D. 1858, was proved and approved the last Will and Testament of Margaret Follmer dec'd of which the preceding is a true copy, and that Letters Testamentary with a copy of the Will annexed, were granted to Charles Follmer and Henry Lantz executors in said Will named.

Witness my hand.
F. Lazarus, Dep Regr

C11 LENA LANTZ C1

LENA LANTZ was born in 1808 in Huntingdon Co., PA and died before 1870, Frankstown Twp., Blair Co., PA. She married RICHARD BANCROFT. He was born in 1807 in England and died in 1867, Frankstown Twp., Blair Co., PA. His will is recorded in Will Book B Page 434 Blair County, PA.

Children of LENA LANTZ and RICHARD BANCROFT are:

1. SARAH ELLEN BANCROFT (C111)

References: 25-Frankstown Twp Blair Co PA H1171

The Last Will
and Testament
of
Richard Bancroft

[F.B. N.O. 6 3 67.
Seven Dollars & a half
U.S. Int Revenue Stamp]

Last will and Testament of Richard Bancroft of Frankstown Township Blair County and State of Pennsylvania

In the name of God Amen: I Richard Bancroft being in feeble health and considering the uncertainty of this mortal life, and being of sound mind and memory do publish this my last will and Testament in manner & form as follows to wit that is to say

Item 1st It is my will that all my just debts and funeral Expenses be paid by my Executors as soon after my death as convenient out of any money I may have at the time of my death, or from the sale of such property as they may think best to dispose of not otherwise bequeathed

Item 2nd I will and bequeath to my beloved wife Rose Ann, all the Items mentioned and Specified in an Article of Agreement made between her and me before our marriage, which Articles is now laying in Thaddeus Banks Law-office And in addition she is to live with my daughter Sarah Ellen intermarried with Samuel Metzker on the place now occupied by my daughter if she desires to do so And Should my beloved wife herein before mentioned get sick and have much trouble so that what I have given her and which is mentioned in this Item Should not be sufficient to Keep my wife, then my executors Shall pay to my wife such a sum as shall Keep her. such addition only to be paid ~~paid~~ to her in case of sickness or much trouble

Item 3rd It is my will that my Executors hereinafter named shall receive two hundred dollars each for their services, to be paid out of the proceeds of my real and personal property that I may be in possession of at the time of my death

Item 4th, I give and bequeath to my daughter Sarah Ellen intermarried with Samuel Metzker, one of the three farms of which I am now in possession, she to make the choice of either of three; The same to be and remain in her Keeping and possession during her lifetime and further that the farm she chooses shall be considered as having been in her possession from the First of April last, and she is also to pay fifty ($50) rent for the place on which she now lives to be paid to my Executors, this rent being for the present year commencing on the First of April last

Item 5th. It is my will that after my daughter has chosen her farm, my Executors shall, if they think best, dispose of the other two farms, and after all just and lawful claims shall have been paid by my Executors hereinafter named, out of the proceeds of the sale of the two farms above mentioned in this Item then the remainder of the proceeds (excepting certain Legacies hereinafter named) I desire my Executors to invest in Government Bonds, and this to be divided equally among my Grand-Children when each shall arrive at the age of twenty-three years (23)

Item 6th, I will and bequeath to each of my five step-children (to wit Eliza Kemberling Intermarried with Samuel Gibson Mary Ann Kemberling Intermarried with Enoch Harpster Susan Kemberling Intermarried with Thomas Bancroft, John Kemberlings heirs and Catharine Hart Intermarried with Oliver Hart, one hundred dollars ($100) to be paid to them by my Executors out of the proceeds of the two farms mentioned in Item 5th, within three years after my death and not sooner than two years after my death with this provision; that whereas it appears that Enoch Harpster aforementioned in this Item received from the hands of James Condron certain moneys belonging to John Kemberling therefore I desire my Executors to withhold payment of the one hundred dollars which Mary Ann above named, is to receive until said Enoch Harpster pays John Kemberlings heirs the amount which he received from the hands of James Condron in case he fails to do this then my Executors to withhold out of the amount out of the one hundred dollars ($100) coming to the aforesaid Mary Ann, to pay the original amount due John Kemberlings heirs Said Enoch Harpster is to pay interest on the amount due John Kemberlings heirs until their claim is satisfied commencing one year after my death, and I further desire that the money coming to John Kemberlings heirs may remain in the hands of my Executors until said heirs arrive at the age of twenty-one (21) years

Item 7th I will and bequeath to my Brother Thomas Bancroft three hundred dollars, to William Bancroft son of Samuel Bancroft I give and bequeath three hundred dollars the same not to be paid until five or six years after my death said money to remain in the hands of my Brother Thomas Bancroft who shall pay it as he thinks best and most useful to said William Bancroft

~~Item~~ 8th. I will & bequeath to John Town three hundred dollars.

Item 9th I will & bequeath to each of my three sisters Mary, Ellen and Sarah in England two hundred;

Item 10th I will and bequeath to the boy I raised. Thomas Ireland Bancroft one horse, saddle and bridle in addition to the above, I also give and bequeath to the said Thomas

Ireland Bancroft two hundred dollars which is to remain in the hands of my Executors until the aforesaid Thomas Ireland Bancroft shall arrive at the age of twenty-three years. It is further my desire that he shall be free to go and hire himself wherever he can get a good situation I also leave him under the spiritual care of Father Welsh of St. Mary's Catholic church Hollidaysburg, that he may be baptized and taught in the Religion of his parents who are dead. if such Should be his desire

Lastly I hereby appoint my Brother Thomas Bancroft and William Geesey as Executors of this my last will & Testament and should either of the above named persons refuse to serve then I appoint Levi B Crumbaker in his stead: hereby revoking all former wills by me made In witness whereof I have hereunto set my hand and seal this seventh? day of May A.D. 1867

R. Bancroft [seal]

Signed sealed published and declared by the above named Richard Bancroft to be his last Will & Testament in the presence of us who at his request and in his presence have subscribed our names as witnesses thereto

Seth R McCune
John Brennan
Jesse Crumbaker

Blair County SS:

Before me the Register of Wills &c in & for the County of Blair personally appeared John Brennan & Jesse Crumbaker who being duly sworn did depose and say that they were personally present & saw & heard Richard Bancroft, sign seal Execute publish pronounce the hereto attached instrument of writing as and for his last will & testament that they signed their names as witnesses thereto in the presence of each other & in the presence & at the request of the said testator & that at the time of signing the same the said testator was of sound & disposing mind Memory & understanding to the best of their Knowledge & belief

Sworn & Subscribed before me the 3rd of June A.D. 1867
R.M. Innes
Register

Jesse Crumbaker
John Brennan

Blair County SS:

Before me the Register of Wills &c in and for the County of Blair personally appeared Thomas Bancroft & William Geesey who being duly sworn did depose and say that as Executors of the last will & Testament of Richard Bancroft dec'd they will well and truly administer the goods & chattels rights & credits of said deceased according to the provisions of the said will and according to law & further that the whole of the Real & personal property devised in said

487

will does not in value exceed the sum of fifteen thousand Dollars to the best of their knowledge and belief

Sworn & subscribed before me the 3rd of June A.D. 1867.
D M Jones
Register

Thomas Bancroft
William Gesey

Thomas Bancroft & William Gesey Executors of the Last Will & Testament of Richard Bancroft deceased

Fees 5.50 [illegible] Paid

Memorandum: Letters Testamentary were this day issued to Thomas Bancroft and William Gesey on the estate of Richard Bancroft deceased.
An Inventory of the Goods & Chattels rights & credits which were of the said deceased to be Exhibited in 30 days days and a just & true acct. calculation & reckoning of their administration to be filed in one year from the date hereof or when thereunto legally required.
Given under my hand & official seal at Hollidaysburg the 3rd day of June A.D. 1867. Appraisement filed [illegible] 10th A.D. 1867. Partial Acct. by Wm Gesey also Partial Acct by Thos. Bancroft filed & certified to Orphans Court to July term 1871

C12 JOHN LANTZ C1

JOHN LANTZ was born on 03 Aug 1809 in Huntingdon Co., PA and died 01 Aug 1864 in Altoona, Blair Co., PA. He married CATHARINE MARKEY in 1829 in Huntingdon Co., PA, daughter of DAVID MARKEY and MARIA ELIZABETH KUNTZ. She was born on 16 Jun 1815 in Frankstown Twp., Huntingdon Co., PA, and died 02 Jun 1882 of heart disease in Altoona, Blair Co., PA. He was a millwright and carpenter by occupation. He is listed in the tax lists for Allegheny Twp., Blair Co., PA, 1846-1850. Both are buried at Hutchinson Cemetery, Altoona, Blair Co., PA. Both died intestate without a will and administration her estate issued 05 Jun 1882 and Blair Co., PA OC Book C Page 376, 403-404.

Some known land transactions were:

02 Apr 1830 – 68 acres deed Henderson Twp., Huntingdon Co., PA to JOHN LANTZ from JOHN KYLER and wife

08 Aug 1832 – 2 acres deed Allegheny Twp., Huntingdon Co., PA to JOHN LANTZ from his father & mother

25 Mar 1850 – 500 acres deed Allegheny Twp., Blair Co., PA to CATHARINE LANTZ from Administrators of SAMUEL ANDERSON deceased

12 Nov 1859 – Lot 11 Block O Adeline Street Altoona, Blair County, PA deed to CATHARINE LANTZ from WILLIAM C. FURGESON and wife ISABELLA M. FURGESON

10 Jun 1864 – Lot 1 Block G of Harriet Street where Collinsville Road intersects, Altoona, Blair Co., PA deed to JOHN LANTZ from WILLIAM LOUDON Heirs

Children of JOHN LANTZ and CATHARINE MARKEY are:

1. DAVID LANTZ, born in 1830 in Huntingdon Co., PA; died 28 Jun 1899 in Richmond, Wayne Co., IN. He married (1) RACHEL. He married (2) MARY. She was born in 1840 in Baden, Germany. She was a dressmaker and he was a carpenter by occupation.
2. ANNA ELIZABETH LANTZ (C122)
3. JOHN MAXWELL LANTZ (C123)
4. ISAAC LANTZ, born in Sep 1840, Huntingdon Co., PA; died 10 Oct 1895, of Typhoid Fever, Seattle, King Co., WA; married ANNA M. He was buried on 19 Oct 1895, at Hutchinson Cemetery, Altoona, Blair Co., PA. He served in Civil War Co. E 184th OH Infantry Union Army 9 Feb 1865-20 Sep 1865. He was a carpenter by occupation.
5. JACOB MARTIN LANTZ (C125)
6. JOSEPH H. LANTZ, born in 1845, Huntingdon Co., PA; died 08 Jul 1895, National Soldiers Home, Fortress Monroe, Hampton, Elizabeth City Co., VA; married JANE "JENNIE" FORSCHT on 10 Nov 1870 in Hollidaysburg, Blair Co., PA; born 1851, PA. In 1881, they resided at 1003 1/2 11th Avenue, Altoona, Blair Co., PA. He was a carpenter by occupation. He served in Civil War in Union Army 12th Regt., Co. L PA Vol Cavalry, on 06 Apr 1864, mustered in at Hollidaysburg, Blair Co., PA and on 20 Jul 1865, was discharged. He is buried at Hampton National Cemetery, Elizabethtown (now Hampton), VA, Plot 7124.
7. DANIEL LLOYD LANTZ, born on 24 Apr 1851, Huntingdon Co., PA; died 05 Oct 1889, Hit by Train, Wilmore, Cambria Co., PA; married ELIZA JANE GROVE on 12 Nov 1871 in Blair Co., PA; born 1841, PA. He is buried at Hutchinson Cemetery. Altoona, Blair Co., PA
8. SYLVESTER BLAIR KNIGHT LANTZ (C128)

References: 3, 24-Allegheny Twp Blair Co PA H59, 25-Logan Twp Blair Co PA H934, 26-Logan Twp Blair Co PA H41, 27-Richmond Wayne Co IN H208, 1, 11-Allegheny Twp, 12, 9, 23-Allegheny Twp Huntingdon Co PA, 13, 14, 15, 16, 11, 2, 17, 22-Allegheny Twp Huntingdon Co PA, 43, 44, 27-Richmond Twp Wayne Co IN H25, 27-Logan Twp Blair Co PA H74, 27-Jackson Twp Cambria Co PA H148

JOHN MAXWELL LANTZ

CATHERINE (MUNDORFF) LANTZ

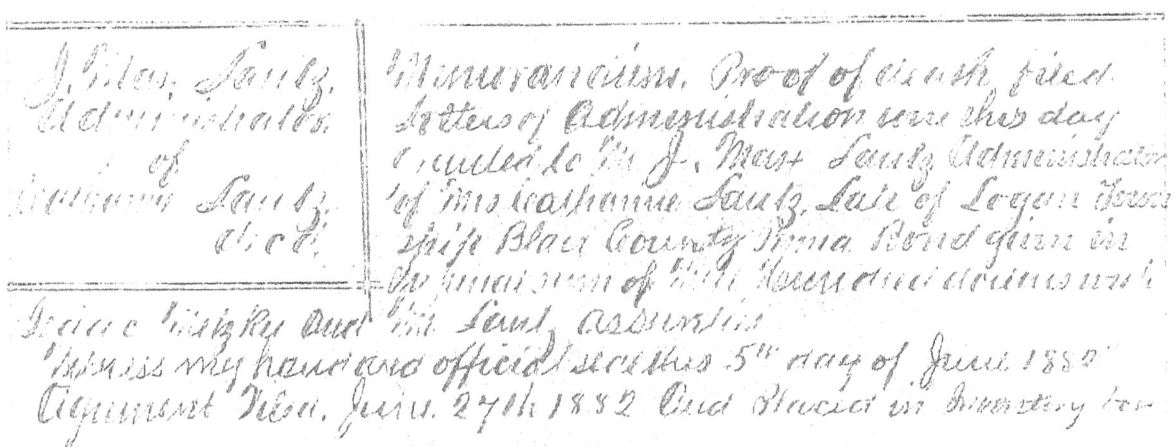

J. Max. Lantz,
Administrator
of
Catharine Lantz,
dec'd.

Memorandum. Proof of death filed
Letters of Administration were this day
granted to Mr J. Max Lantz Administrator
of Mrs Catharine Lantz, late of Logan Township Blair County Penna. Bond given in
the sum of [illegible]
[illegible] and [illegible] Lantz, assurities
Witness my hand and official seal this 5th day of June 1880
Argument filed. June 27th 1882 and placed in Inventory [illegible]

Acct. Statement

of

J. Max Lantz Administrator of the Estate of Catharine Lantz, Dec'd

1882	Dr.	$	
June 6	To Balance after mutual divisions		50
" "	To $.50 from each of the Eight heirs	4	00
" "	To Dividend from Trustees of W. M. Lloyd's Estate	18	05
June 27	To Rent from J. M. Burket	10	00
Aug 18	To Note, J. Martin Lantz	45	00
" 28	To " S. B. Lantz	40	00
"	To Homestead @ Appraisement	3300	00
		$3417	55
1882	Cr.		
June 5	Car fare		78
" "	By Letters of Administration	3	50
" "	By Atty's Fee	5	00
" 6	By 4 Carriages	12	00
" "	By Advertising in Sentinel	2	50
" 27	By Funeral Expenses (J. M. Burket)	25	29
" "	By Casket &c. John Hickley	74	00
" 7	By Lot in Cemetery — J. Hutchinson	10	00
" 2	By Professional Services Dr. M. J. Burch	1	00
" 7	By Removal of the Remains of Jno. Lantz to Cemetery	12	00
" 2	By Expenses to J. Martin Lantz	3	00
" 27	By Car fare to Altoona & Buggy to Hollidaysburg	7	00
"	By Attorney's Fee & Acknowledgments	4	25
	By Fence around Lot & Grave Stones	145	00
June 30	By S. Meyers Florist	4	00
"	By Note & Interest	182	50
"	By $365.71⅝ to each of the Eight heirs	2925	73
		$3417	55

J. Brunner Register fee .50 J. J. Brown Clerk ... Appraisers

J. Max Lantz, Administrator
Lock Haven, Pa.
Aug 9, 1882

State of Pennsylvania }
County of Clinton } ss.

Before me, the subscriber, a Notary Public in and for said County, personally appeared J. Max Lantz, Administrator of the estate of Catharine Lantz deceased, who being duly affirmed doth depose and say that the above stated account is just and true to the best of his knowledge and belief.

Affirmed and subscribed this 9th day of August, A.D. 1882.

J. Max Lantz

Jno. W. McCormick,
Notary Public.

"Pased and allowed on oath of Accountant this 23d day of August A.D. 1882"

C13 WILLIAM LANTZ C1

WILLIAM LANTZ was born in 1813 in Huntingdon Co., PA and died in Dec 1884 in Blair Co., PA. He married JANE E. SONG. She was born on 14 Apr 1815 in PA and died 01 Dec 1883 in Blair Co., PA. He was a carpenter by occupation. They are buried at Presbyterian Cemetery, Hollidaysburg, Blair Co., PA.

Children of WILLIAM LANTZ and JANE SONG are:

1. SARAH ANN LANTZ (C131)
2. WILLIAM MARTIN LANTZ was born on 19 Mar 1844 in Huntingdon Co., PA; died on 12 Mar 1863 in Willow Dam near Williamsburg, Blair Co., PA.
3. EMMA J. LANTZ was born in 1847 in Blair Co., PA; married J. M. CAHOO on 25 Dec 1874 in Zion Evangelical Lutheran Church, Frankstown, Blair Co., PA.

References: 26-Logan Twp Blair Co PA H23, 24-Allegheny Twp Blair Co PA H56

C31 ELIZABETH LANTZ C3

ELIZABETH LANTZ was born on 10 Aug 1805 in Northumberland PA and died 29 Mar 1882 in Fayette Co., IA. She married PHILIP NEWCOMER in Northumberland Co., PA. He was born on 25 Apr 1793 in PA and died 05 Nov 1867 in Fayette Co., IA. Both are buried in Grandview Cemetery, Fayette, Fayette Co., IA

Children of ELIZABETH LANTZ and PHILIP NEWCOMER are:

1. JOHN SAMUEL NEWCOMER (C311)
2. DANIEL NEWCOMER

3. SUSAN NEWCOMER (C313)
4. EMANUEL NEWCOMER, born in 1840 in PA
5. LEVI NEWCOMER, born in 1839 in PA. Served as a Captain in Civil War from IA.
6. PHILIP NEWCOMER, born in 1833 in PA.
7. MARGARET NEWCOMER (C317)
8. CATHERINE L. NEWCOMER (C318)
9. HANNAH ELIZABETH NEWCOMER (C319)
10. JOSEPH T. NEWCOMER, born in 1848 in IL.
11. SARAH C. NEWCOMER, born in 1842 in PA.
12. SILAS NEWCOMER (C31C)
13. HENRY NEWCOMER, born in 1831 in PA.
14. ELIZA A. NEWCOMER, born in 1837 in PA.

References: 67, 24-Lancaster Stephenson Co IL H307, 25-Westfield Twp Fayette Co IA H1448, 27-Fayette Fayette Co IA H129, 45

PHILIP NEWCOMER AND ELIZABETH LANTZ

C33 HENRY LANTZ C3

HENRY LANTZ was born on 25 Jan 1809 and died in 1887 in PA. He married SARAH FOLLMER (CA3) daughter of ABRAHAM FOLLMER and MARGARETHA LANTZ (CA). She was born in 1815 in PA. His will is recorded in Will Book 8 Page 75 Northumberland Co., PA.

Children of HENRY LANTZ and SARAH FOLLMER are:

1. WILLIAM DAVID LANTZ, born 20 Jul 1846 in Northumberland Co., PA.; died 28 Dec 1911; married HENRIETTA CASH. No children.
2. SARAH A, LANTZ, born 23 Mar 1850 in Northumberland Co., PA; died 09 Feb 1912 in Northumberland Co., PA.
3. HENRY LANTZ (C333)
4. ABRAHAM LANTZ, born in 1838 in Northumberland Co., PA.

References: 5, 24-Turbot Twp Northumberland Co PA H88, 25-Turbot Twp Northumberland Co PA H1226, 26-Turbot Twp Northumberland Co PA H61, 27-Turbot Twp Northumberland Co PA H503

C34 SARAH LANTZ C3

SARAH LANTZ was born on 18 Mar 1811 and died in 1882 in Northumberland Co., PA. She married DANIEL FOLLMER. He was born in 13 Apr 1806 in PA and died in 19 Aug 1887 in Northumberland Co., PA. He is buried in the Follmer Lutheran Church Cemetery in Milton, Northumberland Co., PA. His will is recorded in Will Book 8 Page 152 Northumberland Co., PA.

Children of SARAH LANTZ and DANIEL FOLLMER are:

1. MARY FOLLMER, born in 1831 in Northumberland Co., PA.
2. WILLIAM G. FOLLMER (C341)
3. MARGARET ANN FOLLMER, born in 1836 in Northumberland Co., PA.
4. CHARLES FRANKLIN FOLLMER (C344)
5. SARAH ELMIRA FOLLMER (C345), born in 1840 in Northumberland Co., PA.
6. DANIEL HENRY FOLLMER (C346)
7. SUSANNAH LUCRETIA FOLLMER, born in 1846 in Northumberland Co., PA.
8. JOHN S. FOLLMER (C348)
9. MARTIN FOLLMER, born in 1861 in Northumberland Co., PA.
10. ELMIRA FOLLMER, born in 1839 in Northumberland Co., PA.

References: 5, 26-Turbot Twp Northumberland Co PA H109, 25-Turbot Twp Northumberland Co PA H1254/55, 24-Turbot Twp Northumberland Co PA H72, 27-Turbot Twp Northumberland Co PA H389, 45, 36, 67

Daniel Follmer. Decd. Will.

I Daniel Follmer of Turbut Township in the county of Northumberland and
State of Pennsylvania being of Sound mind memory and understanding do make
this my last will and testament hereby revoking and making Void all former
wills by me at any time heretofore made. And first I direct that my body be
decently interred in the Follmer Cemetry Situate in Turbut Township
Northumberland County in a Christianlike manner And as to such Worldly goods
& Estate as it hath pleased God to intrust me with I dispose of the same
as follows I direct that all my debts and funeral Expenses be paid as soon
after my decease as possible out of the first money that Shall come into the
hands of my Executor from any portion of my estate real or personal Item
I give and bequeath unto my beloved wife Sarah all my household goods of every
Kind and description for and during her natural life also the Sum of Three
Hundred Dollars ($300.) in money absolutely to be paid to her by my hereinafter
named Executor out of my Estate as soon after my decease as can be done
Consistently with a proper Settlement of my debts and funeral expenses and it is
further my will that if at any time my beloved wife Sarah Should find that
the said sum of Three Hundred Dollars is not sufficient for her wants and
Comfort in that case my Executor shall provide for her out of my estate such
additional and further sum of money as she may deem necessary for said wants Item
It is further my will and I hereby direct that my beloved wife have and enjoy
during her natural life the exclusive and free and uninterrupted use and enjoyment
of that portion of my mansion house Situate in Turbut Township now occupied
by myself and wife consisting of four chambers on Second floor and three on the
first floor she to have the Selection of the same together with the use and enjoyment
of so much of the cellar as she may require for her own use and wants. Item it
is further my will that my beloved wife have and enjoy the free use of both
rear and front yard surrounding said mansion house also the priviledge of
using the Water on said premises and so much of the garden as she may require
for her own use during her natural life time. Item it is further my will and I
hereby give and bequeath unto my beloved wife Sarah three cows to be selected
by her out of my Stock of cattle for and during her natural life time the
use and profits thereof to be exclusively for her sole benefit and I further
direct my hereinafter named Executor to provide out of my estate such feed
and furnish such pasture, Stabling, bedding and such other needful things
as said cows may Require for their proper Comfort and well being both
Summer and winter and that during the Summer Season they be taken to
and from pasture with the other cattle on the farm. it is further my will and
I hereby instruct and require my said Executor to furnish out of my estate
to my beloved wife Sarah whatever wheat she may need for her own use during her
natural life and that the same be taken to the mill and returned to her in flour
free of any expence to her and further that she be provided with all fire wood
properly prepared for use and with such coal as her wants may require It is
further my desire and I hereby instruct my said Executor to furnish to my beloved wife
each and every year during her said life time out of my estate such number of Shoats
(pigs) as she may need for her own use together with such corn and other feed
as may be necessary for the proper fattening of the same Item I give and bequeath
unto my daughter Margaret Ann Follmer the sum of Two Hundred Dollars
$200. for services rendered me since her arrival at full age Item I give and bequeath
unto my daughter Susannah Lucetia Follmer the sum of One Hundred
Dollars $100. for services rendered me since her arrival at full age Both said

last mentioned legacies to be paid by my said Executor as soon after my decease
as possible. Item I hereby direct my hereinafter named Executor to dispose of at public
sale the ballance of my goods chattels. Stock and farming implements not herein
before bequeathed to my beloved wife Sarah: as soon after my decease as he
may deem expedient. Collect all claims demands notes &c due and owing to
me in any manner from any source and after the payments of my [illegible] debts
funeral expenses and the special legacies hereinbefore bequeathed to my
beloved wife Sarah and my two daughters Margaret Ann and Susannah
Lucetia distribute the ballance share and share alike amongst all my
Children hereinafter named. Item I give and devise unto my son William G.
Follmer and his heirs all that certain piece or parcel of land with the
appurtenances situate in Turbut Township County of Northumberland
and State of Pennsylvania and bounded and described as follows to
wit Bounded on the north by lands of John Hoy. on the South by the
State road leading from the Borough of Milton to Limestoneville. East
by lands of Thomas Ritter and West by public road leading from said
State Road to Follmer Church and other lands of testator containing nine
acres more or less the exact amount to be ascertained by measurement.
In the said William G paying therefor into my estate at the rate of one
Hundred and Seventy dollars for each and every acre But should my
said son William G Follmer be dissatisfied with the said price per acre
then it is my will that my said hereinafter named Executor shall choose
one person my son William G. choose one person and the two thus
chosen select a third who after being duly sworn shall proceed to put
a fair valuation upon the said above described piece or parcel of land
which valuation shall be binding and conclusive upon all parties and
paid for accordingly by my said son William G. Follmer and whereas
one acre and twenty nine and one seventh perches of the above described
piece and parcel of land was paid for by me to one John Hoy. but the
Deed for which was executed by said Hoy in the name of my said
son William G. Follmer. It is therefore my will and I hereby do order
and direct that if my said son William refuses to account to my
Estate for said one acre and twenty nine and one seventh perches
of land at the rate of one Hundred and Seventy Dollars per acre or
so much as the said three persons so selected as aforesaid shall value
the same, then and in that case he the said William G. shall receive the
sum of two Hundred Dollars less out of my estate than the rest of my
Children said piece or parcel of land above described devised to my said
son William G to be paid for by him at and immediately after the decease of
my beloved wife Sarah. the same to remain as part of my Estate until
after the decease of my said wife when my said son William G. only is to
have possession thereof. Item It is further my will and I hereby direct that
immediately after the decease of my beloved wife that all my heirs shall
come together at such time and place as may be designated by my
said Executor and if possible that they agree amongst themselves upon
a fair and equitable valuation of all my Real Estate not hereinbefore disposed
of But in the event of their not being able to agree then said heirs or a
majority of them shall select three competent and judicious persons who
after being duly sworn shall proceed having due respect to the true value thereof
to inquire whether my said Real Estate can be conveniently parted and divided so
as to accomodate all my Children without prejudice to and spoiling the whole

Daniel Follmer, Decd. Will.

I Daniel Follmer of Turbut Township in the County of Northumberland and State of Pennsylvania being of Sound mind memory and understanding do make this my last will and testament hereby revoking and making void all former wills by me at any time heretofore made. And first I direct that my body be decently interred in the Follmer Cemetery Situate in Turbut Township Northumberland County in a Christianlike manner And as to such Worldly goods & Estate as it hath pleased God to intrust me with I dispose of the same as follows I direct that all my debts and funeral Expenses be paid as soon after my decease as possible out of the first money that Shall come into the hands of my Executor from any portion of my estate real or personal Item I give and bequeath unto my beloved wife Sarah All my household goods of every Kind and description for and during her natural life also the Sum of Three Hundred Dollars ($300.) in money absolutely to be paid to her by my hereinafter named Executor out of my Estate as soon after my decease as can be done consistently with a proper Settlement of my debts and funeral expenses and it is further my will that if at any time my beloved wife Sarah Should find that the said Sum of Three Hundred Dollars is not Sufficient for her wants and comfort in that case my Executor shall furnish her out of my estate such additional and further Sum of money as she may deem necessary for said wants Item It is further my will and I hereby direct that my beloved wife have and enjoy during her natural life the exclusive and free and uninterrupted use and enjoyment of that portion of my mansion house Situate in Turbut Township now Occupied by myself and wife consisting of four chambers on Second floor and three on the first floor she to have the Selection of the same together with the use and enjoyment of so much of the cellar as she may require for her own use and wants. It is further my will that my beloved wife have and enjoy the free use of both rear and front yard Surrounding said Mansion house also the priviledge of using the Water on said premises and so much of the garden as she may require for her own use during her natural life time It is further my will and I hereby give and bequeath unto my beloved wife Sarah three cows to be selected by her out of my Stock of Cattle for and during her natural life time the use and profits thereof to be exclusively for her sole benefit and I further direct my hereinafter named Executor to provide out of my estate such feed and furnish such pasture. Stabling. bedding and such other needful thing as said cows may Require for their proper Comfort and well being both Summer and winter and that during the summer Season they be taken to and from pasture with the other cattle on the farm. it is further my will and I hereby instruct and require my said Executor to furnish out of my estate to my beloved wife Sarah whatever wheat she may need for her own use during her natural life and that the same be taken to the mill and returned to her in flour free of any expense to her and further that she be provided with all fire wood properly prepared for use and with such coal as her wants may require It is further my desire and I hereby instruct my said Executor to furnish to my beloved wife each and every year during her said life time out of my estate such number of Shoats (pigs) as she may need for her own use together with such corn and other feed as may be necessary for the proper fattening of the same Item I give and bequeath unto my daughter Margaret Ann Follmer the sum of Two Hundred Dollars $200. for services rendered me since her arrival at full age Item I give and bequeath unto my daughter Susannah Lucretia Follmer the sum of One Hundred Dollars $100. for services rendered me since her arrival at full age Both said

last mentioned legacies to be paid by my said Executor as soon after my decease
as possible. Item I hereby direct my hereinafter named Executor to dispose of at public
sale the ballance of my goods chattels. Stock and farming implements not herein
before bequeathed to my beloved wife Sarah. as soon after my decease as he
may deem expedient Collect all claims demands notes &c due and owing to
me in any manner from any source and after the payments of my just debts
funeral Expenses and the Special legacies herein before bequeathed to my
beloved wife Sarah and my two daughters Margaret Ann and Susannah
Executor distribute the ballance share and share alike amongst all my
Children hereinafter named. Item I give and devise unto my son William G.
Follmer and his heirs all that certain piece or parcel of land with the
appurtenances Situate in Turbut Township County of Northumberland
and State of Pennsylvania and bounded and described as follows to
wit Bounded on the North by lands of John Hoy. on the South by the
State Road leading from the Borough of Milton to Limestoneville. East
by lands of Thomas Ritter and West by public Road leading from said
State Road to Follmer Church and other lands of testator containing nine
acres more or less the exact amount to be ascertained by measurement
he the said William G. paying therefor into my estate at the rate of one
Hundred and Seventy dollars for each and every acre But should my
said Son William G. Follmer be dissatisfied with the said price per acre
then it is my will that my said hereinafter named Executor shall choose
one person my son William G. choose one person and the two thus
chosen select a third who after being duly sworn shall proceed to make
a fair valuation upon the said above described piece or parcel of land
which valuation shall be binding and conclusive upon all parties and
paid for accordingly by my said son William G. Follmer and whereas
one acre and twenty nine and one seventh perches of the above described
piece and parcel of land was paid for by me to one John Hoy. but the
Deed for which was executed by said Hoy in the name of my said
son William G. Follmer. It is therefore my will and I hereby do order
and direct that if my said son William refuses to account to my
Estate for said one acre and twenty nine and one seventh perches
of land at the rate of one Hundred and Seventy Dollars per acre or
so much as the said three persons so selected as aforesaid shall value
the same, then and in that case he the said William G. shall receive the
sum of two Hundred Dollars less out of my estate then the rest of my
children said piece or parcel of land above described devised to my said
son William G. to be paid for by him at and immediately after the decease of
my beloved wife Sarah. the same to remain as part of my Estate until
after the decease of my said wife when my said son William G. only is to
have possession thereof. Item It is further my will and I hereby direct that
immediately after the decease of my beloved wife that all my heirs shall
come together at such time and place as may be designated by my
said Executor and if possible that they agree amongst themselves upon
a fair and equitable valuation of all my Real Estate not hereinbefore disposed
of But in the event of their not being able to agree then said heirs or a
majority of them shall select three competent and judicious persons who
after being duly sworn shall proceed having due respect to the true value thereof
to inquire whether my said Real Estate can be conveniently parted and divided so
as to accommodate all my Children without prejudice to and spoiling the whole

County of Northumberland. S.S.
C. F. Follmer do Swear that as Executor of the foregoing last will and Testament & codicil annexed of Daniel Follmer deceased I will well and truly administer the goods and chattles, rights and credits of said deceased, agreeably to law and that I will comply with the provisions of the law relating to collateral inheritances and I do further swear that he died on the 19th day of August A. D. 1887

C. F. Follmer

Be it remembered that on this 29th day of August A. D. 1887, before me was proved approved and insinuated in due and common form of law the last will and testament and codicil thereto of Daniel Follmer late of Turbut Township, deceased, who died on the 19th day of August A. D. 1887, and that Letters testamentary with a copy of the said will annexed were granted to Charles Franklin Follmer, the executor named in said will.

Witness my hand,
Uriah Bloom,
Register.

C35 MARGARET LANTZ C3

MARGARET LANTZ was born on 14 Aug 1813 and died 18 Mar 1895 in Lockport, Niagara Co., NY. She married JOHN ESHBACH on 01 Sep 1831. He was born in 1838 in PA.

Children of MARGARET LANTZ and JOHN ESHBACH are:

1. INFANT DAUGHTER ESHBACH, born and died 08 Jun 1832.
2. RHUBEN PERRY ESHBACH, born on 13 May 1833; died 10 Nov 1834.
3. MARGARET CATHERINE ESHBACH (C353)
4. THEODORE S. ESHBACH (C354)
5. ELLA JANE ESHBACH, born on 27 Mar 1839; died 21 May 1839.
6. ISAIAH J. ESHBACH, born on 02 May 1840; died 15 May 1843.
7. URIAH H. ESHBACH (C357)
8. ANNA MARY ESHBACH, born on 23 Aug 1844 in NY; died 09 Feb 1912 in Lockport, Niagara Co., NY.
9. DAVID J. ESHBACH (C359)
10. MINERVA E. ESHBACH, born 05 Nov 1849 in Lockport, Niagara Co., NY; died 27 Jan 1881 in NY; married LUTHER WINTERSTEEN. No children.
11. DANIEL LANTZ ESHBACH, born on 09 May 1853 in Lockport, Niagara Co., NY; died 16 Mar 1864 in Lockport, Niagara Co., NY.
12. CHRISTIAN ALICE ESHBACH (C35C)

References: 5, 24-Lockport Niagara Co NY H644, 26-Lockport Niagara Co NY H375

C36 DANIEL LANTZ C3

DANIEL LANTZ was born on 11 Nov 1815 in PA and died 01 May 1891 in Constantine, St.

Joseph Co., MI. He was a Reformed Minister at Constantine and White Pigeon, MI. He married MARY HACKENBERG in PA. She was born in 1821 in PA and died 01 Aug 1910 in Chicago, Cook Co., IL. His daughter Mrs. Nicodemus had a Bible which originally belonged to HENRY LANTZ, who left it to his son, DANIEL, from whom it passed to this DANIEL and then to his daughter.

Children of DANIEL LANTZ and MARY are:

1. MARY LANTZ, born 08 Dec 1843 in PA; married JACOB F. NICODEMUS; No children.
2. JULIA C. LANTZ (C362)
3. DANIEL OLEVIANUS LANTZ (C363)
4. HARRIET LOUISE LANTZ (C364)

References: 5, 25-Constantine St Joseph Co MI H894, 26-Constantine St Joseph Co MI H169, 46-D/DOL/25576, 46-D/DL/Vol 1 Page 286, 46-D/MH/20029

C38 ANNA LANTZ C3

ANNA LANTZ was born on 07 Sep 1820 and died in 1878. She married HENRY AUSTIN in Milton, Northumberland Co., PA. He was born in 1816 in PA. They moved from MILTON, PA, in 1850 and went West. ELIZABETH NEWCOMER and family started with them. They each drove horses and covered wagons. Mr. NEWCOMER was ahead, took the wrong road and they never saw each other again. AUSTINs stopped in OH for five years and then on to MI.

Children of ANNA LANTZ and HENRY AUSTIN are:

1. MARY E. AUSTIN, born in Feb 1843 in PA, married JAMES R. CARTER in 1891; born in Feb 1828 in VA as his 2nd wife; No children.
2. SARAH J. AUSTIN (C382)
3. MARGARET AUSTIN (C383)
4. MARTHA L. AUSTIN (C384)
5. ELMIRA J. AUSTIN (C385)
6. HENRY F. AUSTIN, in 1861 in Clinton Co., MI, four children, two of which died in infancy.

References: 5, 24-Greenbush Twp Clinton Co MI H29, 25-Greenbush Twp Clinton Co MI H127, 26-Greenbush Twp Clinton Co MI H64, 29-Dist 12 Greenbush Clinton Co MI H236

C39 CHRISTIANA LANTZ C3

CHRISTIANA LANTZ was born on 21 Mar 1823 and died in 1901 at Watsontown, PA. She married PHILIP WINTERSTEEN in PA. He was born in 1819 in PA. He was a carpenter by occupation.

Children of CHRISTIANA LANTZ and PHILIP WINTERSTEEN are:

1. DANIEL JEREMIAH WINTERSTEEN, born on 09 Sep 1844 in Columbia Co., PA; died 10 Oct 1848 in Columbia Co., PA.
2. JOHN SAMUEL WINTERSTEEN, born 04 Feb 1847 in Columbia Co., PA.
3. HENRY MARTIN WINTERSTEEN (C393)

4. MARY E. WINTERSTEEN, born 04 Jun 1850 in Columbia Co., PA; died Apr 1921; unmarried.
5. JACOB LUTHER WINTERSTEEN, born 02 Apr 1853 in Columbia Co., PA; died before 1931, one son.
6. SARAH CHRISTENA WINTERSTEEN (C396)
7. WILLIAM FRANKLIN WINTERSTEEN (C397)
8. CHARLES ROLLEN WINTERSTEEN, born 15 Sep 1861 in Columbia Co., PA; died 11 Apr 1862 in Columbia Co., PA.
9. SIMON LANTZ WINTERSTEEN (C399)

References: 5, 24-Madison Twp Columbia Co PA H74, 25-Mifflin Twp Columbia Co PA H1539, 26-Watsontown Northumberland Co PA H25, 27-Watsontown Northumberland Co PA H89

C41 MARTIN GASS C4

MARTIN GASS was born 1816 in Northumberland Co., PA. He married (1) ANNA HOWER in Northumberland Co., PA, daughter of JACOB HOWER. She was born on 05 Dec 1815 in PA and died 22 Jan 1850 in Northumberland Co., PA. He married (2) MARY in Northumberland Co., PA. She was born in 1816 in PA. He was a farmer by occupation.

Children of MARTIN GASS and ANNA are:

1. ELIZABETH JANE GASS (C411)
2. RICHARD A. GASS (C412)
3. JACOB A. GASS; born in 17 Oct 1848 in Northumberland Co., PA; died 25 Jan 1909 in Northumberland Co., PA; married SARAH JANE KEEFER in Northumberland Co., PA, daughter of GEORGE KEEFER; born Nov 1848 in Northumberland Co., PA; He engaged in a grocery business by occupation. They were Democrats and members No children.
4. GEORGE W. GASS (C414)

Child of MARTIN GASS and MARY are:

5. MARTHA GASS, born in 1858 in Northumberland Co., PA.

References: 24-Augusta Twp Northumberland Co PA H7, 25-Augusta Twp Northumberland Co PA H723, 26-Upper Augusta Twp Northumberland Co PA H211, 29-Dist 0161 Sunbury Northumberland Co PA H171, 27-Upper Augusta Twp Northumberland Co PA 167 H307, 67

C42 HENRY L GASS C4

HENRY L. GASS was born on 29 Jul 1805 in Northumberland Co., PA and died 01 Jul 1897 in Northumberland Co., PA. He married (2) JULIA ANN CONRAD in Northumberland Co., PA. She was born in 1803 in PA and died 16 Dec 1857 in Northumberland Co., PA. They are buried in the Eden Lutheran and Evangelical Cemetery, Plum Creek Road, Sunbury, Northumberland Co., PA.

Children of HENRY GASS and are:

1. WILLIAM GASS, born in 27 Jan 1830 in Northumberland Co., PA; died 29 May 1888 in

Northumberland Co., PA. Buried in the Eden Lutheran and Evangelical Cemetery, Plum Creek Road, Sunbury, Northumberland Co., PA. He was blind.
2. MARIA GASS, born in 1832 in Northumberland Co., PA.
3. JULIAN GASS, born in 1834 in Northumberland Co., PA.
4. JACOB C. GASS (C424)
5. ANNA GASS, born in 1836 in Northumberland Co., PA.
6. SUSANNAH GASS, born in 03 Mar 1838 in Northumberland Co., PA; died 27 Oct 1857 in Northumberland Co., PA. Buried in the Eden Lutheran and Evangelical Cemetery, Plum Creek Road, Sunbury, Northumberland Co., PA.
7. ELIAS GASS (C427)
8. GEORGE WASHINGTON GASS, born in 1843 in Northumberland Co., PA.
9. HARRIET LOUISA GASS, born in 1843 in Northumberland Co., PA.
10. ELIZABETH GASS, born in1845 in Northumberland Co., PA.

References: 67, 24-Lower Augusta Twp Northumberland Co PA H288, 25-Lower Augusta Twp Northumberland Co PA H911

C43 JOSEPH GASS C4

JOSEPH GASS was born on 21 Dec 1810 in Northumberland Co., PA and died 28 Dec 1879 in Northumberland Co., PA. He married MARIA RAKER in Northumberland Co., PA. She was born on 27 Jul 1814 in PA and died 25 Oct 1871 in Northumberland Co., PA. He was a farmer by occupation. They were Democrats and members of the Reformed Church. Both are buried in Lantz's Emmanuel Cemetery, Sunbury, Northumberland Co., PA.

Children of JOSEPH GASS and MARIA RAKER are:

1. MARTIN R. GASS, born on 06 Jul 1836 in Northumberland Co., PA; died 12 Jan 1888; married (1) MARY ANN in Northumberland Co., PA; born on 20 Sep 1835 in PA; died 16 Oct 1862 in Northumberland Co., PA; married (2) ABIGAIL in Northumberland Co., PA; born on 18 Nov 1837 in PA; died 26 Jul 1892 in Northumberland Co., PA. They are buried in the Eden Lutheran and Evangelical Cemetery, Plum Creek Road, Sunbury, Northumberland Co., PA.
2. SAMUEL GASS (C432)
3. MARY ANN GASS, born on 29 Jul 1840 in Northumberland Co., PA; died 18 Sep 1900 in Sunbury, Northumberland Co., PA.
4. LUCENDIA GASS, born on 25 Mar 1842 in Northumberland Co., PA; died Feb 1843 in Sunbury, Northumberland Co., PA.
5. JOSEPH GASS (C435)
6. BARBARA ALICE GASS, born on 24 Feb 1847 in Northumberland Co., PA; died in Snyder Co., PA.
7. ISAAC GASS, born on 15 Jul 1849 in Northumberland Co., PA; died 09 Aug 1849 in Northumberland Co., PA. Buried in Lantz's Emmanuel Cemetery, Sunbury, Northumberland Co., PA.
8. RICHARD F. GASS, born on 19 Nov 1852 in Northumberland Co., PA. Graduate of Franklin & Marshall Theological Seminary at Lancaster, PA.; married SARAH LYDIA. in Northumberland Co., PA; born in 1860 in MD. 27-Sunbury Northumberland Co PA 169 H220

References: 67, 45, 24-Lower Augusta Twp Northumberland Co PA H206, 25-Lower Augusta Twp Northumberland Co PA H771

C44 WILLIAM GASS C4

WILLIAM GASS was born on 15 Sep 1815 in Northumberland Co., PA and died 23 Mar 1897 in Northumberland Co., PA. He married SUSANNA STRICKLAND in Northumberland Co., PA. She was born on 27 Jan 1820 in PA and died 29 May 1888 in Northumberland Co., PA. They are buried in the Eden Lutheran and Evangelical Cemetery, Plum Creek Road, Sunbury, Northumberland Co., PA.

Children of WILLIAM GASS and SUSANNA STRICKLAND are:

1. JACOB GASS, born 18 Aug 1842 in Northumberland Co., PA; died 11 May 1858 in Northumberland Co., PA. He is buried in the Eden Lutheran and Evangelical Cemetery, Plum Creek Road, Sunbury, Northumberland Co., PA.
2. JOSEPH A. GASS (C442)
3. SAMUEL W. GASS, born in 1848 in Northumberland Co., PA. Moved out West.
4. ISAAC N. GASS (C444)
5. HARRIET A. GASS, born 1853 in Northumberland Co., PA; died before 1911 in Northumberland Co., PA; married FRANCIS CAMPBELL in Northumberland Co., PA.
6. EMMA J. GASS, born 1856 in Northumberland Co., PA; married (1) JOHN TAYLOR in Northumberland Co., PA; married (2) CHARLES FEESE in Northumberland Co., PA.
7. ANNIE E. GASS, born 1860 in Northumberland Co., PA; married CYRUS TUCKER in Northumberland Co., PA.

References: 67, 25-Shamokin Northumberland Co PA H1187, 25-Shamokin Northumberland Co PA H368

C49 LYDIA GASS C4

LYDIA GASS was born 1819 in Northumberland Co., PA. She married DAVID O. E. MAIZE in Northumberland Co., PA. He was born in 1819 in PA.

Children of LYDIA GASS and DAVID MAIZE are:

1. ELBRIDGE MAIZE, born in 1842 in Northumberland Co., PA.
2. MARY MAIZE, born in 1844 in Northumberland Co., PA.
3. JACOB MAIZE, born in 1846 in Northumberland Co., PA.
4. SUSAN MAIZE, born in 1848 in Northumberland Co., PA.
5. S. MAIZE, born in 1851 in Northumberland Co., PA.
6. A. MAIZE, born in 1857 in Northumberland Co., PA.

References: 24-Sunbury Northumberland Co PA H25, 25-North Ward Lewisburg Union Co PA H1412

C51 REBECCA LANTZ C5

MARGARET REBECCA LANTZ was born on 15 Jan 1806 and died in 19 Nov 1840 in Northumberland Co., PA. She married GEORGE KEEFER in PA. He was born in 24 Jul 1798 in

Oley Twp., Berks Co., PA and died in 10 Sep 1879 in Northumberland Co., PA. Both are buried in Lantz's Emmanuel Cemetery, Sunbury, Northumberland Co., PA. They were Democrats and members of the German Reformed Church.

Children of MARGARET LANTZ and GEORGE KEEFER are:

1. SAMUEL L. KEEFER (C511)
2. MARGARET KEEFER (C512)
3. HANNAH KEEFER (C513)
4. PETER KEEFER (C514)
5. MARY MAGDALENA KEEFER (C515)

References: 5, 45, 36, 66, 67

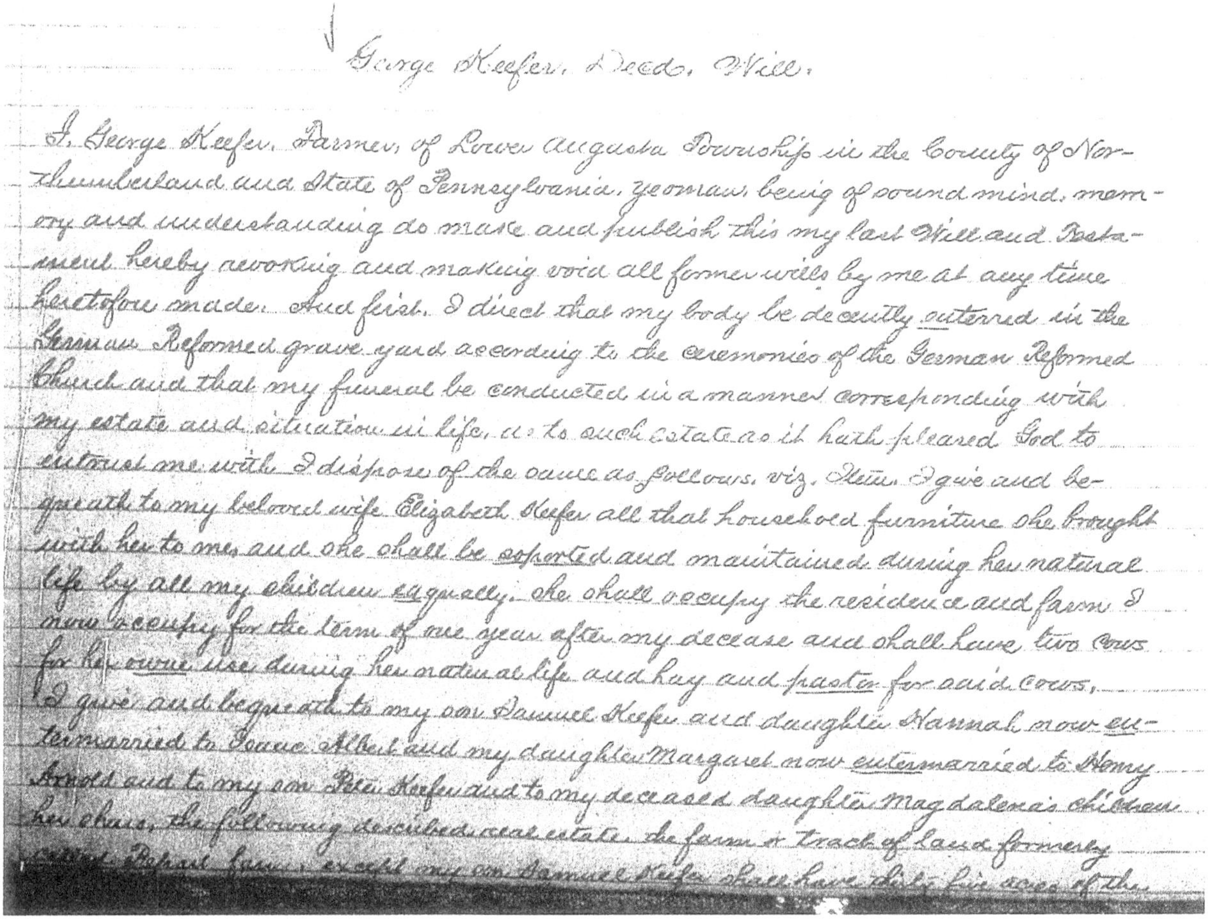

George Keefer, Decd. Will.

I, George Keefer, Farmer, of Lower Augusta Township in the County of Northumberland and State of Pennsylvania, yeoman, being of sound mind, memory and understanding do make and publish this my last Will and Testament hereby revoking and making void all former wills by me at any time heretofore made. And first. I direct that my body be decently interred in the German Reformed grave yard according to the ceremonies of the German Reformed Church and that my funeral be conducted in a manner corresponding with my estate and situation in life, as to such estate as it hath pleased God to entrust me with I dispose of the same as follows, viz. Item. I give and bequeath to my beloved wife Elizabeth Keefer all that household furniture she brought with her to me, and she shall be suported and maintained during her natural life by all my children equally. she shall occupy the residence and farm I now occupy for the term of one year after my decease and shall have two cows for her owne use during her natural life and hay and paster for said cows. I give and bequeath to my son Samuel Keefer and daughter Hannah now intermarried to Isaac Albert and my daughter Margaret now intermarried to Henry Arnold and to my son Peter Keefer and to my deceased daughter Magdalena's children her share, the following described real estate the farm & tract of land formerly called [illegible] farm, except my son Samuel Keefer shall have [illegible] five acres of the foregoing named farm and the balance shall be equally divided, that is to my sons Samuel, Margaret, Peter and Magdalena's children, share and share alike, and that John Zimmerman, the father of the children of my deceased daughter Magdalena shall receive the proceeds of their share out of said mentioned farm and shall have the same until the children will be of age without interest for the same, I give to my daughter Kitty Ann and Jane and Alice, one cow and one bed and bedding, bureau & ½ doz. chairs and furniture besides to the amount of ten dollars, and I give any one of my sons that will farm the farm for their mother for the term before mentioned one of best horses, and I give and bequeath all the balance of my real and personal estate to all my children share and share alike. In Witness Whereof, I the said testator have to this my last will and Testament set my hand and seal the twenty eight day of May A.D. 1864

George Keefer (seal)

The words balance of was interlined before the the signing. Signed, sealed, published and declared by the said testator as and for his last will and Testament in the presence of us who in his presence and at his request and in the presence of each other have subscribed our names as witness thereto.

Daniel Beckley.
Jacob Cable.

State of Pennsylvania }
County of Northumberland } ss

Be it remembered that on this 20th day of September A.D. 1879, before me Urias Bloom, Dep. Register for the Probate of Wills and granting of Letters of Administration in and for said County, personally appeared Daniel Beckley and Jacob Cable, the subscribing witnesses to the foregoing instrument of writing purporting to be the last will and Testament of George Keefer late of Lower Augusta Township, County and State aforesaid, deceased, who being duly sworn according to law did depose and say that they were personally present at the execution of the same and saw and heard the testator therein named sign, seal, publish, pronounce and declare the same as and for his last will and Testament and that at the time of so doing he was of sound mind, memory and understanding to the best of their knowledge and belief.

Sworn and subscribed before me, }
Urias Bloom, Dep. Register. }

Daniel Beckley.
Jacob Cable.

Be it remembered that on this 20th day of September A.D. 1879, before me was proved, approved and insinuated the last Will and Testament of George Keefer late of Lower Augusta Township, County and State aforesaid deceased, who died on the 11th day of September A.D. 1879, and that Letters of Administration with the will annexed upon the said estate were granted to Samuel L. Keefer and George W. Keefer who entered into bond with Jacob Fagely and Peter Keefer as sureties in the sum of five thousand dollars.

Witness my hands.

Lend. Shipman.
Register.

C53 ANNA LANTZ C5

ANNA LANTZ was born on 09 Jun 1809 in Augusta Twp., Northumberland Co., PA and died 22 Nov 1878 in Augusta Twp., Northumberland Co., PA. She married DAVID HAUCK on 12 Mar 1829 in Northumberland Co., PA. He was born on 05 Nov 1805 in Upper Hanover Twp., Montgomery Co., PA and died 27 Feb 1867 in Augusta Twp., Northumberland Co., PA. Both are buried in Lantz's Emmanuel Cemetery, Sunbury, Northumberland Co., PA. His will is recorded in Will Book 5, Page 398 Northumberland Co., PA.

Children of ANNA LANTZ and DAVID HAUCK are:

1. ELIZABETH HAUCK (C531)
2. MARY HAUCK (C532)
3. ANDREW HAUCK(C533)
4. AMELIA C. HAUCK, born in 1839 in Northumberland Co., PA.
5. HENRY L. HAUCK (C535)
6. DAVID K. HAUCK (C536)
7. ARNNIE L. HAUCK, born in 1846 in Northumberland Co., PA.
8. WILLIAM A. HAUCK, born in 1848 in Northumberland Co., PA.
9. JOHN R. HAUCK (C539)
10. PETER F. HAUCK, born in 1852 in Northumberland Co., PA.
11. SAMUEL L. HAUCK, born on 14 Nov 1832 in Northumberland Co., PA; died 28 Nov 1840 in Northumberland Co., PA; buried in Lantz's Emmanuel Cemetery, Sunbury, Northumberland Co., PA.

References: 5, 45, 24-Lower Augusta Northumberland Co PA H147, 25-Lower Augusta Northumberland Co PA H933, 36

C54 MAGDALINE LANTZ C5

MAGDALINE LANTZ was born on 27 Oct 1811 in Northumberland Co., PA and died 03 Mar 1886 in Northumberland Co., PA. She married JOHN STERNER. He was born on 04 Aug 1809 in PA and died 24 Nov 1886 in Northumberland Co., PA. Both are buried in the Lantz Lutheran Cemetery, Sunbury, Northumberland Co., PA.

Children of MAGDALINE LANTZ and JOHN STERNER are:

1. SAMUEL STERNER, born in 1833 in Northumberland Co., PA.
2. ABRAHAM STERNER, born in 1835 in Northumberland Co., PA.
3. HENRY STERNER, born in 1837 in Northumberland Co., PA.
4. CASANDRA STERNER, born in 1839 in Northumberland Co., PA.
5. JOHN C. STERNER, born on 19 Oct 1840 in Northumberland Co., PA; died 09 Apr 1864.
6. DANIEL STERNER, born in 1842 in Northumberland Co., PA.
7. WILLIAM P. STERNER (C547)
8. GEORGE WASHINGTON STERNER (C548)
9. ALEXANDER STERNER, born in 1848 in Northumberland Co., PA.
10. RICHARD F. STERNER, born in 1850 in Northumberland Co., PA.

References: 24-Lower Augusta Twp Northumberland Co PA H274, 25-Lower Augusta Twp

Northumberland Co PA H833, 26-Lower Augusta Twp Northumberland Co PA H115, 27-Lower Augusta Twp Northumberland Co PA H19

C55 SUSANNAH LANTZ C5

SUSANNAH LANTZ was born on 08 Apr 1814 and died 20 Feb 1901. She married WILLIAM DEPPEN in Northumberland Co., PA, son of GEORGE DEPPEN and MARIA MAGADLENA GREISE. He was born in 1814 in PA and died in 08 Jan 1876 in Northumberland Co., PA. He was a merchant by occupation. They were Republicans and members of the German Reformed Church.

Children of SUSANNAH LANTZ and WILLIAM DEPPEN are:

1. BENJAMIN FRANKLIN DEPPEN (C551)
2. GEORGE WASHINGTON DEPPEN (C552)
3. RICHARD L. DEPPEN (C553)
4. SARAH ALICE DEPPEN, born in 1854 in Northumberland Co., PA; died 08 Jun 1915 in Northumberland Co., PA.
5. SAMUEL DEPPEN, born 1845 in Northumberland Co., PA; died in childhood in Northumberland Co., PA.
6. MARY DEPPEN, born in Northumberland Co., PA; died in childhood in Northumberland Co., PA.
7. WILLIAM DEPPEN, born in Northumberland Co., PA; died in childhood in Northumberland Co., PA.

References: 5, 24-Jackson Twp Northumberland Co PA H61, 25-Zerbe Twp Northumberland Co PA H608, 26-Trevorton Zerbe Twp Northumberland Co PA H38, 36, 67

C56 GERTRUDE "CHARITY" LANTZ C5

GERTRUDE "CHARITY" LANTZ was born on 21 Sep 1815 in Northumberland Co., PA and died 16 Mar 1890 in Northumberland Co., PA. She married PETER CULP in Northumberland Co., PA, son of HENRY CULP and SALOMA. He was born on 22 Apr 1814 in Northumberland Co., PA and died 05 Sep 1850 in Northumberland Co., PA. Both are buried in Lantz Lutheran Cemetery, Sunbury, Northumberland Co., PA

Children of GERTRUDE LANTZ and PETER CULP are:

1. SUSAN CULP, born in 1838 in Northumberland Co., PA; married WILLIAM WEITZEL; both died before 1911.
2. HENRY CULP, born in 1840 in Northumberland Co., PA.
3. SAMUEL CULP, born in 1842 in Northumberland Co., PA; served Civil War.
4. DAVID CULP, born in 1844 in Northumberland Co., PA; served and died in Civil War.
5. RICHARD CULP, born in 1847 in Northumberland Co., PA; served in the Civil War.
6. ALBERT S. CULP (C566)
7. PETER F. CULP (C567)

References: 24-Lower Augusta Twp Northumberland Co PA H19, 25-Lower Augusta Twp Northumberland Co PA H935, 45, 27-Lower Augusta Twp Northumberland Co PA H49, 67

C57 HENRY LANTZ C5

HENRY LANTZ was born on 07 Sep 1817 and died 07 Nov 1865. He married CAROLINE BUSSARD, of Germantown, OH. She was born in 1824 in MD. He was struck in the breast bone by a piece of grindstone when he was four years old and was always in poor health as a result. He grew up on the farm, started to Marshall College, but his health failed and he went West. He taught school in OH and IN, and was a merchant losing several stocks in floods and became deep in debt. In 1852, he started to CA, via NY and Panama. After seven months and twenty days of hardships, he arrived in CA. Finally, he returned and settled up with his creditors. Mr. BENJAMIN FRANKLIN DEPPEN, of Trevorton, PA, owns a booklet *To the Memory of Henry Lantz* which is very interesting and from which the above facts have been gleaned.

Children of HENRY LANTZ and CAROLINE BUSSARD are:

1. MARY MAGDALENA LANTZ, born 09 Aug 1842 in Wabash Co., IN; died 30 Aug 1847 in Wabash Co., IN.
2. SUSANNAH LANTZ (C572)
3. SARAH CATHERINE LANTZ (C573)
4. ANNA LANTZ, born 22 Jan 1851 in Wabash Co., IN; died 23 Apr 1853 in Wabash Co., IN.
5. SAMUEL EDWARD LANTZ (C575)
6. ADA LANTZ (C576)
7. ANNA EMMA LANTZ, born 28 Jan 1860 in Wabash Co., IN; married WILLIAM HENRY WEBBER in 1884.

References: 5, 24-Chester Twp Wabash Co IN H256, 25-Chester Twp Wabash Co IN H70, 27-North Manchester Wabash Co In H290

C58 CATHERINE LANTZ C5

CATHERINE LANTZ was born on 16 Nov 1819 and died 07 Jan 1889. She married JOHN DEPPEN in 1850 in Northumberland Co., PA, son of GEORGE DEPPEN. He was born on 04 Jul 1815 in Northumberland Co., PA and died 11 Dec 1893 in Herndon, Northumberland Co., PA. He was a farmer by occupation. They were members of the Reformed congregation of St. Peter's Church.

Children of CATHERINE LANTZ and JOHN DEPPEN are:

1. MARY DEPPEN (C581)
2. SAMUEL DEPPEN (C582)
3. WILLIAM H. DEPPEN (C583)
4. SUSAN C. DEPPEN (C584)

References: 5, 25-Jackson Twp Northumberland Co PA H413, 26-Jackson Twp Northumberland Co PA H132, 67

C59 SARAH LANTZ C5

SARAH LANTZ was born on 11 Jul 1822 in Northumberland Co., PA and died 06 May

1896 in Northumberland Co., PA. She married HENRY HUMMEL in PA, son of JOHN HUMMEL. He was born in 19 Mar 1830 in Snyder Co., PA and died 01 Nov 1900 in Milton, Northumberland Co., PA. He married (2) RACHEL R. in Northumberland Co., PA. His will is recorded in Will Book 5, Page 230 Northumberland Co., PA. Both HENRY and his first wife are buried Lewisburg Cemetery, Lewisburg, Union Co., PA.

Children of SARAH LANTZ and HENRY HUMMEL are:

1. SUSAN M. HUMMEL (C591)
2. SARAH JANE HUMMEL (C592)
3. CATHARINE A. HUMMEL (C593)
4. WILLIAM F. HUMMEL, born in Sep 1862 in PA.
5. JOHN S. HUMMEL (C595)

References: 26-Chillisquaque Twp Northumberland Co PA H279, 29-Milton Ward 5 Northumberland Co PA H639, 67

Nov-22-1900-
See Release of Dower
Recorded in Deed Book 127 Page 692

Will of Henry Hummel, deceased

In the name of God Amen. - I, Henry Hummel of Milton in the County of Northumberland and State of Pennsylvania, farmer, being of sound mind, memory and understanding, but considering the uncertainty of life, do make and publish this my last will and testament, (hereby revoking any and all Wills heretofore made by me at any time) in Manner following to wit:- First. I will and direct that all just debts that may exist against me at my decease may be settled. - Second. - Inasmuch as I did on the fourteenth day of April A.D. 1899, at the request of my wife Rachael R. Hummel give unto my said wife Rachael R. Hummel the sum of Twenty three hundred dollars ($2300.00/100) in Cash the same was and is in lieu of her exemption under the Act of April 14th 1851 and its supplements, and in lieu of her interest in my estate under the intestate laws of the State of Pennsylvania, and also in lieu of her dower at Common law or under the statutes of this State, and whereas my said wife Rachael R. Hummel, did on the said fourteenth day of April 1899, execute

2 - and deliver to me a written agreement wherein the said parties Covenant and agree that she will never ask claim or attempt to collect any thing out of my estate (but the above is to be in full settlement of all claims and demands whatever which she might have in my estate after my decease) by virtue of the intestate laws of Pennsylvania now passed or that may hereafter be passed, and in consideration thereof I did on said fourteenth day of April 1899 give unto my said wife Rachael R. Hummel absolutely the sum of Twenty three hundred dollars ($2300.00/100) in Cash which was to be and which is in lieu of her interest in my estate under the intestate laws of Pennsylvania now passed or that may hereafter be passed, and in lieu of her exemption under the Act of April 14th 1851 and its supplements and also in lieu of her dower at Common law, or under the statutes of this State: And I direct that she shall not receive any thing further out of my estate or any part thereof whatever. - - - - - - - - -

3 - Third. - All of my Estate, real, personal and mixed, whatsoever and wheresoever, I order and direct to be converted into money by my hereinafter named Executor, as soon as the same can conveniently be done after my decease; And for that purpose I do hereby authorize and empower my Executor hereinafter named to sell and dispose of all my said real estate either by public or private sale or sales, for the best price or prices he can obtain for the same, and by proper deeds or deed of Conveyances or assurances in the law, to be duly executed, acknowledged and perfected to grant, convey, and assure the same to the purchaser or purchasers, thereof in fee simple and the same to be done without asking leave of Court. If at any time before my said Estate is converted into money, my hereinafter named Executor should deem it advisable to take out insurance policies on any of the buildings or personal property as a protection in case of fire, he is hereby authorized and directed so to do and to pay said premiums out of the general funds, and he is to have proper credits

Witnesses { W. K. Armstrong, W. J. Gohrs } Henry Hummel (Seal)

Witnesses { W. K. Armstrong, W. J. Gohrs } Henry Hummel (Seal)

Witness
W. K. Armstrong
W. H. Gohre

Henry Hummel (Seal)

in his accounts for the same. — — — — —

4\. Fourth. — When the whole of my Estate shall have been converted into money as before mentioned, then I will and direct that the same shall be divided into five equal parts or shares, and disposed of as follows, to wit: One full equal fifth part or share thereof I give devise and bequeath unto my beloved daughter Jane, who is intermarried with O. B. Brown of Union County, Pennsylvania to her and her heirs and assigns forever. — One full equal fifth part or share thereof, I give devise and bequeath unto my Son John G. Hummel of Union County Pennsylvania, to him and to his heirs and assigns forever. One full equal fifth part or share thereof, I give, devise and bequeath unto my daughter Susan intermarried with Frank Waldron of West Chillisquaque Township Northumberland County, Pennsylvania, and to her heirs and assigns forever. — One full equal fifth part or share thereof I give devise and bequeath unto my daughter Kate intermarried with Irwin B. Romig of Selinsgrove, Snyder County Pennsylvania, and to her heirs and assigns forever. — — — — — — —

5 And one full equal fifth part or share thereof, I give devise and bequeath unto my son William E. Hummel, who resides with me in Milton Northumberland County Pennsylvania and to his heirs and assigns forever. Fifth. All the money which from time to time I have in my lifetime given to my children have been gifts to them and they are not to have the same charged against them nor to account for or pay back the same. And lastly. I nominate, constitute and appoint my friend Arthur L. Swartz, Esq. of Milton, Northumberland County Pennsylvania, Executor of this my last Will and testament, and I do hereby direct that he shall have out of my said estate for his compensation in serving as Executor hereof a commission of three per centum (3%) on the appraised value of my said estate, and that is all my said Executor is to receive for his services as Executor of my said estate. I declare these presents only to be my last will and testament. In witness whereof, I, Henry Hummel the testator, have to this my will written on six pages of legal cap paper set my hand and seal, this twenty-fifth day of August A. D. One thousand Nine hundred (1900). —

Witness. W. K. Armstrong (
W. H. Gohre)

Henry Hummel (Seal)

Signed, sealed, published and declared by the abovenamed Henry Hummel as and for his last Will and testament, in the presence of us who have hereunto subscribed our names at his request as Witnesses thereto in the presence of the said testator and of each other.

W. K. Armstrong
W. H. Gohre.

State of Pennsylvania
County of Northumberland } ss. Be it Remembered, That on the 5th day of November A. D. 1900, before me the Register for the Probate of Wills and granting of Letters of Administration in and for said County, personally appeared W. K. Armstrong and W. H. Gohre the subscribing witnesses to the foregoing instrument of writing purporting to be the last Will and Testament of Henry Hummel late of the Borough of Milton County and State aforesaid, deceased, who being duly sworn according to law do declare and say that they were personally present at the execution of the same and saw and heard the testator therein named sign, seal, publish, pronounce and declare the same as and for his last Will and testament

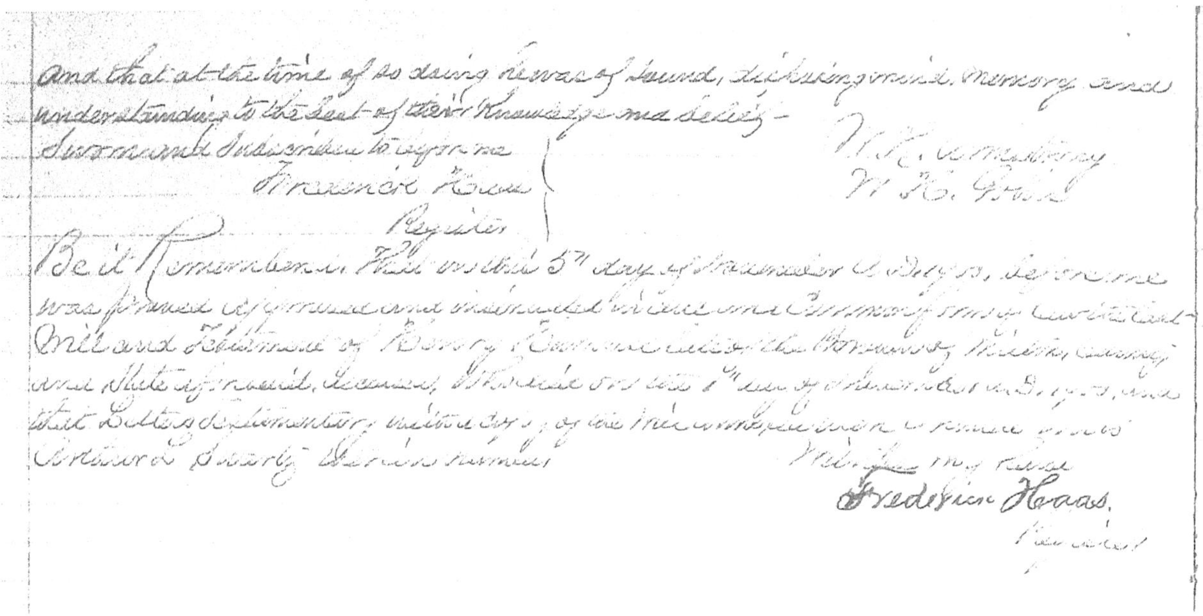
and that at the time of so doing he was of sound, [illegible] mind, memory and understanding to the best of their knowledge and belief -
Sworn and subscribed before me
Frederick Haas
Register
Be it Remembered That on the 5th day of [illegible] before me was proved [illegible]
[illegible]
Frederick Haas,
Register

C5A SAMUEL LANTZ C5

SAMUEL LANTZ was born on 25 Apr 1825 in Northumberland Co., PA and died 27 Aug 1910 in Northumberland Co., PA. He married (1) ANNA WEIMER in 1854 in Northumberland Co., PA. She was born on 03 May 1833 in Northumberland Co., PA and died 20 Dec 1873 in Rockefeller Twp., Northumberland Co., PA. They were farmers by occupation. He married (2) HARRIET E. in 1882 in Northumberland Co., PA.

1. ROSANNA MAGDALINE LANTZ (C5A1)
2. WILLIAM RICHARD F. LANTZ (C5A3)
3. DAVID ALLISON LANTZ (C5A4)
4. ELIZA LANTZ, born 1862 in Northumberland Co., PA.
5. SUSAN LANTZ, born 1865 in Northumberland Co., PA.
6. ELLEN LANTZ (C5A6)

References: 5, 25-Lower Augusta Twp Northumberland Co PA H937, 26-Lower Augusta Twp Northumberland Co PA H76, 27-Lower Augusta Twp Northumberland Co PA H5, 29-Rockafeller Northumberland Co PA H33

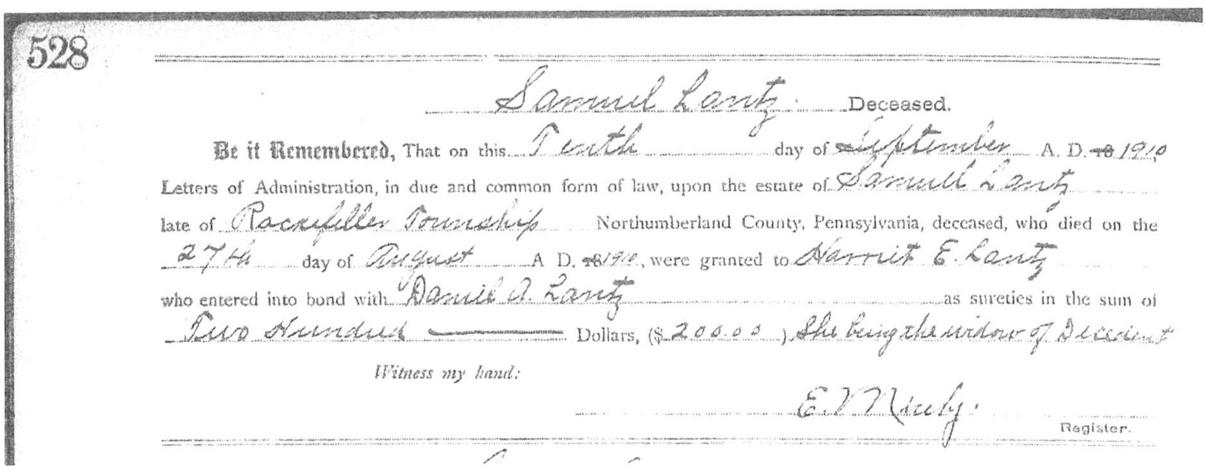
528

Samuel Lantz Deceased.

Be it Remembered, That on this Tenth day of September A. D. ~~18~~1910 Letters of Administration, in due and common form of law, upon the estate of Samuel Lantz late of Rockefeller Township Northumberland County, Pennsylvania, deceased, who died on the 27th day of August A. D. ~~18~~1910, were granted to Harriet E. Lantz who entered into bond with Daniel A. Lantz as sureties in the sum of Two Hundred ——— Dollars, ($200.00) She being the widow of Decedent

Witness my hand:

E. V. Neely
Register.

C82 CHRISTIANA A. LANTZ C8

CHRISTIANA "CHRISTY" A. LANTZ was born in 1826 in Northumberland Co., PA. She married JONAS FOX in Northumberland Co., PA. He was born in 1816 in PA.

Children of CHRISTINA LANTZ and JONAS FOX are:

1. HIRAM E. FOX (C821)
2. LYDIA R. FOX, born in 1847 in Northumberland Co., PA.
3. WILLIAM A. FOX (C823)
4. JOHN FOX, born in 1853 in Northumberland Co., PA.
5. OLIVER JONAS FOX (C825)
6. JORDAN FOX, born in 1856 in St. Joseph Co., MI.
7. FRANKLIN L. FOX, born in 1860 in St. Joseph Co., MI; died 08 Oct 1875 in Kalamazoo Co., MI; buried in Pleasant Valley Cemetery, Kalamazoo Co., MI.
8. ELIZABETH "LIBBIE" FOX, born in 1863 in MI.
9. HENRY LINCOLN FOX (C829)
10. JEREMIAH GRANT FOX (C82A)
11. SHERMAN D. FOX (C82B)

References: 24-Delaware Northumberland Co PA H143, 25-Park St Joseph Co MI H1927, 26-Prairie Ronde Kalamazoo Co MI H45, 36

C83 JOHN LANTZ C8

JOHN LANTZ was born on 11 Sep 1804 in Northumberland Co., PA and died 03 May 1880 in Sandusky Co., OH. He married ELIZABETH DIEFENBACHER on 29 Mar 1827 in Northumberland Co., PA, daughter of PHILIP DIEFFENBACHER and ROSINA MAUSER. She was born on 25 May 1807 in Northumberland Co., PA and died in 17 Nov 1888 in Sandusky Co., OH. She was born on 27 May 1807 in PA. His obituary from the Fremont Journal on 14 May 1880, page 3c4, he and his family had settled near Hessville, Sandusky Co., OH in 1846. They were members of the Reformed Church of Hessville, OH. Both are buried in Washington Chapel Cemetery, Washington Twp., Sandusky Co., OH.

Children of JOHN LANTZ and are: 8 children

1. SIMON SAMUEL LANTZ (C831)
2. ROSANNAH LANTZ (C832)
3. CHRISTIAN M. LANTZ (m), born in 1836 in Northumberland Co., PA. died before 1882.
4. JOHN LANTZ, born in 1839 in Northumberland Co., PA, died before 1882..
5. EMANUEL AURAND LANTZ (f), born in 1849 in Sandusky Co., OH.
6. MARY A. LANTZ (C836)
7. MATILDA LANTZ, married (?) WOLFE.
8. UNKNOWN LANTZ, died before 1882.

References: 24-Washington Twp Sandusky Co OH H1731, 26-Washington Twp Sandusky Co OH H347, 54

C84 JONATHAN LANTZ C8

JONATHAN LANTZ was born on 18 Jun 1812 and died 17 Feb 1894. He married ELIZABETH COUP.

1. LEVI SPELLMAN LANTZ (C841)
2. HENRY H. LANTZ, born in 1838 in PA.
3. WILLIAM C. LANTZ (C843)
4. SIMON P. LANTZ (C844)
5. MARY R. LANTZ, born 03 Aug 1845 and died 18 Mar 1851 in OH.
6. DANIEL F. LANTZ, born on 01 Nov 1847 in OH; married EVELINE R. in MI; born in Mar 1850 in NY; No children.
7. JOHN C. LANTZ, born 15 Mar 1850 in OH; died 04 Nov 1906 in Jersey City, NJ.
8. CLARISSA E. LANTZ, born 10 Jul 1855 in MI; died 22 Oct 1896; married HENRY E. BRIGGS born 1856 MI.
9. MARGARET A. LANTZ (C849)

References: 5, 24-Scott Twp Sandusky Co OH H240, 25-Colon St Joseph Co MI H740, 26-Burlington Calhoun Co MI H260, 27-Constantine St Joseph Co MI H266, 29-Dist 0082 Caledonia Shiawassee Co MI H281, 36

C85 SIMON LANTZ C8

SIMON LANTZ was born on 21 Sep 1814 in Northumberland Co., PA and died 10 Jan 1890 Watsontown, Northumberland Co., PA. He married HARRIET MARSH in Nov 1843, daughter of GRIGGS MARSH. She was born in 1823 in PA. He was educated in the subscription schools and followed farming all his life, He remained on his farm until the spring of 1889 when he moved to Watson town to spend the remainder of his life in retirement. He and his wife were consistent members of the Reformed Church of Watsontown.

Children of SIMON LANTZ and HARRIET MARSH are:

1. SAMANTHA CATHARINE LANTZ (C851)
2. SIMON GRIGGS LANTZ (C852)
3. WILLIAM ISAAC LANTZ, born 1848 and died 1852 in Northumberland Co., PA.
4. ANNIE LOUISE LANTZ, born 1850 and died 1852 in Northumberland Co., PA.
5. HARRIET ELLEN LANTZ, born 1851 and died 1852 in Northumberland Co., PA.
6. DANIEL FRY LANTZ, born 1850 and died before 1870 in Northumberland Co., PA.

References: 5, 24-Delaware Twp Northumberland Co PA H145, 25-Delaware Twp Northumberland Co PA H501, 26-Delaware Twp Northumberland Co PA H93, 27-Delaware Twp Northumberland Co PA H130, 36

C86 LAVINA LANTZ C8

LAVINA LANTZ was born on 30 Apr 1817 in Northumberland Co., PA and died 27 Jan 1862 in Northumberland Co., PA. She married ROBERT HUTCHINSON in 1838 in Northumberland Co., PA. He was born in 1798 in PA and died before 1860 in Northumberland Co., PA.

Children of LAVINA LANTZ and ROBERT HUTCHINSON are:

1. MARY JANE HUTCHINSON (C861)
2. JOSEPH HENRY HUTCHINSON, born on 20 Nov 1842 in Northumberland Co., PA; died 31 Jul 1915 in Northumberland Co., PA; married MARGARET ISABEL EVERET. No children.
3. CHRISTIANA HUTCHINSON, born on 25 Jan 1843 in Northumberland Co., PA; died 06 Nov 1901 in Northumberland Co., PA; married JEFF HARTRANFT, 1864 in Northumberland Co., PA. No children.
4. ROBERT WILSON HUTCHINSON (C864)
5. MARGARET FLORENCE HUTCHINSON, born on 22 Feb 1852 in Northumberland Co., PA; married Rev. J. H. KERR, 1872 in Orangeville, PA. No children.
6. JOHN JAMES GUILFORD HUTCHINSON, born on 07 Apr 1856 in Northumberland Co., PA; died 01 May 1858 in Northumberland Co., PA.

References: 5, 24-Delaware Twp Northumberland Co PA H149, 25-Delaware Twp Northumberland Co PA H476

C87 ROSANNAH LANTZ C8

ROSANNAH LANTZ was born on 21 Oct 1847 in Northumberland Co., PA and died 26 Feb 1861 in Northumberland Co., PA. She married GEORGE P. KAMP in Sep 1847 in Northumberland Co., PA, son of ADAM KAMP and SUSAN REIDER. He was born in 1817 in Bavaria, Germany and died before 1860 in Northumberland Co., PA.

Children of ROSANNA LANTZ and GEORGE KAMP are:

1. CLARINDA KAMP (C871)
2. JOHN TILLMAN KAMP, born 02 Aug 1862 and died Sep 1906 in Northumberland Co., PA.
3. ANNA MARY KAMP, born 02 Aug 1852 and died before 1860 in Northumberland Co., PA.
4. CHARLES FRANKLIN KAMP (C874)
5. SIMON RYNHART KAMP (C875)
6. LUTHER KAMP, died before 1891 in Northumberland Co., PA.
7. WILLIAM S. KAMP, died before 1891 in Northumberland Co., PA.

References: 5, 24-Lewis Northumberland Co PA H114, 25-Turbotville Northumberland Co PA H1097, 36

C88 SALOME LANTZ C8

SALOME LANTZ was born in 1811 in Northumberland Co., PA. She married GEORGE WAGGONER in Northumberland Co., PA. He died in Nov 1843 in Northumberland Co., PA. His will is recorded in Will Book 2 Page 455 Northumberland Co., PA.

Children of SALOME LANTZ and GEORGE WAGGONER are:

1. MARY WAGGONER, born in 1831 in Northumberland Co., PA.
2. LAVINA WAGGONER, born in 1833 in Northumberland Co., PA.
3. ANGELINE WAGGONER, born in 1836 in Northumberland Co., PA.
4. GEORGE R. WAGGONER, born in 1844 in Northumberland Co., PA.

References: 24-Delaware Northumberland Co PA H138

C92 ANGELINA SIEGFRIED C9

ANGELINA SIEGFRIED was born in 1820 in Berks Co., PA. She married 1st DAVID HIGH. He died Aug 1849 in Delaware Co., OH. He died intestate without a will and his estate account #1838 filed Delaware Co., OH, his wife assigned as administrix. She married 2nd JONATHAN TROUTMAN in Delaware Co., OH. He was born 1816 in PA.

Children of ANGELINA SIEGFRIED and DAVID HIGH are:

1. SARAH A. HIGH, born in 1840 Delaware Co., OH.
2. REUBEN HIGH, born in 1842 Delaware Co., OH.
3. SARAH JANE HIGH, born in 1849 Delaware Co., OH.

Children of ANGELINA SIEGFRIED and JONATHAN TROUTMAN are:

4. MARY M. TROUTMAN, born in 1861 in Delaware Co., OH.
5. EMMA E. TROUTMAN, born in 1863 in Delaware Co., OH.

References: 24-Delaware Delaware Co OH H1326, 25-Delaware Delaware Co OH H112

C93 WILLIAM SIEGFRIED C9

WILLIAM SIEGFRIED was born in 1822 in Berks Co., PA and died 09 May 1899 in Delaware Co., OH. He married SUSANNA SWARTZ. She was born in Oct 1829 in PA and died 31 Aug 1905 in Delaware Co., OH. Both are buried in Oak Grove Cemetery, Delaware, Delaware Co., OH

Children of WILLIAM SIEGFRIED and SUSANNA SWARTZ are:

1. SARAH E. SIEGFRIED, born in 1849 Delaware Co., OH.
2. ADAM SIEGFRIED (C932)
3. SAMUEL SIEGFRIED (C933)
4. WILMER WILLIAM SIEGFRIED (C934)
5. CHARLES DANIEL SIEGFRIED (C935)

References: 24-Delaware Delaware Co OH H1325, 25-Delaware Delaware Co OH H99, 26-Delaware Delaware Co OH H166, 29-Dist 0027 Delaware Delaware Co OH H35, 45

C96 BENJAMIN SIEGFRIED C9

BENJAMIN SIEGFRIED was born in 1829 in Berks Co., PA. He married HARRIET. She was born in 1830 in OH.

Children of BENJAMIN SIEGFRIED and HARRIET are:

1. HORACE SIEGFRIED, born in 1857 Delaware Co., OH.
2. MARY SIEGFRIED, born in 1859 Delaware Co., OH.

References: 24-Delaware Delaware Co OH H115

C97 CATHARINE SIEGFRIED C9

CATHARINE SIEGFRIED was born in 1831 in OH. She married EPHRAIM WILLEY in Delaware Co., OH, son of HENRY WILLEY and ELIZABETH. He was born in 1827 in OH.

Child of CATHARINE SIEGFRIED and EPHRAIM WILLEY are:

1. ELMORA WILLEY, born in 1862 in Delaware Co., OH.
2. CATHARINE V. WILLEY, born in 1872 in Delaware Co., OH.
3. MARY P. WILLEY, born in 1876 in Delaware Co., OH.
4. WALTER WILLEY, born in 1879 in Delaware Co., OH.

References: 25-Troy Twp Delaware Co OH H273, 26-Troy Twp Delaware Co OH H30, 27-Troy Twp Delaware Co OH H51

CA2 CHARLES FOLLMER CA

CHARLES FOLLMER was born on 29 Dec 1815 and died 19 May 1883 in Northumberland Co., PA. He married THERESIE ESHBACH in Northumberland Co., PA. She was born on 15 Aug 1815 in PA and died 16 Nov 1864 in Northumberland He is buried in the Paradise Church Cemetery, Northumberland Co., PA.

Children of CHARLES FOLLMER and THERESIE ESHBACH are:

1. LEVI H. FOLLMER (CA21)
2. MARGARET C. FOLLMER (CA22)
3. SARAH E. FOLLMER (CA23)
4. SUSAN B. FOLLMER (CA24)
5. CHARLES D. FOLLMER was born on 03 Jun 1857 in Northumberland Co., PA. He married SUSAN M. KERCHNER in Northumberland Co., PA. She was born on 16 May 1863

References: 67, 29-Dist 0164 Turbot Twp Northumberland Co PA H60, 24-Turbot Twp Northumberland Co PA H24, 25-Turbot Twp Northumberland Co PA H1174

C111 SARAH ELLEN BANCROFT C11

SARAH ELLEN BANCROFT was born in 1842 in Blair Co., PA. She married SAMUEL METZKER in Blair Co., PA. He was born 1841 in PA.

Children of SARAH BANCROFT and SAMUEL METZKER are:

1. MARY LENA METZKER, born 1863 in Blair Co., PA.
2. ROSE ANN METZKER, born 1867 in Blair Co., PA.
3. TAMIE AMELIA METZKER, born 1869 in Blair Co., PA.

References: 26-Huston Twp Blair Co PA H58, 27-Huston Twp Blair Co PA 170 H26

C122 ANNA ELIZABETH LANTZ C12

ANNA ELIZABETH LANTZ was born on 07 Jan 1834 in Eldorado, Altoona, Huntingdon

Co., PA and died 03 Nov 1904, Eldorado, Altoona, Blair Co., PA. She married JOHN METZGER BURKET on 26 Dec 1854 at Zion Evangelical Lutheran Church, Frankstown, PA. He was born on 16 May 1830, Woodbury Twp., Bedford Co., PA and died 01 Aug 1905 at Burket's Station (now south Altoona), PA. His occupation was a RR Laborer in 1870.

Children of ANNA LANTZ and JOHN BURKET are:

1. CATHARINE BURKET, born in 1856 in Blair Co., PA.
2. SYLVESTER BURKET, born in 1858 in Blair Co., PA.
3. ANNA MAY BURKET, born in 1859 in Blair Co., PA.
4. ERMINE ELEANOR BURKET, born in 1862 in Blair Co., PA.
5. DAVID M. BURKET (C1225)
6. MILLIE BURKET, born in 1868 in Blair Co., PA.

References: 25-North Woodbury Twp Blair Co PA H105, 26-Logan Twp Blair Co PA H41, 27-Logan Twp Blair Co PA H74

C123 JOHN MAXWELL LANTZ C12

Rev. JOHN MAXWELL LANTZ was born on 06 Sep 1838 in Altoona, Huntingdon Co., PA and died 21 Aug 1894 in Lewistown, Mifflin Co., PA. He married CATHARINE "KATE" MUNDORFF on 06 Mar 1866 in Blair Co., PA, daughter of ISAAC MUNDORFF and CATHARINE. She was born in Nov 1838 in Lancaster Co., PA. He was a Pump Maker, Teacher and Preacher by occupation. He is buried at Methodist Episcopal Cemetery. According to his obituary

Child of JOHN LANTZ and CATHARINE MUNDORFF is:

1. JOHN MAXWELL LANTZ (C1231)
2. HOWARD O. LANTZ, born Dec 1867 in PA.

References: 26-South Middleton Cumberland Co PA H125, 30-Lewistown Ward 3 Mifflin Co PA H253, 29-Lewistown Mifflin Co PA H434

Rev. J. Max Lantz, D.D.

J. Max Lantz was born in Blair County, Pa., near Altoona, Sept. 6, 1838, and died in Lewistown, Pa., Aug. 21, 1894. He received his early training in the public school, after which he entered the Tuscarora Academy, at Academia, Pa. After graduation, he chose the profession of a teacher, and for three years taught with marked success the high school of Tyrone City, Pa. During this time he was converted and united with the Methodist Episcopal church, the church in which he had been reared. Giving evidence of gifts, grace, and usefulness, he was soon given license as a local preacher. Being convinced that he was called to the work of the ministry, he spent two years in biblical and theological study, and was received into East Baltimore Conference in 1863. The General Conference of 1868 readjusted the work, when Central Pennsylvania Conference was formed, of which Brother Lantz continued a member until the time of his death.

From the beginning he gave evidence of more than ordinary intellectual power, soon began to rise, and for many years filled the best appointments of his Conference. He was a member of the General Conference of 1892. Dickinson College at its last Commencement conferred upon him the degree of Doctor of Divinity. He was a master in the pulpit, stimulating the intellect, arousing the sensibilities, delighting and elevating his congregations to a lofty height of mental and moral excitement. His diffidence caused a reserve of manner that might lead to the impression that he was cold; but such impression soon corrected itself, for on an intimate acquaintance he was found to be gentle, kind, and warm-hearted. He contracted a severe cold, and, though admonished that the greatest care would be necessary, continued to push his work with untiring zeal until he could go no longer.

Juniata Valley Camp Meeting began on Aug. 14. Its spiritual interests being under his supervision, he felt it his duty to be there. He knew it was hazardous, but, like many others, took the risk, which proved fatal. Symptoms of pneumonia developed, and he requested to be taken to his home, in Lewistown, which was done; but all that medical skill and loving hands could do was unavailing.

Dr. Lantz was married in 1866 to Miss Kate Mundorff, of Lancaster County, Pa., who with two sons survives him, one of whom is a student in Dickinson College, the other an attorney-at-law in Lewistown.

The funeral services, after prayer at the house by the Rev. L. M. Smyser, one of his classmates, were held in the Methodist Episcopal church of which he had been the pastor for four years. The services were in charge of the pastor of the family, J. B. Polsgrove, and participated in by the Revs. George Leidy, of Sunbury; M. K. Foster, Presiding Elder of Williamsport District; H. C. Pardoe, of Bedford; and A. R. Lambert and B. H. Hart, of First and Second Churches, Huntingdon. Appropriate addresses were delivered by the Revs. E. J. Gray, D.D., President of Dickinson Seminary; W. W. Evens, D.D., Presiding Elder of Harrisburg District; D. S. Monroe, D.D., Presiding Elder of Altoona District; E. H. Yocum, D.D., Presiding Elder of Danville District; and J. B. Polsgrove, the pastor.

The body was laid to rest in the Methodist Episcopal cemetery, Lewistown, Pa., to wait the resurrection morn. Forty ministers from all sections of the Conference and a large number of laymen attended the funeral and accompanied the remains to the last resting place.

J. B. POLSGROVE.

Rev. JOHN MAXWELL LANTZ

CATHARINE MUNDORFF

C125 JACOB MARTIN LANTZ C12

JACOB MARTIN LANTZ was born on 25 Feb 1844 in Burns Station (now Altoona), Huntingdon Co., PA, and died 30 Jan 1897 in Corner 19th St. & Margaret Ave., Altoona, Blair Co., PA. He married ELIZA BELLE KEPPERLY 15 Apr 1864 in Hollidaysburg, Blair Co., PA, daughter of WILLIAM FREDERICK KEPPERLY and HANNAH HYSSONG. She was born 25 Aug 1844 in Waterside, Huntingdon Co., PA and died 26 Dec 1928 of pneumonia in Altoona, Blair Co., PA. Both are buried in Lot R-560 at Rose Hill Cemetery, Altoona, Blair Co., PA. He purchased on 16 Jan 1868 by deed Lot 14 situate on Maple Street, West Altoona, Blair Co., PA from WILLIAM M. LLOYD & wife, THOMAS MCCAULEY & wife and S. C. BAKER, later know as 2429 Maple Avenue. They were living at 2429 Maple Avenue, Altoona, Blair Co., PA when he died 30 Jan 1897, in front of Curry Canan and Co.'s Wholesale House, Margaret Avenue and 19th Street, Altoona, Blair Co., PA, at Saturday, 7:30 PM. He died from Providential Occuran or heart failure, due to rupture of blood vessel received in a fall. He was buried first on 02 Feb 1897 in the Hutchinson's Cemetery, Altoona, Blair Co., PA where his parents are buried. He was later moved to the Rose Hill Cemetery, Altoona, Blair Co., PA, but his parents and brother still remain buried in the Hutchinson's Cemetery. He was buried by the Hickey Funeral Home of Altoona, Blair Co., PA. He was a carpenter by occupation. They were members of the Methodist Church, 8th Ave., Altoona, Blair Co., PA. He served in the Civil War 12 Regiment, Company E & L PA Volunteer Cavalry, 2/10/1862 - 06/05/1865 Union Army, on 14 Feb 1862, mustered in at Martinsburg, VA, on 29 Feb 1864, reenlisted, and on 05 Jun 1865, was discharged. He received a pension for injuries received during the Civil War, and after his death his widow was also granted a pension. He was member of Encampment 17, Union Veterans Legion, Council 15, Chosen Friends and Post 62 The Red Man, Knights of Pythian and Odd Fellows.

Children of JACOB LANTZ and ELIZA KEPPERLY are:

1. WILLIAM K. LANTZ, born 19 Mar 1866, Altoona, Blair Co., PA; died 03 Jan 1948, of a myocarditis infarction at Altoona, Blair Co., PA; Never married; He was a carpenter by occupation. He is buried in Lot R-560 at Rose Hill Cemetery, Altoona, Blair Co., PA.
2. HARRY G. LANTZ (C1252)
3. FOREST MAXWELL LANTZ (C1253)
4. HOWARD W. LANTZ, born 1873, Altoona, Blair Co., PA; died 1878, Altoona, Blair Co., PA; Never married; He was originally buried in the Hutchison Cemetery and later moved to Lot R-560 at Rose Hill Cemetery, Altoona, Blair Co., PA.
5. ADEN MELVIN LANTZ (C1255)
6. ELBRIDGE GARFIELD LANTZ (C1256)
7. CLYDE RAYMOND LANTZ (C1257)
8. NELLIE MERTEL MAY LANTZ, born 26 Sep 1887, Altoona, Blair Co., PA; died 26 Oct 1959, of uremia Altoona, Blair Co., PA; married ROBERT G. BEACH on 27 Sep 1911 in Altoona, Blair Co., PA; born 26 Mar 1884, PA; died May 1974, Altoona, Blair Co., PA. She is buried at Rose Hill Cemetery, Altoona, Blair Co., PA. Her obituary appeared in the Altoona Mirror on 27 Oct 1959 on page 28.
9. UNKNOWN LANTZ, born Altoona, Blair Co., PA; died Altoona, Blair Co., PA.

References: 3, 4, 30-Altoona Blair Co PA H166, 29-Altoona Blair Co PA H78, 27-Altoona Blair Co PA H402, 26-Altoona Blair Co PA H233, 9, 31, 10-Altoona Blair Co PA H114, 18, 33, 43, 44, 28-Altoona Blair Co PA H286, 46-D/JML/PHY CERT-1897/City Hall Altoona PA

ARMY OF THE UNITED STATES

CERTIFICATE

OF DISABILITY FOR DISCHARGE.

Private Jacob M. Lantz of Captain ______ K Company, (K) of the 12th Penna Regiment of United States Volunteer Cavalry was enlisted by Capt Kenney of the 12 ch Regiment of Cav at Martinsburg Va on the Twenty Ninth day of February 1864, to serve three years; he was born in ______ in the State of ______ is ______ years of age, ______ feet ______ inches high, ______ complexion, ______ eyes, ______ hair, and by occupation when enlisted a ______. During the last two months said soldier has been unfit for duty ______ days.* The Soldier was wounded March 21st 1865 in a skirmish with guerillas in Loudon Co Va by a carbine bullet which entered his left groin and lodged.

STATION: Cumberland Md

DATE: May 31st 1865

J. B. Lewis
Surgeon U.S.V.
In charge of Genl Hospital

I CERTIFY, that I have carefully examined the said Jacob M. Lantz of Captain ______ Company, and find him incapable of performing the duties of a soldier because of[2] Gunshot wound of left groin, and injuries of lumbar region produced by falling from his horse when wounded, which injuries have decidedly impaired the health and strength of the soldier. Physically [illegible] to enlist or [illegible] in the Vets Res Corps. Degree total.

J. B. Lewis
Surgeon. USV.

DISCHARGED, this Fifth day of June 1865, at U.S.A. General Hospital Cumberland Maryland

J. B. Lewis
Surgeon USV
In charge of Genl. Hospital

The soldier desires to be addressed at

Town ______ County ______ State ______

* See Note 1 on the back of this. [2] See Note 2 on the back of this.

[A. G. O. No. 100 & 101—First.] (DUPLICATES.)

No. 1.

INVALID PENSION—ORIGINAL.

Acts of July 14, 1862, and March 3, 1873.

Claimant, Jacob M. Lantz

P. O. Altoona

County, Blair

State, Pennsylvania

Rank, Pri

Company, L

Regiment, 12 Pa Cav

Attorney, Thomas H. Greevy Altoona Pa

Fee, $ 2 contract filed. Material evidence filed since July 8, 1870.

Enlisted Feb. 10, 1863; **Mustered into rank** Feb. 14, 1864.

Discharged June 5, 1865; **Date of completing proof** July 23, 1874.

.... enlistment, from ...., 18 , to ...., 18 , in

Not in the military or naval service since discharged, June 5, 1865, (filed July 9, 1874.)

Rate of pension, $ 2 per month, from July 9, 1874.

Disabled by Gun shot wound of left thigh

Brief for Admission submitted Jany 29, 1875. [illegible], Examiner.

Approved ...., 187 , ..., Reviewer.

Approved at $........ from ...., 187 , ..., Medical Referee.

Declaration filed April 16, 1874, alleging disability from Gun shot wound of thigh, ball still remaining in thigh, received in battle at Hamilton Va March 21st 1865.

Exg Surgeon, Wm. M. Findly, July 15, 1874.

Finds Gun shot wound of left thigh. Dis. 4/4 2.

1 **EXAMINING SURGEON'S CERTIFICATE** 1

IN THE CASE OF AN ORIGINAL APPLICANT.

No. of Application, 191530.

State: Penna. County: Blair.

Post Office: Altoona. July. 15th. 1874.

I hereby certify, That I have carefully examined Jacob M. Lantz, late a Pvt. Co. "L", 12th Regt. Pa. Cav.

Applicant — service

in the service of the United States, who is an APPLICANT for an invalid pension by reason of alleged disability resulting from g. s. w'd of the left thigh.

Degree of disability.

In my opinion the said Jacob M. Lantz is one fourth incapacitated for obtaining his subsistence by manual labor from the cause above stated.

Origin.

Judging from his present condition, and from the evidence before me, it is my belief that the said disability did really originate in the service aforesaid in the line of duty.

Probable duration.

The disability is of indefinite duration.

A more particular description of the applicant's condition is subjoined:

Particular description.

Height, 5' 8", weight, 152; complexion, Ruddy; age, 32; pulse, 70; respiration, 18.

Ball entered in front of the left thigh & to the outer side, shattering the bone somewhat and seems to have traveled back under the Gluteus Maximus to the region of the Spine near the junction of the last Lumbar Vertebra & the Sacrum. He is subject to neuralgic pains of a severe character, and the future may develope more trouble as it has broken open several times.

At present, however, I consider him entitled to one fourth or 2 per mo.

Wm. M. Findley,
Examining Surgeon.

Act of June 27, 1890.

CC DECLARATION FOR WIDOW'S PENSION. CC

To be executed before a Court of Record or some officer thereof having custody of its seal, a Notary Public or Justice of the Peace, whose official signature shall be verified by his official seal, and in case he has none, his signature and official character shall be certified by a Clerk of a Court of Record, or a City or County Clerk.

STATE OF Penna
COUNTY OF Blair } ss:

On this 1 day of May, A. D. one thousand eight hundred and ninety-seven, personally appeared before me, a Alderman of the City of Altoona within and for the county and State aforesaid Belle Lantz aged 52 years, a resident of the City of Altoona, county of Blair, State of Penna who, being duly sworn according to law, declares that she is the widow of Jacob M. Lantz who enlisted under the name of Jacob M. Lantz at ..., on the 10th day of February A.D. 1862 in Co. L. 13th Penna Cavalry as a private (If in State rank, company, and regiment, if in Military service, or vessel, if in Navy.) ... and served at least ninety days in the late War of the Rebellion, in the service of the United States; who was HONORABLY DISCHARGED February 28 1864 & June 5 1865 and died on the 30th day of January 1897 (The cause of death need not be stated.)

That the soldier was not in the Military or Naval service of the United States except as above stated. (If any other service, it should be stated in full.)

That she was married under the name of Eliza Bell Kepperly to said Jacob M. Lantz on the 15 day of April 1864, by John Gorley J.P. at Hollidaysburg Blair Co. there being no legal barrier to said marriage. (If there was a former marriage of claimant or her husband, state it here and how dissolved.)

That she has not remarried since the death of the said Jacob M. Lantz (Name of soldier or sailor.)

That she is without other means of support than her daily labor. That names and dates of birth of all the children now living under sixteen years of age of the soldier are as follows:

Elbridge Garfield born July 13 1881, born ..., 18...
Elida R. born June 10 1885, born ..., 18...
Nellie May born Sept 26, 1887, born ..., 18...

That she has not heretofore applied for pension and the number of her former application is ... (Be careful to fill this part of the blank correctly.) That she makes this declaration for the purpose of being placed on the pension roll of the United States under the provisions of the Act of June 27, 1890.

She hereby appoints ..., of ..., State of ..., her true and lawful attorney to prosecute her claim and receive a fee of $... That her post-office address is 2429 Maple Avenue Altoona county of Blair, State of Penna

Belle Lantz (Claimant's signature.)

Attest: (1) J. A. Emery
(2) C. R. Moore

(3-128 a.)

ACT OF JUNE 27, 1890.

WIDOW'S PENSION.

Claimant Belle Lutz Soldier Jacob W. Lutz

P. O. 2229 Maple Av. Altoona Rank Private, Co. L

County Blair, State Pa. Regiment 12 Pa. Vol. Cav.

Rate, $8 per month, commencing May 3, 1897, and $2 per month additional for each child, as follows:

Elbridge G.	Born, July 12, 1881; Sixteen, 12, 1897	Commencing May 3, 1897
Clide P.	Born, June 12, 1885; Sixteen, 12, 1901	Commencing May 3, 1897
Millie M.	Born, Oct 26, 1887; Sixteen, Oct 25, 1903	Commencing May 3, 1897
	Born, 18; Sixteen, 18	Commencing 18
	Born, 18; Sixteen, 18	Commencing 18
	Born, 18; Sixteen, 18	Commencing 18
	Born, 18; Sixteen, 18	Commencing 18
	Born, 18; Sixteen, 18	Commencing 18

Entitled to $20 per month, Commencing Sept. 8, 1916, Under act of Sept. 8, 1916, Wife During Civil War serv...
a-c 9.2646

Issued Oct 22, 1926 at $50. from Aug 4, 1926 Act of July 3, 1926.

Payments on all former certificates covering any portion of same time to be deducted.

All pension to terminate ...., 189.., date of ....

RECOGNIZED ATTORNEY:

Name Claimant Fee $ — Agent to pay.

P. O. Articles Filed ...., 189..

APPROVALS:

Submitted for ad—, Oct. 14, 1897, Charles Dawes, Examiner.

Approved for ~~for~~ admission

Oct. 23, 1897. S. F. Schaeffer, Legal Reviewer.

The soldier was — pensioned at $8— per month for G. S. W. of left thigh

Enlisted Feby 10, 1862.	Soldier's app'n filed April 16, 1874.
honorably disch'd June 20, 1865.	Clt's app'n under other laws — None, 18
Re-enlisted No, 18	Former marriage of — None, 18
honorably disch'd ...., 18	Death of former —, 18
Died Jany 30, 1897.	Clt's marriage to soldier April 15, 1864.
Declaration filed May 3, 1897.	Clt. not remarried Declares, 18

Claimant is — without other means of support than her daily labor.

Claimant widow, Dr. W. C.

September 19 1916

Widow's Certificate Number 453,917

Name of Soldier (or sailor) Jacob M. Lantz

Service of Soldier (or sailor) 12th Regiment. Company L. Pa. Cavalry

Commissioner of Pensions,

Washington, D. C.

Sir: I am pensioned under the above certificate number, because of the service of the soldier (or sailor) named. I was his wife during the Civil War.

I am 72 years of age, having been born Aug. 25, 1844, at Hopewell Bedford County.

I am entitled to the increase of pension provided by the first section of the Act of September 8, 1916.

(Signature) Belle Lantz

(Postoffice address) 2429 Maple Ave
Altoona Pa

State of Penn'a
County of Blair } S.S. [illegible]
City of Altoona

Before me the undersigned authority duly commissioned and sworn residing in the City of Altoona in the county and state aforesaid personally appeared Mrs Agnes McHale aged 56 years residing at No 2501 Maple Avenue and Mrs Susan Paxson aged 56 years residing at no 2570 West Chestnut Avenue in the City of Altoona aforesaid, who each being sworn in due form of law doth depose and say that they have been personally acquainted with Mrs Belle Lantz for a period of over fifteen years, having resided as neighbors to said Mrs Lantz. The said Mrs Paxson having known the said Mrs Lantz since they were children together. Both affiants know of the death Jacob M Lantz and were present at his home at the time of the funeral and saw him taken to the Cemetery. The date of the death of said Jacob M Lantz was January 30th 1897. The said Mrs Paxson also knew Jacob M Lantz prior to his marraige to said Belle Lantz whose maiden name was Kepperly. and neiter of said parties were married prior to their marraige to each other, and they were married during the war. and both affiants say the said Belle Lantz has not remarried since the death of her husband.

There are three children of said Belle Lantz and Jacob M Lantz under the age of sixteen years to wit;

Elbridge Garfield Lantz born July 13th 1881

Clyde Lantz born June 10th 1885

Nellie May Lantz born September 26th 1887

Affiants know of the birth of these children and ascertain the date by a personal inspection of the family record of said Jacob M Lantz as kept in a book on possession of said Mrs Belle Lantz, and of said children are still living

Affiants know that said Belle Lantz has no ~~other~~ means of support except the result of her own labor and the labor of her children. She has no property except the small amount of personal property, with which said parties kept house, and the value of same is quite trifling Mrs Lantz lives in a small house that was deeded to her and her children by her brother John H Kepperly and she has no income from it and has no support except as stated

Deponents can read and write and have carefully read over the foregoing statement and know the same to be true. Their means of knowledge is derived from their having resided as neighbors to said Mrs Belle Lantz the applicant for pension as herein before set forth.

Sworn and subscribed before me this 20 day of June 1897 —

C. G. Stephens
Alderman

Agnes McHale

Mrs Susan Paxson

Date of death
no prior marr
no remarr
Births
Ind. prop
Income

MEMORANDUM FROM PRISONER OF WAR RECORDS. No.

(This blank to be used only in the arrangement of said records.)

NAME.	RANK.	No. of Reg't.	State	Arm of Service.	Co.	Records of—	Vol.	Page.	Vol.	Page.
Lantz										
~~[illegible]~~ Jacob M	P	12	Pa	C	L	O. R. Ex				

Captured at Winchester Va June 15, 1863, confined at Richmond, Va., [illegible], 1863

Admitted to Hospital at

where he died , 186 , of

Paroled at City Point Va July 19, 1863; reported at Camp Parole, Md., July 20, 1863

~~[illegible]~~ Lantz [illegible] 7-23-74 [illegible] Copied by [illegible]

A Marriage Certificate

By authority of the Commonwealth

This is to certify that on the fifteenth day of April A.D. 1864 before me John Gorley one of the Justices of the peace in and for the County of Blair State of Penna Jacob M Lantz and Eliza [illegible] [illegible] both of said County having plighted the solemn vows of duty and affection were by me legally joined in Marriage each of them declaring themselves of full age and free respectively from prior engagements or other lawfull impediments whereupon I according to the Constitution and laws of the Commonwealth have declared them man and wife — In witness whereof I the said Justice have set my hand seal the day and year written

Jno Gorley J.P. [Seal]

SECOND DEPUTY COMMISSIONER JUL 7 1897

marr

C128 SYLVESTER BLAIR KNIGHT LANTZ C12

SYLVESTER BLAIR KNIGHT LANTZ was born in 1853 in Huntingdon Co., PA and died in Youngstown, Mahoning Co., OH. He married MARY LEONARD, daughter of SIMPSON LEONARD and ELIZABETH. She was born 1858 in PA. He was a pudler by occupation.

Children of SYLVESTER and MARY LEONARD are:

1. ELIZABETH LANTZ, born in 1875 in PA
2. WILLIAM LANTZ, born in 1879 in Youngstown, Mahoning Co., OH

References: 27- Youngstown Mahoning Co OH H6

C131 SARAH ANN LANTZ C13

SARAH ANN LANTZ was born in Oct 1836 in Huntingdon Co., PA. She married JACOB A. BOYCE on 23 Nov 1865 at Zion Evangelical Lutheran Church, Hollidaysburg, Blair Co., PA. He was born in Feb 1835 in PA and died in 1916 in Blair Co., PA.

Children of SARAH LANTZ and JACOB BOICE are:

1. EMMA J. BOYCE, born in Nov 1866 in Blair Co., PA.
2. ANNA C. BOYCE, born in 1869 in Blair Co., PA.
3. SARAH CATHARINE BOYCE, born in Dec 1876 in Blair Co., PA.
4. MARY A. BOYCE, born in Jul 1879 in Blair Co., PA.

References: 27-Logan Twp Blair Co PA H120, 29-District 83 Logan Twp Blair Co PA H439

C311 JOHN SAMUEL NEWCOMER C31

JOHN SAMUEL NEWCOMER was born 03 Jun 1825 in Northumberland Co., PA and died 06 Sep 1908 in Milton, Northumberland Co., PA. He married MATILDA JACOBY in

Northumberland Co., PA, daughter of SAMUEL JACOBY and CATHARINE BACHMAN. She was born in 1834 in PA.

Children of JOHN NEWCOMER and MATILDA JACOBY are:

1. ELIZABETH C. NEWCOMER, born in 1856 in Northumberland Co., PA; married ISAAC SEERS
2. HATTIE M. NEWCOMER, born in 1859 in Northumberland Co., PA; married CHARLES C. GAST; Children: JOHN N. GAST; HELEN M. GAST
3. FRANKLIN A. NEWCOMER (C3113)

References: 67, 26-Turbot Twp Northumberland Co PA H74, 27-Turbot Twp Northumberland Co PA 164 H419

C313 SUSAN NEWCOMER C31

SUSAN NEWCOMER was born on 20 Mar 1828 in Northumberland Co., PA and died in 1901 in Centre Co., PA. She married THOMAS STOVER in Northumberland Co., PA, son of HEINRICH STOBER and MARGARET WOLF. He was born on 15 Sep 1815 in Centre Co., PA and died in 1902 in Centre Co., PA. Both are buried in Livonia Cemetery, Livonia, Centre Co., PA.

Child of SUSAN NEWCOMER and THOMAS STOVER is:

1. ANSENATH M. STOVER (C3131)

References: 67, 29-Dist 0025 Miles Twp Centre Co PA H146, 45

C317 MARGARET NEWCOMER C31

MARGARET NEWCOMER was born on 27 Sep 1827 in Northumberland Co., PA and died 19 May 1864 in Stephenson Co., IL. She married AARON KOSTENBADER in PA. He was born on 22 Feb 1817 in PA and died 21 Sep 1893 in Stephenson Co., IL. Both are buried in Eleroy Cemetery, Eleroy, Stephenson Co., IL.

Children of MARGARET NEWCOMER and AARON KOSTENBADER are:

1. SAMUEL KOSTENBADER (C3171)
2. SUSANNA KOSTENBADER, born on 04 Jan 1851 and died 19 Sep 1885 in Stephenson Co., IL. Buried in Eleroy Cemetery, Eleroy, Stephenson Co., IL.
3. ELIZABETH KOSTENBADER, born in 1853 in Stephenson Co., IL.
4. HENRY KOSTENBADER, born in 1855 in Stephenson Co., IL.
5. JACOB KOSTENBADER, born in 1857 in Stephenson Co., IL.
6. REUBEN KOSTENBADER, born on 19 Mar 1859 and died 20 Oct 1860 in Stephenson Co., IL. Buried in Eleroy Cemetery, Eleroy, Stephenson Co., IL.
7. DANIEL KOSTENBADER, born in 1861 in Stephenson Co., IL.

8. SOLOMON KOSTENBADER, born in 1863 in Stephenson Co., IL.

References: 24-Buckeye Twp Stephenson Co IL H380, 45, 26-Harlem Twp Stephenson Co IL H108, 27-Harlem Twp Stephenson Co IL 176 H135

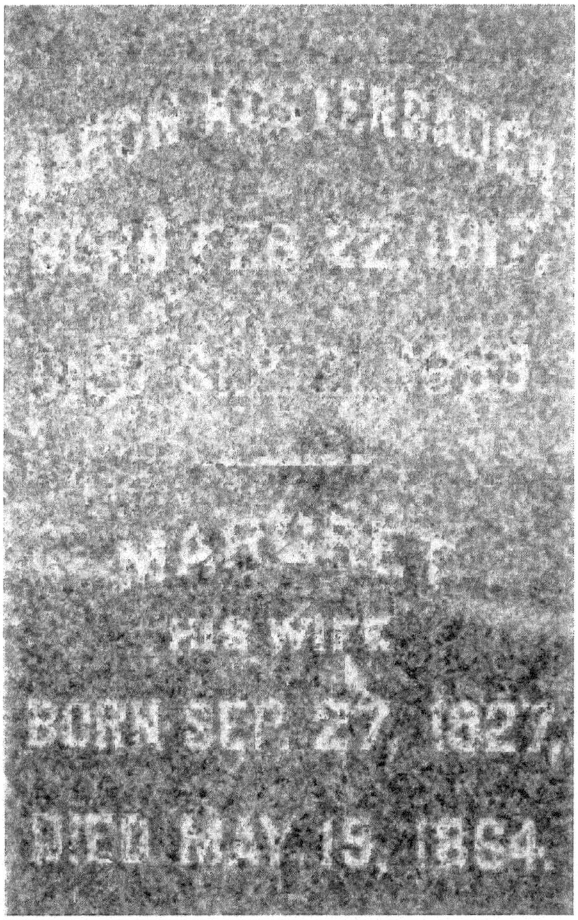

C318 CATHERINE L. NEWCOMER C31

CATHERINE "KATE" L. NEWCOMER was born in 1844 in PA and died 30 Nov 1894 in Fayette Co., IA. She married EDWARD KELLY born in Jan 1844 in PA and died 30 Nov 1912 in Fayette Co., IA. Both are buried in Grandview Cemetery, Fayette, Fayette Co., IA.

Children of CATHERINE NEWCOMER and EDWARD KELLY are:

1. WILLIAM KELLY (C3181)
2. ERNEST KELLY (C3182)
3. JOHN KELLY, born in 1872 in IA
4. MARY E. KELLY, born in 1874 in IA
5. ESTELLA KELLY, born in 1877 in IA
6. EDWARD KELLY, born in 1879 in IA
7. FRANK KELLY, born in Oct 1881 in Fayette Co., IA
8. CATHERINE KELLY, born in 1884 in Fayette Co., IA
9. FLORENCE M. KELLY, born in Feb 1888 in Fayette Co., IA

References: 45, 67, 27-Westfield Fayette Co IA 209 H40, 50-Westfield Fayette Co IA 1885 H33, 29- Dist 0073 Fayette Fayette Co IA H286, 30-Fayette Fayette Co IA 0083 H25

C319 HANNAH ELIZABETH NEWCOMER C31

HANNAH ELIZABETH NEWCOMER was born in Jan 1836 in Northumberland Co., PA. She married (1) WILLIAM A. WOODRING. He was born in 1834 in PA. She married (2) EDMUND C. WHEELOCK in Stephenson Co., IL. He was born in Sep 1842 in VT.

Children of ANNA NEWCOMER and WILLIAM WOODRING are:

1. AQUILLA WOODRING, born in 1858 in IL.
2. LAFOREST WOODRING, born in 1864 in IL.
3. GUY M. WOODRING, born in Dec 1869 in IL.

Child of ANNA NEWCOMER and EDMUND WHEELOCK is:

4. WINSLOW P. WHEELOCK (C3194)

References: 26-Rock Run Twp Stephenson Co IL H69, 27-Davis Stephenson Co IL H13, 29-Dist 0171 Precinct 12 Clear Creek Co CO H277

C31C SILAS NEWCOMER C31

SILAS NEWCOMER was born in 1834 in PA. He married BARBARA. She was born in 1840 in PA.

Children of SILAS NEWCOMER and BARBARA are:

1. HARRY A. NEWCOMER, born in 1864 in IL.
2. CHARLES H. NEWCOMER, born in 1866 in IL.

References: 27-Albany Whiteside Co IL H57

C333 HENRY LANTZ C33

HENRY LANTZ was born on 03 Nov 1843 PA and died after 1930 in Nez Perce Co., ID. He married ABBY VONADA in 1872 in Ilo, ID. She was born in Aug 1847 in PA.

Children of HENRY LANTZ and ABBY VONADA are:

1. CHARLES H. LANTZ (C3331)
2. DANIEL O. LANTZ (C3332)
3. WILLIAM DAVID LANTZ (C3333) was born 18 Apr 1883. He married MAURINE WILKS, 1909.

4. JOHN SIMON LANTZ, born 02 Aug 1888; died 15 Aug 1889.
5. SARAH LANTZ (C3335)

References: 5, 27-Golden Bell Lincoln KS H66, 29-Cold Springs Nez Perce Co ID H37, 31-Dist 51 East Orchards Nez Perce Co ID H131

C341 WILLIAM G. FOLLMER C34

WILLIAM G. FOLLMER was born in Jul 1832 in Northumberland Co., PA. He married ESTHER "HETTIE" in Northumberland Co., PA. She was born in Sep 1837 in PA.

Children of WILLIAM FOLLMER and HETTIE are:

1. NEWTON LUTHER FOLLMER, born in 1860 in Northumberland Co., PA.
2. DANIEL FOLLMER, born in 1862 in Northumberland Co., PA.
3. SARAH "SALLIE" K. FOLLMER, born in 1864 in Northumberland Co., PA.
4. ELLA P. FOLLMER, born in 1866 in Northumberland Co., PA.
5. MINNIE A. FOLLMER, born in 1868 in Northumberland Co., PA.
6. MARY E. FOLLMER, born in Dec 1875 in Northumberland Co., PA.
7. MARGARET I. FOLLMER, born in Apr 1879 in Northumberland Co., PA.

References: 26-Turbot Twp Northumberland Co PA H105, 27-Turbot Twp Northumberland Co PA H391, 29-Dist 0132 Ward 3 Milton Northumberland Co PA H368

C344 CHARLES FRANKLIN FOLLMER C34

CHARLES FRANKLIN FOLLMER was born on 15 Aug 1838 in Northumberland Co., PA. He married ABBIE A. THOMAS in 1872 in Northumberland Co., PA, daughter of WILLIAM F. THOMAS. She was born in 1850 in PA. They were Democrats and members of the Presbyterian Church.

Children of CHARLES FOLLMER and ABBIE THOMAS are:

1. HENRIETTA "ELLIE" F. FOLLMER, born in 1873 in Northumberland Co., PA.
2. ANNIE G. FOLLMER, born in Northumberland Co., PA.

References: 27-Milton Northumberland Co PA 165 H180, 67

C345 SARAH ELMIRA FOLLMER C34

SARAH ELMIRA FOLLMER was born in Oct 1840 in Northumberland Co., PA. She married WILLIAM RAUP in Northumberland Co., PA, son of JOHN RAUP and POLLY CLAPP. He was born on 27 Oct 1839 in Northumberland Co., PA. They were Democrats and in religion were Lutheran.

Children of SARAH FOLLMER and WILLIAM RAUP are:

1. DANIEL F. RAUP (C3451)
2. MARY ELIZABETH RAUP (C3452)
3. SARAH "SALLIE" L. RAUP, born in 1865 in Northumberland Co., PA.
4. IDA C. RAUP (C3454)
5. EMMA "KATIE" CATHERINE RAUP, born in Aug 1871 in Northumberland Co., PA.
6. JOHN NEWTON RAUP (C3456)
7. CLARENCE WILLIAM RAUP (C3457)
8. CHARLES FRANKLIN RAUP (C3458)
9. HARVEY H. RAUP, born in Oct 1879 in Northumberland Co., PA.

References: 67, 26-Lewis Northumberland H214, 27-Turbot Northumberland Co PA 164 H390, 29-Dist 0123 West Chillisquaque Twp Northumberland Co PA H121

C346 DANIEL HENRY FOLLMER C34

DANIEL HENRY FOLLMER was born in 19 Aug 1843 in Northumberland Co., PA and died in Jan 1909 in Northumberland Co., PA. He married REBECCA C. SCHAFFER in 1869 in Northumberland Co., PA, daughter of ELIAS SCHAFFER and ELIZABETH GLAZE. She was born in 1851 in PA. He received his education at the public schools and Milton Academy, and was a farmer by occupation. They were Democrats and were members of the Follmer Lutheran Church where he served as a deacon.

Children of DANIEL FOLLMER and REBECCA are:

1. ROLLAND SYDNEY FOLLMER (C3461)
2. BERTHA GERTRUDE FOLLMER (C3462)

References: 27-Turbot Twp Northumberland Co PA 164 H492, 36, 67

C348 JOHN S. FOLLMER C34

Dr. JOHN S. FOLLMER was born on 18 Jul 1851 in Northumberland Co., PA; died 27 Nov 1926 in Northumberland Co., PA. He married ELIZABETH "LIZZIE" B. VORIS in Northumberland Co., PA daughter of PETER VORIS and CHARITY M. She was born on 11 Oct 1855 in PA and died 11 Jun 1915 in Northumberland Co., PA. He was a druggist by occupation. Both are buried in Harmony Cemetery, Milton, Northumberland Co., PA.

Children of JOHN FOLLMER and LIZZIE are:

1. FREDERICK VORIS FOLLMER (C3481)
2. MALCOLM MURRAY FOLLMER (C3482)

References: 29-Dist 0132 Milton Ward 3 Northumberland Co PA H107, 30-Milton Ward 3 Northumberland Co PA H271, 45

C353 MARGARET CATHARINE ESHBACH C35

MARGARET CATHARINE ESHBACH was born on 14 Sep 1834 in NY and died 24 Nov 1914 in Lockport, Niagara Co., NY. She married WILLIAM J. WALKER in Niagara Co., NY. He was born in 05 Oct 1834 in London, England and died 14 May 1895 in Niagara Co., NY. He was a dyer by occupation. Both are buried in Cold Springs Cemetery in Lockport, Niagara Co., NY.

Children of MARGARET C. ESHBACH and WILLIAM WALKER are:

1. JOHN WILLIAM WALKER, born on 05 Mar 1860 in Niagara Co., NY; died 20 Mar 1935 in Niagara Co., NY; buried in Cold Springs Cemetery in Lockport, Niagara Co., NY.
2. GEORGE W. WALKER, born 1862 in Niagara Co., NY, of VA.
3. HARVEY DANIEL WALKER, born on 23 Aug 1864 in Niagara Co., NY, died 02 May 1927, buried in Cold Springs Cemetery in Lockport, Niagara Co., NY, of NE, four daughters.
4. CHARLES HENRY WALKER, born on 23 Apr 1867 in Niagara Co., NY; died 17 Mar 1926; buried in Cold Springs Cemetery in Lockport, Niagara Co., NY, Doctor, Specialist in Cancer, of NYC, NY.
5. FRANK OLIVER WALKER, born on 05 Mar1869 in Niagara Co., NY; died 19 Dec 1935; buried in Cold Springs Cemetery in Lockport, Niagara Co., NY.
6. ALBERT J. WALKER, born 1876 in Niagara Co., NY, died before 1931.
7. STELLA WALKER, born 1879 in Niagara Co., NY; married (?) HAVENS, 1920-1930 Lockport, NY and divorced prior to 1930; No children.

References: 5, 26-Lockport Ward 3 Niagara Co NY H363, 27-Lockport Niagara Co NY H12, 29-Lockport Ward 5 Niagara Co NY H26, 45, 31-Dist 22 Lockport Niagara Co NY H106

C354 THEODORE S. ESHBACH C35

THEODORE S. ESHBACH was born on 27 Nov 1836 in NY and died 01 Jan 1913 in Buffalo, Erie Co., NY.

Children of THEODORE ESHBACH and (?) are:

1. ALBERT ESHBACH
2. ELLA ESHBACH, married (?) BARBER.

References: 5

C357 URIAH H. ESHBACH C35

URIAH H. ESHBACH was born on 19 Aug 1842 in NY and died 08 Jun 1915 in Detroit, Wayne Co., MI. He married DELLA DODGE on 04 Feb 1892 in Detroit, Wayne Co., MI, daughter of DANIEL DODGE and MARIA COSTELLO.

Child of URIAH H. ESHBACH and DELLA DODGE is:

1. GRACE ESHBACH, born in MI, married (?) DAVIS, Chicago, IL.

References: 5, 59

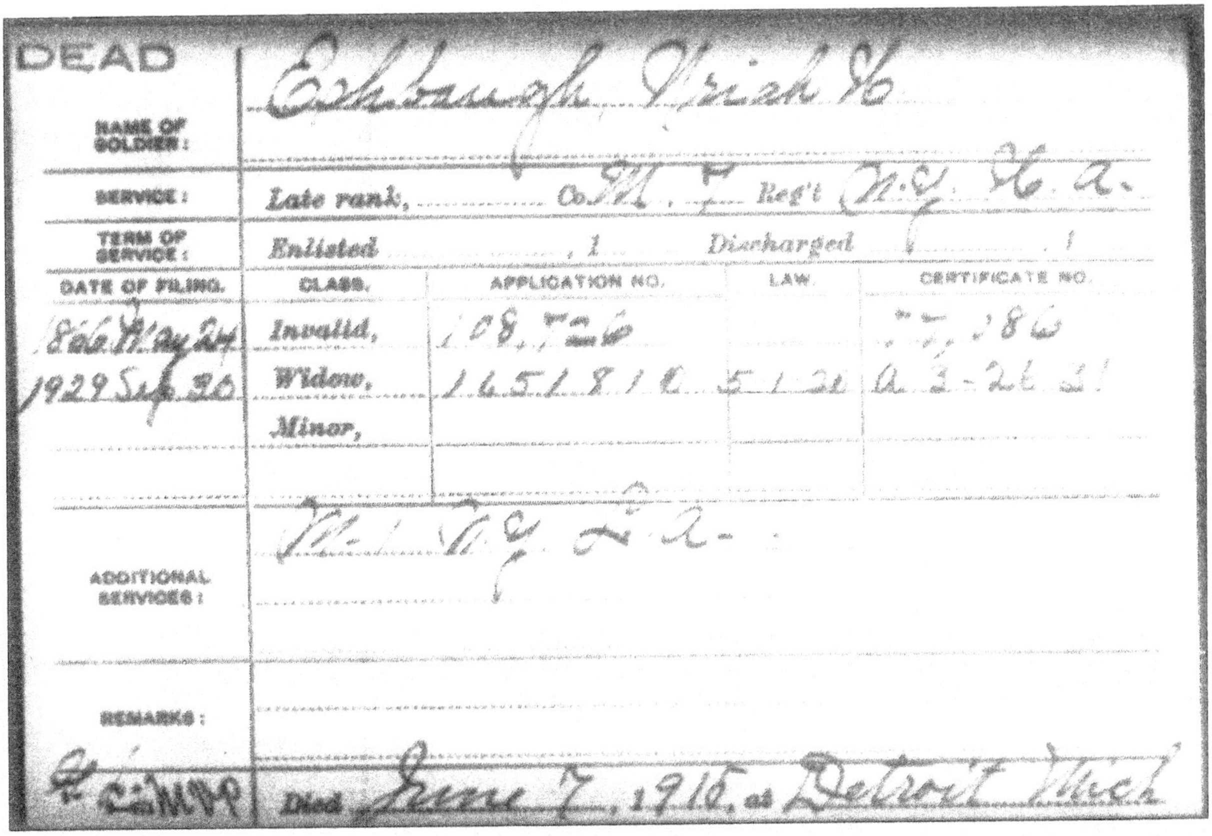
DEAD

NAME OF SOLDIER: Eshbaugh, Uriah H.

SERVICE: Late rank, Co. M, 7 Reg't N.Y. H.A.

TERM OF SERVICE: Enlisted , 1 Discharged , 1

DATE OF FILING.	CLASS.	APPLICATION NO.	LAW.	CERTIFICATE NO.
1866 May 24	Invalid,	108,726		77,286
1929 Sep 20	Widow,	1651810	5 1 20	A 3-26-31
	Minor,			

ADDITIONAL SERVICES: M. 1 N.Y. L.A.

REMARKS:

Died June 7, 1916, at Detroit Mich

C359 DAVID J. ESHBACH C35

DAVID J. ESHBACH was born on 12 Dec 1846 in NY. He married ELIZA in NY. She was born in Jul 1851 in NY. He resided at 174 Waterman St., Lockport, NY.

Child of DAVID J. ESHBACH and ELIZA is:

1. CHARLES F. ESHBACH (C2591)

References: 5, 29-Dist 137 Buffalo Ward 17 Erie Co NY H128

C35C CHRISTIAN ALICE ESHBACH C35

CHRISTIAN ALICE ESHBACH was born on 28 Sep 1858 in Lockport, Niagara Co., NY. She married WILLIAM GASCOYNE in Niagara Co., NY. He was born in Aug 1863 in NY and died before 1910 in Niagara Co., NY.

1. MARGARET ROUSEY GASCOYNE (C35C1)
2. CORA B. GASCOYNE (C35C2)

3. WILLIAM ROY GASCOYNE, died before 1910 in Niagara Co., NY.

References: 5, 29-Lockport Ward 3 Niagara Co NY H171, 30-Lockport Ward 3 Niagara Co NY H104, 31-Lockport Niagara Co NY H30, 10-Lockport Ward 3 Niagara Co NY H216

C362 JULIA C. LANTZ C36

JULIA C. LANTZ was born 16 May 1846 in PA. She married DANIEL A. GLASGOW in St. Joseph Co., MI. He was born Aug 1844 in MI.

Children of JULIA LANTZ and DANIEL GLASGOW are:

1. JOHN GLASGOW, born on 04 Jun 1869 in Constantine, St. Joseph Co., MI.
2. DANIEL GLASGOW, born on 20 Dec 1873 in Constantine, St. Joseph Co., MI.
3. MARY GLASGOW, born in 09 Sep 1878 in Ogle Co., IL.
4. LOUIE A. GLASGOW, born in Oct 1891 in Ogle Co., IL.

References: 5, 26-Constantine St Joseph Co MI H99, 27-Forreston Ogle Co IL H92, 29-Washinton Twp Elkhart Co IN H52

C363 DANIEL OLEVIANUS LANTZ C36

DANIEL OLEVIANUS LANTZ was born on 14 May 1847 in PA and died 12 Oct 1911 in Chicago, Cook Co., IL. He married ELIZABETH ZOLLINGER, daughter of JOHN ZOLLINGER. She was born in Jun 1856 in PA.

Children of DANIEL LANTZ and ELIZABETH are:

1. NETTIE M. LANTZ, born on 10 May 1876 in Cook Co., IL.
2. BENJAMIN O. LANTZ, born on 20 Oct 1878 in Cook Co., IL.
3. JESSIE C. LANTZ (f), born on 21 Oct 1885 in Cook Co., IL.
4. JOHN LANTZ, born on 20 Jul 1883 and died 27 Mar 1888 in Cook Co., IL.

References: 5, 46-D/DOL/25576, 27-Clyde Cook Co IL H21, 29-Chicago Ward 12 Cook Co IL H145

C364 HARRIET LOUISE LANTZ C36

HARRIET LOUISE LANTZ was born on 30 Apr 1849 in PA and died 15 Dec 1911. She married BENJAMIN O. GLADDING in St. Joseph Co., MI. He was born on 05 Aug 1847 in MI.

Children of HARRIET LANTZ and BENJAMIN GLADDING are:

1. WILLIAM O. GLADDING, born in 1875 in Constantine, St. Joseph Co., MI.
2. MARY L. GLADDING, born in Sep 1879 in Constantine, St. Joseph Co., MI.
3. EMILY GLADDING, born on 24 Jan 1882 in Constantine, St. Joseph Co., MI.

References: 27-Constantine St Joseph Co MI H339, 37-Chicago Ward 35 Cook Co IL H195

C382 SARAH JANE AUSTIN C38

SARAH JANE AUSTIN was born on 16 Sep 1845 in OH and died 27 Jun 1922 in Clinton Co., MI. She married WILLIAM H. SILVERS in MI. He was born in Apr 1841 in OH and died in 1916 in Clinton Co., MI. Both are buried in Union Home Cemetery, Saint Johns, Clinton Co., MI.

Children of SARAH AUSTIN and WILLIAM SILVERS are:

1. FRANKLIN H. SILVERS (C3821)
2. ANNA J. SILVERS, born in Mar 1870 in Clinton Co., MI.
3. MARGARET J. SILVERS, born in 1872 in Clinton Co., MI.
4. ALBERT EUGENE SILVERS, born in Mar 1875 in Clinton Co., MI.
5. MARTHA SILVERS, born in 1877 in Clinton Co., MI.
6. WILLIAM P. SILVERS (C3826)
7. EMMA E. SILVERS, born in Jan 1883 in Clinton Co., MI.
8. MANNING J. SILVERS (C3828)
9. CHARLOTTE "LOTTIE" MAY SILVERS, born in May 1891 in Clinton Co., MI.
10. UNKNOWN SILVERS, born in and died before 1900 in Clinton Co., MI.
11. UNKNOWN SILVERS, born in and died before 1900 in Clinton Co., MI.

References: 26-Greenbush Twp Clinton Co MI H93, 27-Greenbush Twp Clinton Co MI H179, 29-Greenbush Twp Clinton Co MI H228, 45

C383 MARGARET AUSTIN C38

MARGARET AUSTIN in Sep 1851 in Clinton Co., MI. She married (?) YOUDAN. He died before 1900 in Clinton Co., MI.

Children of MARGARET AUSTIN and (?) YOUDAN are:

1. MARY YOUDAN, born in Dec 1880 in Clinton Co., MI.
2. DAISY YOUDAN, born in Feb 1884 in Clinton Co., MI.
3. ROSELO YOUDAN, born in Dec 1888 in Clinton Co., MI.
4. FRANK YOUDAN, born in Oct 1895 in Clinton Co., MI.
5. UNKNOWN YOUDAN, born before 1900 in Clinton Co., MI.
6. UNKNOWN YOUDAN, born in and died before 1900 in Clinton Co., MI.
7. UNKNOWN YOUDAN, born in and died before 1900 in Clinton Co., MI.
8. UNKNOWN YOUDAN, born in and died before 1900 in Clinton Co., MI.

References: 5, 29- Greenbush Twp Clinton Co MI H276

C384 MARTHA L. AUSTIN C38

MARTHA L. AUSTIN was born in Nov 1856 in Clinton Co., MI. She married JOHN WESTBROOK in MI. He was born in Nov 1852 in OH.

Child of MARTHA AUSTIN and JOHN WESTBROOK is:

1. FRANCIS GUY WESTBROOK, born in Oct 1880 in Clinton Co., MI.

References: 5, 29- Greenbush Twp Clinton Co MI H275

C385 ELMIRA J. AUSTIN C38

ELMIRA J. AUSTIN was born in 1857 in Clinton Co., MI. She married JOSHUA O. CORKIN in 1881 in Clinton Co, MI. He was born in Feb 1853 in Ireland.

Children of ELMIRA AUSTIN and JOSHUA CORKIN are:

1. MAUD L. CORKIN, born in Apr 1882 in MI.
2. JOSHUA E. CORKIN, born in Sep 1885 in MI.
3. HARRY B. CORKIN, born in Mar 1889 in MI.
4. BESSIE B. CORKIN, born in Sep 1890 in MI; married ELMER BURKE in SD; born in 1898 in SD.
5. FRANCIS "FRANK" B. CORKIN, born in Mar 1892 in MI.
6. GEORGE F. CORKIN (C3856)
7. ELSA H. CORKIN, born in Sep 1896 in MI.
8. LILLIAN M. CORKIN (f), born in Sep 1899 in SD.
9. UNKNOWN CORKIN, born after 1880 and died before 1900.
10. UNKNOWN CORKIN, born after 1880 and died before 1900.
11. UNKNOWN CORKIN, born after 1880 and died before 1900.
12. UNKNOWN CORKIN, born after 1900 and died before 1910 in SD.

References: 29-Rondell Twp Brown Co SD H152, 30-La Prairie Spink Co SD H20. 31-Covington Twp Dakota Co SD H33

C393 HENRY MARTIN WINTERSTEEN C39

HENRY MARTIN WINTERSTEEN was born on 01 Apr 1849 in Columbia Co., PA. He married ANNA J. BEAVER in Northumberland Co., PA, daughter of JOHN S. BEAVER and MARGARET A.. She was born in Apr 1857 in PA.

Children of HENRY WINTERSTEEN and ANNA are:

1. LULA M. WINTERSTEEN, born in 1879 in Northumberland Co., PA.
2. FRANK WINTERSTEEN born in Northumberland Co., PA., resided McEwensville, PA.
3. SON WINTERSTEEN born in Northumberland Co., PA.
4. DAUGHTER WINTERSTEEN born in Northumberland Co., PA.

References: 5, 29-Turbot Twp Northumberland Co PA H132, 27-Delaware Twp Northumberland Co PA H58

C396 SARAH CHRISTENA WINTERSTEEN C39

SARAH CHRISTENA WINTERSTEEN was born on 01 Oct 1856 in Columbia Co., PA. She married Dr. WILLIAM E. METZGER in PA. He was born in Jul 1850 in PA. He was a physician by occupation.

Children of SARAH WINTERSTEEN and WILLIAM METZGER are:

1. FRANCIS G. METZGER, born in 1876 in Union Co., PA.

2. WILLIAM C. METZGER, born in 1877 in Union Co., PA.
3. FREDDIE W. METZGER, born in Feb 1880 in Union Co., PA.
4. THOMAS S. METZGER, born in Jan 1884 in Union Co., PA.
5. FRANK R. METZGER, born in Mar 1887 in Union Co., PA.
6. CARRIE MAY METZGER (C3966)
7. RUTH METZGER, born in Aug 1891 in Union Co., PA.
8. JOHN R. METZGER, born in Aug 1894 in Union Co., PA.

References: 5, 29-Gregg Twp Union Co PA H47, 27-Alvira Gregg Twp Union Co PA H92

C397 WILLIAM FRANKLIN WINTERSTEEN C39

WILLIAM FRANKLIN WINTERSTEEN was born on 26 Jan 1859 in Columbia Co., PA and died before 1931.

Child of WILLIAM FRANKLIN WINTERSTEEN is:

1. SON WINTERSTEEN, resides in Dayton, OH.

References: 5

C399 SIMON LANTZ WINTERSTEEN C39

SIMON LANTZ WINTERSTEEN was born on 15 Jun 1865 in Columbia Co., PA.

Child of SIMON LANTZ WINTERSTEEN is

1. RAYMOND WINTERSTEEN

References: 5

C411 ELIZABETH JANE GASS C41

ELIZABETH JANE GASS was born in 1844 in Northumberland Co., PA and died before 1911 in Northumberland Co., PA. She married WILLIAM MACKERT in Northumberland Co., PA. He was born in 1845 in Germany.

Children of ELIZABETH GASS and WILLIAM MACKERT are:

1. JACOB F. MACKERT (C4111)
2. MARTIN C. MACKERT, born in Sep 1879 in Northumberland Co., PA.

References: 67, 27-Lower Augusta Northumberland Co PA 154 H25

C412 RICHARD A. GASS C41

RICHARD A. GASS was born on 12 Oct 1845 in Northumberland Co., PA. He married EMILY A. GARINGER in 1872 in Northumberland Co., PA, daughter of CHARLES GARINGER and DEBORAH HAAS. She was born in Jun 1852 in PA. He engaged in a mercantile business until he became a traveling salesman for Chase Brothers Nursery Company. They were Democrats and members of the Reformed Church.

Children of RICHARD GASS and EMILY are:

1. LAURA G. GASS, born in Jul 1874 in Northumberland Co., PA.
2. CARRIE D. GASS, born in Nov 1875 in Northumberland Co., PA.
3. CHARLES M. GASS, born in 04 May 1878 in Northumberland Co., PA. He graduated in 1900 with a dentistry degree from Pennsylvania College. He has since has been practicing dentistry in Sunbury, PA. He was a member of Modern Woodman and the Reformed Church.
4. EDWARD F. GASS (C4124)

References: 29-Dist 0163 Sunbury Northumberland Co PA H264, 67

C414 GEORGE W. GASS C41

GEORGE W. GASS was born in Jan 1850 in Northumberland Co., PA. He married MARTHA A. in Northumberland Co., PA. She was born Oct 1856 in PA.

Children of GEORGE GASS and MARTHA are:

1. PETER S. GASS (C4141)
2. MARTIN H. GASS (C4142)
3. GERTRUDE GASS, born Aug 1882 in Northumberland Co., PA.
4. CLYDE J. GASS, born Jun 1885 in Northumberland Co., PA.
5. MABEL GASS, born Mar 1888 in Northumberland Co., PA.
6. GEORGE C. GASS, born Oct 1891 in Northumberland Co., PA.
7. RALPH W. GASS, born Apr 1896 in Northumberland Co., PA.

References: 27-Upper Augusta Twp Northumberland Co PA 167 H307, 27-Dist 0163 Sunbury Northumberland H216, 30-Ward 6 Sunbury Northumberland 0116 H271

C424 JACOB C. GASS C42

JACOB C. GASS was born on 04 Nov 1835 in Northumberland Co., PA and died 01 Aug 1912 in Northumberland Co., PA. He married (1) ANGELINE about 1857 in Northumberland Co., PA. She was born in 1833 in PA and died in 1864 in Northumberland Co., PA. He married (2) JUDITH about 1865 in Northumberland Co., PA. She was born on 11 Feb 1835 in PA and died 06 Nov 1906 in Northumberland Co., PA. He married (3) SUSANNAH MALICK in 1911 in Northumberland Co., PA. He and his first wife are buried in the Eden Lutheran and Evangelical Cemetery, Plum Creek Road, Sunbury, Northumberland Co., PA.

Children of JACOB GASS and ANGELINE are:

1. SUSAN E. GASS, born in 1858 in Northumberland Co., PA.
2. MARIA M. GASS, born in 1860 in Northumberland Co., PA.
3. SARAH A. GASS, born in 1863 in Northumberland Co., PA.

Children of JACOB GASS and JUDITH are:

4. AMELIA CATHARINE GASS, born in 1867 in Northumberland Co., PA.
5. SABINA J. GASS (C4245)
6. SAMUEL E. GASS (C4246)

7. GEORGE GASS, born in 1870 in Northumberland Co., PA; died in 1872 in Northumberland Co., PA. Buried in the Eden Lutheran and Evangelical Cemetery, Plum Creek Road, Sunbury, Northumberland Co., PA.
8. JULIAN GASS, born in Feb 1873 in Northumberland Co., PA.
9. ADAM D. GASS (C4249)
10. CLAYTON E. GASS (C424A)

References: 25-Lower Augusta Twp Northumberland Co PA H774, 26-Lower Augusta Twp Northumberland Co PA H233, 27-Lower Augusta Twp Northumberland Co PA 154 H30, 45, 29-Dist 0157 Shamokin Northumberland Co Pa H194, 30-Upper Augusta Twp Northumberland Co PA 0121 H99

C427 ELIAS GASS C42

ELIAS GASS was born in 1841 in Northumberland Co., PA. He married MARGARET in Northumberland Co., PA. She was born in 1841 in PA.

Children of ELIAS GASS and MARGARET are:

1. WILLIAM C. GASS, born 1862 in Northumberland Co., PA.
2. GEORGE W. GASS, born 1863 in Northumberland Co., PA.
3. ROBERT M. GASS, born 1865 in Northumberland Co., PA.
4. FLORA GASS, born 1867 in Northumberland Co., PA.
5. JOHN GASS, born 1869 in Northumberland Co., PA.

References: 26-Upper Augusta Twp Northumberland Co PA H2

C432 SAMUEL GASS C43

SAMUEL GASS was born on 10 Mar 1838 in Northumberland Co., PA and died 05 Nov 1901 in Northumberland Co., PA. He married SARAH in Northumberland Co., PA. She was born on 26 Feb 1840 in PA and died 04 Jul 1905 in Northumberland Co., PA.

Children of SAMUEL GASS and SARAH are:

1. ELENOR A. GASS, born in 1866 in Northumberland Co., PA.
2. DANIEL C. GASS, born in 1867 in Northumberland Co., PA.
3. SARAH IDA GASS, born in 1872 in Northumberland Co., PA.

References: 27-Lower Augusta Twp Northumberland Co PA H34

C435 JOSEPH GASS C43

JOSEPH GASS was born on 13 Dec 1844 in Northumberland Co., PA. He married RUTH SHIPMAN in Northumberland Co., PA, daughter of Judge ABRAHAM SHIPMAN. She was born in Aug 1845 in PA. He was a farmer by occupation.

Children of JOSEPH GASS and RUTH SHIPMAN are:

1. HORATIO WARREN GASS (C4351)
2. GEORGE NEVIN GASS, died in infancy in Northumberland Co., PA.
3. RICHARD IRA GASS, born in Mar 1876 in Northumberland Co., PA. Minister of the Reformed Church in Mainville, PA.
4. FOSTER W. GASS, born on 26 Nov 1880 in Northumberland Co., PA; died 28 Apr 1946 in Northumberland Co., PA; married RACHEL AMANDA GRIER in Northumberland Co., PA, daughter of ALBERT C. GRIER and CATHARINE GANN; born in 1870 in PA; died 16 Apr 1905 in Northumberland Co., PA. They are buried in the Eden Lutheran and Evangelical Cemetery, Plum Creek Road, Sunbury, Northumberland Co., PA.

References: 67, 27-Lower Augusta Twp Northumberland Co PA 154 H35, 29-Dist 0146 Rockefeller Twp Northumberland Co PA H77, 30-Rockefeller Twp Northumberland Co PA 0095 H48

C442 JOSEPH A. GASS C44

JOSEPH A. GASS was born on 08 Sep 1844 in Northumberland Co., PA. He married ISABELLA A. HAUSEWART on 28 May 1873 in Northumberland Co., PA, daughter of SAMUEL L. HAUSEWART and HULDA FARLEY. She was born in Dec 1847 in PA. He engaged in a fertilizer and farm equipment business in Sunbury, PA. They were Democrats and members of the Zion Lutheran Church.

Children of JOSEPH GASS and ISABELLA HAUSEWART are:

1. HULDA SUSANNA GASS, born in Apr 1875 in Northumberland Co., PA. Teacher by

2. MARGARET S. GASS (C4422)
3. HARRIET A. GASS, born in Oct 1878 in Northumberland Co., PA. Worked as a stenographer in York, PA.
4. ISABELLA M. GASS (C4424)
5. SAMUEL J. GASS (C4425)
6. FRANCIS C. GASS, born in Apr 1888 in Northumberland Co., PA.
7. NELLIE P. GASS, born in Feb 1891 in Northumberland Co., PA.

References: 67, 29-Dist 0163 Sunbury Northumberland Co PA H278

C444 ISAAC N. GASS C44

ISAAC N. GASS was born Jul 1851 in Northumberland Co., PA; died before 1911 in Northumberland Co., PA. He married AMY in Northumberland Co., PA. She was born in Feb 1854 in PA.

Child of ISAAC GASS and AMY is:

1. DAISY V. GASS, born in Jan 1879 in Northumberland Co., PA.

References: 27-Shamokin Northumberland Co PA 163 H44, 29-Dist 0160 Sunbury Northumberland Co PA H120

C511 SAMUEL L. KEEFER C51

SAMUEL L. KEEFER was born on 28 Mar 1828 and died Aug 1916. He married (1) BARBARA A. SAVIDGE in 1851 in Northumberland Co., PA daughter of GEORGE SAVIDGE. She was born on 29 May 1830 and died 06 Aug 1862 in Northumberland Co., PA. He married (2) HARRIET MALICK in Northumberland Co., PA, daughter of W. MALICK. She was born in Oct 1843 in PA. He and 1st wife are buried in Lantz's Emmanuel Cemetery, Sunbury, Northumberland Co., PA. They were Democrats and members of the Reformed Church.

Children of SAMUEL L. KEEFER and BARBARA SAVIDGE are:

1. AMELIA KEEFER, born in 1855 in Northumberland Co., PA, died in 1929.
2. PETER RICHARD KEEFER (C5111)

Children of SAMUEL L. KEEFER and HARRIET MALICK are:

3. JANE "JENNIE" KEEFER, born in 1866 in Northumberland Co., PA, died in 1914.
4. DAVID F. KEEFER, born in 1869 in Northumberland Co., PA.
5. CHARLES MILTON KEEFER, born in May 1874 in Northumberland Co., PA.
6. HARRY OTTO KEEFER, born in Apr 1882 in Northumberland Co., PA.
7. EVA T. KEEFER, born in Nov 1887 in Northumberland Co., PA.

References: 5, 25-Lower Augusta Northumberland Co PA H846, 26-Lower Augusta Northumberland Co PA H69, 27-Lower Augusta Northumberland Co PA H13, 29-Sunbury Northumberland Co PA H127, 45, 36, 67

C512 MARGARET KEEFER C51

MARGARET KEEFER was born on 27 Jul 1832 in PA and died 26 Apr 1904 in Sunbury, Northumberland Co., PA. She married HENRY ARNOLD on 25 Mar 1855 in Northumberland Co., PA. He was born on 03 May 1832 in Northumberland Co., PA and died 06 May 1900 in Sunbury, Northumberland Co., PA. Both are buried in Lantz Lutheran Cemetery, Sunbury, Northumberland Co., PA.

Child of MARGARET KEEFER and HENRY ARNOLD is:

1. SAMUEL ARNOLD (C5121)
2. REBECCA JANE ARNOLD, born 26 Feb 1856/7 in Northumberland Co., PA; died 20 Dec 1918 in Winfield, Cowley Co., KS; married JOHN AL BELTZ on 05 Oct 1886 in Cuyahoga Co., OH; born 23 Jul 1839 in Germany; died 02 Mar 1901 in Winfield, Cowley Co., KS.
3. PETER A. ARNOLD, born 1859 in Northumberland Co., PA.
4. MAY C. ARNOLD, born 1860 in Northumberland Co., PA.
5. HANNAH ANNIE ARNOLD, born in 15 Apr 1864 in Northumberland Co., PA; died 12 Aug 1942 in Northumberland Co., PA; married CHARLES H. LEISENRING in Northumberland Co., PA; born in 1861 in PA; She is buried in Lantz Lutheran Cemetery, Sunbury, Northumberland Co., PA.
6. MARGARET ANN ARNOLD (C5126)
7. LILLIE K. ARNOLD, born Sep 1868 in Northumberland Co., PA.
8. GEORGE W. ARNOLD, born in 16 Jan 1874 in Northumberland Co., PA; died 19 Jan 1910 in Northumberland Co., PA; buried in Lantz Lutheran Cemetery, Sunbury, Northumberland Co., PA.
9. EMMA ARNOLD, born 1879 in Northumberland Co., PA.

References: 45, 25-Upper Augusta Northumberland Co PA H691, 26-Upper Augusta Northumberland Co PA H70, 27-Upper Augusta Northumberland Co PA H273, 29-Sunbury Northumberland Co PA H277, 10-Dist 161 Ward 3 Sunbury Northumberland Co PA, 67

C513 HANNAH KEEFER C51

HANNAH KEEFER was born on 01 Mar 1827 in Northumberland Co., PA and died 05 Jan 1918 in Northumberland Co., PA. She married ISAAC ALBERT in Northumberland Co., PA, son of CHRISTIAN ALBERT and MARY. He was born 31 Dec 1828 in Northumberland Co., PA and died 29 Sep 1906 in Northumberland Co., PA. Both are buried in Herndon Cemetery, Herndon, Northumberland Co., PA.

Children of HANNAH KEEFER and ISAAC ALBERT are:

1. FRANKLIN ALBERT, born in 1853 in Northumberland Co., PA.
2. UNKNOWN ALBERT, born in Northumberland Co., PA.

References: 45, 29-Dist 0125 Jackson Twp Northumberland Co PA H155, 25-Jackson Twp Northumberland Co PA H359, 67

C514 PETER KEEFER C51

PETER KEEFER was born on 03 Mar 1838 in Northumberland Co., PA and died 11 May 1909 in Northumberland Co., PA. He married AMELIA A. HAAS in Northumberland Co., PA. She was born on 19 Nov 1839 in PA and died 24 Jul 1906 in Northumberland Co., PA. He was a contractor by profession specializing in bridge building for more than thirty years and was engaged in a mercantile business for a period of ten years. They were Democrats and members of the Reformed Church. Both are buried in Pomfret Manor Cemetery, Sunbury, Northumberland Co., PA.

Child of PETER KEEFER and AMELIA HAAS is:

1. GEORGE F. KEEFER (C5141)

References: 66, Jackson Twp Northumberland Co PA H81, 26-Upper Augusta Twp Northumberland Co PA 167 H95, 45, 67

C515 MARY MAGDALENA KEEFER C51

MARY MAGDALENA KEEFER was born 18 Dec 1835 in Northumberland Co., PA and died 27 Feb 1863 in Northumberland Co., PA. She married JOHN F. ZIMMERMAN in Northumberland Co., PA. He was born 05 Feb 1829 in PA. Both are buried in Lantz's Emmanuel Cemetery, Sunbury, Northumberland Co., PA.

Children of MARY KEEFER and JOHN ZIMMERMAN are:

1. DAVID A. ZIMMERMAN (C5151)
2. HANNAH A. ZIMMERMAN, born in 1859 in Northumberland Co., PA.
3. AARON PETER ZIMMERMAN (C5153)

References: 45, 25-Lower Augusta Twp Northumberland Co PA H896, 26-Lower Augusta Twp Northumberland Co PA H343

C531 ELIZABETH HAUCK C53

ELIZABETH HAUCK was born on 18 Nov 1835 and died 11 Oct 1905 in Lower Augusta Twp., Northumberland Co., PA. She married DANIEL D. HEILMAN in 26 Sep 1856 in Northumberland Co., PA, son of DANIEL HEILMAN and GERTRUDE DIEHL. He was born on 25 Dec 1829 in Lower Augusta Twp., Northumberland Co., PA and died 30 Jun 1904 in Lower Augusta Twp., Northumberland Co., PA.

Children of ELIZABETH HAUCK and DANIEL HEILMAN are:

1. JOHN C. HEILMAN, born1857 in Northumberland Co., PA. Moved to IN, killed at the age of 25
2. MARGARET ANNIE HEILMAN, born1861 in Northumberland Co., PA, married ROBERT CHARLES, resides Scranton, PA.
3. CLARA ELIZABETH HEILMAN, born on 08 Apr 1868 in Lower Augusta Twp., Northumberland Co., PA; died 28 Jul 1932 in Sunbury, Northumberland Co., PA;

Northumberland Co., PA; died 28 Jul 1932 in Sunbury, Northumberland Co., PA; married ANDREW JACKSON SMITH on 08 Jan 1888 in Northumberland Co., PA.
4. DANIEL F. HEILMAN, born1876 in Northumberland Co., PA.

References: 5, 25-Lower Augusta Northumberland Co PA H893, 26-Lower Augusta Northumberland Co PA H163, 27-Lower Augusta Northumberland Co PA H52, 36

C532 MARY M. HAUCK C53

MARY M. HAUCK was born on 13 Aug 1831 in Northumberland Co., PA and died 24 Jan 1914 in Sunbury, Northumberland Co., PA. She married REUBEN WOLFE on 24 Oct 1861 in Northumberland Co., PA, son of ABRAHAM WOLFE. He was born on 21 Jan 1830 in Northumberland Co., PA and died 08 Oct 1910 in Sunbury, Northumberland Co., PA.

Child of MARY HAUCK and REUBEN WOLFE is:

1. ALICE WOLFE, born 1858 in Lower Augusta Twp., Northumberland Co., PA.
2. CLARA A. WOLFE, born Sep 1862 in Lower Augusta Twp., Northumberland Co., PA; married (?) KNISS.
3. DAVID C. WOLFE, born Dec 1864 in Lower Augusta Twp., Northumberland Co., PA.
4. MACKEY WOLFE, born 1866 in Lower Augusta Twp., Northumberland Co., PA.
5. ELLEN WOLFE, born 1867 in Lower Augusta Twp., Northumberland Co., PA
6. ANTHONY WOLFE, born 07 Nov 1867 in Lower Augusta Twp., Northumberland Co., PA and died 16 May 1900 in PA. He married EMMA ELIZA FASOLD on 21 Dec 1887 in Northumberland Co., PA. She was born on 09 Jun 1869 in Purdytown, PA and died 01 Dec 1911 in Sunbury, Northumberland Co., PA.
7. AMELIA WOLFE, born 1869 in Lower Augusta Twp., Northumberland Co., PA.
8. SAMUEL G. WOLFE, born 1873 in Lower Augusta Twp., Northumberland Co., PA.

References: 26-Lower Augusta Northumberland Co PA H26, 27-Lower Augusta Northumberland Co PA H104, 29-Sunbury Northumberland Co PA H225

C547 WILLIAM P. STERNER C54

WILLIAM P. STERNER was born in Jun 1844 in Northumberland Co., PA. He married ELMIRA M. She was born in May 1847 in PA.

Children of WILLIAM STERNER and ELMIRA are:

1. MARY L. STERNER, born in 1866 in Northumberland Co., PA.
2. CASANDER STERNER, born in 1867 in Northumberland Co., PA.
3. WILLIAM H. STERNER, born in 1869 in Northumberland Co., PA.
4. JAMES B. STERNER (C5474)
5. ABRAHAM STERNER, born in 1875 in Northumberland Co., PA.
6. ANNIE D. STERNER, born in 1876 in Northumberland Co., PA.
7. JASPER STERNER, born in Dec 1879 in Northumberland Co., PA.
8. MYRTLE STERNER, born in Jan 1888 in PA.

References: 26-Lower Augusta Twp Northumberland Co PA H116, 27-Sunbury Northumberland

Co PA H3, 29-Dist 0029 West Scott Twp Columbia Co PA H47

C548 GEORGE WASHINGTON STERNER C54

GEORGE WASHINGTON STERNER was born on 21 May 1846 in Northumberland Co., PA; died 25 Mar 1924 In Northumberland Co., PA. He married ELLEN N. She was born on 21 Feb 1847 in PA and died 26 May 1905 in Northumberland Co., PA. Both are buried in the Lantz Lutheran Cemetery, Sunbury, Northumberland Co., PA.

Children of GEORGE STERNER and ELLEN are

1. ANNIE H. STERNER, born in 1872 in Northumberland Co., PA; died 25 Aug 1926 in Northumberland Co. PA; married (?) ZARTMAN. They are buried in the Lantz Lutheran Cemetery, Sunbury, Northumberland Co., PA.
2. CORA E. STERNER, born in Mar 1874 in Northumberland Co., PA
3. SARAH JENNIE STERNER, born in Mar 1876 in Northumberland Co., PA.
4. JOSIE N. STERNER, born in Sep 1879 in Northumberland Co., PA; died 1961 in Northumberland Co., PA; buried in the Lantz Lutheran Cemetery, Sunbury, Northumberland Co., PA.
5. WALTER STERNER, born on 15 Mar 1893 in Northumberland Co., PA; died 01 Jan 1894 in Northumberland Co., PA; buried in the Lantz Lutheran Cemetery, Sunbury, Northumberland Co., PA.
6. HERMAN STERNER, born in Apr 1894 in Northumberland Co., PA.

References: 45, 27-Lower Augusta Twp Northumberland Co PA H19, 29-Lower Augusta Twp Northumberland Co PA H47

C533 ANDREW HAUCK C53

ANDREW HAUCK was born in 1837 in Northumberland Co., PA. He married ESTHER. She was born in 1837 in PA.

Children of ANDREW HAUCK and ESTHER are:

1. DANIEL H. HAUCK, born 1861 in Northumberland Co., PA.
2. DAVID A. HAUCK, born 1863 in Northumberland Co., PA.
3. MARGARET HAUCK, born 1865 in Northumberland Co., PA.

References: 24-Lower Augusta Twp Northumberland Co PA H106

C535 HENRY L. HAUCK C53

HENRY L. HAUCK was born in 1841 in Northumberland Co., PA. He married HANNAH in Northumberland Co., PA. She was born in 1843 in PA.

Children of HENRY HAUCK and HANNAH are:

1. WILFORD HAUCK, born 1867 in Northumberland Co., PA.
2. ANNIE HAUCK, born 1871 in Northumberland Co., PA.

3. CHARLES HAUCK, born 1874 in Northumberland Co., PA.

References: 27-Upper Augusta Northumberland Co PA 167 H233

C536 DAVID K. HAUCK C53

DAVID K. HAUCK was born in Sep 1843 in Northumberland Co., PA. He married AMELIA C. in Northumberland Co., PA. She was born in Mar 1848 in PA.

Child of DAVID HAUCK and AMELIA is:

1. GERTRUDE L. HAUCK (C5361)

References: 27-Sunbury Northumberland Co PA 168 H221, 27-Dist 0159 Sunbury Northumberland Co PA H302

C539 JOHN R. HAUCK C53

JOHN R. HAUCK was born in Sep 1850 in Northumberland Co., PA. He married CLARA in Northumberland Co., PA. She was born Jul 1851 in PA.

Child of JOHN HAUCK and CLARA is:

1. JENNIE HAUCK, born in Aug 1877 in Northumberland Co., PA.

References: 29-Dist 0163 Sunbury Northumberland Co PA H211

C551 BENJAMIN FRANKLIN DEPPEN C55

BENJAMIN FRANKLIN DEPPEN was born Jun 1847 in Northumberland Co., PA. He married SUSAN HERB in Northumberland Co., PA. She was born in Jan 1859 in PA and died in 1888 in Northumberland Co., PA. He was a Philadelphia & Reading Railway Company Agent in 1880. They were Republicans.

Children of BENJAMIN DEPPEN and SUSAN HERB are:

1. SAMUEL H. DEPPEN (C5511)
2. LAURA A. DEPPEN, born in Jul 1873 in Northumberland Co., PA.
3. SUSAN M. DEPPEN, born in Nov 1884 in Northumberland Co., PA.
4. WILLIAM RALPH DEPPEN (C5514)

References: 5, 27-Zerbe Twp Northumberland Co PA H130, 29-Zerbe Twp Northumberland Co PA H86, 30-Zerbe Twp Northumberland Co PA H94, 10-Zerbe Twp Northumberland Co PA H121, 36, 67

C552 GEORGE WASHINGTON DEPPEN C55

GEORGE WASHINGTON DEPPEN was born 08 Jul 1849 in Northumberland Co., PA and died Jan 1909 in Northumberland Co., PA. He married in 1874 ANGELINE HERB. She was born in Mar 1854 in PA. He was a merchant, bank cashier and county officer of Sunbury, Somerset Co., PA.

Children of GEORGE DEPPEN and ANGELINE HERB are:

1. WILLIAM E. DEPPEN, born in 1875 in Northumberland Co., PA, resided Nanticoke, PA.
2. HARRY L. DEPPEN, born in 1878 in Northumberland Co., PA, married HELEN and resided Sunbury, Somerset Co., PA.
3. SUSAN ANNE DEPPEN (C5523)
4. SARAH E. DEPPEN (C5524)
5. GEORGE H. DEPPEN, born in Sep 1882 in Northumberland Co., PA, resided Sunbury, Somerset Co., PA.
6. CLARA M. DEPPEN, born Jul 1884 in Northumberland Co., PA, married ROBERT E. JAMES. They resided Dover, OH.
7. FRANK R. DEPPEN (C5527)
8. CLARENCE H. DEPPEN, born Oct 1891 in Northumberland Co., PA

References: 5, 27-Sunbury Northumberland Co PA H42, 29-Sunbury Northumberland Co PA H138, 30-Dist 0114 Sunbury Ward 4 Northumberland Co PA H219, 67

C553 RICHARD LAWTON DEPPEN C55

RICHARD LAWTON DEPPEN was born in Aug 1851 and died in 1928. He married CATHERINE BENRY in Northumberland Co., PA. She was born in Jan 1852 in PA. He was a merchant in Shamokin, PA.

Children of RICHARD DEPPEN and CATHERINE BENRY are:

1. CARRIE DEPPEN (C5531)
2. WILLIAM C. DEPPEN, born in Mar 1886 in Northumberland Co., PA, married and resided in WV.
3. RICHARD LAWTON DEPPEN, born Jul 1890 in Northumberland Co., PA, married and resided in CT.

References: 5, 29-Shamokin Northumberland Co PA H87, 30-Shamokin Ward 1 Northumberland Co PA H68

C566 ALBERT S. CULP C56

ALBERT S. CULP was born in 1849 in Northumberland Co., PA. He married ANNA R. She was born in 1852 in PA.

Children of ALBERT CULP and ANNA are:

1. SAMUEL CULP, born in 1873 in Northumberland Co., PA.
2. CHARLES L. CULP, born in 1873 in Northumberland Co., PA.
3. SARAH C. CULP, born in 1873 in Northumberland Co., PA.

References: 27-Lower Augusta Twp Northumberland Co PA H20, 67

C567 PETER F. CULP C56

PETER F. CULP was born on 14 Nov 1850 in Northumberland Co., PA and died in 1921 in Northumberland Co., PA. He married ANNA HEILMAN in 1873 in Northumberland Co., PA, daughter of DANIEL HEILMAN and MARGARET SMELTZER. She was born in Jan 1853 in PA and died 1921 in Northumberland Co., PA. They were Democrats and members of the Reformed Church. Both are buried in Lantz Lutheran Cemetery, Sunbury, Northumberland Co., PA.

Children of PETER CULP and ANNA HEILMAN are:

1. MINNIE CULP, born in 1870 in Northumberland Co., PA.
2. GERTRUDE CULP (C5672)
3. MARGARET CULP, born in 1875 in Northumberland Co., PA; married EDWARD BARTHOLOMEW in Northumberland Co., PA.
4. CREIGHTON GLENN CULP (C5674)
5. TRUEMAN CULP, born in Dec 1879 in Northumberland Co., PA.
6. PEARL VERNON CULP (C5676)
7. ROYAL PALMER CULP (C5677)
8. ALBERT BERNARD CULP (C5678)
9. BESSIE BLANCHE CULP, born in Nov 1893 in Northumberland Co., PA.
10. BRYAN DARLINGTON CULP, born in Sep 1896 in Northumberland Co., PA.

References: 27-Lower Augusta Twp Northumberland Co PA H50, 45, 29-Dist 0146 Rockefeller Twp Northumberland Co PA H210, 30-Dist 0095 Rockefeller Twp Northumberland Co PA H200, 67

C572 SUSANNAH LANTZ C57

SUSANNAH LANTZ was born on 21 May 1845 in IN and died 29 Dec 1880. She married JACOB N. BONAWITZ in 1868. He was born in 1838 in OH. He was a stone mason by occupation.

Children of SUSANNAH LANTZ and JACOB BONAWITZ are:

1. ARDEN A. BONAWITZ, born on 24 Aug 1870 and died 29 Oct 1870 in IN.
2. MARSHALL BONAWITZ (C5722)
3. LOUIE BELLE BONAWITZ (C5723)

References: 5, 27-North Manchester Wabash Co IN H440

C573 SARAH CATHERINE LANTZ C57

SARAH CATHERINE LANTZ was born on 08 Aug 1847 in IN and died 10 Jul 1905 in Wabash Co., IN. She married ABNER HEETER in 1868. He was born in May 1837 in OH and died after 1910 in Wabash Co., IN..

Child of SARAH CATHERINE LANTZ and ABNER HEETER is:

1. EVA HEETER (C5731)

References: 29-Noble Wabash Co IN H289, 30-Dist 0143 North Manchester Ward 3 Wabash Co IN H28

C575 SAMUEL EDWARD LANTZ C57

SAMUEL EDWARD LANTZ was born on 23 Jul 1856. He married PHENA WILLS in 1878 in Wabash Co., IN. She was born in 1858 in IN.

Children of SAMUEL LANTZ and PHENA WILLS are:

2. JESSE VIOLA LANTZ, born 28 Jun 1879 in Wabash Co., IN; married HARRY HILL, 1898.
3. GEORGIA YOUNG LANTZ (C5752)

References: 27-North Manchester Wabash Co In H291

C576 ADA LANTZ C57

ADA LANTZ was born on 10 Jun 1858 in IN. She married ALBERT WILSON in 1889 in IN. He was born in Jul 1850 in IN

Children of ADA LANTZ and ALBERT WILSON are:

1. HARRY L. LANTZ WILSON, born on 25 Sep 1890 in Wabash Co., IN.
2. EMMA MARGARET WILSON (C5762)
3. CHARLES MELVIN WILSON, born on 01 Apr 1895 in Wabash Co., IN.

References: 5, 29-Chester Wabash Co IN H528, 30-North Manchester Wabash Co IN H85

C581 MARY DEPPEN C58

MARY DEPPEN was born 1851 in Northumberland Co., PA. She married ALBERT HOLSHUE in Northumberland Co., PA. He was born in 1852 in PA.

Children of MARY DEPPEN and ALBERT HOLSHUE are:

1. STEPHEN H. HOLSHUE (C5811)
2. FLORENCE H. HOLSHUE, born 01 Sep 1890, three children that died in infancy.

References: 5, 30-Shamokin Ward 2 Northumberland Co PA H208, 67

C582 SAMUEL DEPPEN C58

SAMUEL DEPPEN was born on 05 Sep 1853 in Northumberland Co., PA. He married LUCY ANN ZARTMAN in 1873 in Northumberland Co., PA, daughter of ADAM ZARTMAN and SUSAN FORNEY. She was born in Oct 1858 in PA. He was a farmer by occupation.

Children of SAMUEL DEPPEN and LUCY ZARTMAN are:

1. CARRIE DEPPEN (C5821)
2. MAMIE D. DEPPEN, born Mar1880 in Northumberland Co., PA; married CALVIN ZEIGLER. They resided in Washington, DC.
3. SUSAN C. DEPPEN, born Jul 1884 in Northumberland Co., PA; married JOHN E. WITMER. They resided Harrisburg, PA.

References: 5, 27-Jackson Northumberland Co PA H79, 29-Jackson Northumberland Co PA H6, 67

C583 WILLIAM H. DEPPEN C58

WILLIAM H. DEPPEN was born on 15 Mar 1856 in Northumberland Co., PA and died in 10 Dec 1877 in Northumberland Co., PA. He married KATIE TRESSLER in Northumberland Co., PA.

Children of WILLIAM DEPPEN and KATIE TRESSLER are:

1. IRVIN E. DEPPEN (C5831)
2. WILLIAM H. DEPPEN (C5832)

References: 5, 67

C584 SUSAN C. DEPPEN C58

SUSAN C. DEPPEN was born on 24 Jul 1860 in Northumberland Co., PA. She married WILLIAM BOWER on 24 May 1884 in Northumberland Co., PA son of JACOB BOWER and ______ HAAS. He was born Jan 1858 in PA. He was a school teacher and was the owner of the first livery in the area. They were Democrats and members of the Reformed Church.

Children of SUSAN DEPPEN and WILLIAM BOWER are:

1. KATIE BOWER, born on 05 Jul 1888 and died 18 Jul 1911 in Northumberland Co., PA.
2. WALTER BOWER, born 23 Oct 1893.
3. UNKNOWN CHILD, died in infancy.

References: 5, 29-Jackson Northumberland Co PA H222, 67

C591 SUSAN HUMMEL C59

SUSAN M. HUMMEL was born in Jan 1856 in PA. She married FRANK P. WALDRON on 18 Jan 1877 in Northumberland Co., PA. He was born in Sep 1853 in PA. They were Democrats and members of the Reformed Church.

Children of SUSAN HUMMEL and FRANK WALDRON are:

1. SARAH E. WALDRON, born in Nov 1878 in Northumberland Co., PA; married JOHN E. STAMM in Northumberland Co., PA; born 1872 in PA.
2. WILLIAM C. WALDRON, born in Sep 1881 in Northumberland Co., PA; married GRACE RUNDEO; resided in Reading.
3. ANNIE M. WALDRON, born in Aug 1884 in Northumberland Co., PA.
4. GEORGE O. WALDRON, born in Feb 1891 in Northumberland Co., PA; died age 12 in Northumberland Co., PA.

5. JOHN L. WALDRON, born in Mar 1897 in Northumberland Co., PA.
6. HENRY H. WALDRON; died age six in Northumberland Co., PA.

References: 29-West Chillisquaque Twp Northumberland Co PA H287, 27-Turbot Twp Northumberland Co PA H392, 30-Turbot Twp Northumberland Co PA H32, 67

C592 SARAH JANE HUMMEL C59

SARAH JANE HUMMEL was born in Mar 1858 in PA. She married B. OGDEN BROWN in PA. He was born IN Mar 1856 in PA

Children of SARAH HUMMEL and OGDEN BROWN are:

1. ELIAS HENRY BROWN, born in Sep 1884 in PA.
2. LESTER WILSON BROWN, born in Apr 1886 in PA.
3. BERTHA MAY BROWN, born in Feb 1889 in PA.

References: 29-East Buffalo Twp Union Co PA H38, 30-East Buffalo Twp Union Co PA H72

C593 CATHARINE A. HUMMEL C59

CATHARINE "KATE" A. HUMMEL was born in 1860 in PA and died before 1900-1907 in Snyder Co., PA. She married IRVIN B. ROMIG in PA. He was born in Sep 1859 in PA.

Children of CATHARINE HUMMEL and IRVIN ROMIG are:

1. AMELIA C. ROMIG, born in Sep 1885 in PA.
2. SARAH M. ROMIG, born in Nov 1888 in PA.
3. ANNA MAY ROMIG, born in May 1898 in PA.

References: 29-Selinsgrove Snyder Co PA H59, 67

C595 JOHN S. HUMMEL C59

JOHN S. HUMMEL was born in Sep 1864 in PA. He married ANNA M. GILLINGER in PA. She was born in Sep 1868 in PA.

Child of JOHN HUMMEL and ANNA GILLINGER is:

1. JACKSON H. HUMMEL, born in Feb 1890 in PA and died before 1910 in Union Co., PA.

References: 29-East Buffalo Twp Union Co PA H218, 67

C5A1 ROSANNA MAGDALINE LANTZ C5A

ROSANNA MAGDALINE LANTZ was born in Aug 1853 in Northumberland Co., PA. She married LEWIS MILLER in Northumberland Co., PA. He was born in Feb 1843 in PA

Children of ROSA MAGDALINE LANTZ and LEWIS MILLER are:

1. ELLEN MILLER

2. GEORGE MILLER, killed on P. R. R.

References: 29-Sunbury Northumberland Co PA H268

C5A3 WILLIAM RICHARD F. LANTZ C5A

WILLIAM RICHARD F. LANTZ was born in Apr 1856 in Northumberland Co., PA. He married MARY J. HEIM in Northumberland Co., PA. She was born in Jun 1856 in PA.

Children of WILLIAM LANTZ and MARY HEIM are:

1. MAY LANTZ, born in in Northumberland Co., PA.
2. SAMUEL H. LANTZ, born in Oct 1884 in Northumberland Co., PA.
3. ELLA LANTZ, born in Northumberland Co., PA.
4. AMELIA A. LANTZ, born in Sep 1896 in Northumberland Co., PA.

References: 29-Rockefeller Northumberland Co PA H146, 30-Sunbury Ward 8 Northumberland Co PA H448

C5A4 DAVID ALLISON LANTZ C5A

DAVID ALLISON LANTZ was born on 27 Jan 1859 in Rockefeller Twp., Northumberland Co., PA and died 11 Jul 1934 in Sunbury, Northumberland Co., PA. He married MARY JEANETTA LYTLE on 27 Sep 1884 in Northumberland Co., PA. She was born on 04 Mar 1865 in Lower Augusta Twp., Northumberland Co., PA

Children of DAVID LANTZ and MARY LYTLE are:

1. MAUDE L. LANTZ (C5A41)
2. LULU LANTZ (C5A42)
3. BERTHA L. LANTZ (C5A43)
4. PEARL L. LANTZ (C5A44)
5. CARRIE LANTZ, born in Apr 1896 in Sunbury, Northumberland Co., PA.
6. UNKNOWN TWIN, died in infancy.
7. UNKNOWN TWIN, died in infancy.
8. ELBERT W. LANTZ (C5A48)

References: 5, 29-Sunbury Northumberland Co PA H228, 30-Sunbury Ward 7 Northumberland Co PA H151

C5A6 ELLEN LANTZ C5A

ELLEN "ELLA" LANTZ was born in 1870 in Northumberland Co., PA. She married LEWIS GILBERT in Northumberland Co., PA.

Children of ELLEN LANTZ and LEWIS GILBERT are:

1. SAMUEL GILBERT
2. HELEN GILBERT

References: 5

C821 HIRAM E. FOX C82

HIRAM E. FOX was born in Aug 1844 in Northumberland Co., PA. He married SARAH C. in MI. She was born in May 1845 in MI.

Children of HIRAM FOX and SARAH are:

1. JOHN F. FOX, born in Jan 1872, in MI.
2. MARIA FOX, born in 1875, in MI.
3. WILLIAM FOX, born in Nov 1877, in MI.
4. HIRAM J. FOX (C8214)
5. SHERMAN H. FOX, born in Feb 1891, in MI.

References: 27-Flowerfield St Joseph Co MI 194 H35, 29- Dist 0092 Marcellus Cass Co MI H93, 30-Volinia Cass Co MI 0117 H213

C823 WILLIAM A. FOX C82

WILLIAM A. FOX was born in 1850 in Northumberland Co., PA and died 1914 in Cass Co., MI. He married LUCY J. MCMILLAN in MI. She was born in 1860 and died 1931 in Cass Co., MI. Both are buried in Bly Cemetery, Marcellus, Cass Co., MI.

References: 45

C825 OLIVER JONAS FOX C82

OLIVER JONAS FOX was born in Apr 1855 in MI and died 1928 in Cass Co., MI. He married LIDDIE in MI. She was born in Feb 1862 in MI and died 1926 in Cass Co., MI. Both are buried in Bly Cemetery, Marcellus, Cass Co., MI.

Children of OLIVER FOX and LIDDIE are:

1. ROY O. FOX (C8251)
2. BLANCHE FOX, born in Mar 1890, in MI.
3. CLINT J. FOX (C8253)
4. FLOSSIE B. FOX (C8254)

References: 29-Dist 0133 Bangor Van Buren Co MI H203, 30-Flowerfield St. Joseph Co MI

0127 H207, 10-Dist 222 Springville Wexford Co MI H59, 45

C829 HENRY LINCOLN FOX C82

HENRY LINCOLN FOX was born in 1864 in MI and died 1927 in Cass Co., MI. He married LILLIE J. in MI. She was born in 1870 in MI and died 1954. Both are buried in Bly Cemetery, Marcellus, Cass Co., MI.

Child of HENRY FOX and LILLIE is:

1. MABLE E. FOX, born in Sep 1890 in St. Joseph Co., MI.
2. CHESTER L. FOX, born in 1909 in MI; died 1988 in MI. Buried in Bly Cemetery, Marcellus, Cass Co., MI.

References: 29-Dist 0112 Flowerfield St Joseph Co MI H30, 30-Prairie Ronde Kalamazoo Co MI 0160 H188, 45

C82A JEREMIAH GRANT FOX C82

JEREMIAH GRANT FOX was born in 22 Nov 1865 in MI and died 02 Feb 1942 in Kalamazoo Co., MI. He married ALICE M. in England. She was born in Sep 1868 in MI and died 1947 in Kalamazoo Co., MI. Both are buried in Schoolcraft Cemetery, Schoolcraft, Kalamazoo Co., MI.

Child of JEREMIAH FOX and ALICE is:

1. ETHEL W. FOX (C82A1)

References: 29-Dist 0112 Flowerfield St Joseph Co MI H137, 45, 30-Prairie Ronde Kalamazoo Co MI H165

C82B SHERMAN D. FOX C82

SHERMAN D. FOX was born in 08 Feb 1868 in MI and died 13 Jan 1950 in Kalamazoo Co., MI. He married MINERVA J. in MI. She was born in Jun 1874 in MI and died 1936 in Kalamazoo Co., MI. Both are buried in Schoolcraft Cemetery, Schoolcraft, Kalamazoo Co., MI.

Children of SHERMAN FOX and MINERVA are:

2. FLOYD W. FOX, born in Feb 1894, in MI; died 1913 in Kalamazoo Co., MI; buried in Schoolcraft Cemetery, Schoolcraft, Kalamazoo Co., MI.
3. FLORENCE FOX, born in Dec 1895, in MI.
4. CLAYTON FOX, born in Apr 1898, in MI.
5. ADA FOX, born in 1903, in Kalamazoo Co., MI.
6. JESSIE FOX (m), born in 1905, in Kalamazoo Co., MI.
7. OLA FOX, born in 1908, in Kalamazoo Co., MI.
8. ELI S. FOX, born in 1913, in Kalamazoo Co., MI; died 1970 in Kalamazoo Co., MI; buried in Schoolcraft Cemetery, Schoolcraft, Kalamazoo Co., MI.

References: 29-Dist 0128 Praire Ronde Kalamazoo Co MI H42, 30- Praire Ronde Kalamazoo Co MI 0160 H157, 31-Dist 55 Schoolcraft Kalamazoo Co MI H78, 45

C831 SIMON SAMUEL LANTZ C83

SIMON SAMUEL LANTZ was born in 1831 in Northumberland Co., PA and died 16 Feb 1901 in Hessville, Sandusky Co., OH. He married MARY WAGGONER in 1852, daughter of JOHN WAGGONER. She was born in 1830 and died in 18 Nov 1879 in Washington Twp., Sandusky Co., OH.

Children are:

1. SARAH E. LANTZ, born in 1853 in Sandusky Co., OH m. (?) POSEY in Sandusky Co., OH.
2. VIENNA ELIZABETH LANTZ, born in 1857 in Sandusky Co., OH.
3. MARY C. LANTZ, born in 1858 in Sandusky Co., OH m. (?) POHLMAN in Sandusky Co., OH.
4. LOUISA M. LANTZ, born in Sep 1860 in OH; died 1952 in OH; married GEORGE W NEFF; born on 21 Apr 1860 in OH; died 02 Oct 1942 in Gibsonburg, Sandusky Co., OH.
5. SIMON EDWIN LANTZ, born in 1863 in Sandusky Co., OH.
6. NANCY ALEMEDA LANTZ, born in 1864 in Sandusky Co., OH.
7. MOSES F. LANTZ, born in 1872 in Sandusky Co., OH.
8. CHARLES A. LANTZ, born in 1876 in Sandusky Co., OH.

References: 25-Washington Sandusky Co OH H673, 26-Washington Sandusky Co OH H322, 27-Washington Sandusky Co OH H226

C832 ROSANNAH LANTZ C83

ROSANNAH LANTZ was born in 05 Oct 1835 in Northumberland Co., PA and died 05 Jul 1909 in Center Twp., Wood Co., OH. She married ISAAC WARD on 10 Aug 1851 in Wood Co., OH. He was born on 07 Mar 1827 in Perry Co., OH and died 27 Mar 1903 in Wood Co., OH. Both are buried in Scotch Ridge Cemetery, Pemberville, OH.

Child of ROSANNAH LANTZ and ISAAC WARD is:

1. HIRAM WARD, born in 1852 in Wood Co., OH.
2. ISAAC WARD, born in 1854 in Wood Co., OH.
3. LEMUEL WARD, born in 1855 in Wood Co., OH.
4. JULIA WARD, born in 1857 in Wood Co., OH.
5. EMMA WARD, born in 1860 in Wood Co., OH.
6. ERVIN JOHN WARD, born in 1862 in Wood Co., OH.
7. LEWIS A. WARD, born in 1864 in Wood Co., OH.
8. ELSIE E. WARD, born in 1866 in Wood Co., OH.
9. ELIZABETH CELESTIER WARD, born in 1868 in Wood Co., OH.
10. SARAH M. WARD, born in 1873 in Wood Co., OH.
11. LAURA L. WARD, born in 1875 in Wood Co., OH.
12. NELLIE O. WARD, born in Aug 1879 in Wood Co., OH.

References: 46-D/RL/629-4333-57, 26-Center Twp Wood Co OH H31, 27-Center Twp Wood Co OH H342

C836 MARY A. LANTZ C83

MARY A. LANTZ was born in Mar 1828 in Northumberland Co., PA. She married JOHN S. WARD. He was born in Jun 1826 in OH.

Children of MARY LANTZ and JOHN WARD are:

1. JOHN S. WARD, born in 1862 in San Joaquin Co., CA.
2. ALEXANDER B. WARD, born in 1865 in San Joaquin Co., CA.
3. DAVID L. WARD, born in 1866 in San Joaquin Co., CA.
4. LOUISA B. WARD, born in 1873 in San Joaquin Co., CA.
5. FRANCIS M. WARD, born in Feb 1875 in KS.

References: 27-Dent San Joaquin Co CA H49, 29-Dist 142 Westminster Orange Co CA H661

C841 LEVI SPELLMAN LANTZ C84

LEVI SPELLMAN LANTZ was born on 29 Jul 1836 and died 1904. He married SARAH J. LEINBACH. They resided in Chicago, IL.

Children of LEVI LANTZ and SARAH LEINBACH are:

1. CARL CLIFTON LANTZ, married HENRIETTA ROHRER. They resided in NYC, NY.
2. MARTHA ALICE LANTZ, married D. P. THORPE. They resided in Detroit, MI.
3. WALTER HENRY LANTZ, married MARY DAVIDSON. They resided in Chicago, IL.
4. MAE LANTZ, married HARRY W. LEONARD. They resided in Saratoga Springs, NY.

References: 5, 25-Colon St Joseph Co MI H731

C843 WILLIAM C. LANTZ C84

WILLIAM C. LANTZ was born on 24 Jun 1840. He married HARRIET E. SEARLE. She was born in Jul 1844 in NY. They resided at 528 Colfax Ave., South Bend, IN.

Children of WILLIAM LANTZ and HARRIET SEARLE are:

1. ADA M. LANTZ, born 29 Jul 1866 in St. Joseph Co., IN; married GEORGE M. STUDEBAKER in St. Joseph Co., IN.
2. VERNA E. LANTZ, born 28 Jan 1871 in St. Joseph Co., IN; married T. D. MOTT in St. Joseph Co., IN.
3. WILLIAM SEARLE LANTZ, born 12 Jul 1889 in St. Joseph Co., IN.

References: 5, 26-South Bend Wards 2 and 3 St Joseph Co IN H777, 27-South Bend St Joseph Co IN H500, 29-Dist 123 Portage St Joseph Co IN H15

C844 SIMON P. LANTZ C84

SIMON P. LANTZ was born on 21 Apr 1843 in PA. He married EMMA D. She was born in Dec 1852 in KY. They resided at 310 Townsend St., Lansing, MI.

Child of SIMON LANTZ and EMMA is:

1. FLORENCE LANTZ, born in Sep 1876 in IN.

References: 5, 29-Dist 38 Lansing Ward 3 Ingham Co MI H10

C849 MARGARET A. LANTZ C84

MARGARET A. LANTZ was born in Mar 1859 in MI. She married ALMON E. DAVIS. He was born in Mar 1855 in NY died before 1910 in Goshen, Elkhart Co., IN. They resided at 420 S. 6th St., Goshen, IN.

Children of MARGARET LANTZ and ALMON DAVIS are:

1. WILLIAM S. DAVIS, born Mar 1883 in MI.
2. MILDRED DAVIS, born in 1894 in IN

References: 5, 31-Dist 30 Goshen Elkhart Co IN H258, 31-Ward 4 Goshen Elkhart Co IN H123, 29-Dist 22 Goshen Elkhart Co IN H199, 30-Ward 4 Goshen Elkhart Co IN H187

C851 SAMANTHA CATHARINE LANTZ C85

SAMANTHA CATHARINE "KATE" LANTZ was born on 25 Nov 1844 in Northumberland Co., PA and died 25 Nov 1923. She married GEORGE W. ROMBACH in 27 Sep 1864 in Northumberland Co., PA, son of SILAS RAMBACH. He was born in 22 Feb 1840 in Luzerne Co., PA.

Children of SAMANTHA LANTZ and GEORGE ROMBACH are:

1. HATTIE N. ROMBACH, born 10 Sep 1866 in Northumberland Co., PA.
2. DELA G. ROMBACH, born 22 Jan 1873 in Northumberland Co., PA; married MARY TIMBERLAKE. They resided Haverford, PA.

3. HOWARD W. ROMBACH (C8513)

References: 5, 26-Delaware Northumberland Co PA H193, 27-Watsontown Northumberland Co PA H183, 27-Dist 167 Watsontown Northumberland Co PA H40, 36

C852 SIMON GRIGGS LANTZ C85

SIMON GRIGGS LANTZ was born on 22 Sep 1855 in Northumberland Co., PA. He married ANNIE E. ORWIG. They resided in Watsontown, PA.

Children of SIMON LANTZ and ANNIE ORWIG are:

1. WILLIAM MARSH LANTZ, born in Dec 1880 in Northumberland Co., PA.
2. GLENN OTTO LANTZ (C8522)
3. UNKNOWN LANTZ, born and died before 1880 in Northumberland Co., PA.
4. UNKNOWN LANTZ, born and died before 1880 in Northumberland Co., PA.

References: 5, 29-Dist 168 Watsontown Northumberland Co PA H108

C861 MARY JANE HUTCHINSON C86

MARY JANE HUTCHINSON was born on 17 Aug 1840 and died 22 Mar 1893. She married SIMON LILLEY in 1865 in Northumberland Co., PA. He was born in Sep 1833 in PA.

Children of MARY HUTCHINSON and SAMUEL LILLEY are:

1. MARGARET E. LILLEY (C8611)
2. MARY E. LILLEY, born 06 Feb 1868 in Northumberland Co., PA; married CHARLES QUIGLEY. Resided in Newberry, PA.
3. IDA L. LILLEY, born May 1872 in Northumberland Co., PA; died 1910; married ELMER BENDRE. No children.
4. HATTIE LILLEY, born May 1878 in Northumberland Co., PA; resided in Newberry, PA.
5. SIMON M. LILLEY, born Apr 1880 in Northumberland Co., PA; married RACHEL GLAZE. Resided in McEwansville, PA.
6. EDITH LILLEY, born Dec 1882 in Northumberland Co., PA; married FRANK WARNER. Resided in Watsontown, PA.

References: 5, 26-Lewis Northumberland Co PA H39, 27-Delaware Northumberland Co PA H131, 29-Dist 127 Lewis Northumberland Co PA H163

C864 ROBERT WILSON HUTCHINSON C86

Rev. ROBERT WILSON HUTCHINSON was born on 10 Feb 1848 in Northumberland Co., PA.. He married ALICE GUILFORD. They resided Six Lakes, MI.

Children of Rev. ROBERT HUTCHINSON and ALICE GUILFORD are:

1. DAUGHTER HUTCHINSON, married SAMUEL SHULL. They resided Howard City,

MI.
2. MAUD HUTCHINSON

References: 5

C871 CLARINDA KAMP C87

CLARINDA KAMP was born on 05 Jan 1849 in Northumberland Co., PA. She married BENJAMIN VAN NOSTRAND in 1870, Watsontown, Northumberland Co., PA. He was born in 1847 in NY.

Children of CLARINDA KAMP and BENJAMIN VAN NOSTRAND are:

1. MABEL VAN NOSTRAND, born 19 Apr 1874 in St. Joseph Co., MI; married HARVEY HUFFMAN, 1894 in St. Joseph Co., MI. Three daughters and two sons.
2. GEORGE VAN NOSTRAND (C8712)
3. KATE VAN NOSTRAND, born 27 Feb 1879; died Mar 1924; married SAM BROWN, Jun 1914. No children.
4. FAY VAN NOSTRAND, born 20 Feb 1884 in St. Joseph Co., MI; married MAUDE WILLIAMSON, 1905. Six children.
5. HATTIE VAN NOSTRAND, born 29 May1886 in St. Joseph Co., MI; married 1905. Two sons.

References: 5, 27-Three Rivers St Joseph Co MI H125

C874 CHARLES FRANKLIN KAMP C87

CHARLES FRANKLIN KAMP was born on 15 Oct 1854 in Northumberland Co., PA and died May 1916 in Northumberland Co., PA. He married HATTIE KELLER.

Children of CHARLES KAMP and HATTIE KELLER are:

1. CARL KAMP, married. One son.
2. JOSEPHINE KAMP, married, One son.

References: 5

C875 SIMON RYNHART KAMP C87

SIMON RYNHART KAMP was born on 08 Oct 1856 in Northumberland Co., PA and died Aug 1919 in Northumberland Co., PA. He married SUSAN SHIRDEL in Northumberland Co., PA. She was born in Dec 1866 in PA

Children of SIMON KAMP and SUSAN SHIRDEL are:

1. SHIRDEL KAMP, born in Jul 1885 in PA, married. Resided in Ridley Park, PA. Two sons.
2. BESSIE KAMP, born in Oct 1883 in PA, married.

3. ABAGAIL KAMP, born in Jun 1887 in PA, married. Resided in Los Angles, CA.Three children.
4. FREEMAN KAMP, born in Nov 1894 in PA, died before 1931.

References: 5, 29-Leiperville Delaware Co PA H174

C932 ADAM SIEGFRIED C93

ADAM SIEGFRIED was born on 25 Mar 1857 Delaware Co., OH and died 04 Jun 1942 in Delaware Co., OH. He married IDA S. DAVIS in OH. She was born in 1867 in OH and died 09 Jul 1914 in Delaware Co., OH. Both are buried in Oak Grove Cemetery, Delaware, Delaware Co., OH.

Children of ADAM SIEGFRIED and IDA DAVIS are:

1. PAUL D. SIEGFRIED, born in 1893 in OH; died 24 Oct 1918; buried in Oak Grove Cemetery, Delaware, Delaware Co., OH.
2. RUTH H. SIEGFRIED, born in 1898 in OH.

References: 30-Ward 2 Delaware Delaware Co OH H132, 45

C933 SAMUEL SIEGFRIED C93

SAMUEL SIEGFRIED was born in 1861 Delaware Co., OH and died 06 Jun 1936 in Delaware Co., OH. He married MARTHA ANN THOMAS in Delaware Co., OH. She was born in Aug 1865 in OH and died 10 Dec 1933. Both are buried in Oak Grove Cemetery, Delaware, Delaware Co., OH.

Child of SAMUEL SIEGFRIED and MARTHA THOMAS is:

1. MABEL S. SIEGFRIED, born Jul 1891 in Delaware Co., PA.

References: 29-Dist 0027 Delaware Delaware Co OH H38, 45

C934 WILMER WILLIAM SIEGFRIED C93

WILMER WILLIAM SIEGFRIED was born in 02 Apr 1864 Delaware Co., OH and died 26 Oct 1949 in Delaware Co., OH. He married GWENDOLYN in Delaware Co., OH. She was born in Dec 1876 in OH. He is buried in Oak Grove Cemetery, Delaware, Delaware Co., OH.

Children of WILMER SIEGFRIED and GWENDOLYN are:

1. WILMER H. SIEGFRIED, born in 1902 in Delaware Co., OH.
2. SAMUEL CORWIN SIEGFRIED, born in 1904 in Delaware Co., OH.

References: 29-Dist 0027 Delaware Delaware Co OH H35, 30-Delaware Delaware Co OH 0032 H190, 45

C935 CHARLES DANIEL SIEGFRIED C93

CHARLES DANIEL SIEGFRIED was born in 08 Dec 1869 Delaware Co., OH and died 01 Mar 1939 in Delaware Co., OH. He married MARY EVELYN GROSS in Delaware Co., OH. She was born 29 Aug 1870 in OH and died 02 Jun 1944 in Delaware Co., OH. Both are buried in Oak Grove Cemetery, Delaware, Delaware Co., OH.

Children of CHARLES SIEGFRIED and MARY GROSS are:

1. RAYMOND M. SIEGFRIED, born in 28 Feb 1898 in Delaware Co., OH; died 03 Nov 1957 in Delaware Co., OH; buried in Oak Grove Cemetery, Delaware, Delaware Co., OH.
2. NORMAN E. SIEGFRIED, born in Mar 1900 in Delaware Co., OH.
3. CATHARINE G. SIEGFRIED, born in 1902 in Delaware Co., OH.

References: 29-Dist 0027 Delaware Delaware Co OH H72, 30-Ward 2 Delaware Delaware Co OH H158, 45

CA21 LEVI H. FOLLMER CA2

LEVI H. FOLLMER was born on 05 Jan 1841 in Northumberland Co., PA. He married ELLEN R. WATTS in Northumberland Co., PA. She was born in Jan 1839 in PA.

Child of LEVI FOLLMER and ELLEN WATTS is:

1. ELIZABETH FOLLMER, born in Dec 1873 in Northumberland Co., PA.

References: 67, 29-Dist 0127 Lewis Northumberland Co PA H159

CA22 MARGARET C. FOLLMER CA2

MARGARET C. FOLLMER was born 11 Nov 1842 in Northumberland Co., PA. She married SAMUEL P. LERCH in Northumberland Co., PA. He was born on 23 Oct 1839 in PA.

Children of MARGARET FOLLMER and SAMUEL LERCH are:

1. Rev. CHARLES D. LERCH, was born on 17 Nov 1868 in Northumberland Co., PA.
2. SAMUEL E. LERCH, was born on 23 Aug 1871 in Northumberland Co., PA.
3. MARY T. LERCH, was born on 15 Aug 1874 in Northumberland Co., PA.
4. AMY F. LERCH, was born on 23 Feb 1878 in Northumberland Co., PA.
5. MAGGIE I. LERCH, was born on 14 May 1883 in Northumberland Co., PA.
6. SALLIE E. LERCH, was born on 14 May 1883 in Northumberland Co., PA.

References: 67, 27-Lewis Twp Northumberland Co PA 153 H146, 29-Lewis Twp Northumberland Co PA 153 H239

CA23 SARAH E. FOLLMER CA2

SARAH E. FOLLMER was born 08 Jan 1846 in Northumberland Co., PA. She married

WILLIAM H. MILLER in Northumberland Co., PA. He was born in Nov 1840 in PA and died 1909 in Northumberland Co., PA.

Children of SARAH FOLLMER and WILLIAM MILLER are:

1. FANNIE M. MILLER, born in 1871 in Northumberland Co., PA.
2. MARGARET "MAGGIE" I. MILLER, born in Apr 1878 in Northumberland Co., PA.
3. ROSIE T. MILLER, born in Dec 1879 in Northumberland Co., PA.
4. CARRIE E. MILLER, born in Jun 1884 in Northumberland Co., PA.

References: 67, 29-Dist 0168 Watsontown Northumberland Co PA H39, 27-Turbot Twp Northumberland Co PA 164 H494

CA24 SUSAN B. FOLLMER CA2

SUSAN B. FOLLMER was born on 14 Nov1847 in Northumberland Co., PA. She married JOSIAH BAKER. He was born 17 Jun 1856 in PA.

Children SUSAN FOLLMER and JOSIAH BAKER are:

1. SAMUEL E. BAKER, born in Jul 1877 in Northumberland Co., PA.
2. CYRUS O. BAKER, born in 1879 in Northumberland Co., PA.
3. SALLIE BAKER, born in Feb 1880 in Northumberland Co., PA.
4. DAISY I. BAKER, born in Dec 1882 in Northumberland Co., PA.
5. LUCY R. BAKER, born in Mar 1884 in Northumberland Co., PA.
6. MARGARET "MAGGIE" E. BAKER, born in Aug1888 in Northumberland Co., PA.

References: 67, 27-Turbot Twp Northumberland Co PA H373, 29-Dist 0164 Turbot Twp Northumberland Co PA H157, 29-Turbot Twp Northumberland Co PA 0120 H139

C1225 DAVID M. BURKET C122

DAVID M. BURKET was born in Aug 1867 in Blair Co., PA. He married BERTHA M. in Blair Co., PA. She was born in Jan 1874 in Blair Co., PA.

Children of DAVID BURKET and BERTHA are:

1. CHARLES E. BURKET, born 21 May 1894 in Blair Co., PA.
2. ELIZABETH MARY BURKET, born 22 Sep 1896 in Altoona, Blair Co., PA.
3. MILDRED BEATRICE BURKET, born 06 Sep 1899 in Altoona, Blair Co., PA.
4. JOHN MAXWELL BURKET, born 28 Aug 1901 in Altoona, Blair Co., PA.
5. MARY E. BURKET, born 1909 in Altoona, Blair Co., PA.

References: 29-Dist 0055 Ward 6 Altoona Blair Co PA H205, 30-Ward 6 Altoona Blair Co PA 0050 H143, 64

C1231 JOHN MAXWELL LANTZ C123

JOHN MAXWELL LANTZ was born in 1872 in Mechanicsburg, PA. He married VERNA T. TAYLOR, daughter of WILLIAM F. TAYLOR and EMMA HAUPT on 21 Oct 1896 in Tyrone, Blair Co., PA. She was born in 1876 in Hopewell, PA.

Children of JOHN LANTZ and VERNA TAYLOR are:

1. RICHARD T. LANTZ, born in 1898 in PA.
2. WILLIAM R. LANTZ, born in 1899 in PA.
3. EMILY K. LANTZ, born in 1903 in PA.
4. ELIZABETH H. LANTZ, born in 1905 in PA.

References: 30-Dist 0018 Gregg Centre Co PA H71, 10-Dist 86 Mount Union Ward 3 Huntingdon Co PA H311

C1252 HARRY G. LANTZ C125

HARRY G. LANTZ was born in Apr 1869, Altoona, Blair Co., PA and died in 1925 in Altoona, Blair Co., PA. He married NELLIE M. FORD 1889 in Blair Co., PA, daughter of WILLIAM FORD and CATHARINE MARSHALL. She was born in Jul 1869 in Altoona, Blair Co., PA, and died in 1959 in Hollidaysburg, Blair Co., PA. Both are buried at Greenlawn Cemetery, Hollidaysburg, Blair Co., PA. He was a machinist by occupation.

Children of HARRY LANTZ and NELLIE FORD are:

1. DOROTHY LANTZ, born 1903 in Altoona, Blair Co., PA.
2. CORA MAY LANTZ was born on 20 May 1888 in Altoona, Blair Co., PA. She married AUBREY GROVER NONEMAKER on 24 Jan 1912 in Altoona, Blair Co., PA. He was born in 1890 in Altoona, Blair Co., PA.
3. CHESTER GARFIELD LANTZ was born on 22 Sep 1889 in Altoona, Blair Co., PA.
4. WILLIAM MARTIN LANTZ was born on 21 Dec 1891 in Altoona, Blair Co., PA and died on 16 Jun 1961 in Hollidaysburg, Blair Co., PA. He married (1) ELEANOR. She was born in 1894 in PA. He married (2) ALICE LUCRETIA GLASS on 03 Aug 1932 in Greensburg, PA, daughter of FRANCIS XAVIER GLASS and REBECCA JANE YINGLING. She was born on 24 Sep 1894 in East Freedom, PA and died on 13 Oct 1972 in Hollidaysburg, Blair Co., PA. He and is 2nd wife are buried in Greenlawn Cemetery, Hollidaysburg, Blair Co., PA
5. RALPH R. LANTZ (12525)

References: 29-Dist 67 Altoona Ward 9 Blair Co PA H55, 30-Dist 0056 Altoona Ward 9 Blair Co PA H178, 10-Dist 72 Altoona Ward 9 Blair Co PA H258

C1253 FOREST MAXWELL LANTZ C125

FOREST MAXWELL LANTZ was born on 21 Mar 1870, Altoona, Blair Co., PA; died 21 Aug 1948, of a cerebral hemorrhage in Altoona, Blair Co., PA. He married CATHARINA H. LUCKARDT in 1893 in Blair Co., PA, daughter of CHARLES LUCKARDT and MARGARETHA. She was born Oct 1874 in Baltimore, MD, and died 06 Mar 1925 of pneumonia in Altoona, Blair Co., PA. He was a bridge builder by occupation and helped build Dome on Library of Congress Washington DC. During WW II he was employed by the War

Department as an Inspector of Locomotives being sent overseas. He worked as a machinist for the PRR 22 Nov 1898-Aug 1937. Both are buried in Lot O-315-317 at Rose Hill Cemetery, Altoona, Blair Co., PA. His obituary appeared in the Altoona Mirror, Altoona, Blair Co., PA on 23 Aug 1948 on page 26.

Children of FOREST LANTZ and CATHARINA LUCKARDT are:

1. ALPHARATA LANTZ was born on 04 Nov 1894 in Altoona, Blair Co., PA; died in 1978 in Altoona, Blair Co., PA; buried in Lot O-315-317 at Rose Hill Cemetery, Altoona, Blair Co., PA.
2. MARGARET LANTZ, born on 31 Oct 1895 in Altoona, Blair Co., PA, died before 1900 in Altoona Blair Co., PA.
3. RUTH LANTZ, born on 20 Dec 1896 in Altoona, Blair Co., PA; died on 14 Apr 1984 in Altoona, Blair Co., PA; buried in Lot O-315-317 at Rose Hill Cemetery, Altoona, Blair Co., PA.
4. CATHARINE LANTZ, born on 08 Dec 1899 in Altoona, Blair Co., PA; died on 04 Feb 1994 in Altoona, Blair Co., PA.
5. JENNIE LANTZ, born on 09 Sep 1905 in Altoona, Blair Co., PA; died on 03 Jun 1965 in Altoona, Blair Co., PA; buried in Lot O-315-317 at Rose Hill Cemetery, Altoona, Blair Co., PA.
6. HELEN LANTZ, born on 03 Jan 1907 in Pittsburgh, Allegheny Co., PA; died on 03 Jul 1908 in Altoona, Blair Co., PA; buried in Lot O-315-317 at Rose Hill Cemetery, Altoona, Blair Co., PA.

References: 30-Dist 0056 Altoona Ward 9 Blair Co PA H216, 10-Dist 72 Altoona Ward 9 Blair Co PA H172

C1255 ADEN MELVIN LANTZ C125

ADEN MELVIN LANTZ was born on 22 Dec 1877 in Altoona, Blair Co., PA and died 05 Jan 1963, Altoona, Blair Co., PA. He married J. MARY ALLEN in 1901 in Blair Co., PA. She was born 1885 in PA, and died 08 Jan 1954 in Altoona, Blair Co., PA. He was machinist by occupation. His obituary appeared in the Altoona Mirror, Altoona, PA on 07 Jan 1963 on page 20. They were members of the Lady of Lourdes Catholic Church.

Children of ADEN LANTZ and J. ALLEN are:

1. ADEN W ILLIAM L ANTZ, born on 17 Nov 1899 in Lilly, PA; died on 23 Apr 1963 in Altoona, Blair Co., PA; married MARY S. SELWITZ; born on 02 Jun 1902 in Altoona, Blair Co., PA; died on 04 Mar 2001 in Hialeah, FL. Both are buried in Lot L-380-382 at Rose Hill Cemetery, Altoona, Blair Co., PA.
2. VALORIE LANTZ, born on 17 Mar 1903 in Altoona, Blair Co., PA.
3. NELLIE MAY LANTZ, born on 06 Jan 1905 in Altoona, Blair Co., PA, married (?) CASSIDY; resided Hollidaysburg, PA.
4. PAUL LANTZ, born in 1908 in Altoona, Blair Co., PA.
5. HOWARD LANTZ, born in 1910 in Altoona, Blair Co., PA.
6. AGNES F. LANTZ (C12556)
7. WINIFRED LANTZ, born in 1915 in Altoona, Blair Co., PA.

8. SARAH JANE LANTZ, born in Apr 1918 in Altoona, Blair Co., PA; married (?) BOLAND.
9. ROBERT LANTZ, born in 1924 in Altoona, Blair Co., PA.
10. HELEN LANTZ (C1255A)

References: 10-Dist 72 Altoona Ward 9 Blair Co PA H293, 30-Dist 0056 Altoona Ward 9 Blair Co PA H206, 31-Dist 28 Altoona Blair Co PA H46, 40-Altoona Blair Co PA 7-13A H261, 40-Altoona Blair Co PA 7-49 H122

C1256 ELBRIDGE GARFIELD LANTZ C125

ELBRIDGE GARFIELD LANTZ was born on 13 Jul 1881 in Altoona, Blair Co., PA, and died 04 Dec 1950 of a myocarditis infarction in Altoona, Blair Co., PA. He married (1) BESSIE MAY CARTWRIGHT on 11 Sep 1903 in Youngstown, Mahoning Co., OH, daughter of JAMES CARTWRIGHT and MARGARET E. "BESSIE" GUNNETT. She was born 12 Nov 1888 in Oreminea, Blair Co., PA, and died 19 May 1927 in Altoona, Blair Co., PA. He married (2) WILLIVENE D. EAGLER in 1932 in Altoona, Blair Co., PA, daughter of JAMES EAGLER and MERRILL PENNINGTON. She was born 12 Jul 1904 in La Jose, PA, and died 09 Jul 1989 in Altoona, Blair Co., PA. 1904-1910 for a few years was a Semi-Pro Baseball Player in Pittsburgh, Allegheny Co., PA and 1910-1940, blacksmith and machinist PRR retiring after 30 years service. All are buried in Lot R-534 at Rose Hill Cemetery, Altoona, Blair Co., PA. Her obituary

Children of ELBRIDGE LANTZ and BESSIE CARTWRIGHT are:

1. CLYDE RAYMOND LANTZ (C12561)
2. HELEN MARGARET LANTZ, born Jan 1906, Pittsburgh, Allegheny Co., PA; died 03 Jul 1908, Altoona, Blair Co., PA; never married; She was buried in Fairview Cemetery by the Hickey Funeral Home of Altoona, Blair Co., PA. Helen died of malnutrition. Her funeral was held at 2429 Maple Avenue, Altoona, Blair Co., PA. She was buried on 07 Apr 1904, Buried Rose Hill Cemetery, Altoona, Blair Co., PA.
3. MAE BESSIE LANTZ, born 31 Dec 1908, Altoona, Blair Co., PA; died 27 Feb 1985, Philadelphia, Philadelphia Co., PA; married GEORGE J. HAUSER, 26 Sep 1927, Altoona, Blair Co., PA; born 08 Mar 1901, PA; died 30 Jun 1974, Philadelphia, Philadelphia Co., PA. They are buried at Cedar Hill Cemetery Philadelphia, Philadelphia Co., PA.
4. FREDA JOSEPHINE LANTZ, born 18 May 1922, Altoona, Blair Co., PA; died 20 Dec 1999, Corning, Steuben Co., NY; married JAMES WESLEY GOOD, 22 Dec 1939, Cumberland, MD; born 18 Jul 1916, Lilly, Cambria Co., PA; died 03 Sep 1996, Corning, NY. They are buried at Beaver Dams Cemetery, Beaver Dams, NY.

Children of ELBRIDGE LANTZ and WILLIVENE EAGLER are:

5. ADELBERT G. LANTZ, born 19 Aug 1933, Altoona, Blair Co., PA; died 05 Oct 1957, from an auto accident Altoona, Blair Co., PA. He served in the Korean War in the U.S. Air Force. He is buried at Rose Hill Cemetery Altoona, Blair Co., PA.

References: 43, 44, 10-Altoona Blair Co PA H143, 32-Altoona Blair Co PA H597, 40-Altoona Blair Co PA H224, 46-D/EGL/100671/DOH PA, 46-M/EGL&BMC/1903Pg67/Mahoning Co OH, 46-DBMC/47923/DOH PA

RUTH ANNA MAE LANTZ, GEORGE HOWARD LANTZ, DELBERT LANTZ and BESSIE MAE (LANTZ) HAUSER

CLYDE RAYMOND LANTZ

Date of birth is incorrect on grave stone, his WW I and WW II draft registration says 1881 and his father's Civil War Pension Record below also says 1881

ELBRIDGE (AL) LANTZ

Retired PRR blacksmith and former baseball player, died unexpectedly at his home, 2429 Maple avenue, Monday morning at 12:30 o'clock.

Mr. Lantz was born in Altoona, July 13, 1880, the son of Jacob M. and Bell (Kepperly) Lantz. He was active in Blair county baseball circles at one time and a member of the Pittsburg semi-professional baseball circles. Mr. Lantz retired from the Pennsylvania Railroad in 1940 after 30 years of service. He was twice married, his first wife, Bessie (Cartwright) Lantz died 23 years ago.

Surviving are his second wife, Mrs. Willivene (Eagler) Lantz, one son, Delbert of Altoona; two daughters, Mrs. George Houser of Janesville, Wis.; Mrs. James Good of Hastings and a step-son, Roy J. Eagler of Altoona; 11 grandchildren, two brothers and one sister, Aden, Clyde and Mrs. Nellie Beech, all of Altoona. A son, Clyde Lantz, died two years ago.

He was a member of the Presbyterian church.

Friends will be received at the N. A. Stevens mortuary.

MRS. BESSIE LANTZ

[illegible] of E. G. Lantz of 2919 Pine avenue, died at the Altoona hospital last [illegible]ning at 6.55 o'clock of a compli[illegible] of diseases. She was the daugh[illegible] of Mr. and Mrs. James Cartwright, [illegible]ceased, formerly of Springfield [illegible], and was aged 39 years, 2 [illegible] and 7 days. She was mar[illegible] Sept. 8, 1903, to E. G. Lantz and [illegible] since then at the above ad[illegible] Four children were born to [illegible], the second, Helen, preceding [illegible] brother to the grave. With the [illegible] and three children survive, Clyde [illegible] and Freda, all at home. The [illegible] brothers and sisters also sur[illegible] George W. of Ormenia, Mrs. [illegible] Black and Mrs. Ella Stevens [illegible]liamsburg, Mrs. A. J. Black of [illegible] and Mrs. John Gingrich of [illegible]town, Pa. The deceased was a [illegible]ber of the Eighth Avenue Meth[illegible] church where funeral services [illegible] be held on Sunday at 3.30 p. m. [illegible]ment will be made in Rose Hill [illegible]metery. MAY 20

CARDS OF THANKS.

We desire to return our sincere thanks for the kindness and sympathy extended us by friends and neighbors, during the illness and death of our Beloved Wife and Mother. Also for the beautiful floral offerings and use of automobiles as well as those who offered the use of same but were not needed.

MR. ELBRIDGE G. LANTZ AND FAMILY.

MAY 26

C1257 CLYDE RAYMOND LANTZ C125

CLYDE RAYMOND LANTZ was born on 10 Jun 1885, Altoona, Blair Co., PA and died 11 Sep 1951, of a myocarditis infarction in Altoona, Blair Co., PA. He married PEARL AYERS 1909 in Blair Co., PA, daughter of DANIEL AYERS and SOPHIA. She was born 15 May 1890 in PA and died Feb 1966 in Altoona, Blair Co., PA. He was a laborer by occupation. Both are buried at Lot R-590 at Rose Hill Cemetery, Altoona, Blair Co., PA. His obituary appeared in the Altoona Mirror, Altoona, PA on 11 Sep 1951, page 36.

Children of CLYDE LANTZ and PEARL AYERS are:

1. EDNA RUTH LANTZ, born in 1910 in Altoona, Blair Co., PA; married P. J. LAMBERT.
2. VIOLA E. LANTZ (C12572)
3. DOROTHY LANTZ, born in 1920 in Altoona, Blair Co., PA, married (?) HESS

References: 30-Dist 0056 Altoona Ward 9 Blair Co PA H166, 10-Dist 72 Altoona Ward 9 Blair Co PA H286, 31-Dist 28 Altoona Blair Co PA H99, 40-Altoona Blair Co PA 7-40A H100

C2591 CHARLES F. ESHBACH C259

CHARLES F. ESHBACH was born in Jan 1874 in NY and died before 1930 in Buffalo, Erie Co., NY. He married CATHERINE in Buffalo, Erie Co., NY. She was born in1873 in NY.

Child of CHARLES ESHBACH and CATHERINE is:

1. MILDRED ESHBACH, born 1904 in Buffalo, Erie Co., NY.

References: 30-Dist 0120 Buffalo Ward 13 Erie Co NY H187, 10-Dist 0120 Buffalo Ward 13 Erie Co NY H176

C3113 FRANKLIN A. NEWCOMER C311

FRANKLIN A. NEWCOMER was born in 31 Dec 1866 in Northumberland Co., PA. He married JENNIE L. B. CLEWELL in Northumberland Co., PA, daughter of GODFREY WILLIAM CLEWELL and CATHARINE ARTLEY. She was born in Nov 1870 in PA. They were Independents where political issues were concerned and members of the Lutheran Church of Christ at Milton, PA.

Children FRANKLIN NEWCOMER and are:

1. FRANKLIN C. NEWCOMER, born in Jun 1895 in Northumberland Co., PA
2. JOHN WILLIAM NEWCOMER, born in 1905 in Northumberland Co., PA

References: 67, 29-Dist 0164 Turbot Twp Northumberland Co PA H123

C3131 ANSENATH M. STOVER C313

ANSENATH M. STOVER was born on 16 Feb 1859 in Stephenson Co., IL and died in 1918 in Centre Co., PA She married JOHN HOSTERMAN DELONG in PA, son of JOHN DELONG and LUCRETIA JAYNES. He was born on 29 Jan 1854 in Centre Co., PA and died in 1923 in Centre Co., PA. Both are buried in Livonia Cemetery, Livonia, Centre Co., PA.

Children of ANSENATH STOVER and JOHN DELONG are:

1. THOMAS STOVER DELONG, born on 28 Apr 1882 and died 03 Mar 1885 in Centre Co., PA. Buried in Livonia Cemetery, Livonia, Centre Co., PA.
2. CHARLES A. DELONG, born in Nov 1883 in Centre Co., PA.
3. ARCTURA DELONG, born in Jul 1886 in Centre Co., PA.
4. SUSAN LUCRETIA DELONG, born on 28 Nov 1888 and died 23 Mar 1890 in Centre Co., PA. Buried in Livonia Cemetery, Livonia, Centre Co., PA.
5. JOHN DELONG, born on 23 Nov 1896 and died in Dec 1896 in Centre Co., PA. Buried in Livonia Cemetery, Livonia, Centre Co., PA.

References: 29-Dist 0025 Miles Twp Centre Co PA H145, 45, 30-Miles Twp Centre Co PA 0026 H224

JOHN HOSTERMAN DELONG

ANSENATH M. STOVER

C3171 SAMUEL KOSTENBADER C317

SAMUEL KOSTENBADER was born in Sep 1848 in Stephenson Co., IL. He married MARY ANN in Stephenson Co., IL. She was born in Dec 1852 in IL.

Children of SAMUEL KOSTENBADER and MARY ANN are:

1. LAURA M. KOSTENBADER, born in 1877 in Stephenson Co., IL.
2. AARON S. KOSTENBADER, born in 1879 in Stephenson Co., IL.
3. CLEO J. KOSTENBADER, born in Jun 1886 in Stephenson Co., IL

References: 27-Harlem Twp Stephenson Co IL 176 H135, 29-Dist 0098 Harlem Twp Stephenson Co IL H122

C3181 WILLIAM KELLY C318

WILLIAM KELLY was born on 18 Jan 1866 Fayette Co., IA and died 19 Oct 1936 in Fayette Co., IA. He married MARY E. born on 25 Apr 1868 in MN and died 22 Apr 1955 in Fayette Co., IA. Both are buried in Grandview Cemetery, Fayette, Fayette Co., IA.

Children of WILLIAM KELLY and MARY are:

1. PAUL L. KELLY, born in 1901 in Fayette Co., IA.
2. HELLEN L. KELLY, born in 1901 in Fayette Co., IA.

References: 45, 29- Dist 0073 Fayette Fayette Co IA H286, 30-Fayette Fayette Co IA 0083 H25

C3182 ERNEST KELLY C318

ERNEST KELLY was born in 1869 in Fayette Co., IA and died in 1948 in Fayette Co., IA. He married ELIZABETH MARIAN DURFEY in Fayette Co., IA. She was born in 1878 IA and died in 1966 in Fayette Co., IA. Both are buried in Wadena Cemetery, Wadena, Fayette Co., IA.

Children of ERNEST KELLY and ELIZABETH are:

1. NELLY JANET KELLY, born in 15 Jun 1910 in Fayette Co., IA; died 20 Mar 1998 in Goose Creek, Berkeley Co., SC; married (1) THOMAS JOSEPH BERGEN; born on 09 Mar 1910 in Volga, Clayton Co., IA; died 12 Sep 1967 in Elkader, Clayton Co., IA She and 2nd husband are buried in Saint Joseph's Cemetery, Elkader, Clayton Co., IA; married (2) William N. Bjerke; born on May 14, 1904 in Ulen, Clay Co., MN; died Nov. 11, 1991; buried Concordia Cemetery, Fertile, Polk Co., MN.
2. RUSSELL R. KELLY, born in 1914 and died in 1915 in Fayette Co., IA. Buried in Wadena Cemetery, Wadena, Fayette Co., IA.

References: 45

C3194 WINSLOW P. WHEELOCK C319

WINSLOW P. WHEELOCK was born in Oct 1879 in Stephenson Co., IL. He married CORA M. in Stephenson Co., IL. She was born in 1878 in IA.

Children of WINSLOW WHEELOCK and CORA are:

1. GUY WHEELOCK, born in 1902 in CO.
2. MYRTLE WHEELOCK, born in 1905 in CO.
3. NELLIE F. WHEELOCK, born in 1912 in CO.
4. CORA W. WHEELOCK, born in 1916 in CO.

References: 10-Dist 60 Aroya Cheyenne Co CO H12, 31-Dist 48 Fort Collins Larimer Co CO H86

C3331 CHARLES H. LANTZ C333

CHARLES H. LANTZ was born on 20 May 1876 in PA. He married BERTHA WILKS 1904.

Children of CHARLES LANTZ and BERTHA WILKS are:

1. CHARLES D. LANTZ
2. DOROTHY LANTZ, born 15 Aug 1909

References: 5

C3332 DANIEL O. LANTZ C333

DANIEL O. LANTZ was born on 20 May 1876 in PA. He married MYRTLE RISDEN in Lewiston, ID. She was born in 1883 in WA.

Children of DANIEL O. LANTZ and MYRTLE RISDEN are:

1. ELNA M. LANTZ (C33321)
2. ETTA LANTZ (C33322)
3. DANIEL O. LANTZ, born 29 Jul 1903 in ID; married GEORGIA WARREN, 1928 in ID.
4. EMMA LANTZ (C33324)
5. WILLIAM LANTZ, born 24 Aug 1907 in ID.
6. CECIL LANTZ, born 10 May 1915 in ID.

References: 5, 30-Dist 0216 Mason Nez Perce Co ID H159, 10-Dist 136 Morrow Lewis Co ID H37

C3333 WILLIAM DAVID LANTZ C333

WILLIAM DAVID LANTZ was born on 18 Apr 1883 in KS. He married MAURINE

"MAMIE" WILKS, 1909. She was born in 1891 in WA.

Children of WILLIAM DAVID LANTZ and MAURINE WILKS are:

1. JOHN D. LANTZ, born 02 Oct 1910 in Morrow Co., ID.
2. ETHEL MAY LANTZ, born 04 Feb 1911 in Morrow Co., ID.

References: 5, 31-Dist 51 East Orchards Nez Perce Co ID H131, 10-Dist 136 Morrow Co ID H2

C3335 SARAH C. LANTZ C333

SARAH C. LANTZ was born on 13 Dec 1890 in KS. She married ALPHA E. HOWERTON. He was born in 1887 in MO.

Children of SARAH LANTZ and ALPHA HOWERTON are:

1. LENA A. HOWERTON, in 1914 in ID
2. CECIL E. HOWERTON, in 1917 in ID.
3. ROY M. HOWERTON, in 1918 in ID.
4. EDNA HOWERTON, in 1921 in Nez Perce Co., ID
5. HELEN HOWERTON, in 1930 in Nez Perce Co., ID.

References: 5, 10-Dist 141 Gifford Nez Perce Co ID H129, 31-Dist 50 Webb Nez Perce Co ID H38

C3451 DANIEL F. RAUP C345

DANIEL F. RAUP was born in Sep 1861 in Northumberland Co., PA. He married CLARA V. HOTTENSTEIN in Northumberland Co., PA. She was born in Feb 1858 in PA.

Children of DANIEL RAUP and CLARA HOTTENSTEIN are:

1. GERTRUDE RAUP, born in May 1883 in Northumberland Co., PA.
2. IZORA E. RAUP, born in Jan 1888 in Northumberland Co., PA.
3. HOMER D. RAUP, born in Jun 1890 in Northumberland Co., PA.
4. STANLEY K. RAUP, born in Dec 1896 in Northumberland Co., PA.

References: 29-Dist 0164 Turbot Twp Northumberland Co PA H121, 30-Kelly Twp Union Co PA 0165 H97

C3452 MARY ELIZABETH RAUP C345

MARY ELIZABETH RAUP was born in Sep 1863 in Northumberland Co., PA. She married ELMER STRINE in Northumberland Co., PA. He was born in Sep 1864 in PA.

Children of MARY RAUP and ELMER STRINE are:

1. SARAH STRINE, born in Feb 1884 in Northumberland Co., PA.
2. HELEN STRINE, born in Apr 1886 in Northumberland Co., PA.

References: 29-Dist 0133 Ward 4 Milton Northumberland Co PA H125

C3454 IDA C. RAUP C345

IDA C. RAUP was born in Mar 1868 in Northumberland Co., PA. She married WILLIAM P. HOTTENSTEIN in Northumberland Co., PA. He was born in May 1863 in PA.

Children of IDA RAUP and WILLIAM HOTTENSTEIN are:

1. MERRILL F. HOTTENSTEIN, born Jan 1892 in Northumberland Co., PA.
2. WILFRED E. HOTTENSTEIN, born Feb 1895 in Northumberland Co., PA.

References: 29-Dist 0164 Turbot Twp Northumberland Co PA H135, 30-Turbot Twp Northumberland Co PA 0120 H119

C3456 JOHN NEWTON RAUP C345

JOHN NEWTON RAUP was born in Jun 1872 in Northumberland Co., PA; married BESSIE M. KRUMM in Northumberland Co., PA. She was born in Jul 1877 in PA.

Children of JOHN RAUP and BESSIE KRUMM are:

1. CLARA E. RAUP, born in Oct 1894 in Northumberland Co., PA.
2. WILLIAM F. RAUP, born in Jul 1897 in Northumberland Co., PA.

References: Dist 0234 Milton Northumberland Co PA H83

C3457 CLARENCE WILLIAM RAUP C345

CLARENCE WILLIAM RAUP was born in 1875 in Northumberland Co., PA; married (1) NINA YOUNG in Northumberland Co., PA; married (2) FLORENCE WERTZ in Northumberland Co., PA.

Child of CLARENCE RAUP and NINA YOUNG is:

1. CATHERINE E. RAUP, born in 1901 in Northumberland Co., PA.

Children of CLARENCE RAUP and FLORENCE WERTZ are:

2. DOROTHY E. RAUP, born in 1909 in Northumberland Co., PA.

3. SARAH I. RAUP, born in 1911 in Northumberland Co., PA.
4. RUTH RAUP, born in 1919 in Northumberland Co., PA.

References: 30-Ward 3 Milton Northumberland Co PA 0074 H421, 10-Dist 188 White Deer Union Co PA H23

C3458 CHARLES FRANKLIN RAUP C345

CHARLES FRANKLIN RAUP was born in Dec 1878 in Northumberland Co., PA. He married CORA B. MILLER in Rockford, Winnebago Co., IL, daughter of JOHN L. MILLER and LOIS A. She was born in 1882 in IL.

Child of CHARLES RAUP and CORA MILLER is:

1. BARBARA J. RAUP, born in 1924 in IL.

References: 10-Dist 197 Ward 4 Rockford Winnebago Co IL, 31-Dist 32 Rockford Winnebago Co IL H674

C3461 ROLLAND SYDNEY FOLLMER C346

ROLLAND SYDNEY FOLLMER was born on 27 Jul 1871 in Northumberland Co., PA. He married MARY M. UTT in Mar 1891 in Northumberland Co., PA, daughter of DAVID UTT and MARGARET J. FOLLMER. They were Democrats and members of the Follmer Lutheran Church.

Children of ROLLAND FOLLMER and MARY UTT are:

1. RHEA M. FOLLMER, born in Northumberland Co., PA.
2. BERTHA M. FOLLMER, born in Northumberland Co., PA.
3. SCHAEFFER U. FOLLMER, born in Northumberland Co., PA.

References: 67

C3462 BERTHA GERTRUDE FOLLMER C346

BERTHA GERTRUDE FOLLMER was born in 1875 in Northumberland Co., PA. She married J. WESLEY WOLFE in Northumberland Co., PA.

Child of BERTHA FOLLMER and J. WOLFE is:

1. GLENN WOLFE, born Northumberland Co., PA.

References: 67

C3481 FREDERICK VORIS FOLLMER C348

FREDERICK VORIS FOLLMER was born on 13 Dec 1885 in Northumberland Co., PA and died 02 May 1971 in Northumberland Co., PA. He married ELLA BROWN in Northumberland Co., PA. She was born on 13 Nov 1891 in PA and died 01 Sep 1976 in Northumberland Co., PA. Both are buried in Harmony Cemetery, Milton, Northumberland Co., PA.

Child of FREDERICK FOLLMER and ELLA BROWN is:

1. MARY ELIZABETH FOLLMER, born in 1924 in Northumberland Co., PA.

References: 45, 31-Dist 29 Milton Northumberland Co PA H122

C3482 MALCOLM MURRAY FOLLMER C348

MALCOLM MURRAY FOLLMER was born on 14 Feb 1890 in Northumberland Co., PA and died 09 Jul 1858 in Northumberland Co., PA. He married GRACE PHOEBE GODCHARLES. in Northumberland Co., PA. She was born on 27 Oct 1889 in PA and died 10 Apr 1986 in Northumberland Co., PA. Both are buried in Harmony Cemetery, Milton, Northumberland Co., PA.

Child of MALCOLM FOLLMER and GRACE GOODCHARLES is:

1. PHOEBE G. FOLLMER, born in 1923 in Northumberland Co., PA.

References: 45, 31-Dist 30 Milton Northumberland Co PA H192

C35C1 MARGARET ROUSEY GASCOYNE C35C

MARGARET ROUSEY GAŚCOYNE was born in Nov 1886 in Niagara Co., NY. She married FRANK FELLOWS in Lockport, Niagara Co., NY.

Child of MARGARET GASCOYNE and FRANK FELLOWS is:

1. MILTON L. FELLOWS, born 1907 Lockport, Niagara Co., NY.

References: 30-Lockport Ward 3 Niagara Co NY H104

C35C2 CORA B. GASCOYNE C35C

CORA B. GASCOYNE was born Aug 1891 in Niagara NY. She married (?) STANDER in Niagara Co., NY. He died before 1940 in Niagara Co., NY.

Child of CORA GASCOYNE and (?) STANDER is:

1. CHARLES H. STANDER, born 1919 in Lockport, Niagara Co., NY.

References: 40-Lockport Niagara Co NY H114, 31-Lockport Niagara Co NY H30, 10-Lockport Ward 3 Niagara Co NY H216

C3821 FRANKLIN H. SILVERS C382

FRANKLIN H. SILVERS was born in Feb 1868 in Clinton Co., MI and died in 1920 in Clinton Co., MI. He married LYDIA E. MOWAT in Clinton Co., MI, daughter of GEORGE MOWAT. She was born in Oct 1877 in MI. He is buried in Mount Rest Cemetery, Saint Johns, Clinton Co., MI.

Child of FRANKLIN SILVERS and IDA is:

1. OTTO F. SILVERS, born in Jan 1899 in Clinton Co., MI.
2. UNKNOWN SILVERS, born and died before 1910 in Clinton Co., MI.
3. UNKNOWN SILVERS, born and died before 1910 in Clinton Co., MI.

References: 29-Bingham Twp Clinton Co MI H72, 30-St Johns Ward 1 Clinton Co MI H296, 45

C3826 WILLIAM P. SILVERS C382

WILLIAM P. SILVERS was born in Jan 1879 in Clinton Co., MI and died in 1948 in Clinton Co., MI. He married LILLIE C. in Clinton Co., MI. She was born in 1879 in MI and died 1976 in Clinton Co., MI. Both are buried in Mount Rest Cemetery, Saint Johns, Clinton Co., MI.

Child of WILLIAM SILVERS and LILLIE is:

1. MAXINE SILVERS, born in 1913 in Clinton Co., MI.

References: 31-Dist 13 Greenbush Twp Clinton Co MI H71, 45

C3828 MANNING J. SILVERS C382

MANNING J. SILVERS was born in Jun 1886 in Clinton Co., MI and died 1965 in Clinton Co., MI; married NINO STEADMAN in Clinton Co., MI, daughter of __________ STEADMAN and MARY A. She was born in 1891; died in 1949 in Clinton Co., MI. Both are buried in Union Home Cemetery, Saint Johns, Clinton Co., MI.

Child of MANNING SILVERS and NINO STEADMAN is:

1. MARTHA E. SILVERS, born in 1929 in MI.

References: 31-Dist 1026 Nankin Wayne Co MI H403, 45

C3856 GEORGE F. CORKIN C385

GEORGE F. CORKIN was born in Oct 1893 in MI. He married EMMA. She was born in 1909 in KS.

Children of GEORGE CORKIN and EMMA are:

1. GEORGE F. CORKIN, born in 1931 in Dakota Co., NE.
2. ELMIRA CORKIN, born in 1933 in Dakota Co., NE.
3. EMMA LOU CORKIN, born in 1935 in Dakota Co., NE.
4. ROBERT CORKIN, born in 1937 in Dakota Co., NE.
5. WILLIAM CORKIN, born in 1938 in Dakota Co., NE.

References: 40-St Johns Precinct Dakota Co NE

C3966 CARRIE MAY METZGER C396

CARRIE MAY METZGER was born in Oct 1889 in Union Co., PA. She married JOHN D. MEEK in Union Co., PA. He was born in 1884 in PA.

Children of CARRIE METZGER and JOHN MEEK are:

1. DONALD F. MEEK, born in 1912 in Union Co., PA.
2. HELEN R. M. MEEK, born in 1920 in Union Co., PA.

References: 10-Gregg Twp Union Co PA H83

C4111 JACOB F. MACKERT C411

JACOB F. MACKERT was born in Jun 1874 in Northumberland Co., PA. He married IDA MAY in Northumberland Co., PA. She was born in Feb 1879 in PA.

Children of JACOB MACKERT and IDA are:

1. WILLIAM "WILLIE" J. MACKERT, born in Nov 1896 in Northumberland Co., PA; married ELVENA A. in Northumberland Co., PA; born in 1900 in PA.
2. V. CHARLES MACKERT (C41112)
3. HELEN MACKERT, born in Oct 1899 in Northumberland Co., PA.
4. EDWARD WALTER MACKERT (C41114)
5. MABLE I. MACKERT, born in Oct 1908 in Northumberland Co., PA.
6. C. SARAH MACKERT, born in Oct 1910 in Northumberland Co., PA.

References: 29-Dist 0160 Sunbury Northumberland Co PA H207, 30-Ward 8 Sunbury Northumberland Co PA 0118 F433, 10-Dist 137 Sunbury Northumberland Co PA H286, 31-Dist 72 Sunbury Northumberland PA H225, 31-Dist 75 Sunbury Northumberland PA H177

C4124 EDWARD F. GASS C412

EDWARD F. GASS was born in 12 Dec 1883 in Sunbury, Northumberland Co., PA. He married FRANCES E. BRAND on 03 Sep 1909 in Northumberland Co., PA, daughter of WILLIAM F. BRAND and LAURA TAYLOR. He is a member and founder of the firm of WETZEL & GASS of Sunbury, PA dealing in electrical equipment and supplies.

Children of EDWARD GASS and FRANCES BRAND are:

1. CHARLES J. GASS, born in 1911 in Northumberland Co., PA.
2. WILLIAM F. GASS, born in 1912 in Northumberland Co., PA.
3. LAURA J. GASS, born in 1916 in Northumberland Co., PA.

References: 10-Dist 137 Ward 8 Sunbury Northumberland Co PA H327, 40-Sunbury Northumberland Co PA 49-95 H247

C4141 PETER S. GASS C414

PETER S. GASS was born May 1878 in Northumberland Co., PA. He married MARY “NETTIE” A. in Northumberland Co., PA. She was born in 1881 in PA.

Children of PETER GASS and MARY are:

1. HANNAH MILDRED GASS, born in 1904 in Northumberland Co., PA.
2. THELMA L. GASS, born in 1909 in Northumberland Co., PA.
3. BAILEY G. GASS, born in 1913 in Northumberland Co., PA.

References: 31-Dist 69 Sunbury Northumberland Co PA H410, 30-Ward 3 Steelton Dauphin Co PA 0122 H293, 10-Dist 32 Hemlock Columbia Co PA H57

C4142 MARTIN H. GASS C414

MARTIN H. GASS was born Nov 1880 in Northumberland Co., PA. He married KATIE in Northumberland Co., PA. She was born in 1880 in PA.

Children of MARTIN GASS and KATIE are:

1. MARTIN E. GASS, born in 1906 in Northumberland Co., PA.
2. RUTH E. GASS, born in 1908 in Northumberland Co., PA.
3. PAUL H. GASS, born in 1917 in Northumberland Co., PA.

References: 30-Ward 9 Sunbury Northumberland 0119 H259, 10-Dist 86 Lower Augusta Twp Northumberland Co PA H81

C4245 SABINA J. GASS C424

SABINA J. GASS was born in 1868 in Northumberland Co., PA. She married JACOB BROCIOUS in Northumberland Co., PA. He was born in 1866 in PA.

Children of SABINA GASS and JACOB BROCIOUS are:

1. CORA J. BROCIOUS, born in 1895 in Northumberland Co., PA.
2. CLAYTON L. BROCIOUS (C42452)

References: 30-Upper Augusta Twp Northumberland Co PA 0121 H99

C4246 SAMUEL E. GASS C424

SAMUEL E. GASS was born in Jan 1869 in Northumberland Co., PA. He married MARGARET E. in Northumberland Co., PA. She was born in Feb 1866 in PA and died before 1910 in Northumberland Co., PA.

Children of SAMUEL GASS and MARGARET are:

1. HERMAN L. GASS (C42461)
2. DAISY A. GASS, born in Oct 1895 in Northumberland Co., PA.
3. IRVIN E. GASS, born in May 1899 in Northumberland Co., PA.
4. MARGARET M. GASS, born in May 1901 in Northumberland Co., PA.
5. CLARA A. GASS, born in May 1905 in Northumberland Co., PA.

References: 29-Dist 0162 Sunbury Northumberland Co PA H340, 30-Ward 7 Sunbury Northumberland Co PA 0117 H7

C4246 ADAM D. GASS C424

ADAM D. GASS was born in Jun 1877 in Northumberland Co., PA. He married EDITH J. in Northumberland Co., PA. She was born in 1889 in Northumberland Co., PA.

Children of ADAM GASS and EDITH are:

1. JACOB R. EMERSON GASS, born in 1907 in Northumberland Co., PA.
2. GORDON E. GASS, born in 1908 in Northumberland Co., PA.
3. CHARUS L. GASS, born in 1909 in Northumberland Co., PA.
4. WILLIAM GASS, born in 1912 in Northumberland Co., PA.
5. WARREN W. GASS, born in 1917 in Northumberland Co., PA.
6. D. ALBERT GASS, born in 1925 in Northumberland Co., PA.

References: 30-Upper Augusta Twp Northumberland Co PA 0121 H100, 10-Dist 86 Lower Augusta Twp Northumberland Co PA H17, 31-Dist 24 Upper Augusta Twp Northumberland Co PA H33

C4246 CLAYTON E. GASS C424

CLAYTON E. GASS was born in Nov 1878 in Northumberland Co., PA. He married LOTTIE M. in Northumberland Co., PA. She was born in 1883 in PA.

Children of CLAYTON GASS and LOTTIE are:

1. ELMER GASS, born in 1907 in Northumberland Co., PA.
2. HENRY J. GASS, born in 1912 in Northumberland Co., PA.
3. MABEL M. GASS, born in 1913 in Northumberland Co., PA.

References: 30-Upper Augusta Twp Northumberland Co PA 0121 H101, 10-Dist 140 Upper Augusta Twp Northumberland Co PA H106

C4351 HORATIO WARREN GASS C435

HORATIO WARREN GASS was born on 09 Sep 1868 in Northumberland Co., PA. He graduated on 21 May 1898 with a medical degree from Medico-Chirurgical College in Philadelphia, PA. He married GERTRUDE E. KUEBLER on 28 Jun 1900 in Northumberland Cc., PA, daughter of GEORGE E. KUEBLER and SARAH FASOLD. He practiced first at the Aetna Hospital in Berks County, PA and moved to Sunbury, PA in 1901 to start a private practice. He was the jail physician at Sunbury from 1906 to 1908 and then employed as the medical examiner for the Mutual Life and Traveler's Insurance Companies and for the Ancient Order of United Workmen. They were Democrats and members of the Reformed Church.

Child of HORATIO GASS and GERTRUDE KUEBLER is:

1. MARK KUEBLER GASS

References: 67

C4422 MARGARET S. GASS C442

MARGARET "MAGGIE" S. GASS was born in Nov 1876 in Northumberland Co., PA. She married GEORGE S. CONRAD in Northumberland Co., PA. He was born 1879 in PA.

1. NEIL CONRAD, born in 1907 in Northumberland Co., PA.

References: 30-Ward 8 Sunbury Northumberland Co PA 0118 H403

C4424 ISABELLA M. GASS C442

ISABELLA M. GASS was born in Jun 1881 in Northumberland Co., PA. She married CHARLES SCHLEGEL in Northumberland Co., PA. He was born in 1880 in PA.

Children of ISABELLA GASS and CHARLES SCHLEGEL are:

1. MARIAN SCHLEGEL, born in 1907 in Northumberland Co., PA.
2. CHARLES KENNETH SCHLEGEL, born in 1909 in Northumberland Co., PA.

References: 30-Ward 9 Sunbury Northumberland Co PA 0119 H200, 30-Dist 136 Ward 7 Sunbury Northumberland Co PA H156

C4425 SAMUEL J. GASS C442

SAMUEL J. GASS was born on 27 Jun 1883 in Northumberland Co., PA. He married GRACE G. in Northumberland Co., PA. She was born in 1888 in PA.

Child of SAMUEL GASS and GRACE is:

1. HAROLD S. GASS, born in 1921 in Northumberland Co., PA.

References: 31-Dist 74 Sunbury Northumberland Co PA H499

C5111 PETER RICHARD KEEFER C511

PETER RICHARD KEEFER was born 01 Aug 1859 in Northumberland Co., PA. He married EMMA R. CROWL on 24 Feb 1881, daughter of JACOB CROWL and SUSAN HUEY. She was born in Aug 1857 in PA. He was a carpenter and house builder by occupation. They were Democrats and members of the Reformed Church.

Child of PETER KEEFER and EMMA HUEY is:

1. MARY BELLE KEEFER, born in Sep 1886 in Northumberland Co., PA.

References: 67, 29-Dist 0163 Sunbury Northumberland Co PA H135

C5121 SAMUEL ARNOLD C512

SAMUEL L. ARNOLD was born in Jan 1856 in Northumberland Co., PA. He married ESTHER J. in Northumberland Co., PA. She was born in Sep 1855 in PA.

Child of SAMUEL ARNOLD and ESTHER is:

1. WILLIAM L. ARNOLD, born in Aug 1881 in Northumberland Co., PA.

References: 29-Dist 0161 Sunbury Northumberland Co PA H203, 30-Sunbury Northumberland Co PA 0112 H231

C5126 MARGARET ANN ARNOLD C512

MARGARET ANN ARNOLD was born on 05 Aug 1866 in Northumberland Co., PA and died 05 Sep 1953 in Elizabethtown, Lancaster Co., PA. She married ISAAC JONES REITZ on

02 Aug 1882 in Northumberland Co., PA. He was born on 01 Jul 1863 in Northumberland Co., PA and died 08 Feb 1949 in Sunbury, Northumberland Co., PA.

Child of MARGARET ARNOLD and ISAAC REITZ is:

1. MAUDE A. REITZ (C51261)

References: 29-Sunbury Northumberland Co PA H107, 30-Sunbury Ward 9 Northumberland Co PA H187

C5141 GEORGE F. KEEFER C514

GEORGE F. KEEFER was born on 10 Aug 1864 in Northumberland Co., PA. He graduated in June 1886 from Bucknell College, Lewisburg, PA. For four years he pursued civil engineering and surveying in the service of the Civil Engineers Corps and then in 1890 embarked in a business on his own in that field. He married ELLEN "ELLA" R. KUEBLER in 1895 in Northumberland Co., PA.

Child of GEORGE KEEFER and ELLA KUEBLER is:

1. PAUL FREDERICK KEEFER, was born in 1898 in Northumberland Co., PA; married HELEN R. in Northumberland Co., PA; born in 1898 in PA.
2. SARAH ALICE KEEFER, was born in 1904 in Northumberland Co., PA.
3. GEORGE W. KEEFER, was born in 1912 in Northumberland Co., PA.

References: 66, 10-Dist 140 Upper Augusta Twp Northumberland Co PA H108, 31-Dist 78 Upper Augusta Twp Northumberland Co PA H132, 40-Upper Augusta Twp Northumberland Co PA H153 & H154

C5151 DAVID A. ZIMMERMAN C515

DAVID A. ZIMMERMAN was born in Jun 1857 in Northumberland Co., PA. He married MARY A. BARTHOLOMEW in Northumberland Co., PA, daughter of CHARLES BARTHOLOMEW. She was born in May 1856 in PA.

Children of DAVID ZIMMERMAN and MARY are:

1. EMERY ZIMMERMAN, born in Jul 1877 in Northumberland Co., PA; died before 1910 in Schenectady, Schenectady Co., NY.
2. ELLEN I. ZIMMERMAN, born in Jul 1882 in Northumberland Co., PA.
3. SPENCER D. ZIMMERMAN, born in Dec 1890 in Northumberland Co., PA.

References: 29-Dist 0134 Ward 4 Schenectady Schenectady Co NY H81, 30-Ward 6 Schenectady Schenectady Co NY 0194 H201

C5153 AARON PETER ZIMMERMAN C515

AARON PETER ZIMMERMAN was born in 06 Jan 1861 in Northumberland Co., PA and died 15 Jul 1928 in Northumberland Co., PA. He married ELIZABETH S. ZIMMERMAN in Northumberland Co., PA. She was born 12 May 1863 in PA and died 18 Oct 1938 in Northumberland Co., PA. Both are buried in Shamokin Cemetery, Shamokin, Northumberland Co. PA.

Children of AARON ZIMMERMAN and ELIZABETH are:

1. MABLE C. ZIMMERMAN, born in Aug 1882 in Shamokin, Northumberland Co., PA.
2. LULA HELEN ZIMMERMAN, born in Oct 1891 in Shamokin, Northumberland Co., PA.
3. RUTH M. ZIMMERMAN, born in Jul 1894 in Shamokin, Northumberland Co., PA.

References: 45, 29-Dist 0152 Shamokin Northumberland Co PA H266

C5361 GERTRUDE L. HAUCK C536

GERTRUDE L. HAUCK was born in Sep 1878 in Northumberland Co., PA. She married FRANK A. NEFF in Northumberland Co., PA. He was born in 1876 in PA.

Child of GERTRUDE HAUCK and FRANK NEFF is:

1. DAVID A. NEFF, born in 1908 in Northumberland Co., PA.

References: 30-Ward 2 Sunbury Northumberland Co PA 0112 H278

C5511 SAMUEL H. DEPPEN C551

SAMUEL H. DEPPEN was born in1877 in Northumberland Co., PA.

Children of SAMUEL H. DEPPEN are:

1. FRANK DEPPEN, born in 1899 in Northumberland Co., PA.
2. DONALD DEPPEN, born in 1905 in Northumberland Co., PA, resided NYC, NY.

References: 5, 10-Zerbe Twp Northumberland Co PA H121

C5474 JAMES B. STERNER C547

JAMES B. STERNER was born in May 1873 in Northumberland Co., PA. He married HARRIET E. RINKER in Columbia Co., PA, daughter of BENJAMIN F. RINKER and JANE HANNAH. She was born in 1878 in PA.

Children of JAMES STERNER and HARRIET RINKER are:

1. ROBERT B. STERNER, born in 1906 in Bloomsburg, Columbia Co., PA; married MARGARET MCCORMICK in Columbia Co., PA, daughter of ________ MCCORMICK and ROSA; born in 1917 in MI.
2. CATHRYNE A. STERNER, born in 1913 in Bloomsburg, Columbia Co., PA.

References: 30-Ward 4 Bloomsburg Columbia Co PA 0011 H36, 10-Dist 15 Ward 4 Bloomsburg Columbia Co PA H50, 40-Bloomsburg Columbia Co PA 19-21 H7

C5514 WILLIAM RALPH DEPPEN C551

WILLIAM RALPH DEPPEN was born in Dec 1882 in Northumberland Co., PA. He married EVA KLINE TREVORTON in Northumberland Co., PA. She was born in 1885 in PA.

Children of WILLIAM RALPH DEPPEN and EVA KLINE TREVORTON are:

1. ROBERT DEPPEN, born in 1910 in Northumberland Co., PA.
2. JOHN DEPPEN, born in 1912 in Northumberland Co., PA.
3. MARGARET DEPPEN, born in 1918 in Northumberland Co., PA.

References: 5, 10-Zerbe Twp Northumberland Co PA H120

C5523 SUSAN ANNE DEPPEN C552

SUSAN ANNE DEPPEN was born in 1879 in Northumberland Co., PA and died in 1917 in Brooklyn, Susquehanna Co., PA. She married ROY C. SHADDUCK. He was born in 1887 in PA.

Child of SUSAN DEPPEN and ROY SHADDUCK is:

1. THOMAS D. SHADDUCK, born in 1914 in Brooklyn, Susquehanna Co., PA.

References: 5, 10-Dist 64 Brooklyn Susquehanna Co PA H10

C5524 SARAH E. DEPPEN C552

SARAH "SALLIE" E. DEPPEN was born in Feb 1880 in Northumberland Co., PA. She married JAMES MCDONALD in Northumberland Co., PA. He was born in1874 in PA.

Children of SARAH DEPPEN and JAMES MCDONALD are:

1. MARY A. MCDONALD, born in 1908 and died in 1926 in Sunbury, Northumberland Co., PA.
2. ROBERT D. MCDONALD, born in 1911 in Sunbury, Northumberland Co., PA.
3. SARA E. MCDONALD, born in 1917 in Sunbury, Northumberland Co., PA.

References: 5, 30-Dist 0118 Sunbury Ward 8 Northumberland Co PA H267, 10-Dist 0118 Sunbury Ward 8 Northumberland Co PA H383

C5527 FRANK R. DEPPEN C552

FRANK R. DEPPEN was born Jan 1886 in Northumberland Co., PA. He married MARY E. in Northumberland Co., PA. She was born in 1887 in PA.

Children of FRANK DEPPEN and MARY are:

1. HELEN K. DEPPEN, born in 1909 in unbury, Northumberland Co., PA.
2. RICHARD P. DEPPEN, born in 1913 in PA.
3. DONALD P. DEPPEN, born in 1916 in PA.
4. DIANE G. DEPPEN, born in 1929 in PA.

References: 5, 30-Dist 0114 Sunbury Ward 4 Northumberland Co PA H219, Dist 138 Nescopeck Luzerne Co PA H318, 31-Dist 3 Danville Montour Co PA H152

C5531 CARRIE DEPPEN C553

CARRIE DEPPEN was born in Sep 1882 in Northumberland Co., PA. She married E. J. AYRES in Northumberland Co., PA.

Child of CARRIE DEPPEN and E. J. AYRES is:

1. CATHERINE AYRES, resided Jersey City, NJ.

References: 5

C5672 GERTRUDE CULP C567

GERTRUDE CULP was born in 1874 in Northumberland Co., PA. She married JACOB E. DRUMM in Northumberland Co., PA. He was born in 1866 in PA.

Children of GERTUDE CULP and JACOB DRUMM are:

1. DORA DRUMM, born in 1888 in Northumberland Co., PA.
2. FRANKLIN DRUMM, born in 1907 in Northumberland Co., PA.
3. ELMER DRUMM, born in 1914 in Northumberland Co., PA.

References: 10-Dist 86 Lower Augusta Twp Northumberland Co PA H63

C5674 CREIGHTON GLENN CULP C567

CREIGHTON GLENN CULP was born in 1877 in Northumberland Co., PA and died in 1957 in Northumberland Co., PA. He married FLORENCE GERTRUDE READER in Northumberland Co., PA. She was born in 1882 in PA and died in 1960 in Northumberland Co., PA. Both are buried in Lantz Lutheran Cemetery, Sunbury, Northumberland Co., PA.

Children of CREIGHTON CULP and FLORENCE READER are:

1. LEROY CULP, born on 27 May 1900 in Northumberland Co., PA; died 01 Mar 1921 in Northumberland Co., PA; buried in Lantz Lutheran Cemetery, Sunbury, Northumberland Co., PA.
2. CHARLES M. CULP, born in 1902 in Northumberland Co., PA.
3. WILLIAM P. C. CULP, born in 1905 in Northumberland Co., PA.
4. MARY B. CULP (C56744)
5. RALPH W. CULP (C56745)
6. MARLYN R. CULP, born in 1913 in Northumberland Co., PA.
7. PAUL P. CULP (C56747)

References: 30-Sunbury Northumberland Co PA 0118 H358, 10-Dist 137 Sunbury Northumberland Co PA H4, 45, 31-Dist 45 Northumberland Twp Northumberland Co PA H263, 67

C5676 PEARL VERNON CULP C567

PEARL VERNON CULP was born in Jan 1882 in Northumberland Co., PA and died in 1953 in Northumberland Co., PA. He married MARY E. HEWITT in Northumberland Co., PA. She was born in 1886 in PA and died in 1958 in Northumberland Co., PA. Both are buried in Lantz Lutheran Cemetery, Sunbury, Northumberland Co., PA.

Children of PEARL CULP and MARY are:

1. GEORGE A. CULP, born in 1905 in Northumberland Co., PA and died in 1952 in Northumberland Co., PA.
2. PETER L. CULP, born in 1909 in Northumberland Co., PA.

References: 30-Dist 0119 Sunbury Ward 9 Northumberland Co PA, 45, 67

C5677 ROYAL PALMER CULP C567

ROYAL PALMER CULP was born in May 1884 in Northumberland Co., PA and died in 1953 in Northumberland Co., PA. He married STELLA M. LYTLE in Northumberland Co., PA. She was born in 1884 in PA and died in 1968 in Northumberland Co., PA.

Child of ROYAL CULP and STELLA is:

1. HELEN M. CULP, born 1908 in Northumberland Co., PA.

References: 30-Lower Augusta Twp Northumberland Co PA H146, 67

C5678 ALBERT BERNARD CULP C567

ALBERT BERNARD CULP was born in Mar 1886 in Northumberland Co., PA. He married ETHEL B. WEITZEL in Northumberland Co., PA. She was born in 1886 in PA and died 1919 in Northumberland Co., PA. She is buried in Lantz Lutheran Cemetery, Sunbury, Northumberland Co., PA.

Children of ALBERT CULP and ETHEL WEITZEL are:

1. ALFRED B. CULP, born in 1905 in Northumberland Co., PA; died in 1962 in Northumberland Co., PA; buried in Lantz Lutheran Cemetery, Sunbury, Northumberland Co., PA.
2. LOT F. CULP, born in 1907 in Northumberland Co., PA; died in 1919 in Northumberland Co., PA; buried in Lantz Lutheran Cemetery, Sunbury, Northumberland Co., PA.
3. MILDRED N. CULP, born in 1909 in Northumberland Co., PA; died in 1910 in Northumberland Co., PA; buried in Lantz Lutheran Cemetery, Sunbury, Northumberland Co., PA..

References: 30-Rockefeller Twp Northumberland Co PA 0095 H25, 67

C5722 MARSHALL BONAWITZ C572

MARSHALL BONAWITZ was born on 29 Apr 1872 in IN. He married ORILLA WILLIAMS in 1891 in IN. She was born in Feb 1871 in IN.

Children of MARSHALL BONAWITZ and ORILLA WILLIAMS are:

1. LAWRENCE BONAWITZ, born Aug 1892 in Grant Co., IN.
2. TIGNER W. BONAWITZ, born in Dec 1895 in Grant Co., IN.
3. LAURA LOU BONAWITZ, born in Jul 1897 in Grant Co., IN.
4. KATHRYN BONAWITZ, born in Jun 1898 in Grant Co., IN.
5. JOSEPHINE BONAWITZ, born on 03 Jun 1901 and died 10 Dec 1905 in Grant Co., IN.
6. JENETTE BONAWITZ, born in 1903 in Grant Co., IN.
7. ROBERT BONAWITZ

References: 5, 30-Ward 1 Marion Grant Co IN 0050 H294, 29-Dist 0026 Center Twp Grant Co IN H255

C5723 LOUIE BELLE BONAWITZ C572

LOUIE BELLE BONAWITZ was born on 14 Sep 1877 and died 11 Mar 1907. She married MARION ADAMS in 1900.

Child of LOUIE BONAWITZ and MARION ADAMS is:

1. MARY KATHRYN ADAMS, born 25 Jul 1905

References: 5

C5731 EVA HEETER C573

EVA HEETER was born on 14 Oct 1870. She married JOSEPH B. BIXLER in 1892. He was born in Feb 1863 in IN.

Children of EVA HEETER and JOSEPH BIXLER are:

1. RUTH ESTELLA BIXLER, born 25 Feb 1894 in IN.
2. MARY HELEN BIXLER, born 22 May 1900 in IN.
3. PAUL ABNER BIXLER, born 02 Apr 1903; died 18 Jun 1905.
4. ABNER LAWRENCE BIXLER, born 13 May 1908, Wenatchee, WA.

References: 5, 29-Dist 114 Chester Wabash Co IN H634, 30-Dist 0143 North Manchester Ward 3 Wabash Co IN H28

C5752 GEORGIA YOUNG LANTZ C575

GEORGIA YOUNG LANTZ was born on 18 Jun 1889. She married N. ROY CONSTANT in 1908, El Dorado, KS.

Child of GEORGIA LANTZ and ROY CONSTANT is:

1. HUGH RAYMOND CONSTANT, born 26 Oct 1912, Wichita, KS.

References: 5

C5762 EMMA MARGARET WILSON C576

EMMA MARGARET WILSON was born on 11 May 1892 in Wabash Co., IN. She married RUSSELL SHEAK. He was born in 1893 in IN.

Children of EMMA WILSON and RUSSELL SHEAK are:

1. HENRYWILSON SHEAK, born 30 Sep 1913 in IN.
2. MAE MERRITT SHEAK, born on 03 Jul 1916 in IN.
3. CHARLES SHEAK, born in 1918 in IN.
4. MARY E. SHEAK, born in 1923 in IN.
5. JOHN HENRY SHEAK, born in 1925 in IN.
6. ALICE SHEAK, born in 1938 in IN.

References: 5, 10-Dist 22 Logansport Ward 1 Cass Co IN H122, 31-Dist 394 Chicago Cook Co IL H84, 40-North Manchester Wabash Co IN 85-2A H6

C5811 STEPHEN H. HOLSHUE C581

STEPHEN H. HOLSHUE was born in 1878. He married GERTRUDE M. SLUSHER. She was born in 1882 in PA.

Child of STEPHEN HOLSHUE and GERTRUDE SLUSHER is:

1. RUSSELL E. HOLSHUE, born in 1902 in PA.

References: 5, 10-Dist 110 St Clair North Ward Schuylkill Co PA H45

C5821 CARRIE DEPPEN C582

CARRIE DEPPEN was born in 1879 in Northumberland Co., PA. She was married. W. P. ZARTMAN in PA. He was born in 1875 in PA.

Child of CARRIE DEPPEN and W. ZARTMAN is:

1. ELWOOD ZARTMAN, born in 1902 in Northumberland Co., PA.

References: 5, 30-Dist 0101 Shamokin Ward 3 Northumberland Co PA H1

C5831 IRVIN E. DEPPEN C583

IRVIN E. DEPPEN was born on 10 Feb 1877. He married LULU K. FAIRCHILDS in PA. She was born in Jan 1878 in PA.

Child of IRVIN DEPPEN and LULU FAIRCHILDS is:

1. ELWOOD F. DEPPEN, born in Mar 1898 in PA.

References: 5, 29-Dist 41 Halifax Dauphin Co PA H291

C5832 WILLIAM H. DEPPEN C583

WILLIAM H. DEPPEN was born in 1879 in PA. He married DELIA V. GEIST in PA. She was born in 1884 in PA.

Child WILLIAM DEPPEN and DELLA GEIST is:

1. JOSEPH W. DEPPEN, born in 1915 in PA.

References: 5, 10-Dist 99 Harrisburg Ward 10 Dauphin Co PA H158

C5A41 MAUDE L. LANTZ C5A4

MAUDE L. LANTZ was born in Apr 1886 in Northumberland Co., PA. She married RENO J. SOLOMON in Northumberland Co., PA. He was born in 1885 in PA

Child of MAUDE LANTZ and RENO SOLOMON is:

1. FERN E. SOLOMON, born in 1926 in PA.

References: 5, 31-Dist 13 Limestone Union Co PA H3

C5A42 LULU LANTZ C5A4

LULU LANTZ was born in Jan 1888 in Northumberland Co., PA. She married WILLIAM H. LONG in Northumberland Co., PA. He was born in 1885 in PA and died before 1940 in Northumberland Co., PA.

Children of LULU LANTZ and WILLIAM LONG are:

1. MILDRED E. LONG, born in 1912 in Northumberland Co., PA.
2. BERTHA F. LONG, born in 1914 in Northumberland Co., PA.
3. DORIS M. LONG (C5A423)
4. WILLIAM L. LONG, born in 1923 in Northumberland Co., PA.

References: 5, 31-Dist 72 Sunbury Northumberland Co PA H214, 40-Sunbury Northumberland Co PA 49-94 H295

C5A43 BERTHA L. LANTZ C5A4

BERTHA L. LANTZ was born in Mar 1890 in Northumberland Co., PA. She married JAMES W. SHIPE in Northumberland Co., PA. He was born in 1885 in PA.

Children of BERTHA LANTZ and JAMES SHIPE are:

1. BERTHA MARY SHIPE, born 1919 in Schuylkill Co., PA.
2. JAMES W. SHIPE, born 1922 in Schuylkill Co., PA.

References: 5, Dist 108 Schuylkill Haven Schuylkill Co PA H297

C5A44 PEARL L. LANTZ C5A4

PEARL L. LANTZ was born in Sep 1892 in Northumberland Co., PA. She married JOHN C. HILBISH in Northumberland Co., PA. He was born in 1888 in PA.

Child of PEARL LANTZ and JOHN HILBISH is:

1. JOHN LANTZ HILBISH, born in 1922 in Northumberland Co., PA.

References: 5, 40-Sunbury Northumberland Co PA 49-96 H223

C5A48 ELBERT W. LANTZ C5A4

ELBERT W. LANTZ was born in 1905 in Northumberland Co., PA. He married ALICE E. SHINDLE in Northumberland Co., PA. She was born in 1907 in PA.

Child of ELBERT LANTZ and ALICE SHINDLE is:

1. BARBARA A. LANTZ, born in 1928 in Northumberland Co., PA.

References: 5, 31-Dist 29 Milton Northumberland Co PA H85

C8214 HIRAM J. FOX C821

HIRAM J. FOX was born in Jan 1886, in MI. He married ETHEL H. in MI. She was born in 1890 in MI.

Children of HIRAM FOX and ETHEL are:

1. GLADYS G. FOX, born in 1916 in Cass Co., MI.
2. ORLO D. FOX, born in 1918 in Cass Co., MI.

References: 10-Dist 140 Volinia Cass Co MI H184, 31-Dist 22 Volinia Cass Co MI H59

C8251 ROY O. FOX C825

ROY O. FOX was born in Nov 1883, in MI and died 1943 in Cass Co., MI. He married ARLIE B. in MI. She was born on 14 Jun 1885 in MI and died 1971 in Cass Co., MI. Both are buried in Bly Cemetery, Marcellus, Cass Co., MI.

Children of ROY FOX and ARLIE are:

1. MARGERY FOX, born in 1905 in Van Buren Co., MI.
2. MARIE FOX, born in 1907 in Van Buren Co., MI.
3. MARION E. FOX, born in 1907 in Van Buren Co., MI.
4. SHIRLEY FOX, born in 1921 in Van Buren Co., MI; died 1993 in Cass Co., MI; married _______ WRIGHT; She is buried in Bly Cemetery, Marcellus, Cass Co., MI.

References: 31-Dist 27 Porter Van Buren Co MI H190, 10-Dist 203 Porter Van Buren Co MI H102

C8253 CLINT J. FOX C825

CLINT J. FOX was born in Jun 1893, in MI. He married HAZEL in MI. She was born in 1893 in MI.

Children of CLINT FOX and HAZEL are:

1. PEARL FOX, born in 1921 in MI.
2. RAYMOND FOX, born in 1922 in MI.
3. OLIVER FOX, born in 1923 in MI.
4. RACHEL FOX, born in 1925 in MI.
5. EVA FOX, born in 1921 in MI.
6. ROY FOX, born in 1921 in MI.

References: 31-Dist 27 Wexford Twp Wexford Co MI H97

C8254 FLOSSIE B. FOX C825

FLOSSIE B. FOX was born in Mar 1895 in MI. She married CHARLES E. DRAKE in MI. He was born in 1892 in MI.

Children of FLOSSIE FOX and CHARLES DRAKE are:

1. DONALD E. DRAKE, born 1913 in MI.
2. COY B. DRAKE, born 1914 in MI.

3. LUCILLE L. DRAKE, born 1918 in MI.
4. JOYCE E. DRAKE, born 1925 in MI.
5. EMERSON DRAKE, born 1927 in MI.

References: 10-Dist 203 Porter Van Buren MI H112

C82A1 ETHEL W. FOX C82A

ETHEL W. FOX was born in Oct 1891 in MI and died 1984 in Kalamazoo Co., MI. She married CLARENCE ARCHIE BRADFORD in MI, son of CALVIN P. BRADFORD and CATHERINE F. BARTLETT. He was born on 30 Sep 1889 in Attica, Harper County, Kansas and died 1979 Kalamazoo Co., MI. Both are buried in Schoolcraft Cemetery, Schoolcraft, Kalamazoo Co., MI.

Children of ETHEL FOX and CLARENCE BRADFORD are:

1. WARD BRADFORD, born 1911 in MI.
2. CELENA BRADFORD, born 1914 in MI.
3. HERBERT BRADFORD, born 1915 in MI.
4. ALENA BRADFORD, born 1918 in MI.
5. ELINOR BRADFORD, born 1919 in MI.

References: 45, 31-Dist 145 Wyoming Twp Kent Co MI H3, 10-Dist 12 Courtland Twp Kent Co MI H203

C8513 HOWARD W. ROMBACH C851

HOWARD W. ROMBACH was born on 10 Aug 1875 in Northumberland Co., PA. He married (1) IONE MORGAN. She was born in May 1875 in PA and died in 1925 in Northumberland Co., PA. He married (2) MARGARET H. BAIRD in 1927 who had been previously married to a HARPER.

Children of HOWARD ROMBACH and IONE MORGAN are:

1. FRED WILSON ROMBACH, born 13 Oct 1898; married JEAN ROCHE, 1921, Watsontown, Northumberland Co., PA.
2. MARGARET KATHERINE ROMBACH (C85132)

References: 5, 29-Dist 168 Watsontown Northumberland Co PA H106, 10-Dist 0123 Watsontown Ward 1 Northumberland Co PA H156, 31-Dist 82 Watsontown Northumberland Co PA H259

C8522 GLENN OTTO LANTZ C852

GLENN OTTO LANTZ was born in May 1893 in Northumberland Co., PA. He married SARA ESTHER HUBBARD. She was born in 1893 in PA.

Children of GLENN LANTZ and SARA HUBBARD are:

1. DOROTHY ELIZABETH LANTZ, born on 01 Mar 1919 in OK.

2. DORIS MAY LANTZ, born on 09 May 1923 in PA.

References: 5, 31-Dist 14 Frenchtown Hunterdon Co NJ H193

C8611 MARGARET E. LILLEY C861

MARGARET E. LILLEY was born on 19 Jan 1866 in Northumberland Co., PA. She married JOHN WELSH in Northumberland Co., PA. He was born in Mar 1858 in PA.

Child of MARGARET LILLEY and JOHN WELSH is:

1. FLORENCE H. WELSH, born in Feb 1892 in Northumberland Co., PA.

References: 5, 29-Dist 168 Watsontown Northumberland Co PA H2

C8712 GEORGE VAN NOSTRAND C871

GEORGE VAN NOSTRAND was born on 28 Jan 1876 in St. Joseph Co., MI. He married EMMA HOFFMAN in 1898.

Children of GEORGE VAN NOSTRAND and EMMA HOFFMAN are:

1. WILDA VAN NOSTRAND, born 11 Oct 1898; married RALPH CROUNS, 1917. Two daughters.
2. LENA VAN NOSTRAND, married PAUL SEIBERT, 1927.

References: 5

C12525 RALPH R. LANTZ C1252

RALPH R. LANTZ was born on 06 Feb 1894 in 2424 Maple Avenue, Altoona, Blair Co., PA and died in 1969 in Hollidaysburg, Blair Co., PA. He married MARY E. KENNEDY on 14 Nov 1914 in Cumberland, MD. She was born in 1897 in PA.

Child of RALPH LANTZ and MARY KENNEDY is:

1. HARRY C. LANTZ, born in 1915 in Blair Co., PA.

References: 10-Dist 92 Hollidaysburg Blair Co PA H54

C12556 AGNES F. LANTZ C1255

AGNES F. LANTZ was born on 17 Nov 1911 in Altoona, Blair Co., PA and died on 21 May 2000 in Altoona, Blair Co., PA. She married PAUL F. KELLY on 09 May 1933 in Cumberland, MD. He was born in 1915 in PA.

Children of AGNES LANTZ and PAUL KELLY are:

1. PAUL T. KELLY
2. RICKE M. KELLY
3. DONNA F. KELLY, born on 20 Apr 1938 in Altoona, Blair Co., PA; died 21 Feb 1989 in Altoona, Blair Co., PA; married JOHN J. ARNSPARGER on 15 Oct 1960 in Altoona, Blair Co., PA.
4. RONALD R. KELLY, born on 20 Apr 1938; died 16 Oct 1998.
5. THOMAS KELLY

References: Obit of AFL, Obit of DFK, 40-Altoona Blair Co PA 7-49 H122

C1255A HELEN W. LANTZ C1255

HELEN W. LANTZ married PETE KEIRN on 14 Dec 1932 in Altoona, Blair Co., PA, son of HARVEY J. KEIRN and ROSE A. BRANDT. He was born on 16 Dec 1911 in Altoona, Blair Co., PA and died 30 Oct 1991 in Altoona, Blair Co., PA.

Children of HELEN W. LANTZ and PETE KEIRN are:

1. PAUL R. KEIRN
2. JANET M. KEIRN, married (?) STITT
3. JOSEPH E. KEIRN

References: Obit

Retired business president

Pete Keirn, 79, of Box 75A, RD 3, died at 4 p.m. Wednesday, Oct. 30, 1991, at his residence, following an extended illness.

Mr. Keirn retired as president of Keystone Radiator Inc. in 1986, after 50 years' in the business.

He was born Dec. 16, 1911, in Altoona, the son of Harvey J. and Rose A. (Brandt) Keirn, and Dec. 14, 1932, in Altoona, married Helen W. Lantz.

Surviving are his wife, three children: Paul R., Janet M. Stitt and Joseph E. of Altoona, nine grandchildren and seven great-grandchildren.

Mr. Keirn was a member of the Cathedral of the Blessed Sacrament.

He was also a charter/life member of Star of the Sea Council, Knights of Columbus and was a life member of the National Radiator Association.

Friends will be received from 2 to 4 and 7 to 9 p.m. Friday at the Jones Funeral Home.

Pete Keirn

KEIRN — The funeral of Pete Keirn of Box 75A, Altoona RD 3, will be held with a Mass of Christian Burial at 10 a.m. Saturday at the Cathedral of the Blessed Sacrament. Interment at Calvary Cemetery. Friends will be received from 2 to 4 and 7 to 9 p.m. Friday at Jones Funeral Home, where a wake service will be held in the evening.

C12561 CLYDE RAYMOND LANTZ C1256

CLYDE RAYMOND LANTZ was born on 10 Oct 1904 in Pittsburgh, Allegheny Co., PA, and died 24 Nov 1947 of coronary heart disease-cardiac vercular in Altoona, Blair Co., PA. He married CATHERINE WILNORA GOOD 09 Mar 1929 in Marsteller, Cambria Co., PA, daughter of BENJAMIN FRANKKLIN GOOD and MARTHA ADELINE MARKS. She was born 28 Apr 1912 in Barr Twp., Cambria Co., PA, and died 23 Oct 1973 in Altoona, Blair Co., PA. In 1910, he was a tinner, in 1936, a machinist and 1941-1945, laborer & helper for the PRR. In 1951, she worked at the Puritan Knitting Mills, Altoona, Blair Co., PA and 1961-1970, Ward Secretary, Altoona Hospital, Altoona, Blair Co., PA. Both are buried in Lot F-53-56 at Rose Hill Cemetery, Altoona, Blair Co., PA.

Children of CLYDE LANTZ and CATHERINE GOOD are:

1. RAYMOND GARFIELD LANTZ (C125611)
2. RUTH ANNA MAE LANTZ (C125612)
3. GEORGE HOWARD LANTZ (C125613)
4. DONALD WAYNE LANTZ (C125614)

References: 32-Altoona Blair Co PA H598, 43, 40-Altoona Blair Co PA H254, 46-M/CRL&CWG/30998 Vol79 Pg698/Cambria Co PA, 46-D/CWG/9620773/DOH PA

CLYDE RAYMOND LANTZ, CATHERINE WILNORA (GOOD) LANTZ and RAYMOND GARFIELD LANTZ

RAYMOND GARFIELD LANTZ

DORIS FAYE (BRUCKMAN) LANTZ, RAYMOND GARFIELD LANTZ, RUTH ANNA MAE LANTZ, CATHERINE WILNORA (GOOD) LANTZ, GEORGE HOWARD LANTZ, RAYMOND CLYDE LANTZ and DONALD WAYNE LANTZ

DONALD WAYNE LANTZ

GEORGE HOWARD LANTZ

CLYDE RAYMOND LANTZ, CATHERINE WILNORA (GOOD) LANTZ, RAYMOND GARFIELD LANTZ, GEORGE HOWARD LANTZ and RUTH ANNA MAE LANTZ

CLYDE RAYMOND LANTZ CATHERINE WILNORA (GOOD) LANTZ

C12572 VIOLA E. LANTZ C1257

VIOLA E. LANTZ was born on 12 Jan 1913 in Altoona, Blair Co., PA and died on 02 Jun 1997 in Stevens, PA. She married (1) ALFRED E. HUPERT in Altoona, Blair Co., PA. He died in 1936 in Altoona, Blair Co., PA. She married (2) LOUIS P. HEALY in Altoona, Blair Co., PA. He died in 1972 in Altoona, Blair Co., PA.

Children of VIOLA LANTZ and ALFRED HUPERT are:

1. PATRICIA LEE HUPERT, born in 1930 in Altoona, Blair Co., PA.
2. SHIRLEY ANN HUPERT, born in 1933 in Altoona, Blair Co., PA.
3. JOAN HUPERT, born in 1936 in Altoona, Blair Co., PA.

References: 40-Altoona Blair Co PA 7-40A H100

C33321 ELNA M. LANTZ C3332

ELNA M. LANTZ was born on 17 Feb 1900 in ID. She married SYLVESTER LUNDERS, 1921 in ID. He was born in 1892 in OK.

Children of ELNA LANTZ and SYLVESTER LUNDERS are:

1. HOWARD E. LUNDERS, born in 1924 in Morrow Co., ID.
2. DALE LUNDERS, born in 1925 in Morrow Co., ID.
3. MARY LOUISE LUNDERS, born in 1928 in Morrow Co., ID.

References: 5, 31-Dist 13 Morrow Lewis Co ID H2, 40- Morrow Lewis Co ID 31-11 H13

C33322 ETTA LANTZ C3332

ETTA LANTZ was born on 15 Jun 1901 in ID. She married M. COVINGTON in 1924.

Child of ETTA LANTZ and M. COVINGTON is:

1. HELEN LORMEL COVINGTON

References: 5

C33324 EMMA LANTZ C3332

EMMA LANTZ was born on 18 Jun 1905 in ID. She married J. RAYMOND FALLWELL in 1922 in ID. He was born in 1903 in OK.

Children of EMMA LANTZ and J. FALLWELL

1. MARGARET FALLWELL, born in 1923 in ID.
2. BERNICE FALLWELL, born in 1925 in ID.
3. MADELIN, born in 1939 in ID.

References: 5, 31-Dist 51 East Orchards Nez Perce ID H73, 40-West Orchards Nez Perce ID 35-38 H239

C41112 V. CHARLES MACKERT C4111

V. CHARLES MACKERT was born in Mar 1898 in Northumberland Co., PA. He married FRANCES M. in Northumberland Co., PA. She was born in 1901 in PA.

Child of V. MACKERT and FRANCES is:

1. MARY ELLEN MACKERT, born in 1922 in Northumberland Co., PA.

References: 31-Dist 75 Sunbury Northumberland Co PA H177

C41114 EDWARD WALTER MACKERT C4111

EDWARD WALTER MACKERT was born in 1901 in Northumberland Co., PA. He married MARGUERITE in Northumberland Co., PA. She was born in 1903 in PA.

Child of EDWARD MACKERT and MARGUERITE is:

1. ESTHER L. MACKERT, born 1923 in Northumberland Co., PA.

References: 31-Dist 75 Sunbury Northumberland Co PA H383, 40-Upper Augusta Twp Northumberland Co PA H42

C42452 CLAYTON L. BROCIOUS C4245

CLAYTON L. BROCIOUS was born in 1895 in Northumberland Co., PA. He married CARRIE E. in Northumberland Co., PA. She was born in 1893 in PA.

Child of CLAYTON BROCIOUS and CARRIE is:

1. ROBERT W. BROCIOUS, born in 1823 in Northumberland Co., PA.

References: 31-Dist 74 Sunbury Northumberland Co PA H187

C42461 HERMAN L. GASS C4246

HERMAN L. GASS was born in Nov 1893 in Northumberland Co., PA. He married KATHERINE B. in Northumberland Co., PA. She was born in 1898 in PA.

Children of HERMAN GASS and KATHERINE are:

1. E. JANE GASS, born in 1922 in PA.
2. RICHARD B. GASS, born in 1923 in PA.
3. DALE I. GASS, born in 1929 in PA.

References: 31-Dist 5 Berwick Columbia Co PA H103

C51261 MAUDE A. REITZ C5126

MAUDE A. REITZ was born 04 Dec 1884 in Northumberland Co., PA and died 16 Apr 1955 in Sunbury, Northumberland Co., PA. She married WILLIAM HENRY CONRAD on 25 Aug 1910 in Northumberland Co., PA. He was born on 27 Nov 1882 in East Sunbury, Northumberland Co., PA and died 18 Jan 1960 in Sunbury, Northumberland Co., PA.

Children of MAUDE REITZ and WILLIAM CONRAD are:

1. WILLIAM H. CONRAD, born in 1912 in Sunbury, Northumberland Co., PA.
2. MARTHA J. CONRAD, born in 1914 in Sunbury, Northumberland Co., PA.
3. ROBERT R. CONRAD, born in 1916 in Sunbury, Northumberland Co., PA.
4. NANCY S. CONRAD, born in 1926 in Sunbury, Northumberland Co., PA.

References: 30-Sunbury Ward 9 Northumberland Co PA H187, 31-Sunbury Northumberland Co PA H272

C56744 MARY B. CULP C5674

MARY B. CULP was born in 1908 in Northumberland Co., PA. She married _____ KEEFER in Northumberland Co., PA.

Children of MARY CULP and ______ KEEFER are:

1. SHIRLEY M. KEEFER, born in 1928 in Northumberland Co., PA.
2. ROBERT L. KEEFER, born in 1929 in Northumberland Co., PA.

References: 31-Dist 45 Northumberland Twp Northumberland Co PA H263

C56745 RALPH W. CULP C5674

RALPH W. CULP was born on 13 May 1910 in Northumberland Co., PA and died 30 May 1963 in Northumberland Co., PA. He married LORENA D. in Northumberland Co., PA. She was born in 1910 in PA. He is buried in Lantz Lutheran Cemetery, Sunbury, Northumberland Co., PA.

Children of RALPH CULP and LORENA are:

1. DOROTHY L. CULP, born 1930 in Northumberland Co., PA.
2. WOODROW L. CULP, born 1932 in Northumberland Co., PA.
3. VIRGINIA M. CULP, born 1934 in Northumberland Co., PA.
4. GEORGIA A. CULP, born 1936 in Northumberland Co., PA.
5. SANDRA K. CULP, born 1939 in Northumberland Co., PA.

References: 40-sunbury Northumberland Co PA 49-96 H353

C56747 PAUL P. CULP C5674

PAUL P. CULP was born in 1916 in Northumberland Co., PA. He married SARAH L. in Northumberland Co., PA. She was born in 1914 in PA.

References: 40-sunbury Northumberland Co PA 49-92 H240

C5A423 DORIS M. LONG C5A42

DORIS M. LONG was born in 1921 in Northumberland Co., PA. She married REGINALD T. MERIDEN in Northumberland Co., PA. He was born in 1917 in PA.

Child of DORIS LONG and REGINALD MERIDEN is:

1. CAROL M. MERIDEN, born in 1939 in Northumberland Co., PA.

References: 40-Sunbury Northumberland Co PA 49-94 H295

C85132 MARGARET KATHERINE ROMBACH C8513

MARGARET KATHERINE ROMBACH was born on 12 Jun 1906 in Northumberland Co., PA. She married J. LESTER GEORGE in 1927 in Northumberland Co., PA. He was born in 1903 in PA.

Children of MARGARET ROMBACH and J. GEORGE are:

1. WILLIAM HOWARD GEORGE, born in 1926 in PA.
2. BARBARA JEAN GEORGE, born on 03 Mar 1928 in PA.

References: 5, 31-Dist 26 Phillipsburg Centre Co PA H199

C125611 RAYMOND GARFIELD LANTZ C12561

RAYMOND GARFIELD LANTZ was born on 29 Jul 1929 in Altoona, Blair Co., PA, and died 11 Mar 2006 in Altoona, Blair Co., PA. He married DORIS FAYE BRUCKMAN 12 Jan 1951 in Winchester, Frederick Co., VA, daughter of CHARLES HERBERT BRUCKMAN and MARY IRENE DETWILER. She was born 02 Oct 1930 in Altoona, Blair Co., PA, and died 11 Feb 2004 in Pensacola, Escambia Co., FL. He served in the U.S. Navy 12 Sep 1946-21 Feb 1950, on 13 Aug 1946, enlisted at Pittsburgh, PA, on 15 May 1949, advanced to rank of AM3 and on 21 Feb 1950, was honorably discharged at NAS Key West, FL. He was a bartender most of 1955-1979 at various establishments in Altoona, Blair Co., PA, an electronic repair technician for a short time during that period and finally in 1980 was from 1980, Owner & Operator of Ray's Handy Store till he retired. She was a nurse's aide 1961-1968 Altoona Hospital, Altoona, Blair Co., PA and in 1970 Laundry Worker, Penn Alto Hotel, Altoona, Blair Co., PA for a number of years until retired.

Child of RAYMOND LANTZ and DORIS BRUCKMAN is:

1. RAYMOND CLYDE LANTZ (C1256111)

References: 43, 44, 46-B/DFB/154546/DOC PA, 46-D/DFL/14946309/Escambia Co FL, 46-B/RGL/1041310-1929/DOH PA, 46-D/RGL/P12307661/DOH PA, 46-M/RGL&DFB/1819310/DOH VA

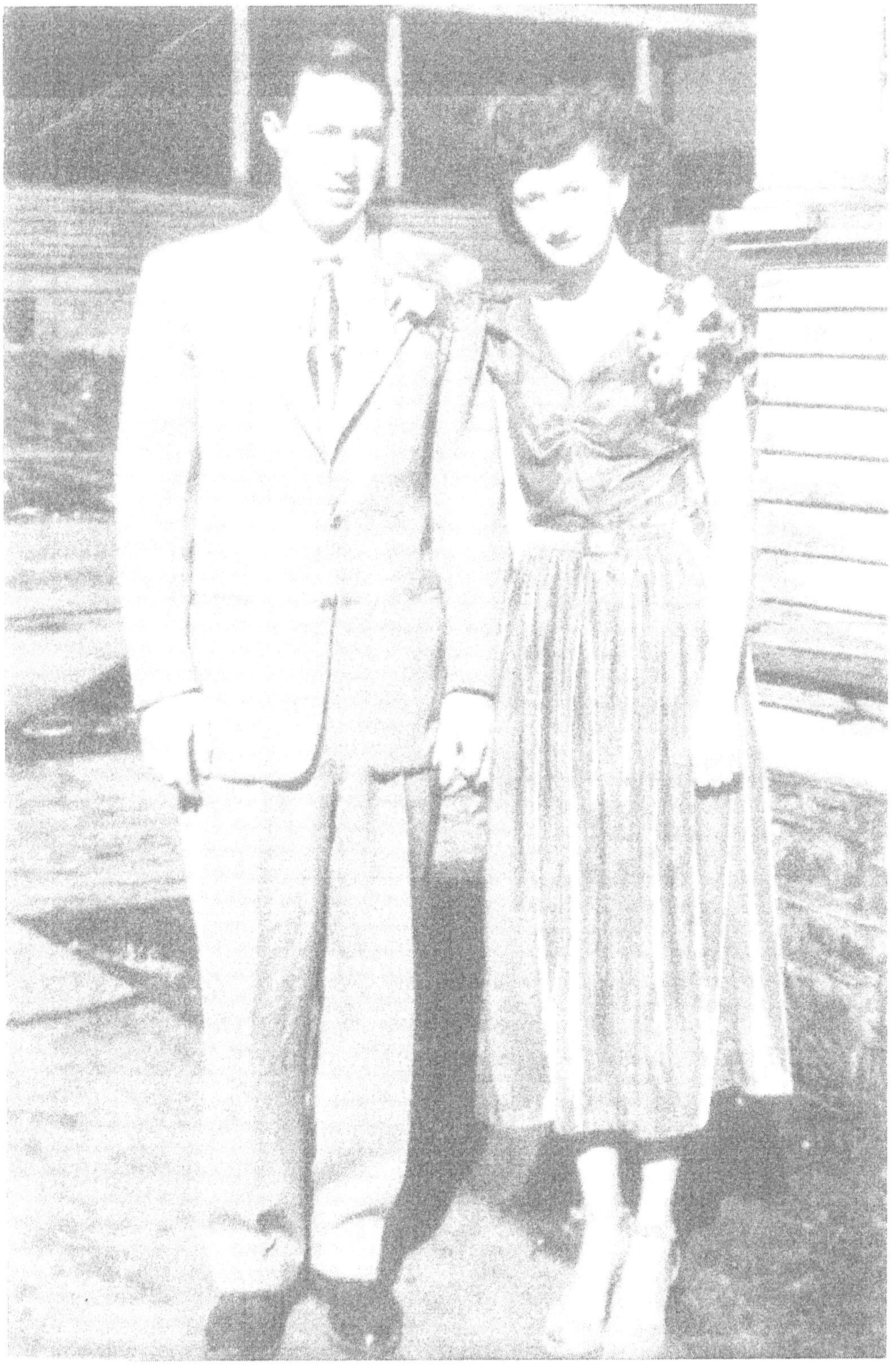

RAYMOND GARFIELD LANTZ and DORIS FAYE (BRUCKMAN) LANTZ

RAYMOND CLYDE LANTZ

C125612 RUTH ANNA MAE LANTZ C12561

RUTH ANNA MAE LANTZ was born on 05 Feb 1935 in Altoona, Blair Co., PA and died 27 Nov 1993 in Scranton, Lackawanna Co., PA. She married (1) JAMES ROBERT RHODES on 18 Jun 1955 at Altoona, Blair Co., PA. He was born on 02 Nov 1934 in Altoona, Blair Co., PA and died 23 Aug 1992 in Clarks Summit, PA. They were divorced in Feb 1967. She married (2) RICHARD JAMES DAVEY on 08 Jul 1967 in Scranton, PA. He was born on 18 Feb 1927, Blakely, PA and died 26 May 2002 in Jessup, PA.

Children of RUTH LANTZ and JAMES RHODES are:

1. ROBERT JAMES RHODES (C1256121)
2. STEPHEN DUANE RHODES (C1256122)
3. JEFFREY MARTIN RHODES (C1256123)
4. ERIC WILLIAM RHODES (C1256124)

Children of RUTH LANTZ and RICHARD DAVEY are:

5. CATHERINE RUTH DAVEY (C1256125)
6. RICHARD JAMES DAVEY, born 13 May 1969, Peckville, PA. He is member of Oriental Star Lodge 588, Free and Accepted Masons, Peckville, PA.
7. CHARLES RICHARD DAVEY (C1256125)

References: 6-Robert James Rhodes

C125613 GEORGE HOWARD LANTZ C12561

GEORGE HOWARD LANTZ was born on 18 Jul 1938 in Barnesboro, Cambria Co., PA. He married PATRICIA MASTALSKI on 13 Aug 1960 in Coupon, PA, the daughter of MICHAEL MASTALSKI and HELEN FULTONOVICH. She was born on 16 Aug 1940 in Altoona, Blair Co., PA, and died 14 Jan 1996 in Richmond, VA. She is buried Blair Co., PA. He resides in Richmond, VA.

Children of GEORGE LANTZ and PATRICIA MASTALSKI are:

1. GEORGE "BUTCH" MICHAEL LANTZ was born on 29 Dec 1962 in Altoona, Blair Co., PA.
2. HELEN MAY LANTZ was born on 23 Oct 1968 in Richmond, Richmond Co., VA.
3. MELISSA RENEE LANTZ was born on 20 Aug 1970 in Richmond, Richmond Co., VA.

References: 6-George Howard Lantz

C125614 DONALD WAYNE LANTZ C12561

DONALD WAYNE LANTZ was born on 06 Mar 1941 in Altoona, Blair Co., PA and died 24 Apr 1998 in Altoona, Blair Co., PA. He married CAROLYN JOAN EMIGH on 17 Jun 1967 in Altoona, Blair Co., PA, the daughter of CARL REED EMIGH and ALMA ANNA DIXON.

She was; born 23 Oct 1944, PA. He served in the U.S. Army from 15 Feb 1960 to 14 Feb 1963. He is buried Rose Hill Cemetery Altoona, Blair Co., PA.

Children of DONALD LANTZ and CAROLYN EMIGH are:

1. TIMOTHY WAYNE LANTZ was born on 04 Mar 1969 in Altoona, PA. He married BRENDA M. CRIST on 19 Jun 1999 in Altoona PA, the daughter of EUGENE F. CRIST and DARLENE M. SCHENK. She was born on 29 Aug 1974 in Altoona, Blair Co. PA. Both are graduates of Penn State University. He is Web Manager for Dickinson College. She has a masters in Counseling and is a school counselor and an avid rider and trainer of horses. She can be found at her websites pkinpa.com and kissdressage.com He is an artist and has created a Tarot deck and somewhere nearing 50 book covers and his website is stygiandarkness.com.
2. DAWN RENEE LANTZ (C1256142)

References: 6-Carolyn (Emigh) Lantz, 6-Brenda (Crist) Lantz

DONALD WAYNE and CAROLYN JOAN (EMIGH) LANTZ

TIMOTHY WAYNE and BRENDA M. (CRIST) LANTZ

C1256111 RAYMOND CLYDE LANTZ C125611

RAYMOND CLYDE LANTZ was born on 20 Nov 1951 in Altoona, Blair Co., PA. He married (1) CHRISTINA IRENE LANTZ, 30 Aug 1969 in Duncansville, PA, daughter of ROBERT ALLEN LANTZ and ANNA DELL HUMERICK. She was born 16 Nov 1951 in Altoona, Blair Co., PA. They were divorced 09 Dec 1975, Hollidaysburg, Blair Co., PA; He married (2) DIANNA LEE CROSSLEY 26 Mar 1977 in Pensacola, Escambia Co., FL, daughter of NOEL NELSON CROSSLEY and SANDRA LEE SHAW. She was born 01 Nov 1956 in Pontiac, Oakland Co., MI. He served in the U.S. Navy 30 Apr 1969- 31 May 1989 and retired 29 Apr 1999. His current occupation is as a Software Engineer/Computer Programmer. DIANNA LEE CROSSLEY is a Native American with 1/4 Blood Degree of the Huron Potawatomi Tribe. He is the author of this book and currently resides at 8939 Abbington Drive, Pensacola, FL 32534-5347. He is a graduate of Embry Riddle Aeronautical University.

Child of RAYMOND LANTZ and CHRISTINA LANTZ is:

1. YVONNE MARIE LANTZ (C12561111)

Child of RAYMOND LANTZ and DIANNA CROSSLEY is:

2. NELSON GARFIELD LANTZ (C12561112)

References: 43, 44, 46-B/RCL/199333-51/DOH PA, 46-B/DLC/6125/Oakland Co MI, 46-M/RCL&DLC/77-559/Escambia Co FL, 46-B/YML/1970/Prince George's Co MD, 46-M/RCL&CIL/73729/Blair Co PA, 46-DIV/RCL&CIL/530-1975/Blair Co PA

YVONNE MARIE LANTZ

NELSON GARFIELD LANTZ

RAYMOND CLYDE, DIANNA LEE (CROSSLEY) & NELSON GARFIELD LANTZ

RAYMOND CLYDE LANTZ Battle of Pensacola Florida re-enactment

C1256121 ROBERT JAMES RHODES C125612

ROBERT JAMES RHODES was born on 29 Jul 1957 in Altoona, PA. He married (1) KATHY KAPUSCINSKI on 14 Aug 1982 in Scranton, PA and they were divorced 19 Dec 1984. He married (2) KRISTIN WARE on 09 Aug 1985 in Chinchilla, as her 2nd marriage also, PA, daughter of HARRY LLOYD WARE and GLORIA FRASCATORI. She was born on 21 Feb 1953 in Philadelphia, PA. He graduated Keystone College, AS Computer Information Systems in 1997 and retired in 2010 from PA Department of Public welfare as Management Information Systems Coordinator. He is a member and Past Master, Oriental Star Lodge 588, Free and Accepted Masons, Peckville, PA. She retired from Clarks Summit State as a Psychiatric Aide.

Family of ROBERT RHODES and KRISTIN WARE is:

1. JESSICA NICOLE COLVIN, born 23 Feb 1983, Scranton, PA.
2. ROBERT JAMES RHODES, born 08 Oct 1987, Scranton, PA. He graduated from Wyotech Blairsville campus Automotive Paint and Restoration in 2008.

References: 6-Robert James Rhodes

ROBERT JAMES RHODES, KRISTIN (WARE) RHODES, ROBERT JAMES RHODES & JESSICA NICOLE COLVIN

C1256122 STEPHEN DUANE RHODES C125612

STEPHEN DUANE RHODES was born on 27 Nov 1958 in Altoona, PA. He married (1) BEVERLY AMELIA JASON on 18 Aug 1979 in Scranton, PA and they were divorced 21 May 1992. He married (2) BETHANY SUE LEADER on 24 Jul 1993 in Dunmore, PA, the daughter of ROBERT ARNOLD LEADER and VALERI GWEN JONES. She was born on 20 Jul 1962 in Scranton, PA. He is a member and Past Master, Oriental Star Lodge 588, Free and Accepted Masons, Peckville, PA.

Children of STEPHEN LANTZ and BETHANY LEADER are:

1. STEPHANY RUTH RHODES, born on 30 Apr 1994 in Denver, CO.
2. SARAH RHYS RHODES, born on 16 Jul 1996 in St. Louis Park, MN.

References: 6-Robert James Rhodes

SARAH RHYS RHODES, STEPHEN DUANE RHODES, STEPHANY RUTH RHODES & BETHANY SUE (LEADER) RHODES

C1256123 JEFFREY MARTIN RHODES C125612

JEFFREY MARTIN RHODES was born on 03 Sep 1962 in Scranton, PA. He married DELANE FAYE RIBOLINI, 18 Aug 1984 in Scranton, PA, daughter of LEWIS EUGENE RIBOLINI and JUNE FAYE LOGAN. She was born 13 Mar 1963 in Wilkes Barre, PA. He is a member of Acacia Lodge 579, Free and Accepted Masons, Taylor, PA.

Children of JEFFREY RHODES and DELANE RIBOLINI are:

1. CASSANDRA FAYE RHODES, born on 04 Jul 1985, Scranton, PA; married (1) NICHOLAS MARK ACRI, on 23 Jun 2007, Taylor, PA and divorced on 28 July 2008; married (2) MATTHEW WILLIAM DECKER on 16 July 2011.
2. TARA ALMA RHODES, born on 30 May 1988, Scranton, PA
3. ADAM JOSEPH RHODES, born on 10 May 1993, Scranton, PA. He is member of Acacia Lodge 579, Free and Accepted Masons, Taylor, PA.

References: 6-Robert James Rhodes

C1256124 ERIC WILLIAM RHODES C125612

ERIC WILLIAM RHODES was born on 26 Mar 1964 in Scranton, PA. He married PATRICIA ANN HEIST on 27 May 1989 in North Hampton, PA, daughter of JOHN CYRUS HEIST and MARGARET PAVLOCHIN. She was born on 29 Oct 1964 in Allentown, PA. He received in 1986 BS Electrical Engineering from Penn State University, MBA in 1992 from Marywood University and is a member of Oriental Star Lodge 588, Free and Accepted Masons, Peckville, PA. She received in 1986 BS Marketing from Penn State University.

Children of ERIC RHODES and PATRICIA HEIST are:

1. JOHN RICHARD RHODES, born on 22 Apr 1994, Binghamton, NY.
2. BRIAN THOMAS RHODES, born on 01 Dec 1995, Binghamton, NY.
3. JULIA MARGARET RHODES, born on 15 Feb 1999, Binghamton, NY.

References: 6-Robert James Rhodes

JOHN RICHARD RHODES, BRIAN THOMAS RHODES, JULIA MARGARET RHODES, PATRICIA ANN (HEIST) RHODES & ERIC WILLIAM RHODES

C1256125 CATHERINE RUTH DAVEY C125612

CATHERINE RUTH DAVEY was born 01 Apr 1968 in Peckville, PA. She married ROBERT WILLIAM GERICHTEN on 30 May 1992 in Peckville, PA, son of WILLIAM ANTHONY GERICHTEN and VICTORIA ZABICKI. He was born 23 Aug 1968 in Queens, NY. They were divorced 02 Jan 2002. She married (2) PATRICK JOHN DEMPSEY on 08 mar 2002 in Jessup, PA as his 3rd marriage, son of JOHN JOSEPH DEMPSEY and ANN MARIE SPEICHER. He was born 03 May 1961 in Scranton, PA

Family of CATHERINE DAVEY and PATRICK DEMPSEY is:

1. SEAN PATRICK DEMPSEY, born on 22 Dec 1989 in Scranton, PA
2. JUSTIN JEROME DEMPSEY, born on 26 Apr 1992 in Scranton, PA
3. ERICA CATHERINE GERICHTEN, born on 22 Feb 1995, Scranton, PA.
4. DOUGLAS WILLIAM GERICHTEN, born on 09 July 1997, Scranton, PA.

References: 6-Robert James Rhodes

PATRICK JOHN DEMPSEY, CATHERINE RUTH (DAVEY) DEMPSEY, DOUGLAS WILLIAM GERICHTEN, JUSTIN JEROME DEMPSEY, ERICA CATHERINE GERICHTEN & SEAN PATRICK DEMPSEY

C1256127 CHARLES RICHARD DAVEY C125612

CHARLES RICHARD DAVEY was born on b. 22 Sep 1971 in Peckville, PA. He married SHARON KIM WETTER on 26 Aug 1995 in Scranton, PA. She was born on 05 Jan 1968. They are divorced. He married (2) APRIL MARIE GREEN on 18 Jul 2008 in Throop, PA. She was born on 28 May 1974 in Scranton, PA. He is a member Oriental Star Lodge 588, Free and Accepted Masons, Peckville, PA

Children of CHARLES DAVEY and SHARON WETTER are:

1. DYLAN RICHARD DAVEY, born on 20 Sep 2000, Scranton, PA.
2. RYAN ROBERT DAVEY, born on 28 Aug 2002, Scranton, PA

Children of CHARLES DAVEY and APRIL GREEN are:

3. CHARLES RICHARD DAVEY, born on 2 Mar 2006, Scranton, PA
4. ARIANA RUTH DAVEY, born on 23 Nov 2009, Scranton, PA

References: 6-Robert James Rhodes

C1256142 DAWN RENEE LANTZ C125614

DAWN RENEE LANTZ was born on 04 Nov 1971 in Altoona, PA. She married GEOFFREY MOSEBEY on May 10 1997 in Altoona, PA the son of WILLIAM LYLE. MOSEBEY, Jr. and CAROLYN J. CULBERTSON. He was born on 13 Feb 1972 in Addis Ababa, Ethiopia. Both are graduates of Penn State University. His father was a famous spy and enemy of Marxism and communism who worked for the CIA in India, Africa and the Middle East and his mother as well was also a famous spy who worked for the CIA in counter terrorism in Africa and the Middle East. He is also a 2nd great grandson of the famous Confederate spy WILLIAM LESLIE MOSEBEY.

Children of DAWN LANTZ and GEOFFREY MOSEBEY are:

1. CONNOR MOSEBEY was born on 09 Apr 2001 in Chambersburg, PA.
2. QUINN MOSEBEY was born on 02 May 2004 in Altoona, PA.

References: 6-Dawn (Lantz) Mosebey

CONNOR, DAWN RENEE (LANTZ), QUINN and GEOFFREY MOSEBEY

CONNOR MOSEBEY

QUINN MOSEBEY

C12561111 YVONNE MARIE LANTZ C1256111

YVONNE MARIE LANTZ was born on 18 Mar 1970 in Camp Springs, Prince George's Co., MD. She married ROBERT STEVENS.

Children of Yvonne Lantz and ROBERT STEVENS are:

1. ASHLEIGH E. STEVENS was born on 01 Sep 1987 in Altoona, Blair Co., PA.
2. ROBERT STEVENS was born in Altoona, Blair Co., PA.

References: 6-Yvonne Marie (Lantz) Stevens

C12561112 NELSON GARFIELD LANTZ C1256111

NELSON GARFIELD LANTZ was born on 25 Jun 1979 in Honolulu, HI. He married (1) SHAWN MARIE GILBERT on 10 Jan 2004 in Pensacola, Escambia Co., FL, daughter of RICHARD CONRAD GILBERT and SHEILA MARIE ROBISON. She was born 11 Jul 1977 in Birmingham, Jefferson Co., AL. They were divorced 09 Dec 1975, Pensacola, Escambia Co., FL. He married (2) RYAN SUMMER THORP, 02 Jul 2009 in Pensacola, Escambia Co., FL, daughter of KEITH EDWARD THORP and MERCEDES GAY SULLIVAN. She was born 02 Apr 1990 in St. Petersburg, Pinellas Co., FL.

Family of NELSON LANTZ and SUMMER THORP is:

1. ISABELLA ANNE MARIE BOLAR, born on 29 Dec 2007, Pensacola, Escambia Co., FL.
2. JOCELYN ROSE LANTZ, born on 20 Nov 2009, Pensacola, Escambia Co., FL.

References: 43, 44, 46-M/NGL&RST/2009ML001721 Escambia Co FL, 46-B/JRL/109-2009-109762/Escambia Co FL, 46-B/RST/109-1990-052983/Escambia Co FL,46-B/ISAMB/109-2007-249036/Escambia Co FL, 46-B/NGL/79008371/DOH HI

JOCELYN ROSE LANTZ, RYAN SUMMER (THORP) LANTZ, NELSON GARFIELD LANTZ, & ISABELLA ANNE MARIE BOLAR

C125611111 ASHLEIGH E. STEVENS C12561111

ASHLEIGH E. STEVENS was born on 01 Sep 1987 in Altoona, Blair Co., PA.

Child of ASHLEIGH STEVENS is:

1. JASIAH EDWARD STEVENS was born in 2005 in Altoona, Blair Co., PA.

References: 6-Yvonne Marie (Lantz) Stevens

CHAPTER V

D JOHANN GEORGE LANTZ I

JOHANN (HANS) GEORGE LANTZ was born 21 Aug 1751 in Albany Twp., Berks Co., PA, and died 04 Apr 1827 in Lincoln Co., NC. He married (1) FRANCES "FANNY" ELIZABETH ANTHONY 1778, daughter of PAULUS ANTHONY and ANNA SECHLER. She was born 1756, and died 07 Dec 1791 in Lincoln Co., NC. He married (2) SUSANNAH the widow DIETZ after 1794. She died after Jul 1845.

"His name is recorded in the LANTZ Family Bible, housed at the Catawba College Library, as JOHANN GEORGE LANTZ, although "HANS" is often the name listed on later documents."

"HANS GEORGE LANTZ moved to Lincoln Co., NC in 1787. He made frequent trips back to the old home and visited his brothers in Maryland and Pennsylvania. He married, first, FANNIE ANTHONY, and after her death, the widow (SUSANNAH) DIETZ. He received the large family Bible that belonged to his Pioneer father, JACOB LANTZ of Berks Co., PA."

"Several records of that time in Lincoln Co. mentions George and his family. Census of Lincoln Co. for 1810 mentions GEORGE LANTZ and family. Court records regarding GEORGE LANTZ and the DIETZ children. Records for jury duty. There are deed records on sale of land to SAMUEL LANTZ on May 25, 1808 (160 acres) and to Jacob Lantz July 12, 1812 for 125 acres."

"HENRY HOOVER, guardian of SAMUEL DIETZ and FREDERICK DIETZ vs. JOHN DEITZ, GEORGE LANTZ and his wife SUSANNAH: Petition the court on hearing the petition of petitioner and the answer of defendants, decreed as follows: That the said prayer of the petitioner be granted as in said petition is set forth and that execution issue against the defendant's bodies, goods, chattels, lands and tenements for the payment and satisfaction of the aforesaid decrees and costs of suit according to act of assembly made and provided for such cases."

"GEORGE was a sponsor for baptisms of his sister SUSANNA's children in 1774, 1776 at Friedens Church at Stony Run. He also sponsored one baptism for his brother HENRY's child in 1778 at New Bethel Zion of Greenwich Twp. He and FANNIE had their son JOHANN JACOB baptized on 29 May, 1783 at the same New Bethel Zion Church. In 1787 GEORGE and FANNIE and family moved to Lincoln Co., NC."

JOHANN GEORGE LANTZ's bible was donated by a descendant Dr. W. A. Lantz to the Catawba College which pictures are included in this section and were provided by JIM DAVIS. The Bible was printed at Nurnberg, Germany in 1770.

His estate file is filed under "GEORGE LORETZ" 1827 Lincoln Co., NC which contained the following dower records for his wife and summons of heirs from the Oct 1827 and Jan 1828 court sessions.

Children of JOHANN LANTZ and FRANCES ANTHONY are:

1. SAMUEL LANTZ (D1)
2. BARBARA LANTZ, born 1781; died 1781 in Lincoln Co., NC.
3. JOHANN JACOB LANTZ (D3)
4. ELIZABETH LANTZ (D4)

Children of JOHANN LANTZ and SUSANNAH DIETZ are:

5. BARBARA LANTZ (D5)
6. MARY "POLLY" LANTZ (D6)
7. ANNA LANTZ (D7)

References: 5, 6-Sarah Mae (Huss) Lantz, 6-Bill Lantz, 6-From Elein Lantz Whitehead to Mrs. Coy F. Lantz, 42-Deed Book Page 62 dated Jan. 1811, 24-Lincoln Co NC H668, 6-Francys P. (Pattie) Lantz Phillips, 60, 6-Jim Davis

State of North Carolina
To the Sheriff of Lincoln County greeting
You are hereby Commanded to Summon Samuel Lentz, Jacob Lentz, Jacob Holman & Betsey his wife John Holman & Barbara his wife Daniel Holman & Polly his wife Jacob Michael & Tina his wife to appear before the Justices of the County Court of Pleas & Quarter Sessions to be held for this County at the Court house in Lincolnton on the fourth Monday after the 4th September next, then & there to answer to the Petition of Susanah Lentz Widow & Relict of George Lentz decd for her Dower of Land belonging to the Estate of the said decd & this you shall in no wise omit under the Penalty by law imposed Witness V McBee Clerk of said Court at office the 3 Monday in July 1827 Vardry McBee

Dower of Land
to be laid off to
Susanah Lentz.

Recd
To January Sess. 1828

Executed

H Cansler Shff

H Cansler charges $2 — Lawyer

State of North Carolina } Court of Pleas and Quarter Sess.
Lincoln County } July 1827

The petition of Susanna Lantz widow and relict of George Lantz late of said County humbly petitioning sheweth to your worships that her late husband George Lantz died lately intestate seized and possessed of several valuable tracts of land in said County viz the tract on which he lived on Rattling Creek (except a small part of said tract conveyed to ~~George~~ Jacob Lantz) Beginning at a red oak runs No 22 West 128 poles to a black oak thence ~~East~~ 66 East 236 poles to a hickory thence South 18 East 136 poles to a black oak and thence to the beginning. Your petitioner prays that the proper parties may be made viz Saml Lantz heir and administrator and Jacob Lantz Jacob Holman & Betsey his wife, John Holman and Barbary his wife. Saml Holman & Polly his wife and Jacob Michael and Anne his wife, and that your worships will issue your order to the sheriff of said County commanding him commanding him to summons a jury of freeholders to ~~lay~~ set off and allot to your petitioner her dower in the above described tract of land: and that said Sheriff and Jury may likewise allot and set off to your petitioner her share of the ~~personal property~~ of her deceased husband

R. B. [illegible]

State of North Carolina

To the Sheriff of Lincoln County Greeting

You are hereby commanded, agreeably to Order of Lincoln County Court of Pleas & Quarter Sessions, October Session 1827 to Summon a Jury of good & lawful men who shall be freeholders unconnected with Susanah Lontz widow & Relict of George Lontz dec^d or with the heirs of the said dec^d either by consanguinity or affinity, to meet on the premises of the said George Lontz deceased, at such time as you shall appoint then & there to lay off to Susanah Lontz widow & Relict as aforesaid her dower of Land out of the Real Estate of the dec^d according to Act of Assembly in such case made & provided, & further to assess her such damages as they may adjudge she is entitled to for detention of dower. And make return thereof to the County Court of Pleas & Quarter Sessions to be held for said County at the Court-house in Lincolnton on the third Monday in January Next, When & Where you shall make known how you have Executed this Writ, Witness V. McBee Clerk of the said Court at Office the fourth Monday after the 4th in September 1827

Vardy McBee

Copy delivered
to S Lantz &
Jno Holman,
Dan'l Holman &
Jacob Auchard
on Saturday 27
1827

31

Susanah Lontz

vs.

The Heirs of
Geo Lontz dec'd

Summons

To October Term 1827

Executed by delivering
to each of the defts
a copy of Petition &
Subpoena

W. H. Carusler Shff

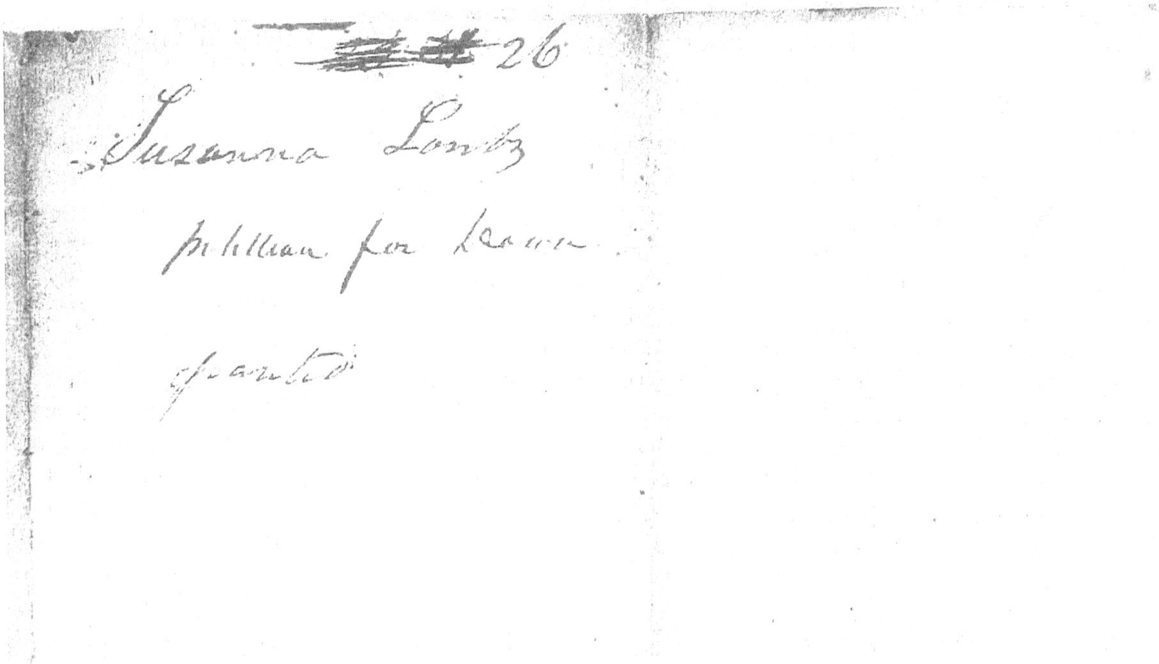
#26
Susanna Lantz

BIBLIA,

Das ist:

Die gantze Heilige Schrifft des Alten und Neuen Testaments,

Wie solche von

Herrn Doctor Martin Luther Seel.

Im Jahr Christi 1522. in unsere Teutsche Mutter-Sprach zu übersetzen angefangen, Anno 1534. zu End gebracht,

und

Vor einigen Jahren bereits

Mit den Summarien Herrn Johann Sauberti Seel.

auch mit dem

Vielfältigen und Lehrreichen Nutzen, über alle Capitel,

des Herrn D. Salomon Glassens Seel.

ausgefertiget,

Anjetzt mit gantz neuen und schönen Kupfer-Bildnissen nebst denenselben beygedruckten Lebens-Läufen, auch andern annehmlichen Figuren samt deren kurtzen Auslegungen und angehengten Moralien ausgezieret, dann von denen vorhin eingeschlichenen Druck-Fehlern auf das fleissigste gereiniget,

Uber dieses sind nicht allein des seel. Hn. Lutheri und seines Geschlechts warhaffte und aus uralten Gemählden genommene Abbildungen und Lebens-Lauf beygefüget, sondern auch zu End des gantzen Wercks, neben den Christlichen Haupt-Symbolis, ein kurtzer und nützlicher Bericht von der Augspurgischen Confession selbsten, wie man sie in dem rechten Original, im Jahr 1530. Kayser Carl dem Fünften überantwortet, beygedruckt worden.

Samt einer Vorrede

Herrn Johann Michael Dilherrns.

Mit Römisch-Kayserl. auch Königl. Polnisch- und Chur-Fürstl. Sächsis. allergnädigsten PRIVILEGIIS.

Nürnberg,

In Verlegung der Johann Andreä Endterischen Handlung.

Anno M DCC LXX.

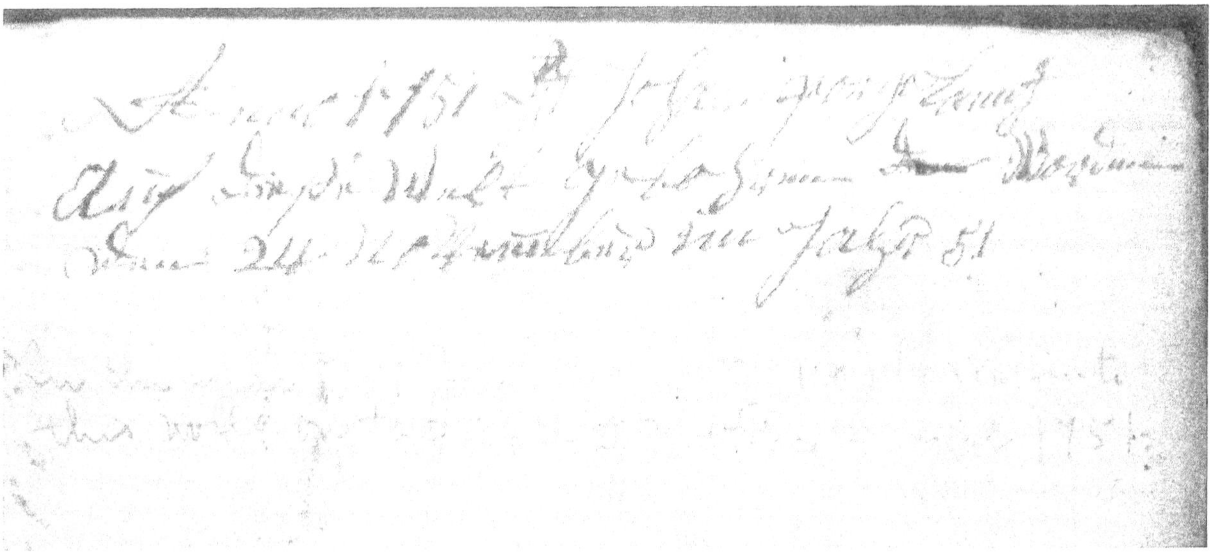

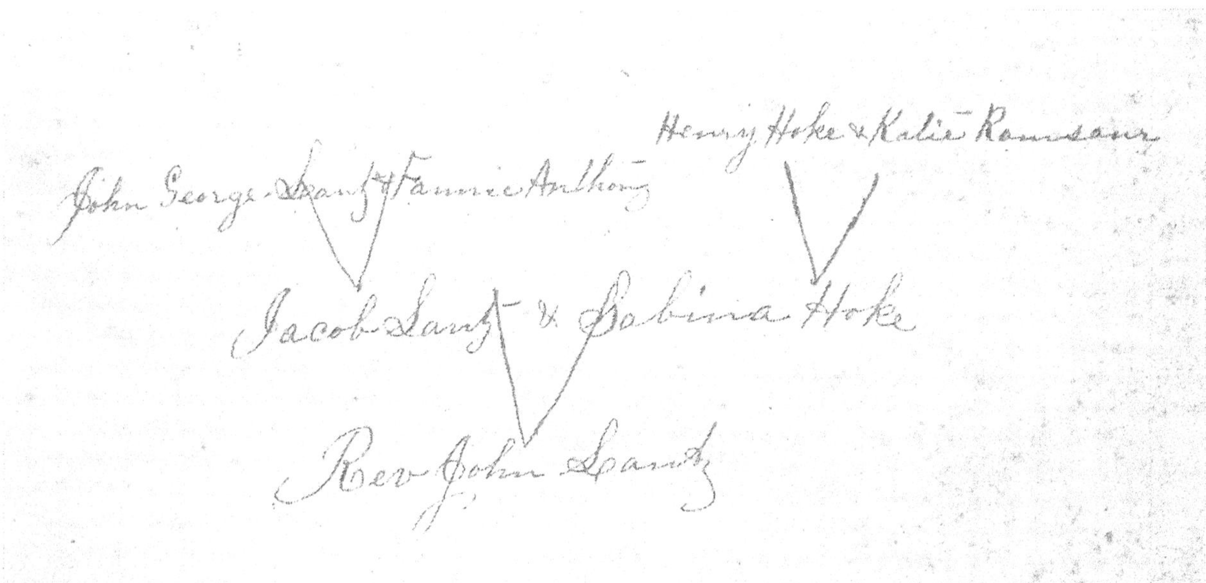

D1 SAMUEL LANTZ D

SAMUEL LANTZ was born 10 Dec 1779 in New Tripoli, Lehigh Co., PA, and died 07 May 1871. He married CATHERINE HILDEBRAND. She was born 13 Jan 1787, and died 17 Nov 1845 in Lincoln Co., NC. "He had a good home in Lincoln Co., NC but sold it during the war and invested in Confederate bonds and lost everything. He and his family moved to IA."

Known Land Transaction:

25 May 1808 – Deed of sale of land from HANS GEORGE LANTZ to SAMUEL LANTZ for 160 acres dated

Children of SAMUEL LANTZ and CATHERINE HILDEBRAND are:

1. FRANCES BARBARA LANTZ (D11)
2. JUDITH LANTZ, born in 1806 in Lincoln Co., NC; married (1) JOSEPH CLAY; died in 1849 in Lincoln Co., NC; No children; married (2) HENRY KILLIAN in Lincoln Co.,

NC. He was born in 1787 in NC.

3. EVE LANTZ
4. MARY E. LANTZ, born in Lincoln Co., NC.
5. ELI LANTZ, died young.
6. BARBARA LANTZ (D16)
7. GEORGE LANTZ (D17)
8. LINNA JANE LANTZ (D18)

References: 6-Sarah Mae (Huss) Lantz, 6-Ann Albright Pepmeyer, 26-Union Twp Lincoln Co NC H211, 5, 24-Lincoln Co NC H639, 25-Lincoln Co NC H39

D3 JOHANN JACOB LANTZ D

JOHANN JACOB LANTZ was born 15 Feb 1783 in New Tripoli, Berks Co., PA, and died 13 Mar 1849 in Catawba Co., NC. He married SARAH "SALLIE" SABINA HOKE on 21 Aug 1806 in Lincoln Co., NC, daughter of JOHN HOKE and KATHERINE RAMSOUR. She was born 21 Dec 1787 in Lincoln Co., NC, and died 13 Jun 1864 in Catawba Co., NC. His will is record in Will Book 1 Page 74 in Catawba Co., NC.

Some known land transactions:

24 Aug 1811 – Deed of sale of land from HENRY HILDEBRAND to JACOB LANTZ for 27 acres - proved by JOHN YODER.

29 Jul 1812 – Deed of sale of land from JOHANN GEORGE LANTZ to JACOB LANTZ for 125 acres - proved by oath of JOHN SEAGLE.

Children of JOHANN LANTZ and SARAH HOKE are:

1. JOHN GEORGE LANTZ (D31)
2. HENRY LANTZ, born 19 Feb 1809 in Lincoln Co., NC.
3. JOHN LANTZ (D33)
4. CATHARINA LANTZ, born 11 Jul 1812 in Lincoln Co., NC. She married JAMES HARTMAN in 14 Jan 1852 in Catawba Co., NC. He was born in 1820 in NC. No children.
5. ELIZABETH N. LANTZ (D35)
6. SARAH LANTZ (D36)
7. JACOB LANTZ (D37)
8. ANNA LANTZ, born 08 Nov 1821 in NC; died 08 Nov 1821 in NC.
9. HANNAH LANTZ, born 05 Jan 1823 in NC; died 08 Oct 1831 in NC.
10. RHODA LANTZ, born 07 Nov 1824 in NC; died 18 Oct 1831 in NC.
11. BARBARA LANTZ, born 28 May 1827 in NC; died 05 Oct 1831 in NC.

References: 6-Sarah Mae (Huss) Lantz, 6-Sarah Sabina Hoke, 5, 24-Catawba Co NC H453, 25-Catawba Co NC H1216, 37, 65,

[illegible] April Session 1841

I [illegible] of the County of [illegible] & State of North Carolina
knowing the uncertainty of this life and being desirous while living and in my
[illegible] of the [illegible] [illegible] [illegible] [illegible] do hereby
make the following disposition of a portion of my property viz:
First I give & bequeath to my wife Sabina during her natural life or
widowhood all that tract of land situate lying and being in the County
and State aforesaid on both sides of Mountain Creek including my
dwelling, beginning at a black oak [illegible] on John [illegible] line near
his corner and runs South 85½ [illegible] poles to a post oak then S 30 E 40
poles to a stone on a ditch then down the ditch North 71 E 12 poles to
a [illegible] then S 35 E [illegible] poles on [illegible] then [illegible] 60½ poles to a stone
[illegible] then [illegible] the creek [illegible] poles to a small black oak on a
line of [illegible] then with said line of [illegible] [illegible] poles [illegible] the [illegible]
Mountain Creek branch to a [illegible] then [illegible] poles to a stake on
the bank of a ditch then [illegible] poles to a [illegible] on a line of [illegible] then
with the line of said [illegible] poles to a stake on the side of the
Buffalo Shoals Road then with said road [illegible] poles to a [illegible]
[illegible] then [illegible] poles to an elder bush then [illegible] poles to a
Maple near John [illegible] line then with his line [illegible] poles to
the beginning containing by estimation 177 acres being lot No. 1 of the [illegible]
I also give and bequeath unto my wife Sabina my negro woman [illegible]
with her son [illegible] during her life or widowhood after her death or marriage
said negro woman with her [illegible] to be sold and the proceeds thereof to be
equally divided among the heirs of my daughter Elizabeth Wilkinson,
I also give unto my wife Sabina a [illegible] [illegible] [illegible] and my buggy
[illegible] two [illegible] to be chosen out of my stock by her three sheep five
head of hogs all to be taken by herself her bed [illegible] [illegible] clothing kitchen
table & cupboard with all the kitchen furniture & one Bureau standing
in the hall room with the [illegible] [illegible]
Item I give and bequeath to my son Henry all that tract of land
lying in the same County on both sides of Mountain Creek, being lot
No. 3 in the division [illegible] Beginning at a black oak John [illegible]
corner and runs with his line [illegible] poles [illegible] a branch to a
post oak then N 15 W [illegible] poles to a post oak then S 35½ W 34 poles to a
post oak then S [illegible] E [illegible] to a black oak [illegible] near the bank of the
old creek then S [illegible] poles to a white oak [illegible] the creek then
S [illegible] E [illegible] poles with [illegible] line to a stake in his field
then North 25 W [illegible] poles to a [illegible] then N 47 W 31 poles to a May Cherry on the
bank of the creek ditch then [illegible] poles to a stake at a bridge on a
ditch then down said ditch N [illegible] poles to a stake near a willow
bush then N 42 W 80 poles to a stake on the side of the Buffalo Shoals road
then N 53 E 20 poles to a haw bush then N 17½ W [illegible] poles to an elder bush
then N 26 W 70 poles to a Maple near John [illegible] line then with his

[illegible] S 83 W 40 poles to the beginning containing by estimation 135 acres valued by me at [illegible] dollars to him his heirs and assigns for ever but the [illegible] [illegible] Henry being under me as guardian for him he is to [illegible] the [illegible] [illegible] as guardian for him by getting the said land. I also give and bequeath to [illegible] [illegible] a negro girl from two to three years old by the name of [illegible] to him his heirs and assigns for ever. Also one bay mare called [illegible] [illegible] [illegible] I give and bequeath to my son John [illegible] a tract of land lying on the [illegible] side of [illegible] Creek in the same County & State. Beginning at a black oak Samuel [illegible] [illegible] [illegible] thence with his line S 3 W [illegible] poles to a stake his corner then N 87 E [illegible] [illegible] 25 to a stake then S 82 E [illegible] poles to a black gum then S 23 E 18 poles to a stake then S 87 E 31 poles to a stake in the orchard then S[illegible] poles to the [illegible] line in the [illegible] of the [illegible] east of the barn then N 72 E 14½ poles to a post oak on [illegible] [illegible] line on the east side of the [illegible] road then N 15 W with [illegible] line 91 poles to a Spanish oak corner of the [illegible] tract then S 64 E 6 poles to a stake on Samuel [illegible] line thence with it to the beginning containing 45 acres 100 perches. Also a lot of land on both sides of said Creek including a meadow Beginning at a [illegible] and [illegible] at [illegible] line [illegible] with it N 82 W 58 poles to a stake on [illegible] [illegible] line thence with it North 17 E 5½ to a [illegible] on [illegible] line the same course 23 poles more to a black oak [illegible] corner then with his line N 57 E 14 poles crossing [illegible] Creek to a stake on the east bank of said Creek [illegible] [illegible] [illegible] & crossing the Creek again S 14 [illegible] poles to the beginning containing 16 acres & 10 perches both tracts together valued by me at [illegible] dollars [illegible] [illegible] I give and bequeath to said son his heirs and assigns for ever. I also give and bequeath to said son John [illegible] my new [illegible] waggon and my two [illegible] [illegible] [illegible] by the names of [illegible] & [illegible] to him his heirs and assigns for ever.

Sixth I give and bequeath to my son John a tract & parcel of land known as the [illegible] land lying on the west side of the [illegible] fork joining lands of John [illegible] Henry [illegible] [illegible] and [illegible] [illegible] beginning at a black gum on the river bank and runs west 112 poles to a black oak in [illegible] land then South 10 E 103 poles to a black oak then North 87 E 116 poles to a hickory on the bank of the river then up the river as it meanders to the beginning containing 46 acres excepting a [illegible] lot that [illegible] [illegible] [illegible] [illegible] in the North east corner of said land, to him his heirs and assigns for ever. Said land is valued by me at [illegible]. I also give and bequeath to my son John a negro girl by the name of Margaret about 7 years old to him his heirs and assigns for ever. I also give to my son a small tract of [illegible] land on the waters of [illegible] Creek conveyed to me by Henry [illegible] beginning at a [illegible] post oak [illegible] corner runs with his line North 112 poles to a chesnut then east 67 poles to a black oak then South 46 poles to a pine on [illegible] [illegible] line then with his line S 86 W 78 poles to a black oak [illegible] corner then South 40 poles to a black oak then [illegible] 4 poles to the beginning 37 acres to him his heirs & assigns for ever.

[illegible]

Fifth I give and bequeath unto my son [illegible] the tract of land on [illegible] [illegible] on Killion Creek beginning at a [illegible] oak [illegible] corner [illegible] with [illegible] line S 83 W 105 [illegible] to a small [illegible] then with [illegible] line N 77 W 42 poles to a small [illegible] corner on the [illegible] then N [illegible] poles to a [illegible] on the east side of [illegible] to a black [illegible] then [illegible] poles to a [illegible] the creek then crossing the creek South 87 [illegible] poles to a [illegible] corner then a new line crossing the creek [illegible] 7 poles to a stake Samuel [illegible] corner then [illegible] the creek [illegible] poles to a stake in the middle of the creek then with another of his lines N 81 E 67 poles to a stake then [illegible] N 87 W 32 poles to a stake four poles North of the [illegible] then a [illegible] then N 83 E 31 poles to a stake in the orchard [illegible] of the [illegible] then [illegible] poles to a stake near the [illegible] of the [illegible] from the [illegible] then [illegible] poles to a post oak on the east side of the [illegible] then [illegible] to the beginning along [illegible] line containing 100 acres valued by me at one thousand dollars [illegible] tract of land I give to him his heirs and assigns for ever. Also a tract of land known as [illegible] the name of [illegible] lying on [illegible] of Killion Creek in the county of Lincoln State of North Carolina beginning at a [illegible] of the [illegible] North [illegible] poles to a [illegible] then [illegible] poles to a hickory [illegible] corner then with his line South [illegible] poles to a [illegible] then to the beginning containing [illegible] acres to him & his heirs for ever but that my son is to have no pay for the [illegible] he holds against me of nearly two hundred dollars with the interest. I also give & bequeath to my son [illegible] one negro boy by the name of [illegible] in consideration for work and labour done for me by said son [illegible] to him his heirs & assigns for ever.

Sixthly. I give & bequeath to my daughter Catharine all that tract or parcel of land willed to my wife [illegible] her life or widowhood with equal rights & privilege with her [illegible] from the time of my death. I also give and bequeath to my daughter Catharine a negro [illegible] by the name of [illegible] to her & her heirs for ever.

Seventh. I give and bequeath unto my daughter Sarah all that tract of land lying on both sides of [illegible] Creek whereon [illegible] Howard [illegible] beginning at a small black oak [illegible] line near his [illegible] and runs S [illegible] E 188 poles to a post oak then S 36 E 40 poles to a [illegible] on a ditch then down the ditch N 17 E 12 poles to a hickory then S 83 E 3 poles to an [illegible] then N 73 E 57 poles to a [illegible] then crossing the [illegible] S 36 E 58 poles to a small black oak on a line of No 5 then with said line N 72 E 40 poles to a white oak [illegible] corner then with his line [illegible] poles to a [illegible] white oak & [illegible] corner then North [illegible] poles to a hickory [illegible] line then with his line South

75 [illegible] 82 poles to a Post oak Said Sheppards Corner then with his line
[illegible] 118 poles to a Post oak [illegible] then 302 poles to a post oak thence
[illegible] poles to a Corner of W Sheppards Corner then with Rowes line 168
to [illegible] poles to the beginning containing 185 acres being lot No 1 of the Plat
with the [illegible] valued to me at 800 dollars but as her husband
[illegible] Harrison holds a note or notes against me to the amount of
[illegible] hundred & fifty dollars payable [illegible] which was to be
[illegible] of them getting said land he is not to bring said note
or notes against my [illegible] or executor or estate but is to have a
lien on the land for the amount to her & her heirs for ever
I also give and bequeath to my daughter Sarah a negro girl of the
name of Hannah to her & her heirs for ever
In witness whereof I have hereunto set my hand and seal
this [illegible] day of July 1835

Jacob Lantz (Seal)

I Jacob Lantz make and declare the following to be a codicil to my
last will & testament & [illegible] that the same shall be taken as a
part of my last will & testament. All my slaves living at my decease
and not willed in the above will and all my personal goods not
willed to none of my sons may be appraised and equally divided
among my sons after paying my just debts or be sold as they
may think proper the heirs of my daughter Elizabeth Wilkinson
to get one part equal to one of my sons & other daughters which
part shall be placed in the hands of a guardian chosen by the
Court for the support of said Elizabeth Wilkinson & her heirs
Given under my hand & seal this 24 day
of October 1835

Jacob Lantz

D4 ELIZABETH LANTZ D

ELIZABETH LANTZ was born 1786, and died after 1850. She married JACOB HALLMAN 13 Aug 1808 in Lincoln Co., NC, son of ANTHONY HALLMAN and ELIZABETH GINGERY. He was born 1787, and died Mar 1851 in Lincoln Co., NC. His will is recorded in Will Book 2 Page 349 in Lincoln Co., NC.

Children of ELIZABETH LANTZ and JACOB HALLMAN are:

1. FRANCES "FANNY" HALLMAN (D41)
2. ANTHONY HALLMAN (D42)
3. ELIZABETH HALLMAN (D43)
4. GEORGE WASHINGTON HALLMAN (D44)
5. SUSANNAH HALLMAN (D45)
6. RHODA "RODY" HALLMAN, born 1826 in Lincoln Co., NC; died 1899 in Lincoln Co., NC.
7. BENJAMIN HALLMAN (D47)
8. ISRAEL HALLMAN, born 1831.
9. MARY CATHERINE HALLMAN (D49)

References: 6-Sarah Mae (Huss) Lantz, 6-Nancy Cason, 24-Lincoln Co NC H272, 65

349

April Sessions 1851
Jacob Hallman's Will

In the name of God Amen I Jacob Hallman of the County of Lincoln and State of North Carolina Being of sound mind and perfect memory blessed be God do on this 24th day of December in the year of our Lord one thousand Eight hundred and fifty make & publish this to be my last Will and Testament in manner and form as follows that is to say 1st I will & bequeath unto my beloved wife Elizabeth during her lifetime My home plantation also all my house and kitchen furniture Excepting such things as she may not wish to keep if any such they may be sold with other property also the old cow My Bay mare and pump horse two head of Sheep one sow and six shoats also choice of two young hogs, and at the death of my wife Elizabeth my will is that all her property be Equally divi-ded between my three daughters Fanny Susannah & Rody by consent or Else put to sale and the money arising from the sale Equally divided between the three above named Daughters 2nd I will and bequeath unto my daughter Fanny Ten acres of Land Including the meadow that is now called hers binding or Running with Clarks Creek and Lockarts creek so as to make the number of acres 3rd I also give and bequeath unto my Son Anthony Fifteen acres of Land Joining his own

Continued 350

Tract of Land commencing at his line and running down to a dead Apple Tree in the flat near to a Cherry Tree and from that across to Wiley Hallmans Line so as to make the fifteen acres also my half of the Waggon after my wifes death 4th I also give and bequeath to my Son George Twelve Acres of Land of the home tract on these Conditions that he George Hallman first give up one note which he holds against me for Twenty five dollars 5th I also give and bequeath unto my Son Benjamin Fifteen acres of Land of the home tract on these Conditions that he Benjamin Hallman pay to his brother Anthony Hallman a sum of money amounting to one hundred and fifteen dollars which Anthony Hallman paid to John Boyd for Benjamin Hallman as security money, the two last Lotts mentioned is to be laid off Joining Fannys lott, 6th I give and bequeath unto my grand Daughter S. M. C. Bridges Ten Acres of my home tract of Land Joining the alove mentioned lotts if She should not live to be of age the Land is to fall back to my Children 7th my further will is that all the ballance of home tract of Land shall be Equally divided between my Son Isreal and Daughters Elizabeth Susannah & Rody, 8th I also give and bequeath unto my daughter Rody my Ball mare and my young Cow also three bed steads and clothing for the same such as her Sisters Received also the saddle and bridle the now

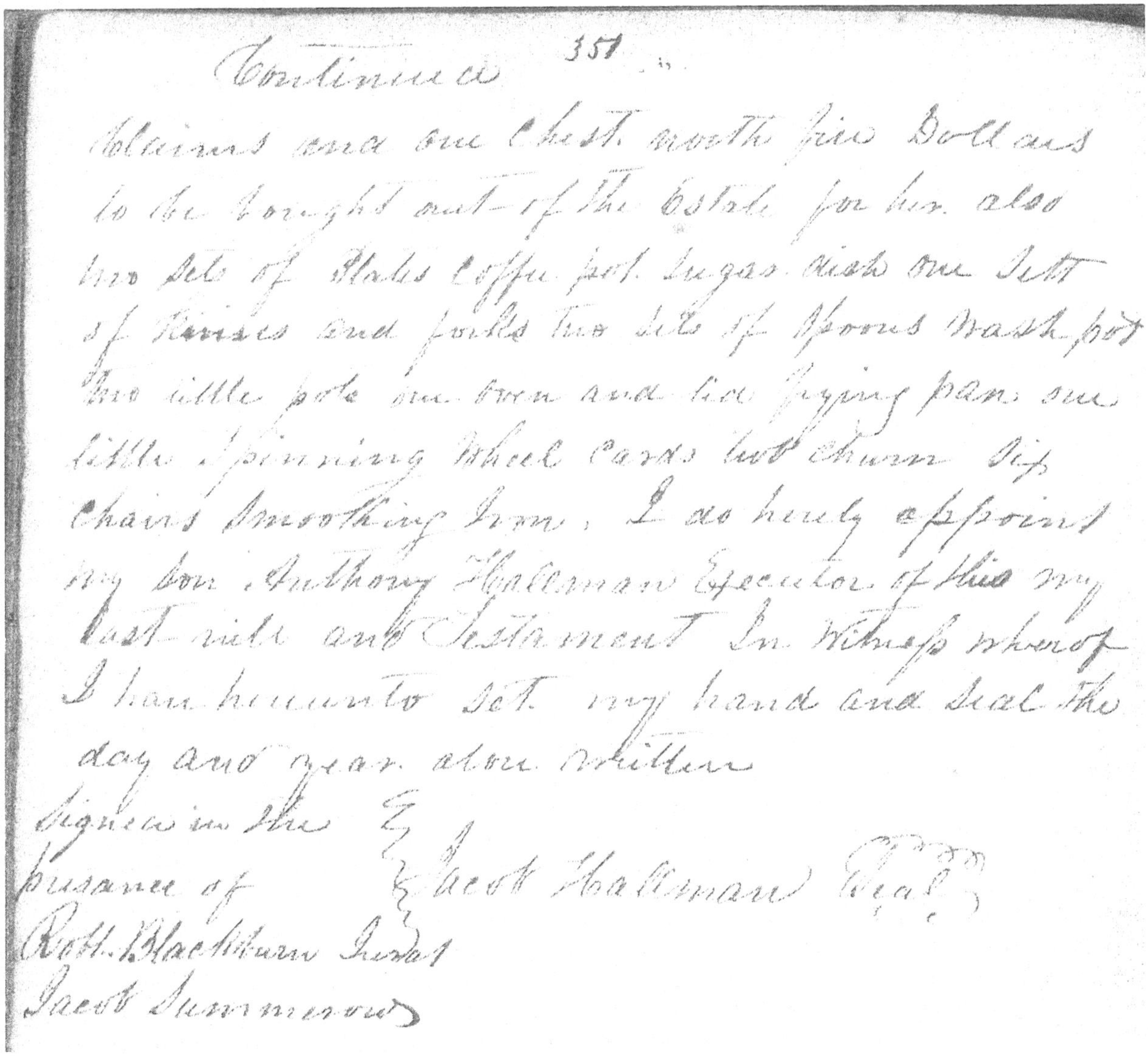
Continued 351
Claims and one Chest worth five Dollars
to be bought out of the Estate for her also
two sets of Plates coffee pot sugar dish one sett
of Knives and forks two sets of Spoons wash pot
two little pots one oven and lid frying pan one
little Spinning Wheel Cards two churn six
Chairs Smoothing Iron. I do hereby appoint
my son Anthony Hallman Executor of this my
last will and Testament In Witness whereof
I have hereunto set my hand and seal the
day and year above written
Signed in the
presence of Jacob Hallman (Seal)
Robt. Blackburn Jurat
Jacob Summerow

D5 BARBARA LANTZ D

BARBARA LANTZ was born 1799, and died 31 Dec 1858. She married (1) JOHN HALLMAN 21 Mar 1814 in Lincoln Co., NC, son of DANIEL HALLMAN. He was born 1795, and died before 1830. She married (2) JACOB CLINE, Sr. 23 Oct 1841 in Lincoln Co., NC. He was born 1765, and died after 1850.

Child of BARBARA LANTZ and JOHN HALLMAN is:

1. DELILA HALLMAN (D51)

References: 6-Sarah Mae (Huss) Lantz, 24-Catawba Co NC H697

D6 MARY LANTZ D

MARY "POLLY" LANTZ was born 05 Oct 1801 in Lincoln Co., NC, and died 18 Nov 1842 in Lincoln Co., NC. She married DANIEL HALLMAN 05 Feb 1824 in Lincoln Co., NC, son of HENRY HALLMAN and RACHEL WARLICK. He was born 19 Jan 1803 in Lincoln Co., NC, and died 13 Jan 1891 in Lincoln Co., NC. His will is recorded in Will Book 4 Page 450 in Lincoln Co., NC.

Children of MARY LANTZ and DANIEL HALLMAN are:

1. ELEANOR HALLMAN (D61)
2. MARGARET HALLMAN, born 1828.
3. ELMIRA HALLMAN (D63)
4. ANDREW HALLMAN (D64)
5. ABEL HALLMAN (D65)
6. PHYLECTOR HALLMAN (D66)
7. MICHAEL HALLMAN (D67)
8. MARY CATHARINE HALLMAN, born 1838. She married (?) WARE.
9. MARTHA EMELINE HALLMAN (D69)

References: 6-Sarah Mae (Huss) Lantz, 24-Lincoln Co NC H213, 25-Lincoln Co NC H188

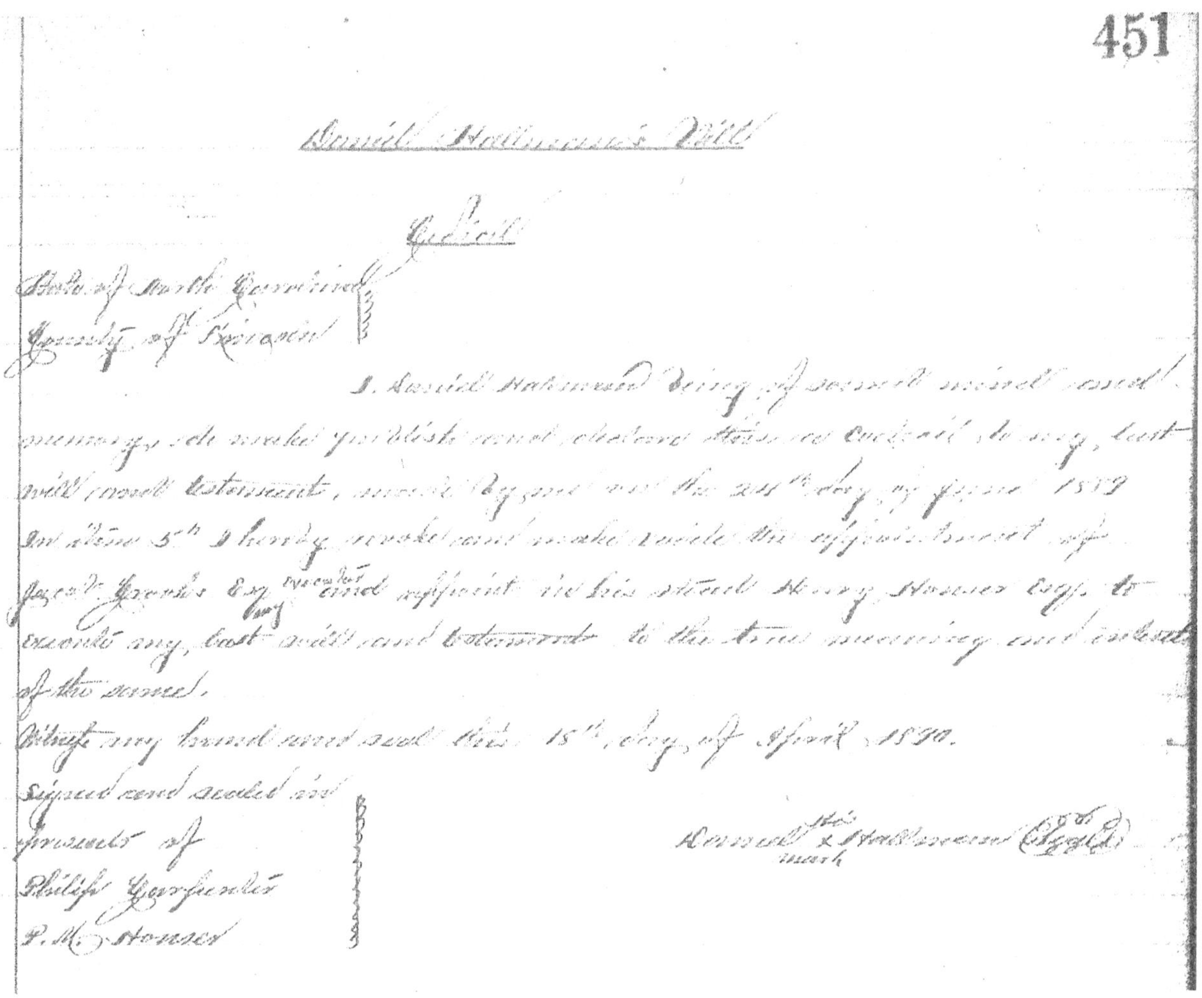

451

Daniel Hallman's Will

Codicil

State of North Carolina }
County of Lincoln }

I, Daniel Hallman being of sound mind and memory do make publish and declare this a Codicil to my last will and testament, made by me on the 20th day of June 1889 In item 5th I hereby revoke and make void the appointment of Jacob Yount's Esq executor and appoint in his stead Henry Houser Esq. to execute my last will and testament to the true meaning and intent of the same.

Witness my hand and seal this 15th day of April 1890.

Signed and sealed in presence of }
Philip Carpenter
P. M. Houser

Daniel his x mark Hallman (Seal)

Daniel Hallman's Will

State of North Carolina
Lincoln County

I Daniel Hallman of the County of Lincoln and State of North Carolina being of sound mind and memory and considering the uncertainty of my earthly existence do make and declare this my last will and testament in manner and form following, that is to say:

1st. I will and bequeath to my daughter Margaret Hartsoe wife of Sylvanus Hartsoe, and to her Children five acres of land including the buildings and all the improvements thereon including spring, orchards, [illegible] shop &c. And at my death, the said five acres and improvements to be valued by three disinterested men to be chosen by her and my executor and the value of the same to be deducted out of her share of my estate.

2nd. I will that all the remainder of my lands and personal belonging to my estate, be sold by executor at public sale for cash and after paying my burial and funeral expenses, together with all my just debts,

the remainder of my estate to be equally divided between all my heirs, namely, to [illegible] heirs her share, and [illegible] Hallman heirs his share, to Myra's heirs, Andrew Hallman, Philetus Houser, Catherine Byers, Abel Hallman, Caroline Hartsoe and Frances Fisher, and Margaret Hartsoe after deducting from Margaret Hartsoe share the value of the premises heretofore mentioned and willed to her & her Children.

3rd I will that the one taking care of me, boarding and clothing the remainder of my life shall be paid by executor twelve dollars and fifty cents per month from this date out of my estate.

4th I will that if Catherine Byers or Frances Fisher should die before my death, and without any living Children, their shares shall be equally divided between all my other heirs.

5th I do hereby constitute and appoint my trusty friend Jacob [illegible] Executor to this my last will and testament to the true intent and meaning of the same.

And lastly I hereby revoke all former wills and testaments heretofore made by me.

Witness my hand & seal this [illegible] day of April 1887

Signed sealed in presence of us
[illegible]
[illegible]

Daniel his X mark Hallman (Seal)

[illegible]

D7 ANNA LANTZ D

ANNA LANTZ was born in 1802. She married JACOB MICHAEL 13 Nov 1820 in Lincoln Co., NC. He was born in 1802 in NC.

Children of ANNA LANTZ and JACOB MICHAEL are:

1. AMBROSE MICHAEL (D71)
2. HENRY MICHAEL, born in 1831 in Lincoln Co., NC.
3. JACOB MICHAEL (D73)
4. MARY M. MICHAEL (D74)
5. NOAH MICHAEL, born in 1838 in Lincoln Co., NC.
6. DANIEL MICHAEL, born in 1841 in Lincoln Co., NC.
7. BARBARA MICHAEL, born in 1843 in Lincoln Co., NC.

References: 24-Lincoln Co NC N668, 25-Lincoln Co NC H1157

D11 FRANCES BARBARA LANTZ D1

FRANCES "FANNY" BARBARA LANTZ was born in 11 Oct 1807 in Lincoln Co., NC and died 30 May 1905 in Lee Co., IA. She married ELIAS JARRETT on 08 Mar 1827 in Lincoln Co., NC, son of JOHANNES JARRETT and ELIZABETH FISHER. He was born 24 Sep 1799 in Lincoln Co., NC and died 20 Jan 1884 in Lee Co., IA. Both are buried in Clay Grove Cemetery, West Point Twp., Lee Co., IA.

Children of FRANCES LANTZ and ELIAS JARRETT are:

1. HARRIET K. JARRETT (D111)
2. SARAH ELIZABETH JARRETT (D112)
3. JOHN E. JARRETT born on 27 Aug 1830 in Lincoln Co., NC; died 14 Jul 1926 in Lee Co., IA; married AREY E. HARRISON; born on 08 Nov 1841 in IA; died 11 Sep 1911 in Lee Co., IA. Both are buried in Clay Grove Cemetery, West Point Twp., Lee Co., IA.
4. CAROLINE JARRETT, born in 1833 in Lincoln Co., NC.
5. MARY ANNA JARRETT (D115)
6. FANNIE LOUISE JARRETT (D116)
7. PHILIP FRANKLIN JARRETT (D117)
8. MARGARET JANE JARRETT (D118)
9. EVA SUSANNAH JARRETT, born in 1842 in Lincoln Co., NC; married JAMES BOYLE.
10. FRANCES EMELINE JARRETT, born on 15 Oct 1843 in Lincoln Co., NC; died 31 May 1852 in Lee Co., IA. She is buried in Clay Grove Cemetery, West Point Twp., Lee Co., IA.
11. ISABEL JARRETT (D11B)
12. CANDACE VIRGINIA JARRETT (D11C)
13. BARBARA JARRETT (D11D)

References: 6-Sarah Mae (Huss) Lantz, 24-Lee Co IA H459, 25-Lee Co IA H512, 26-Marion Twp Lee Co IA H178, 27-Marion Twp Lee Co IA H228, 29-Franklin Twp Le Co IA H57, 45

D16 BARBARA LANTZ D1

BARBARA LANTZ was born 15 Apr 1813 in Lincoln Co., NC, and died in Lee Co., IA. She married JOHN HOOVER 26 Sep 1932 in Lincoln County, NC, son of SOLOMON HOOVER and HANNAH ARNDT. He was born 30 Jul 1807 in Lincoln Co., NC, and died 08 Apr 1887 in Lee Co., IA.

Children of BARBARA LANTZ and JOHN HOOVER are:

1. ROSANNA C. HOOVER, born 12 Aug 1833 in Lincoln Co., NC.
2. MARY E. HOOVER, born on 12 Sep 1835 in Lincoln Co., NC.
3. JULIA HOOVER, born 26 Sep 1837 in Lincoln Co., NC.
4. F. W. HOOVER, born 1838 in Lincoln Co., NC.
5. FRANCES "FANNY" J. HOOVER, born 09 Jan 1840 in Lincoln Co., NC.
6. LINNA JANE HOOVER, born 28 Feb 1843 in Lincoln Co., NC.
7. DORCAS E. HOOVER, born 18 Sep 1844 in Lincoln Co., NC.
8. BARBARA ELENORA HOOVER (D168)
9. SARAH HOOVER, born 19 Apr 1854 in IA.
10. MARLTEA HOOVER, born 24 Nov 1856 in IA.

References: 6-Sarah Mae (Huss) Lantz, 27-Franklin Twp Lee Co IA H54, 29-Franklin Twp Lee Co IA H64, 50-1895 Lee Co Page 183, 25-Franklin Twp Lee Co IA H181

D17 GEORGE LANTZ D1

GEORGE LANTZ was born 28 Aug 1817 in Lincoln Co., NC, and died 26 Jan 1890. He married ELMIRA "MYRA" ELIZABETH ROCKETT 16 Dec 1844, daughter of MIDDLETON ROCKETT and MAHALA BALLEW. She was born 07 Oct 1822 in Lincoln Co., NC, and died

29 Jul 1895.

Children of GEORGE LANTZ and ELMIRA ROCKETT are:

1. TITUS LANTZ, born 07 Feb 1847 in Lincoln Co., NC; died 06 May 1856.
2. SAMUEL HARVEY LANTZ (D172)
3. JOHN MILTON LANTZ (D173)
4. LEANDER WASHINGTON LANTZ (D174)
5. PHILLIP FREDERICK LANTZ (D175)
6. WILLIAM D. LANTZ, born 22 Feb 1855 in West Point, Lee Co., IA; died 15 Feb 1879.
7. GEORGE HENDERSON LANTZ (D177)
8. STEPHEN ANDERSON LANTZ, born 29 Apr 1860 in Van Wert, Decatur Co., IA. He married MARY ELLISON.
9. MAJOR LANTZ, born 05 Apr 1862 in Van Wert, Decatur Co., IA.
10. IDA JANE LANTZ (D17A)
11. ABRAHAM LINCOLN LANTZ, born 1867.

References: 6-Sarah Mae (Huss) Lantz, 27-Long Creek Twp Decatur Co IA H45, 26-Long Creek Twp Decatur Co IA H61, 24-Division 28 Lee Co IA H616, 25-Decatur Twp Decatur Co IA H179, 6-Francys Pattie Lantz Phillips

D18 LINNA JANE LANTZ D1

LINNA JANE LANTZ was born 02 Jan 1821 in Lincoln Co., NC, and died 16 Jul 1898 in Davis Co., IA. She married JAMES ALBRIGHT on 13 Dec 1848 in Lincoln County, NC. He was born 09 Aug 1822 in Rowan Co., NC, and died 08 Feb 1890 in Davis Co., IA.

Children of LINNA LANTZ and JAMES ALBRIGHT are:

1. MARY DOVYANN CATHERINE ALBRIGHT (D181)
2. JOHN LANTZ ALBRIGHT (D182)
3. LINNA JANE ALBRIGHT (D183)

References: 6-Sarah Mae (Huss) Lantz, 24-Lincoln Co NC H673, 25-Franklin Twp Lee Co IA H180, 26-Franklin Twp Lee Co IA H25, 27- Franklin Twp Lee Co IA H29, 65

D31 JOHN GEORGE LANTZ D3

JOHN GEORGE LANTZ was born 18 Jul 1807 in Lincoln Co., NC, and died 05 May 1865. He married THERESA L. DOYLE 23 Jan 1841 in Benton Co., AR. She was born 15 Jul 1819 in TN, and died 29 Jun 1889 in Parker Co., TX.

Children of JOHN LANTZ and THERESA DOYLE are:

1. JACOB BENTON LANTZ (D311)
2. JOHN D. LANTZ, born 06 Dec 1844 in AL; died 09 Jan 1856 in Parker Co., TX..
3. SARAH F. LANTZ (D313)
4. MARION LANTZ, born 11 Mar 1849 in TX; died 09 Jan 1856 in TX; buried in Veal Station Cemetery, Parker Co., Texas.
5. EMMA LANTZ, born 04 Feb 1851 in TX; died 02 Jan 1856 in Parker Co., Texas.
6. GEORGE HOWARD LANTZ, born 08 Sep 1853; died 17 Dec 1856 in Parker Co., Texas.
7. ALBERT COLUMBUS LANTZ (D317)

8. LEONIDAS "LON" LANTZ, born in 1858 in Parker Co., TX; died 1946. He married MINERVA JANE WALLER in 1904 in Parker Co., TX, her 2nd marriage and no children.
9. MARY ALICE LANTZ (D319)
10. HATTIE LANTZ, born 13 Jul 1860 in TX; died 23 Nov 1895. She married W.S. BRITT on 11 Apr 1878.
11. MARTHA LANTZ, born in 1862 in TX.

References: 6-Sarah Mae (Huss) Lantz, 5, 27-Precinct 2 Parker Co TX H181, 26-Precinct 2 Parker Co TX H435, 24-Rusk Twp Rusk Co TX H275

D33 JOHN LANTZ D3

Rev. JOHN LANTZ was born 28 May 1810 in Lincoln Co., NC, and died 26 Jan 1873 in Taneytown, Carroll Co., MD. He married NANCY C. FRAILEY/FRALEY on 13 Apr 1845 in Rowan Co., NC. She was born in 1822 in NC. "The Rev. JOHN LANTZ served St. Matthews Church from 1859 to 1868. He was a native of Lincoln Co., NC and was originally from the Daniel's Reformed Church congregation. He was reared under the ministry of Rev. FRITCHEZ. He was a student at the Academy in Lincolnton, N.C. He studied Theology at York, PA under DR. MAYER. He ended his ministry at Taneytown, MD where he died at the age of 73 years."

Children of JOHN LANTZ and NANCY FRAILEY are:

1. ELLEN ELVIRA LANTZ (D331)
2. SUSANNA CATHRINA LANTZ (D332)
3. HENRIETTA CAROLINE LANTZ (D333)
4. EMMA JANE LANTZ (D334)
5. WILLIE AUGUSTA LANTZ, born in 1863 in NC; died 06 Feb 1959. She was formerly an instructor at Hood College, Frederick, Maryland was later Registrar of Catawba College, Salisbury, N.C. She was 96 when she died and is buried in Newton, N.C.

References: 6-Sarah Mae (Huss) Lantz, 5, 26-Riverheads Augusta Co VA H71, 6-Jim Davis, 65

JOHN LANTZ and NANCY FRAILEY marriage certificate provided by JIM DAVIS

D35 ELIZABETH N. LANTZ D3

ELIZABETH N. LANTZ was born 15 Apr 1815, and died 02 Nov 1892. She married THOMAS WILKINSON Jan 1841 in NC. He was born in 1813 in Catawba Co., NC.

Children of ELIZABETH LANTZ and THOMAS WILKINSON are:

1. MARTHA C. WILKINSON (D351)
2. RUFUS A. WILKINSON (D352)
3. WILLIAM H. WILKINSON (D353)
4. NANCY CAROLINE WILKINSON (D354)
5. GEORGE M. WILKINSON (D355)
6. JACOB M. WILKINSON (D356)
7. DAVID C. KING WILKINSON (D357)
8. JAMES WESLEY WILKINSON (D358)
9. MARY A. E. WILKINSON, born in 13 Jan 1858 in Catawba Co., NC; died young; married L. W. LATHAM
10. SARAH C. WILKINSON (D35A)
11. JOHN F. WILKINSON (D35B)
12. ABSOLEM LANE WILKINSON (D35C)

References: 6-Sarah Mae (Huss) Lantz, 5, 24-Catawba Co NC H440, 25-Catawba Co NC H1518, 26-Caldwell Twp Catawba Co NC H92

D36 SARAH LANTZ D3

SARAH LANTZ was born 25 Dec 1816, and died 02 Nov 1892. She married GEORGE HOWARD Jan 1841 in NC. He died before 1860 in Catawba Co., NC.

Child of SARAH LANTZ and GEORGE HOWARD is:

1. MARY ANN HOWARD (D361)
2. NANCY CATHERINE HOWARD (D362)
3. SALOME HOWARD, born 07 Aug 1847; died 03 Nov 1859 of diphtheria.
4. MARTHA CURTIS HOWARD (D364)
5. FRANCES AUGUSTA HOWARD (D365)
6. JOHN F. HOWARD, born in 1853 in Catawba Co., NC.
7. SUSAN HOWARD, born in 1856 in Catawba Co., NC.

References: 6-Sarah Mae (Huss) Lantz, 5, 25-Catawba Co NC H1217

D38 JACOB LANTZ D3

JACOB LANTZ was born 08 Aug 1819 in Lincoln Co., NC, and died 29 Apr 1864 in Point Lookout Prison, MD. He married LINNA CARPENTER 02 Jan 1845, daughter of JOHN

CARPENTER and MARY RAMSOUR. She was born 14 Sep 1821 in Lincoln Co., NC, and died 08 Sep 1895 in Lincoln Co., NC. "JACOB LANTZ was among the men who taught school at St. Matthews School House near the spring. The school house was built around 1838. He built a two story wooden frame house in 1858 that is still in use by the Coy Lantz Family (as of 2004)."

"During the Civil War, he served as a private with Company E, 57 NC Infantry Regiment, commanded by Captain DANIEL RHYNE of Catawba Co. This company was raised in Catawba Co. on July 4, 1862. IT was mustered into service at Salisbury on July 17, 1862 and assigned to the 57th Regiment, N.C. Troops, as Company E. No letters or visits-home accounts exist. He was captured Nov. 7, 1863 and taken prisoner during the battle at Rappahannock, VA. He died nine months later on Apr. 29, 1864 while in the Union camp at Point Lookout, Maryland and was buried there. Descendants who have visited the site have learned that living conditions at the time were so harsh that many prisoners died of pneumonia as well as wounds. It is recorded that the only protein that prisoners had at the prison were the rats they were able to catch for food. The harsh winter conditions with little shelter and clothing for the prisoners also created severe health hazards. The commander of this prison was recognized for his ability to save money. According to *The Lantz Family Record* published in 1931 (page 48) his mother, Sabina, died when she heard of her son JACOB's death in a prison camp. Civil War Archival Data: "Point Lookout, MD, Reg. 1, Page 270, shows JACOB LANTZ, Pvt. Co. E, 57th NC Regiment Infantry, was captured at Rappahannock Station on Nov. 7, 1863. Date of arrival as prisoner in Washington, D.C. was Nov. 11, 1863. Records of the Federal Provost Marshal indicate that he died April 29, 1864 at Point Lookout Prison, MD. The Civil War Battle at Rappahannock Station occurred during the October-November, 1863, Bristoe Campaign (Culpeper Co. and Fauquier Co., VA). On November 7, 1863, the Union army forced passage of the Rappahannock River at two places. A dusk attack overran the Confederate bridgehead at Rappahannock Station, capturing more than 1,600 men of Jubal Early's Division. The battle on that day resulted in an estimated casualty number of 2,531 (captured, killed, or wounded). JACOB LANTZ, who had survived the Battle of Gettysburg on July 1-3, 1863 (his company, a part of ROBERT HOKE's Brigade, fought during the first day of this battle), was one of those 1,600 Confederates captured during this battle at Rappahannock Station, VA."

LINNA CARPENTER LANTZ was confirmed in St. Matthews Church on June 3, 1838. Her sister, ELIZABETH CARPENTER, married James Summerow. She was widowed almost a year before the war ended. She managed the farm which lost some acreage in those years due to poor economic conditions while caring for young JOHN and SALLY. Among old receipts from 1848-66 is one showing that LINNA paid her state tax of $188 and Co. tax of $226 for the year of 1866. Another receipt shows that she had sold fodder to a Confederate officer during the war. It seems that she was a skilled seamstress and may have taken in some sewing. Cardboard clothing patterns were found in the attic of the house but unfortunately not preserved. Stories passed down from Grandma LAURA tell of a Negro slave woman who had been given to LINNA by her parents as a wedding gift. The woman's fingerprints are said to be those which smeared the faux painted mantel of the living room to test the drying paint. The mantel remains as it was originally spatter painted to resemble black and gray speckled granite."

Children of JACOB LANTZ and LINNA CARPENTER are:

1. NANCY CAROLINE LANTZ, born 15 Feb 1846; died 11 Jun 1858 in Lincoln Co., NC. It has been said that Nancy Caroline died of the flux. Earlier in the year of 1858, she cross-stitched in wool yarn a sampler on perforated paper designed with the golden rule and letters of the alphabet. Ann Lantz Reep has the framed original and patterns for making copies were given to cousins, and many copies were made.
2. INFANT SON LANTZ, born 21 Jun 1848.
3. MARY JANE LANTZ, born 30 Oct 1849; died 07 May 1851 in Lincoln Co., NC.
4. JOHN FRANKLIN LANTZ (D384)
5. SARAH ALICE LANTZ (D385)

References: 6-Sarah Mae (Huss) Lantz, 5, 24-Lincoln Co NC H671, 25-Lincoln Co NC H766

JOHN CHARLES LANTZ (D38454) at Point Lookout Confederate Cemetery

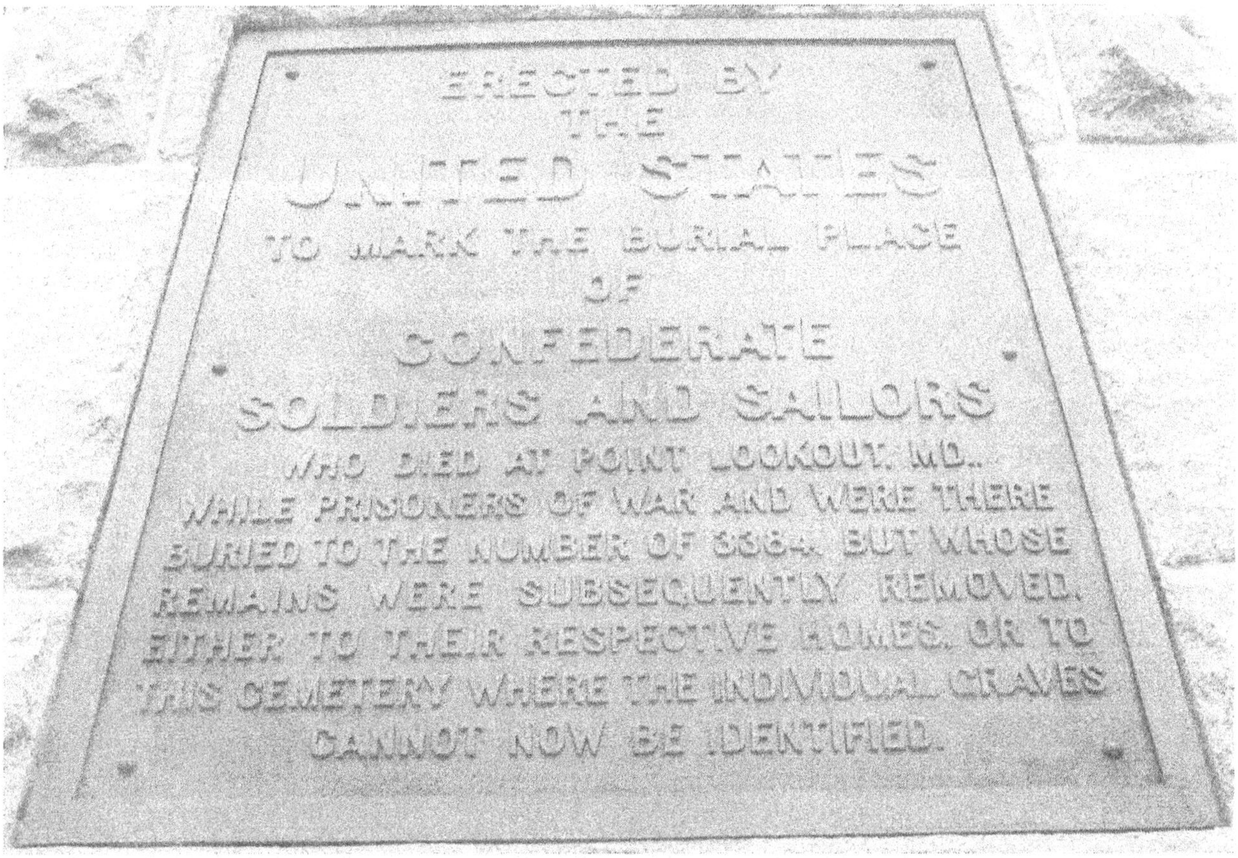

ERECTED BY
THE
UNITED STATES
TO MARK THE BURIAL PLACE
OF
CONFEDERATE
SOLDIERS AND SAILORS
WHO DIED AT POINT LOOKOUT, MD.,
WHILE PRISONERS OF WAR AND WERE THERE
BURIED TO THE NUMBER OF 3384, BUT WHOSE
REMAINS WERE SUBSEQUENTLY REMOVED,
EITHER TO THEIR RESPECTIVE HOMES, OR TO
THIS CEMETERY WHERE THE INDIVIDUAL GRAVES
CANNOT NOW BE IDENTIFIED.

LANGSTON, KINDRED D 4 N. C. CAV.
LANIER, B. D., SGT. I 31 N. C.
LANKFORD, J. L. L 55 N. C.
LANKIN, W. H. C 9 VA.
LANTZ, JACOB E 57 N. C.
LASCAS, A. M. G 52 GA.
LASLEY, CHAS. A. K 48 VA.
LASSITER, WM. N. H 38 N. C.
LAUGHTER, JNO. R. A 25 N. C.
LAWHORN, ALEX. A 42 MISS.
LAWRENCE, T. J. C 20 MISS.

Point Lookout Confederate Cemetery Memorial Plaques

D41 FRANCES "FANNY" HALLMAN D4

FRANCES "FANNY" HALLMAN was born in 1809 in Lincoln Co., NC. She married MOSES CARPENTER; born in 1807 in NC and died in 1858 in Lincoln Co., NC. His will is recorded in Will Book 3 page 19 in Lincoln Co., NC.

Children of FRANCES HALLMAN and MOSES CARPENTER are:

1. JACOB CARPENTER (D411)
2. SUSAN CARPENTER, born in 1833 in Lincoln Co., NC.
3. LOUISA CARPENTER, born in 1835 in Lincoln Co., NC.
4. MOSES CARPENTER, born in 1837 in Lincoln Co., NC.
5. FRANCES CARPENTER, born in 1840 in Lincoln Co., NC.
6. SOPHIA CARPENTER, born in 1842 in Lincoln Co., NC.
7. WILLIAM CARPENTER, born in 1844 in Lincoln Co., NC.
8. BENJAMIN CARPENTER, born in 1846 in Lincoln Co., NC.
9. GEORGE CARPENTER, born in 1847 in Lincoln Co., NC.
10. JONAS M. CARPENTER, born in 1850 in Lincoln Co., NC.

References: 24-Lincoln Co NC H361, 25-Lincoln Co NC H487

D42 ANTHONY HALLMAN D4

ANTHONY HALLMAN was born 02 Feb 1811 in Lincoln Co., NC, and died 06 Dec 1861 in Lincoln Co., NC. He married SUSANNA BOLLINGER 18 Mar 1837 in Lincoln Co., NC, daughter of HENRY BOLLINGER. She was born 17 Mar 1818, and died 12 Nov 1878 in Lincoln Co., NC.

Children of ANTHONY HALLMAN and SUSANNA BOLLINGER are:

1. FRANCES E. HALLMAN (D421)
2. GEORGE HALLMAN, born 1840; died 12 May 1863 in Richmond, VA during Civil War.
3. MARTHA HALLMAN (D423)
4. EMMA HALLMAN (D424)
5. MARY J. HALLMAN, born 1851. She married JOHN MONTGOMERY.
6. JAMES MONROE HALLMAN (D426)
7. MARGARET E. HALLMAN, born 13 Feb 1857; died 20 Nov 1857.
8. WILLIAM SIDNEY HALLMAN (D428)

References: 6-Sarah Mae (Huss) Lantz, 24-Lincoln Co NC H274, 25-Lincoln Co NC H176

D43 ELIZABETH HALLMAN D4

ELIZABETH HALLMAN was born in 1814 in Lincoln Co., NC. She married JOHN S. FISHER on 07 Oct 1837 in Lincoln Co., NC. He was born in 1809 in NC.

Children of ELIZABETH HALLMAN and JOHN FISHER are:

1. SARAH SUSANNA "SURPHRINE" FISHER, born in 1838 in Lincoln Co., NC.
2. HENRY C. FISHER, born in 1843 in Lincoln Co., NC; married MARY A. in NC; born 1844 NC.
3. JACOB D. FISHER, born in 1845 in Lincoln Co., NC.
4. JOSEPH MANGRUM. FISHER (D434)
5. GEORGE FISHER, born in 1853 in NC.
6. JOHN W. FISHER, born in 1857 in NC.

References: 24-Lincoln Co NC H264, 25-Summers Dist Caldwell Co NC H369, 26-Summers Dist Caldwell Co NC H90, 27-Lovelady Twp Caldwell Co NC 053 H197, 27-Catheys Creek Twp Transylvania Co NC 188 H22

D44 GEORGE WASHINGTON HALLMAN D4

GEORGE WASHINGTON HALLMAN was born 23 Jun 1818 in Lincoln Co., NC, and died 05 Jul 1869. He married MARGARET ELIZABETH BAILEY in 1843 in Lincoln Co., NC. She was born 1816, and died 1893.

Children of GEORGE HALLMAN and MARGARET BAILEY are:

1. SAMUEL JACOB HALLMAN (D441)
2. RUTH ELIZABETH HALLMAN, born 08 Jun 1848. She married ALFRED REID THOMPSON.
3. MARCELLUS BAILEY HALLMAN, born 10 Sep 1850 in Shelby, Cleveland Co., NC; died 12 Mar 1894. He married ADDIE FLETCHER LOWRY; born 04 Oct 1862; died 07 Aug 1954.
4. JOHN CALHOUN HALLMAN (D444)
5. MARTHA DEAN HALLMAN, born 10 Oct 1853 in Shelby, Cleveland Co., NC. She married THOMAS LEROY SIMS; born 10 May 1845.
6. MARGARET HALLMAN, born 1855 in Shelby, Cleveland Co., NC; died 28 Sep 1876. She married AUGUSTUS LOVELY ROGERS; born 08 Aug 1849; died 10 Jul 1932.

References: 6-Sarah Mae (Huss) Lantz, 24-Lincoln Co NC H259

D47 BENJAMIN HALLMAN D

BENJAMIN HALLMAN was born 1830. He married MARTHA E. C. SHERRILL on 01 Apr 1848 in Catawba Co., NC, daughter of MASON SHERRILL and MARGARET.

Child of BENJAMIN HALLMAN and MARTHA SHERRILL is:

1. CARDWELL HALLMAN, born 1849.

References: 6-Sarah Mae (Huss) Lantz, 24-Catawba Co NC H214

D45 SUSANNAH HALLMAN D4

SUSANNAH HALLMAN was born in 1823 in Lincoln Co., NC. She married JAMES SUMMEROUR on 10 Jan 1848 in Lincoln Co., NC. He was born in 1810 in Lincoln Co., NC.

Children of SUSANNAH HALLMAN and JAMES SUMMEROUR are:

1. PINKNEY JANE SUMMEROUR, born in 1849 in Lincoln Co., NC.
2. SARAH ANN SUMMEROUR (D452)

References: 24-Lincoln Co NC H210, 25-Lincoln Co NC H178, 26-Union Twp Lincoln Co NC H178, 56, 27-Lincolnton Lincoln Co NC H446

D49 MARY CATHERINE HALLMAN D4

MARY CATHERINE HALLMAN was born 1832. She married JOHN L. BRIDGES 12 May 1849 in Lincoln Co., NC. He was born in 1827 in NC.

Child of MARY HALLMAN and JOHN BRIDGES is:

1. SALOMA M. C. BRIDGES, born before 24 Dec 1850.

References: 6-Sarah Mae (Huss) Lantz, 24-Catawba Co NC H318

D51 DELILA HALLMAN D5

DELILA HALLMAN was born 11 Apr 1815 in Lincoln Co., NC, and died 19 Jul 1904 in Catawba Co., NC. She married ABEL JESSE PROPST, son of JOHN PROPST and CHRISTINA DIETZ. He was born 31 Dec 1808 in Lincoln Co., NC, and died 24 Mar 1892 in Catawba Co., NC.

Children of DELILA HALLMAN and ABEL PROPST are:

1. ELMINA SUSANNAH PROPST
2. ABEL HENRY PROPST
3. JEMIMA ANNA ELIZABETH PROPST, born 05 Sep 1835 in Lincoln (later Catawba) Co., NC.
4. JOHN WILLIAM PROPST (D514)
5. NANCY REBECCA PROPST, born 06 Mar 1846 in Catawba Co., NC.
6. DAVID JESSE PROPST, born 18 Mar 1849 in Catawba Co., NC.
7. FREDERICK ANDREW PROPST, born 31 Dec 1852 in Catawba Co., NC.
8. ELIAS GIRARD PROPST, born 26 Oct 1853 in Catawba Co., NC.
9. MARY ADELINE SYLOMA PROPST, born 14 Feb 1860 in Catawba Co., NC.

References: 6-Sarah Mae (Huss) Lantz, 24-Catawba Co NC H374, 25- Catawba Co NC H575

D61 ELEANOR HALLMAN D6

ELEANOR HALLMAN was born on 24 Dec 1824 Lincoln Co., NC and died 12 Oct 1858 in

Lincoln Co., NC. She married WINEHARDT SAINE 19 Sep 1849 in Lincoln Co., NC. He was born on 17 Oct 1824 in Lincoln Co., NC and died 07 Oct 1892 in Lincoln Co., NC. Both are buried in Bethphage Lutheran Church Cemetery, Crouse, Lincoln Co., NC, along with his 2nd wife.

Children of ELEANOR HALLMAN and WINEHARDT SAINE are:

1. WESLEY SAINE, born 1850 in Lincoln Co., NC.
2. LOGAN SAINE (D612)
3. MARTHA FRANCES SAINE, born 1853 in Lincoln Co., NC.
4. ADOLPHUS D. SAINE (D614)
5. MARY ISABELLA SAINE, born 1856 in Lincoln Co., NC.

References: 24-Lincoln Co NC H900, 25-Lincoln Co NC H810, 26-Liberty Twp Lincoln Co NC H155

D63 ELMIRA HALLMAN D6

ELMIRA "MIRA" HALLMAN was born in 1828 in Lincoln Co., NC. She married SOLOMON SAINE. He was born in 1828 in Lincoln Co., NC and died before 1870 in Lincoln Co., NC.

Children of ELMIRA HALLMAN and SOLOMON SAINE are:

1. NANCY J. SAINE, born 1853 in Lincoln Co., NC.
2. WILLIAM M. SAINE, born 1855 in Lincoln Co., NC.
3. MARY A. E. SAINE, born 1857 in Lincoln Co., NC.
4. DANIEL A. SAINE (D634)
5. MARTIN L. SAINE, born 1862 in Lincoln Co., NC.

References: 25-Lincoln Co NC H899, 26-Liberty Twp Lincoln Co NC H133

D64 ANDREW HALLMAN D6

ANDREW HALLMAN was born 13 Sep 1829 in Lincoln Co., NC. He married MARY SUSANNAH HALLMAN 15 Sep 1859 in Lincoln Co., NC, daughter of ISAAC HALLMAN and MARY ANTHONY. She was born 24 Feb 1836 in Lincoln Co., NC, and died 06 Aug 1893 in Lincoln Co., NC.

Children of ANDREW HALLMAN and MARY HALLMAN are:

1. LAURA J. HALLMAN, born 1861.
2. JOHN F. HALLMAN, born 1864.
3. WILLIAM A. HALLMAN, born 1868.

References: 6-Sarah Mae (Huss) Lantz, 25-Lincoln Co NC H742, 27-Northbrook Twp Lincoln Co NC H11

D65 ABEL HALLMAN D6

ABEL HALLMAN was born on 10 Feb 1832 and died 28 Jan 1905. He married SARAH SELF HOYLE. She was born on 08 Jul 1837 and died 12 Jul 1929.

Children of ABEL HALLMAN and SARAH HOYLE are:

1. JOSEPH A. HALLMAN, born 1872 in Lincoln Co., NC.
2. LEMMEL E. HALLMAN, born 1873 in Lincoln Co., NC.

References: 26-Laurel Hill Twp Lincoln Co NC H36

D66 PHYLECTOR HALLMAN D6

PHYLECTOR HALLMAN was born 24 Jun 1834 in Lincoln Co., NC, and died 06 May 1912 in Lincoln Co., NC. She married (2) EMANUEL SQUIRE HOUSER, son of JACOB HOUSER and CATHERINE HEAVNER. He was born 09 Apr 1826 in Lincoln Co., NC, and died 16 Dec 1910.

Children of PHYLECTOR HALLMAN and EMANUEL HOUSER are:

1. LUTHER ERNEST HOUSER (D661)
2. REUBEN E. HOUSER (D662)
3. UNKNOWN HOUSER, born in and died before 1880 in Lincoln Co., NC.

References: 6-Sarah Mae (Huss) Lantz, 26-Lincoln Co NC H131, 29-Dist 107 Howard Creek Lincoln Co NC H48

D67 MICHAEL HALLMAN D6

MICHAEL HALLMAN was born 1837 and died before 1891. He married CLEMENTINE LUCINDA DELLINGER 21 Feb 1863 in Lincoln Co., NC.

Children of MICHAEL HALLMAN and CLEMENTINE are:

1. EMMA HALLMAN, born in 1864 in Lincoln Co., NC.
2. OTHO HALLMAN, born in 1866 in Lincoln Co., NC.
3. JUNIS HALLMAN, born in 1869 in Lincoln Co., NC.
4. JAMES HALLMAN, born in 1871 in Lincoln Co., NC.
5. ALBERTUS HALLMAN, born in 1876 in Lincoln Co., NC.

References: 27-Ironton Twp Lincoln Co NC H288

D69 MARTHA EMELINE HALLMAN D6

MARTHA EMELINE HALLMAN was born Jul 1841 in NC. She married DANIEL MOSES HARTZOGE on 17 Aug 1865 in NC. He was born on 10 Oct 1838 in NC.

Children of MARTHA HALLMAN and DANIEL HARTZOGE are:

1. JAMES LUTHER HARTSOGE born in 1867 in NC.
2. WILLIAM G. HARTSOGE born on 30 Apr 1867 in NC.
3. SARAH JANE HARTSOGE, born on 09 Aug 1870 in NC.
4. JOHN LAWSON HARTSOGE, born on 29 Aug 1872 in NC.
5. MARY HARTSOGE, born in 1875 in NC.
6. THOMAS EDWARD HARTSOGE, born in 1877 in NC.
7. MIRIEL "MYRA" LENORE REGINE HARTSOGE, born in Sep 1879 in NC.
8. EMMA A. HARTSOGE, born Feb 1883 in NC.
9. JULIA E.. HARTSOGE, born in Aug 1885 in NC.

References: 6-Sarah Mae (Huss) Lantz, 27-Kings Mountain Cleveland Co NC H378, 29-Dist 76 Crowder Mountain Gaston Co NC H396

D71 AMBROSE MICHAEL D7

AMBROSE MICHAEL was born in 1829 in Lincoln Co., NC. He married CYNTHIA A. She was born in 1834 in NC.

Child of AMBROSE MICHAEL and CYNTHIA is:

1. M. S. E. (f) MICHAEL, born in 1860 in Catawba Co., NC.

References: 25-Catawba Co NC H495

D73 JACOB MICHAEL D7

JACOB MICHAEL was born in 1833 in Lincoln Co., NC. He married SARAH S. WEAVER. She was born in 1833 in NC, daughter of CHRISTINA.

Child of JACOB MICHAEL and SARAH WEAVER is:

1. CATHARINA MICHAEL, born in 1857 in Catawba Co., NC.

References: 25-Catawba Co NC H136

D74 MARY M. MICHAEL D7

MARY M. MICHAEL was born in 1836 in Lincoln Co., NC. She married ISAAC REINHARDT in Lincoln Co., NC, as his 2nd wife, son of CHARLES REINHARDT. He was born in 1814 in NC.

Children of MARY MICHAEL and ISAAC REINHARDT are:

1. ZURA "BELLE" J. A. REINHARDT, born1865 in Lincoln Co., NC.
2. NANCY J. REINHARDT, born1868 in Lincoln Co., NC.

References: 26-Rhodesville Twp Lincoln Co NC H104, 27-Howards Creek Twp Lincoln Co NC H69

D111 HARRIET K. JARRETT D11

HARRIET K. JARRETT born in 1825 in Lincoln Co., NC. She married GEORGE W. SAMPLE in Lee Co., IA. He was born in 1823 in IL.

Children of HARRIET JARRETT and GEORGE SAMPLE are:

1. SARAH A. E. SAMPLE, born in 1853 in Lee Co., IA.
2. JOHN SAMPLE, born in 1853 in Lee Co., IA.
3. PHILIP SAMPLE, born in 1858 in Lee Co., IA.
4. MCCLELLAND SAMPLE, born in 1864 in Lee Co., IA.
5. MARGARET SAMPLE, born in 1866 in Lee Co., IA.
6. MARY SAMPLE, born in 1868 in Lee Co., IA.

References: 25-Marion Twp Lee Co IA H831, 26-Marion Twp Lee Co IA H189, 27-Marion Twp Lee Co IA H224

D112 SARAH ELIZABETH JARRETT D11

SARAH ELIZABETH JARRETT was born on 30 May 1829 in Lincoln Co., NC and died 14 Feb 1914 in Fort Madison, Lee Co., IA. She married PHILIP EHART on 21 Nov 1854. He was born in 24 Aug 1829 in Salingenstadt, Germany and died 30 Jul 1876 in Fort Madison, Lee Co., IA.

Children of SARAH JARRETT and PHILIP EHART are:

1. JOHN EHART, born in 1856 in Lee Co., IA; married ISABELL; born in 1858 in IA.
2. MARY EHART, born in 1858 in Lee Co., IA.
3. MARGARET EHART, born in 1861 in Lee Co., IA; married FRANK J. SWANSON; born 1861 in Sweden.
4. EDWARD EHART, born in 1866 in Lee Co., IA.
5. DAISEY LENORE EHART, born on 08 Feb 1873 in Lee Co., IA; died 06 Jun 1943 in Fort Madison, Lee Co., IA; married ISAAC WILSEY TRAVERSE on 28 Dec 1891; born 22 Oct 1872 in Hancock Co., IL; died 12 Apr 1935 in Fort Madison, Lee Co., IA.

References: 25-West Point Twp Lee Co IA H277, 26-Fort Madison Twp Lee Co IA H157, 27-Fort Madison Lee Co IA H79, 29- Fort Madison Lee Co IA H725

D115 MARY ANNA JARRETT D11

MARY ANNA JARRETT was born in 1834 in Lincoln Co., NC. She married AMOS LOGAN. He was born in 1836 in OH.

Children of MARY JARRETT and AMOS LOGAN are:

1. ROBERT A. LOGAN, born in 1859 in Lee Co., IA.
2. SAMUEL LOGAN, born in 1862 in Lee Co., IA.
3. IDA LOGAN, born in 1865 in Lee Co., IA.

4. ANNA LOGAN, born in 1872 in Lee Co., IA.

References: 25-Pleasant Ridge Twp Lee Co IA H38, 26-Pleasant Ridge Twp Lee Co IA H173

D116 FANNIE LOUISE JARRETT D11

FANNIE LOUISE JARRETT was born on 16 Aug 1836 in Lincoln Co., NC and died 30 Sep 1920 in Lee Co., IA She married CHARLES MARTIN. He was born on Oct. 20, 1839 in Prussia and died Feb. 3, 1916 in Lee Co., IA. He was a merchant by occupation. Both are buried in the West Point Cemetery, West Point Twp., Lee Co. IA.

Children of FANNIE JARRETT and CHARLES MARTIN are:

1. NETTIE MARTIN, born in 1862 in Lee Co., IA.
2. KATTIE MARTIN, born in 1863 in Lee Co., IA.
3. EDWARD MARTIN, born in 1867 in Lee Co., IA.
4. EMMA MARTIN, born in Nov 1868 in Lee Co., IA; married (?) DAUBE.
5. WILLIAM MARTIN, born in 1869 in Lee Co., IA.

References: 26-West Point Twp Lee Co IA H139, 27-West Point Twp Lee Co IA H126, 29-West Point Twp Lee Co IA H125, 45

D117 PHILIP FRANKLIN JARRETT D11

PHILIP FRANKLIN JARRETT was born in Feb 1838 in Lincoln Co., NC. Married RACHEL ANN COURTRIGHT born 18 Dec 1841 died 17 Feb 1899 in Lee Co., IA. Both are buried in the Clay Grove Cemetery, West Point Twp., Lee Co., IA.

1. MARY ALICE JARRETT, born in Jul 1873 Lee Co., IA.

References: 27-Marion Twp Lee Co IA H228, 29-Marion Twp Lee Co IA H57, 45

D118 MARGARET JANE JARRETT D11

MARGARET JANE JARRETT was born on 05 Feb 1840 in Lincoln Co., NC and died 16 Sep 1929 in Lee Co., IA. She married JACOB E. MCCRACKEN. He was born 07 Dec 1836 died 16 Sep 1926 in Lee Co., IA. Both are buried in the Clay Grove Cemetery, West Point Twp., Lee Co., IA.

Children of MARGARET JARRETT and JACOB MCCRACKEN are:

1. CHARLEY C. MCCRACKEN, born in 1863 in Lee Co., IA.
2. LAURA O. MCCRACKEN, born in 1865 in Lee Co., IA.

References: 50-Marion Twp Lee Co IA F84, 27- Marion Twp Lee Co IA H273, 45

D11B ISABEL JARRETT D11

ISABEL JARRETT was born in Sep 1846 in IN. She married JAMES STEELE in IA. He was born in Aug 1845 in IA.

Child of ISABEL JARRETT and JAMES STEELE is:

1. ELMA C. STEELE, born in Jan 1883 in IA.

References: 27-Nodaway Twp Page Co IA, 29- Grant Twp Taylor Co IA H68, 30-Grant Twp Taylor Co IA H47

D11C CANDACE VIRGINIA JARRETT D11

CANDACE VIRGINIA JARRETT was born on 21 Oct 1848 in Lee Co., IA and died 17 Oct 1929 in Lee Co., IA. She married JOHN C. COURTRIGHT. He was born in 28 Feb 1846 in OH and died 09 Jul 1900 in Lee Co., IA. Both are buried in Clay Grove Cemetery, West Point Twp., Lee Co., IA.

Children of CANDACE JARRETT and JOHN COURTRIGHT are:

1. O. C. COURTRIGHT, born in Dec 1869 in Lee Co., IA.
2. L. E. COURTRIGHT, born in Dec 1870 in Lee Co., IA.
3. EDWARD E. COURTRIGHT, born in Dec 1873 in Lee Co., IA.
4. V. B. COURTRIGHT, born in Dec 1875 in Lee Co., IA.
5. MERTLE M. COURTRIGHT, born in Oct 1881 in Lee Co., IA.
6. HUGH L. COURTRIGHT, born in Mar 1885 in Lee Co., IA.
7. PEARL C. COURTRIGHT, born in Apr 1889 in Lee Co., IA.

References: 29-Franklin Twp Lee Co IA H57, 45, 27-Franklin Twp Lee Co IA H2

D11D BARBARA JARRETT D11

BARBARA JARRETT was born on 06 Mar 1850 in Lee Co., IA and died 24 Jun 1919 in Lee Co., IA. She married HORACE PATCHEN. He was born on 01 Feb 1841 died 30 Jun 1904 in Lee Co., IA. Both are buried in Clay Grove Cemetery, West Point Twp., Lee Co., IA.

Child of BARBARA JARRETT and HORACE PATCHEN is:

1. HORACE JARRETT PATCHEN born 01 Feb 1883 died 15 Apr 1945.

References: 45, 30-Des Moines Polk Co IA 1227

D168 BARBARA ELENORA M. HOOVER D16

BARBARA ELENORA M. HOOVER was born in Sep 1852 in Lincoln Co., NC. She married FREDERICK W. KOEHLER in Lee Co., IA. He was born Feb 1854 in IA.

Children of BARBARA HOOVER and FREDERICK KOEHLER are:

1. EARL J. KOEHLER, born in Mar 1883 in Lee Co., IA.
2. GOLDIE E. KOEHLER, born in May 1889 in Lee Co., IA.

References: 29-Franklin Twp Lee Co IA H64, 50-Lee Co Page 183

D172 SAMUEL HARVEY LANTZ D17

SAMUEL HARVEY LANTZ was born 29 Sep 1848 in Lincoln Co., NC, and died 1933. He married CORDELIA ANN PIERCY 05 Feb 1891 in Weldon, Decatur, IA, daughter of WILLIAM PIERCY. She was born 05 Aug 1872 in Lucas, Wayne Co., IA, and died 03 Aug 1945.

Children of SAMUEL LANTZ and CORDELIA PIERCY are:

1. ORVIL LANTZ, born and died before 1900 in IA.
2. JOHN CALVIN LANTZ, born in Mar 1892 in IA; died 25 Apr 1924. He married EDNA SELBY Feb 1914.
3. EUNICE M. LANTZ, born on 18 Jul 1895 in IA; died 19 Jul 1969. She married OTTO SORENSEN 25 May 1923 in Kirksville, MO.
4. IRA D. LANTZ, born 21 Jun 1898 in IA; died 12 Jan 1952. He married MAURITA SCOTT 26 Feb 1921.
5. VERN GOLDIE LANTZ, born 29 Apr 1900 in IA; died 01 Jul 1975. He married MARY FRELEN.
6. ELBA LANTZ, born 29 Jan 1902 in IA; died 13 Jul 1980 in Cincinnati, OH. He married LENA BRIGGS 24 Oct 1942 in Kirksville, MO.
7. ROY LANTZ, born 21 Dec 1906 in MO; died 26 Dec 1981.
8. GLADYS LANTZ, born 10 Jun 1908 in MO; died 30 Mar 1995. She married JOHN FEATHERING 04 Jun 1928 in Ft. Madison, Lee Co., IA.
9. RALEIGH LANTZ, born 23 Aug 1910 in MO; died 03 Nov 1994. He married MYRTLE ARNDT 14 Aug 1937.

References: 6-Sarah Mae (Huss) Lantz, 29-Dist 45 Franklin Decatur Co IA H26, 30-Dist 0020 Salt River Adair Co MO H214, 10-Dist 0020 Salt River Adair Co MO H46

D173 JOHN MILTON LANTZ D17

JOHN MILTON LANTZ was born on 14 Mar 1850 in West Point, Lee Co., IA and died 10 Jan 1929. He married MAY LITTLE on 23 Feb 1881 in home of HENRY LITTLE, Van Wert, IA. She was born on 27 Dec 1857 in IA and died 02 Mar 1919.

Children of JOHN LANTZ and MAY LITTLE are:

1. HARRY CLAUDE LANTZ, born 1880 in IA; died 1964. He married PERLE SCOTT.
2. BERNICE LILLIAN LANTZ, born 04 Sep 1883 in IA; died 15 Dec 1921. She married A. T. PAYTON 06 Feb 1909 I nIA.

References: 6-Sarah Mae (Huss) Lantz, 29-Dist 42 Decatur Decatur Co IA H170, 50-1885 Garfield Calhoun Co H3

D174 LEANDER WASHINGTON LANTZ D17

LEANDER WASHINGTON LANTZ was born on 22 Oct 1851 in West Point, Lee Co., IA, and died 03 Oct 1930 in Johnson Co., NE. He married IDA MAY "SARAH" MOFFITT on 17 Jun 1880 in Clarinda, Page Co., IA. She was born on 01 May 1859 in Chillicothe, Peoria Co., IL, and died 30 Mar 1928 in Johnson Co., NE. He was one of the owners of The Smartville Grain and live Stock Company of Smartville, Johnson Co., NE. Both are buried in Tecumseh Cemetery, Tecumseh, Johnson Co., NE.

Children of LEANDER LANTZ and IDA MOFFITT are:

1. GEORGE FRANKLIN LANTZ, born on 17 Jan 1881 in IA.
2. ALFORD CALVIN ROCKETT LANTZ (D1742)
3. FREDERICK VERN LANTZ (D1743)
4. TWILLA MAY LANTZ (D1744)
5. ETHEL BLANCHE LANTZ (D1745)
6. DURWARD BELMONT LANTZ (D1746)
7. IVAN WASHINGTON LANTZ (D1747)
8. WILLIAM ABNER LANTZ, born in 09 May 1898 in NE; died 13 May 1973 in Johnson Co., NE; married BESSIE M. CHANDLER.
9. EARL LEANDER LANTZ, born in 1901 in NE; died 1969. He married SARAH RUTH PEEK CRABBE.

References: 6-Sarah Mae (Huss) Lantz, 29-Dist 23 Helena Johnson Co NE H81, 6-Francys Pattie Lantz Phillips, 45

D175 PHILLIP FREDERICK LANTZ D17

PHILLIP FREDERICK LANTZ was born on 26 Apr 1853 in West Point, Lee Co., IA, and died 08 Jun 1935. He married OLIVE THOMPSON on 19 Apr 1887 in Leon, Decatur Co., IA, daughter of ISAIAH THOMPSON and MALINDA CLAYTON. She was born on 26 Jan 1867, and died 29 Sep 1940.

Children of PHILLIP LANTZ and OLLIE THOMPSON are:

1. RAY ELMER LANTZ (D1751)
2. EDITH LANTZ, born on 09 Aug 1891 in Van Wert, Decatur Co., IA; died 24 Mar 1953 in Hampton, Franklin Co., IA. She married GARY SAYLOR 11 Jun 1910.
3. FERN LANTZ, born on 13 Jun 1894 in Van Wert, Decatur Co., IA; died 08 Apr 1973. She married BASSETT MALLATT 23 Feb 1930.
4. FAYE LANTZ, born in 1895 in Decatur Co., IA.
5. VERA LANTZ, born on 27 Jun 1897 in Van Wert, Decatur Co., IA; died 08 Jun 1981 in Oskaloosa, Mahaska, IA. She married CLYDE JOHNSON 23 Sep 1917.
6. CHRISTA LANTZ, born on 25 Dec 1900 in Van Wert, Decatur Co., IA; died 04 Feb 1996 in Osceola, Clarke Co. IA. She married ROBERT EDGE 25 Dec 1919; born 1897.

References: 6-Sarah Mae (Huss) Lantz, 29-Dist 45 Franklin Decatur Co IA H5, 30-Dist 0045 Franklin Decatur Co IA H28

D177 GEORGE HENDERSON LANTZ D17

GEORGE HENDERSON LANTZ was born on 10 Mar 1859 in West Point, Lee Co., IA, and died 1919. He married NANCY ANN DAVIS in Oct 1880 in Van Wert, Decatur Co., IA. She was born in Apr 1862 in IA, and died 1928.

Children of GEORGE LANTZ and NANCY DAVIS are:

1. ARTHUR LANTZ, born and died before 1900 in IA.
2. VERN R. LANTZ, born in Jun 1885 in IA.
3. LELA LANTZ, born in Dec 1891 in IA.
4. ALPHA LANTZ, born in Jun 1885 in IA.

References: 6-Sarah Mae (Huss) Lantz, 29-Dist 40 Burrell Decatur Co IA H257

D17A IDA JANE LANTZ D17

IDA JANE LANTZ was born on 02 Feb 1864 in Van Wert, Decatur Co., IA, and died 20 Nov 1945 in Eldora, Marshall Co., IA. She married LEANDER R. BEAM on 16 Sep 1885 in Humeston, Wayne Co., IA, son of SAMUEL BEAM and MARY TURLEY. He was born on 11 Feb 1863 in IL and died 23 Jun 1944 in Marshalltown, Marshall Co., IA.

Children of IDA LANTZ and LEANDER BEAM are:

1. BEULAH LEOLINE BEAM, born Aug 1886 in Van Wert, Decatur Co., IA; died 1921. She married WEBSTER DAYTON.
2. BLANCHE ELEANOR BEAM, born Feb 1889 in Van Wert, Decatur Co., IA. She married JAMES CLAIR GIFFORD 27 Jan 1915.
3. RUTH BEAM, born 1891 in Van Wert, Decatur Co., IA. She married CLARK CROWELL.
4. PAUL FRANK BEAM, born 25 Jun 1897 in Van Wert, Decatur Co., IA; died 28 Nov 1930 in Marshalltown, Marshall Co., IA. He married RUTH M. HICKMAN 25 Dec 1920.
5. HOMER ROBINSON BEAM, born Jan 1899 in Van Wert, Decatur Co., IA. He married RUBY WILSON.
6. DARRELL RICHARD BEAM, born 1906 in Van Wert, Decatur Co., IA. He married FREDA BURHAM.

References: 6-Sarah Mae (Huss) Lantz, 29-Dist 49 Long Creek Decatur Co IA H59, 30-Dist 0181 Valley Polk Co IA H108

D181 MARY DOVYANN CATHERINE ALBRIGHT D18

MARY DOVYANN CATHERINE ALBRIGHT was born on 24 Dec 1849 in Lincoln Co., NC and died 29 May 1926 in Davis Co., IA. She married WILLIAM E. PARKER on 28 Oct 1880 in Lee Co., IA.

Children of MARY ALBRIGHT and WILLIAM PARKER are:

1. EMMA R. PARKER, born Dec 1882 in IA
2. JAMES RALPH PARKER (D1812)

References: 29-Fabius Twp Davis Co IA H49, 30-Wyacondah Twp Davis Co IA H25

D182 JOHN LANTZ ALBRIGHT D18

JOHN LANTZ ALBRIGHT was born 05 Mar 1851 in Lincoln Co., NC and died 14 Feb 1924 in Los Angeles, CA. He married DELIAH ARDELLA FINGER 28 Dec 1881 in Lee Co., IA. She was born in Mar 1860 in OH and died before 1910 in Davis Co., IA.

Children of JOHN ALBRIGHT and DELIAH FINGER are:

1. BINA E. ALBRIGHT, born in Sep 1884 in IA.
2. LELLIE J. ALBRIGHT, born in Sep 1887 in IA.
3. ETTA V. ALBRIGHT, born in Aug 1896 in IA.
4. WILLIAM DENNY ALBRIGHT, born in Jul 1899 in IA.

References: 29-West Grove Twp Davis Co IA H100, 30-West Grove Twp Davis Co IA H149

D183 LINNA JANE ALBRIGHT D18

LINNA JANE ALBRIGHT was born 28 May 1861 in Lee Co., IA (near West Point) and died 07 Jul 1919 in West Grove, Davis Co., IA. She married IRA JUDSON FOSTER 27 Feb 1889 in Davis Co., IA. Both are buried in Hopkins Cemetery, Davis Co., IA.

Children of LINNA ALBRIGHT and IRA FOSTER are:

1. LEO CLIFFORD FOSTER (D1831)
2. NOEL FERREE FOSTER (D1832)
3. JAMES LLOYD FOSTER, born on 27 Aug 1893 in IA; died 25 Jan 1966 in Davis Co., IA; buried in Hopkins Cemetery, Davis Co., IA.
4. VERA MABEL FOSTER (D1834)
5. OSCAR JUDSON FOSTER (D1835)

References: 29-Fabius Twp Davis Co IA H50, 30-Fabius Twp Davis Co IA H45, 45

MRS. IRA J. FOSTER

Linna Jane Albright was born near West Point, Lee county, Iowa, May 28, 1861, and died at her home five miles south of West Grove, Iowa, July 7, 1919, age 58 years, 1 month and 9 days.

She was united in marriage to Ira J. Foster, February 27, 1889. To this union were born seven children, two passing away in infancy. Those living are: Leo C., Noel, F., James L., Vera M., Oscar J., all of whom are at home. She also leaves to mourn her loss, one sister, Mrs. W. E. Parker, who lives south of Bloomfield, and one brother, J. L. Albright, of Los Angeles, California.

Early in life she professed faith in Christ and united with the Cumberland Presbyterian church, but later in life she moved her membership to the North Union Baptist church, where she has lived a faithful member for seventeen years. She was a devoted wife and a loving mother. She was untiring in her devotion to her family, and neighbors and friends. She was always ready to help in time of sickness and need. She loved her Savior and the church, and enjoyed doing His will, until He called her to her heavenly home. Evangelist T. H. Dabney conducted the funeral services at Mark, assisted by Bro. Dawkins the pastor, who is a relative of the deceased. The large audience bespoke the high esteem in which sister Foster was held. Rev. 14:13.

D311 JACOB BENTON LANTZ D31

JACOB BENTON LANTZ was born 12 Jan 1843 in AL and died 30 Dec 1909 in Parker Co., TX. He married (2) LILLIE ANN DENTON on 03 Nov 1874 in TX. She was born in Aug 1852 in TN.

Children of JACOB LANTZ and LILLIE DENTON are:

1. ALBERT LANTZ (D3111)
2. SALLIE LANTZ was born 24 Feb 1877 in Parker Co., TX. Not married and lived with her brother CHARLES.
3. FANNIE LANTZ (D3113)
4. MAUD LANTZ (D3114)
5. CHARLES LANTZ born on 15 Aug 1882 in Parker Co., TX. Not married and lived with his sister SALLIE.
6. INA "IVY" LANTZ, born on 02 Nov 1885 in Parker Co., TX.
7. JOHN LANTZ (D3117)
8. GEORGE LANTZ (D3118)
9. LEONIDAS LANTZ (D3119)
10. DOLLIE LANTZ, born on 08 Oct 1895 in Parker Co., TX.

References: 5, 26-Precinct 2 Parker Co TX H435, 27- Precinct 2 Parker Co TX H181, 29-Justice Precinct 2 Parker Co TX H56, 30- Justice Precinct 2 Parker Co TX H37, 10-Justice Precinct 2 Parker Co TX H79, 10- Justice Precinct 2 Parker Co TX H80, 40-Justice Precinct 2 Parker Co TX H54

D313 SARAH F. LANTZ D31

SARAH F. LANTZ was born 12 Jan 1846 in AL and died in 1872 in TX. She married JAMES P. MONROE MATLOCK. Both died of smallpox along with their one-month-old child.

Children of SARAH LANTZ and JAMES MATLOCK are:

1. L. MATLOCK (f), born in 1865 in TX.
2. JOHN W. MATLOCK, born in 1867 in TX.
3. MARTHA E. MATLOCK, born in 1869 in TX, married (?) HILDEBRAND.
4. BETTIE L. MATLOCK (D3134)

References: 5, 27-Precinct 2 Parker Co TX H181

D317 ALBERT COLUMBUS LANTZ D31

ALBERT COLUMBUS LANTZ was born 21 Dec 1856 in TX, and died 21 Apr 1904 in TX. He married ALICE OLIVIA GRISHAM 23 Sep 1886 in TX. She was born 02 Dec 1859 in TX, and died 1949.

Children of ALBERT LANTZ and ALICE GRISHAM are:

1. JOHN ALBERT LANTZ, born 10 Sep 1887 in TX; died 15 Apr 1956. He married BLANCHE GOE.
2. IRL HARRISON LANTZ (D3172)
3. JAMES LEONIDAS LANTZ, born 25 Jul 1892 in TX; died 25 May 1955. He married ELLA MAE BARKER 03 Jan 1925 in TX.

References: 6-Sarah Mae (Huss) Lantz, 5, 29-Dist 97 Denison Ward 2 Grayson Co TX H20, 30-

Dist 0059 Dallas Ward 7 Dallas Co TX H159

D319 MARY ALICE LANTZ D31

MARY ALICE LANTZ was born on 23 Mar 1859 and died 18 Jun 1918 in Poolville, Parker Co., TX. She married JAMES COLEMAN on 23 Mar 1881 in TX. He was born on 01 Jan 1847 in TN and died 21 Dec 1920 in Parker Co., TX. Both are buried in Poolville Cemetery, Poolville, Parker Co., TX.

Children of MARY LANTZ and JAMES COLEMAN are:

1. WALTER L. COLEMAN (D3191)
2. ALBET CARL COLEMAN, born on 09 Jun 1885 in Parker Co., TX; died 04 Mar 1890 in Parker Co., TX; buried in Poolville Cemetery, Poolville, Parker Co., TX.
3. LAURA PEARL COLEMAN, born on 18 Sep 1883 in Parker Co., TX; died 29 Aug 1884 in Parker Co., TX; buried in Poolville Cemetery, Poolville, Parker Co., TX.
4. FLORA LOUISE COLEMAN, born in Nov 1888 in TX.
5. ROY EDWARD COLEMAN (D3195)
6. NELLIE G. COLEMAN, born in Jul 1894 in TX.

References: 5, 29-Dist 70 Justice Precinct 2 Parker Co TX H58, 30-Dist 0068 Weatherford Ward 3 Parker Co TX H248, 45

D331 ELLEN ELVIRA LANTZ D33

ELLEN ELVIRA LANTZ was born in 1847 in NC. She married THOMAS M. SMILEY on 27 May 1875 in Catawba Co., NC. He was born in 1842 in VA.

Children of ELLEN LANTZ and T. SMILEY are:

1. CAROLINA S. SMILEY, born in May 1876, married RICHARD HOGSHEAD.
2. WILLIAM V. SMILEY, married BESS RHODES; resided OH.
3. GRIER R. SMILEY (D3313)
4. ARGYLE J. SMILEY, born in Jul 1881 in VA.

References: 5, 30-Dist 0040 Riverheads Augusta Co VA H70, 29-Dist 34 Moffetts Creek Augusta Co VA H296, 27-Roverhead Augusta Co VA H354, 65

D332 SUSANNA CATHRINA LANTZ D33

SUSANNA CATHRINA LANTZ was born in Jan 1849 in NC. She married Rev. JOHN ALLISON FOIL. He was born in Feb 1848 in NC. They resided at 405 N. Poplar St., Charlotte, NC.

Children of SUSANNA LANTZ and JOHN FOIL are:

1. HELEN LANTZ FOIL, born in 1874 in Catawba Co., NC; married O.P. BEARD.
2. MIRIAM HAMERSLEY FOIL, born in 1876 in Catawba Co., NC

3. ETHEL LANTZ FOIL, born in Feb 1883 in Catawba Co., NC

References: 6-Sarah Mae (Huss) Lantz, 5, 27-Newton Catawba Co NC H12, 29-Dist 47 Newton Catawba Co NC H288

D333 HENRIETTA CAROLINE LANTZ D33

HENRIETTA CAROLINE LANTZ was born in Mar 1850 in NC. She married JACOB A. SILER on 19 Oct 1876 in Catawba Co., NC, son of JOHN SILER and MARY. He died before 1900 in Augusta Co., VA. They resided at 505 S. Mendelshasse, Greensboro, Guilford Co., NC.

Children of HENRIETTA LANTZ and JACOB SILER are:

1. ARTHUR FRALEY SILER, born in Oct 1878 in Augusta Co., VA.
2. JACOB FOIL SILER, born in Nov 1880 in Augusta Co., VA.
3. JESSIE MOSELLE SILER (f), born in Apr 1883 in Augusta Co., VA.

References: 6-Sarah Mae (Huss) Lantz, 5, 30-Dist 0110 Greensboro Ward 4 Guilford Co NC H111, 27-Riverhead Augusta Co VA H458, 65

D334 EMMA JANE LANTZ D33

EMMA JANE LANTZ was born in 1853 and dies in 1902. She married (1) ALFRED STARR on 07 Nov 1878 in Catawba Co., NC. He died before 1880 in VA. She married (2) JACOB H. SWARTZEL in VA. He was born in Oct 1849 in VA

Child of EMMA LANTZ and JACOB SWARTZEL is:

1. KENNETH H. SWARTZEL, born in Jul 1891 in VA.

References: 6-Sarah Mae (Huss) Lantz, 5, 29-Dist 36 Middlebrook Augusta Co VA H29, 65

D351 MARTHA C. WILKINSON D35

MARTHA C. WILKINSON was born in Sep 1839 in Catawba Co., NC. She married WILLIAM J. CALDWELL. He was born in Mar 1835 in NC.

Children of MARTHA WILKINSON and WILLIAM CALDWELL are:

1. GEORGE B. CALDWELL, born in May 1860 in NC.
2. JOHN L. CALDWELL, born in 1861 in NC.
3. JEFFERSON CALDWELL, born in 1862 in NC.
4. FANNIE CALDWELL, born in 1864 in NC.
5. WALTER A. CALDWELL, born in 1866 in NC.
6. IOLA L. CALDWELL, born in Jan 1868 in NC.
7. CANDICE CALDWELL, born in 1870 in NC.
8. WILLIAM W. CALDWELL (D3518)
9. LILLY MAY CALDWELL, born in May 1873 in NC.

10. JACOB CALDWELL, born in 1875 in NC.
11. MARY CALDWELL, born in 1878 in NC.
12. BARTTEL CALDWELL, born in Jan 1882 in NC.

References: 29-Lincolnton Lincoln Co NC H341, 27-Ironton Lincoln Co NC H263, 26-Ironton Lincoln Co NC H336

D352 RUFUS A. WILKINSON D35

RUFUS A. WILKINSON was born on 26 May 1843 in Catawba Co., NC and died 20 Mar 1911 in Mecklenburg Co., NC. He married ELLA SHUFORD. He is buried in Elmwood Cemetery, Charlotte, Mecklenburg Co., NC.

Children of RUFUS WILKINSON and ELLA SHUFORD are:

1. CARRIE WILKINSON, born in 1872 in Lincoln Co., NC.
2. SHUFORD WILKINSON (D3522)
3. MARVIN WILKINSON (D3523)

References: 27-Denver Twp Lincoln Co NC H605, 45

D353 WILLIAM H. WILKINSON D35

WILLIAM H. WILKINSON was born in 1847 in Catawba Co., NC. He married MARY ANN CALDWELL.

Children of WILLIAM WILKINSON and MARY CALDWELL are:

1. AUGUSTUS M. WILKINSON, born in Oct 1872 in Catawba Co., NC.
2. MINNIE WILKINSON, born in 1875 in Catawba Co., NC.
3. TOBIN WILKINSON, born in 1877 in Catawba Co., NC.
4. WILLIAM WILKINSON, born in 1879 in Catawba Co., NC.
5. MAGGIE E. WILKINSON, born in Nov 1881 in NC.
6. JOHN L. WILKINSON, born in Sep 1886 in NC.
7. BEULAH WILKINSON, born in Sep 1889 in NC.
8. MOCK R. WILKINSON, born in Oct 1894 in NC.

References: 27-Mountain Creek Twp Catawba Co NC H197, 29-Paw Creek Twp Mecklenburg Co NC H69

D354 NANCY CAROLINE WILKINSON D35

NANCY CAROLINE WILKINSON was born in 23 Aug 1849 in Catawba Co., NC and died 13 Nov 1922 in Catawba Co., NC. She married WILLIAM A. DRUM. He was born on 16 Nov 1845 in NC and died 18 Dec 1926 in Catawba Co., NC. Both are buried in Pisqah United Methodist Church Cemetery, Catawba, Catawba Co., NC.

Children of NANCY WILKINSON and WILLIAM DRUM are:

1. AMANDA DRUM, born in 1869 in Catawba Co., NC.
2. MARY DRUM, born in 1871 in Catawba Co., NC.
3. ANNA S. DRUM, born in Nov 1873 in Catawba Co., NC.
4. BELZAME DRUM, born in 1877 in Catawba Co., NC.
5. CORA DRUM, born in 1879 in Catawba Co., NC.
6. ALDOLPHUS STAMEY DRUM (D3546)
7. MILTON L. DRUM, born in Oct 1882 in Catawba Co., NC.
8. DORCUS E. DRUM, born in Aug 1884 in Catawba Co., NC.
9. BESSIE E. DRUM, born in Oct 1887 in Catawba Co., NC.
10. NANCY E. DRUM, born in Dec 1889 in Catawba Co., NC.
11. MERTLE P. DRUM, born in Dec 1890 in Catawba Co., NC.

References: 27-Mountain Creek Twp Catawba Co NC H217, 29-Mountain Creek Twp Catawba Co NC H104, 45

D355 GEORGE M. WILKINSON D35

GEORGE M. WILKINSON was born in 1838 in Catawba Co., NC. He married MARY R. SHELTON.

Children of GEORGE WILKINSON and MARY SHELTON are:

1. FANNIE E. WILKINSON, born in 1868 in Catawba Co., NC.
2. MICHAEL W. WILKINSON, born in 1870 in Catawba Co., NC.
3. GEORGE D. WILKINSON, born in 1874 in Catawba Co., NC.
4. DAVID L. WILKINSON, born in 1877 in Catawba Co., NC.

References: 27-Caldwells Twp Catawba Co NC H185

D356 JACOB M. WILKINSON D35

JACOB M. WILKINSON was born in 1842 in Catawba Co., NC. He married MARTHA SUMMIT. She was born in 1848 in NC.

Children of JACOB WILKINSON and MARTHA SUMMIT are:

1. PINKNEY WILKINSON, born in 1863 in Catawba Co., NC.
2. FANNIE WILKINSON, born in 1867 in Catawba Co., NC.
3. DOROTHY WILKINSON, born in 1871 in Catawba Co., NC.
4. SARAH WILKINSON, born in 1873 in Catawba Co., NC.
5. SUSAN CORY WILKINSON, born in 1874 in Catawba Co., NC.
6. MOTTIE C. WILKINSON, born in 1875 in Catawba Co., NC.
7. STEVE P. WILKINSON, born in 1877 in Catawba Co., NC.

References: 27-Caldwells Twp Catawba Co NC H184

D357 DAVID C. KING WILKINSON D35

DAVID C. KING WILKINSON was born in 1853 in Catawba Co., NC. He married JULIA. She was born in Feb 1860 in NC.

Children of DAVID WILKINSON and JULIA are:

1. CARSON WILKINSON, born in Aug 1885 in Lincoln Co., NC.
2. JAMES WILKINSON, born in Mar 1887 in Lincoln Co., NC.
3. EVERET B. WILKINSON, born in Jun 1888 in Lincoln Co., NC.
4. ESSIE P. WILKINSON, born in Jan 1891 in Lincoln Co., NC.
5. HARLAND L. WILKINSON, born in Jul 1894 in Lincoln Co., NC.
6. CONNIE M. WILKINSON, born in Oct 1896 in Lincoln Co., NC.

References: 29-Catawba Springs Twp Lincoln Co NC H235

D358 JAMES WESLEY WILKINSON D35

JAMES WESLEY WILKINSON was born in 1851 in Catawba Co., NC. He married MARY E. She was born in 1855 in NC.

Children of JAMES WILKINSON and MARY are:

1. EVERETT R. WILKINSON (D3581)

References: 30-Statesville Iredell Co NC H153, 10-Statesville Iredell Co NC H662, 31-Statesville Iredell Co NC H121

D35A SARAH C. WILKINSON D35

SARAH C. WILKINSON was born 21 Apr 1836 in NC and died 17 Jun 1901 in Catawba Co., NC. She married THOMAS FLETCHER DRUM in Catawba Co., NC. He was born 05 Nov 1829 in NC and died 13 Feb 1920 in Catawba Co., NC. Both are buried in Pisqah United Methodist Church Cemetery, Catawba, Catawba Co., NC.

Children of SARAH WILKINSON and THOMAS DRUM are:

1. JACOB FRANCIS M. DRUM (D35A1)
2. MARTHA JANE DRUM (D35A2)
3. NANCY CATHERINE DRUM, born 13 Jan 1858 in Catawba Co., NC.
4. GEORGE P. DRUM (D35A4)
5. THOMAS JEFFERSON DRUM (D35A5)
6. CHARLOTTE C. DRUM, born 186 in Catawba Co., NC.
7. ETTA E. DRUM, born 1862 in Catawba Co., NC.
8. IDA R. DRUM, born 1864 in Catawba Co., NC.
9. LAURA C. DRUM, born 1868 in Catawba Co., NC.
10. SARAH S. DRUM, born 1869 in Catawba Co., NC.
11. ELLA F. DRUM, born 1872 in Catawba Co., NC.
12. LILLIE A. DRUM, born 1874 in Catawba Co., NC.
13. EVA S. DRUM, born 1876 in Catawba Co., NC.
14. WILLIE B. DRUM, born 1878 in Catawba Co., NC.

References: 6-Sarah Mae (Huss) Lantz, 29-Dist 35 Catawba Co NC H184, 25-Catawba Co NC H1069, 26-Hamilton Catawba Co NC H237, 27-Catawba Catawba Co NC H226, 45

D35B JOHN F. WILKINSON D35

JOHN F. WILKINSON was born 07 Apr 1845, and died 21 Jun 1894. He married HARRIET L. DRUM. She was born 14 Sep 1850, and died 19 Mar 1936.

Child of JOHN WILKINSON and HARRIET DRUM is:

1. FANNIE JULIA ERA WILKINSON (D35B1)
2. WILLIAM WILKINSON, born in 1869 in Catawba Co., NC.

References: 6-Sarah Mae (Huss) Lantz, 26-Caldwell Twp Catawba Co NC H92

D35C ABSOLEM LANE WILKINSON D35

ABSOLEM LANE WILKINSON was born in 1855 in Catawba Co., NC and died before 1900 in Catawba Co., NC. He married IDA MARY DRUM (D4212), born in May 1872 in Lincoln Co., NC.

Children of ABSOLEM WILKINSON and IDA DRUM are:

1. HENRY R. WILKINSON, born in Jun 1895 in Catawba Co., NC.
2. EFFIE C. WILKINSON, born in Dec 1896 in Catawba Co., NC.
3. ARTY L. WILKINSON, born in Mar 1899 in Catawba Co., NC.

References: 29-Mountain Creek Twp Catawba Co NC H102

D361 MARY ANN HOWARD D36

MARY ANN HOWARD was born 28 Jun 1843 in NC, and died 1923. She married DAVID F. MOOSE in 1861 in Catawba Co., NC. He was born in 1833 in NC.

Children of MARY HOWARD and DAVID MOOSE are:

1. LAURA ETTA MOOSE, born 14 Nov 1861, Newton, Catawba Co., NC.
2. SARAH ANN MOOSE (D3612)
3. DORA FRANCES MOOSE (D3613)
4. GEORGE HOWARD MOOSE (D3514)

References: 6-Sarah Mae (Huss) Lantz, 5, 26-Newton Catawba Co NC H148, 27-Newton Catawba Co NC H162

D362 NANCY CATHERINE HOWARD D36

NANCY CATHERINE HOWARD was born 28 Mar 1845 in Catawba Co., NC. She married GABRIEL POWELL SHERRILL on 20 Nov 1866 in Catawba Co., NC. He was born in 1845 in NC and died in 1898 in Catawba Co., NC.

Children of NANCY HOWARD and GABRIEL SHERRILL are:

1. MARY TULLULA SHERRILL, born on 12 May 1867 in Catawba Co., NC; died 12 Jul 1891; married W. M. SHERRILL. One child.
2. SARAH "SALLIE" ELIZABETH SHERRILL, born on 27 Feb 1869 in Catawba Co., NC; married J. W. LITTLE. Four children.
3. BARBARA PINKNEY SHERRILL, born on 10 Dec 1870 in Catawba Co., NC; married A. C. SHERRILL. One child.
4. SUE AUGUSTA SHERRILL, born on 26 Jul 1873 in Catawba Co., NC; married R. A. WHITE. Three children.
5. MATTIE ZARA SHERRILL, born on 28 Aug 1875 in Catawba Co., NC; married P. N. MOCH. Three children.
6. EMMA LANTZ SHERRILL, born on 22 May 1877 in Catawba Co., NC; married L. A, WHITE. Seven children.
7. ALEXANDER LEE SHERRILL, born on 08 Jan 1879 in Catawba Co., NC; married ELLA BOST. Two children.
8. WADE HAMPTON SHERRILL, born on 08 Sep 1881 in Catawba Co., NC; married BERTIE ROBINSON.
9. CHARLES EDGAR SHERRILL, born on 16 Dec 1884 in Catawba Co., NC; died 27 Jan 1909.
10. RICHARD STOUGH SHERRILL, born on 16 Mar 1890 in Catawba Co., NC.

References: 5, 26-Mountain Creek Catawba Co NC H242, 27-Mountain Creek Catawba Co NC

H298, 29-Dist 44 Mountain Creek Catawba Co NC H40

D364 MARTHA CURTIS HOWARD D36

MARTHA CURTIS HOWARD was born 03 Feb 1849 and died 07 Jun 1880. She married FRANCIS ROBINSON on 01 Aug 1866 in Catawba Co., NC. He was born in 1843 in NC.

Children of MARTHA HOWARD and FRANCIS ROBINSON are:

1. SARAH OLA ROBINSON (D3641)
2. LILLIE S. ROBINSON, born in 1871 in Catawba Co., NC.
3. JOHN FRANKLIN ROBINSON, born in 1873 in Catawba Co., NC.
4. MARY ANNA ROBINSON, born in 1875 in Catawba Co., NC.

References: 5, 26-Mountain Creek Catawba Co NC H227, 27-Mountain Creek Catawba Co NC H290

D365 FRANCIS AUGUSTA HOWARD D36

FRANCES "FANNIE" AUGUSTA HOWARD was born 16 Nov 1850 in Catawba Co., NC and died 12 Feb 1916 in Catawba Co., NC. She married HENRY FRANK POWELL in Jun 1869 in Asheville, NC. He was born in Nov 1850 in NC.

Children of FRANCES HOWARD and HENRY POWELL are:

1. EVA CAROLINE POWELL (D3651)
2. GEORGE A. POWELL, born in Sep 1871 in Catawba Co., NC.
3. SUE E. POWELL, born in Aug 1876 in Catawba Co., NC.
4. JOHN B. POWELL, born in Aug 1879 in Catawba Co., NC.

References: 5, 27-Catawba Catawba Co NC H159, 29-Ashville Ward 4 Buncombe Co NC H251

D384 JOHN FRANKLIN LANTZ D38

JOHN FRANKLIN LANTZ was born 28 Jan 1856 in Lincoln Co., NC, and died 28 Oct 1928 in Lincoln Co., NC. He married LAURA ADELINE ROBINSON 04 Mar 1880 in Lincolnton, Lincoln Co., NC, daughter of MARCUS ROBINSON and MARGARET KISTLER. She was born 05 Jan 1861, and died 21 Oct 1950 in Lincoln Co., NC.

Children of JOHN LANTZ and LAURA ROBINSON are:

1. ALFRED LEE LANTZ, born 05 Feb 1881 and died 18 Nov 1881 in Lincoln Co., NC.
2. BESSIE ERA LANTZ (D3842)
3. ADA CAROLINE LANTZ (D3843)
4. ORA ALICE LANTZ, born 16 Nov 1890 and died 17 Sep 1893 in Lincoln Co., NC.
5. COY FRANKLIN LANTZ (D3845)

References: 6-Sarah Mae (Huss) Lantz, 29-Dist 108 Reepsville Lincoln Co NC H252

JOHN FRANKLIN LANTZ and LAURA ADELINE ROBINSON

JOHN FRANKLIN LANTZ

LAURA ADELINE ROBINSON

Family Farmhouse built in 1858 by JACOB LANTZ (died in Civil War in 1864).... LAURA ADELINE ROBINSON, wife of JOHN FRANKLIN LANTZ, stands in the front.

D385 SARAH ALICE LANTZ D38

SARAH ALICE LANTZ was born on 11 Jul 1859 in Lincoln Co., NC and died 01 Jul 1941 in Lincoln Co., NC. She married WILLIAM PINKNEY RAMSOUR 09 Feb 1888 in Lincoln Co., NC. He was born in Mar 1842 in NC.

Children of SARAH LANTZ and WILLIAM RAMSOUR are:

1. WILLIAM RUSSELL RAMSOUR, born on 20 Apr 1892 in Lincoln Co., NC; died 30 May 1961; married HATTIE A.; born in Aug 1874 in NC.
2. JOHN DOUGLAS RAMSOUR, born on 26 Nov 1898 in Lincoln Co., NC; died 19 Jan 1908 in Lincoln Co., NC.
3. UNKNOWN RAMSOUR, born and died before 1900 in Lincoln Co., NC.

References: 6-Sarah Mae (Huss) Lantz, 5, 29-Dist 108 Reepsville Lincoln Co NC H287

D411 JACOB CARPENTER D41

JACOB CARPENTER was born in Oct 1830 in Lincoln Co., NC and died in 1902 in Gaston Co., NC. He married LUCINDA in Lincoln Co., NC. She was born Oct 1835 in NC.

Children of JACOB CARPENTER and LUCINDA are:

1. ARTHUR M. CARPENTER (D4111)
2. JOHN C. CARPENTER (D4112)
3. EVALINE C. CARPENTER, born in 1856 in Lincoln Co., NC.
4. ELAIN CATHARINE CARPENTER (D4114)
5. EDITH CLARISSA CARPENTER, born in 1860 in Lincoln Co., NC; married LABAN SMITH; born in 1855 in NC; no children.
6. ELVIN CLATON CARPENTER (D4116)
7. WINNIE CARPENTER (D4117)
8. MINNIE CARPENTER, born in Jan 1866 in Lincoln Co., NC; died after 1910 Gaston Co., NC; married (2) TENEY STINES in 1900-1910 in GASTON Co., NC; died before 1910 in Gaston Co., NC; her 2nd no marriage and no children.
9. WILLIAM B. CARPENTER (D4119)
10. ROSA CARPENTER, born in Jan 1870 in Lincoln Co., NC.
11. ALICE CARPENTER (D411B)
12. HARRIS CARPENTER, born in 1874 in Lincoln Co., NC; died before 25 Jul 1902 in NC.

References: 25-Lincoln Co NC H507, 26-Ironton Lincoln Co NC H309, 27-Ironton Lincoln Co NC H68, 29-Gastonia Twp Gaston Co NC H230, 30-Dallas Twp Gaston Co NC H432

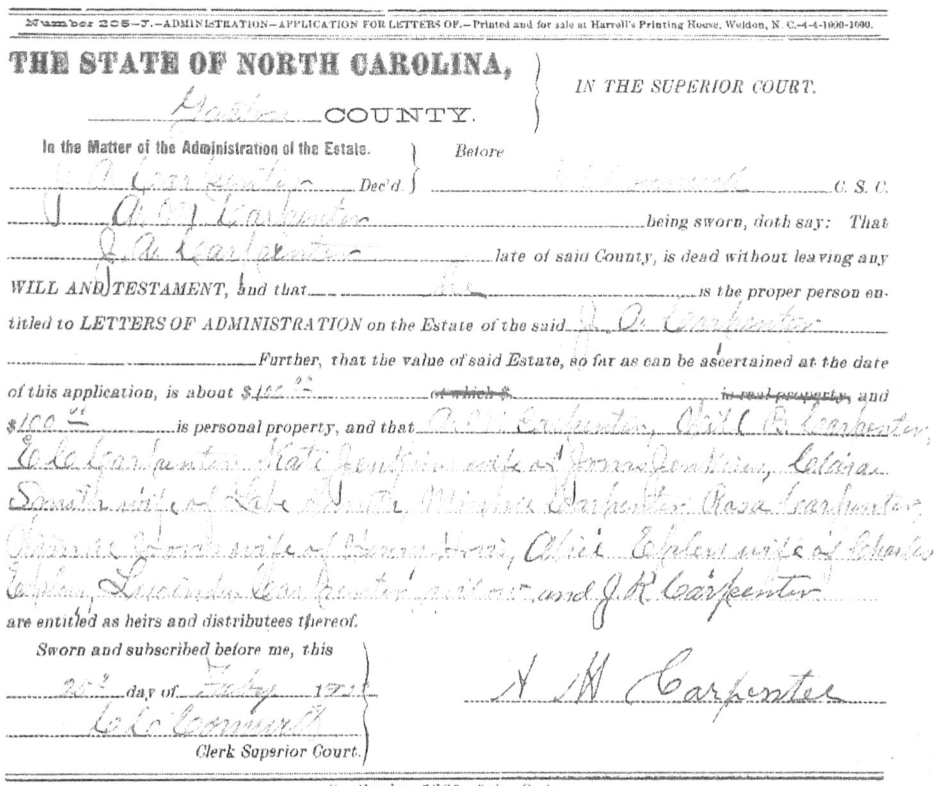

Number 205-J.—ADMINISTRATION—APPLICATION FOR LETTERS OF.—Printed and for sale at Harrell's Printing House, Weldon, N. C.—4-4-1900-1000.

THE STATE OF NORTH CAROLINA, Gaston COUNTY. — *IN THE SUPERIOR COURT.*

In the Matter of the Administration of the Estate. J. A. Carpenter Dec'd. — *Before* [illegible] *C. S. C.*

A. M. Carpenter *being sworn, doth say: That* J. A. Carpenter *late of said County, is dead without leaving any WILL AND TESTAMENT, and that* he *is the proper person entitled to LETTERS OF ADMINISTRATION on the Estate of the said* J. A. Carpenter *Further, that the value of said Estate, so far as can be ascertained at the date of this application, is about* $100.00 ~~of which $~~ ~~is real property,~~ *and* $100.00 *is personal property, and that* A. M. Carpenter, Will B. Carpenter, Ella Carpenter, Kate Jenkins wife of [illegible] Jenkins, Clarissa Smith wife of [illegible] Smith, Minnie Carpenter, Rosa Carpenter, [illegible] wife of [illegible], Alice Eaker wife of Charles Eaker, Lucinda Carpenter widow, and J. R. Carpenter *are entitled as heirs and distributees thereof.*

Sworn and subscribed before me, this 20th *day of* Feby 1902
[illegible]
Clerk Superior Court.

A. M. Carpenter

See Section 1381 of the Code.

A. M. Carpenter, Administrator of the estate of Jacob A. Carpenter, deceased, files this as his final account, to-wit:

1902.	Receipts.	
Nov. 22.	To cash received from sale of personal prpperty	$75.35
	To cash received from sale of one Wagon ---	10000
	To cash received from sale of Horse ----------	65.00
	To cash received from sale of corn ----------	9.00
		$159.35

1901.	Disbursements.	
Nov.9.	Paid Armstrong Undertakers -------	$22.50
Nov.20.	Paid Town Tax for 1901 ----------	13.44
Nov.2.	Paid Anders & Floyd (Livery hire) -	3.50
1902. Feb.25.	Paid C. C. Cornwell, C. S. C. for Letters of Administration and stamp on bond ------------------------	2.25
June 5.	Paid Hanna Bro. (Livery hire) ---	3.00
1901 Nov.23.	Paid C. B. Armstrong, Sheriff 9taxes for 1901) ----------------------	7.48
Nov.2.	Paid Morris Bros in full of acct.	7.20
Nov.1.	Paid Fayssoux & Davis in full of acct. ----------------------------	1.25
1902. Apr.19.	Paid Dr.J. M. Sloan (medical bill)	20.00
Dec.15.	Paid I. N. Alexander (town tax)	7.37
Nov.5.	Paid Gastonia Book Store --------	1.00
	Paid P. M. Gardner in full of acct.	2.40
Nov.22.	Paid W. I. Stowe (auctioneer) ---	3.00
Dec.13.	Paid Gastonia Gazett in full of acct	3.00
Mch.17.	Paid Gastonia Gazett for publishing	
1905	notice to creditors -------------	2.50
Jan.31.	Paid C. B. Armstrong, Sheriff taxes for 1902 ----------------------	5.77
	Paid Hanna Bros. in full of acct.	3.50
1904	Paid Minnie Carpenter in full of account --------------------------	10.00
May 28.	Paid Gastonia Gazett for advertising notice of sale --------------	3.00
	Retained for services rendered in the administration of this estate	7.50

Amounts forward ------------------------ $125.66 $159.35

Retained my account and interest on

same at 4% ------------------------ 36.00

Retained on account for wheat ---- 6.00

Paid C. C. Cornwell C. S. C. for

filing and recording this account - 2.25 $175.91

By balance due Administrator ---- $16.56

Administrator.

Subscribed and sworn to before me, this the 15th day of October, 1904.

Clerk Superior Court, Gaston Co., N. C.

Examined and approved,

C. S. C.

D421 FRANCES E. HALLMAN D42

FRANCES E. HALLMAN was born on 07 Oct 1838 in NC and died 07 Dec 1893 in NC. She married PETER MONROE DRUM in NC. He was born on 05 Apr 1824 in NC and died 19 Dec 1910 in NC.

1. GEORGE DRUM, was born in 1870 in Lincoln Co., NC
2. IDA MARY DRUM (D4212) see (D35C)
3. MARTIN DRUM, was born in 1876 in Lincoln Co., NC.
4. NANCY DRUM, was born in 1879 in Lincoln Co., NC.

References: 29-Mountain Creek Twp Catawba Co NC H102, 29-Mountain Creek Twp Catawba Co NC H102, 27-Lincolnton Lincoln Co NC H292

D423 MARTHA A. HALLMAN D42

MARTHA A. HALLMAN was born on 07 Nov 1843 in Lincoln Co., NC and died 19 Aug 1884 in Catawba Co. NC. She married MORRIS R. BOST on 07 Sep 1868 in Catawba Co., NC. He was born in Aug 1846 in NC.

Children of MARTHA HALLMAN and MORRIS BOST are:

1. SUSAN BOST, born in 1869 in Catawba Co., NC; died before 1880 in Catawba Co., NC.

2. LAURA E. BOST, born in Aug 1870 in Catawba Co., NC.
3. LUTHER A. BOST, born in Sep 1872 in Catawba Co., NC.
4. GEORGE T. BOST, born in Apr 1876 in Catawba Co., NC.
5. W. E. BOST (m), born in 1878 in Catawba Co., NC; died before 1880 in Catawba Co., NC.
6. FANNIE P. BOST, born in Jun 1881 in Catawba Co., NC.

References: 26-Caldwell Twp Catawba Co NC H150, 27-Caldwells Twp Catawba Co NC H9, 29-Dist 46 Newton Twp Catawba Co NC H190

D424 EMMA HALLMAN D42

EMMA HALLMAN was born in 1848 in Lincoln Co., NC and died before 1900 in Catawba Co., NC. She married ADOLPHUS. RUDISILL on 10 Feb 1876 in Catawba Co., NC, son of MARCUS HENRY RUDISILL and FRANCES LAVINA KILLIAN. He was born on 01 Apr 1849 in Catawba Co., NC and died in Aug 1876.

Child of EMMA HALLMAN and ADOLPHUS RUDISILL is:

1. BOB RUDISILL, born in Jun 1884 in NC.

References: 29-Bandy Twp Catawba Co NC H128

D426 JAMES MONROE HALLMAN D42

JAMES MONROE HALLMAN was born 20 Nov 1855 in Lincoln Co., NC and died 11 May 1919 in Lincoln Co., NC. He married (1) MARY JANE CARRA HALLMAN on 09 Jan 1879 in Lincoln Co., NC, daughter of ALFRED HALLMAN and MARY KILLIAN. She was born 31 Jan 1857, and died 16 Apr 1889 in Lincoln Co., NC. He married (2) ESTHER SUSANNA BROWN on 19 Aug 1891 in Lincoln Co., NC, daughter of JOHN BROWN and SUSAN REEL. She was born 16 Aug 1865 in Iron Station, Lincoln Co., NC, and died 20 Jul 1925 in Lincoln Co., NC.

Children of JAMES HALLMAN and MARY HALLMAN are:

1. OTTIS THEODORE HALLMAN, born 21 Dec 1879 in Lincoln Co., NC; died 11 Dec 1934. He married MINNIE IRENE MARTIN 25 Dec 1900 in Lincoln Co., NC. No children.
2. MARY ETTA HALLMAN (D4262)
3. LOTTIE E. HALLMAN, born 13 Jun 1883 in Lincoln Co., NC; died 09 Mar 1884 in Lincoln Co., NC.
4. JAMES LEVY HALLMAN (D4264)
5. BESSIE HALLMAN (D4265)
6. LOOMIS ALFRED HALLMAN, born 21 Mar 1889 in Lincoln Co., NC; died 12 Sep

1889 in Lincoln Co., NC.

Children of JAMES HALLMAN and ESTHER BROWN are:

7. ROBERT BROWN HALLMAN, born 30 Jun 1892 in Lincoln Co., NC; died 16 Sep 1917 in Lincoln Co., NC. He married BEULAH YATES 28 Jun 1911 in Lincoln Co., NC.
8. FANNIE GEORGIANNA HALLMAN (D4268)
9. THOMAS ANTHONY HALLMAN, born 09 Feb 1895 in Lincoln Co., NC; died 17 May 1896 in Lincoln Co., NC.
10. JOHN BLAIR HALLMAN, born 07 Apr 1896 in Lincoln Co., NC; died 14 Mar 1943 in Oklahoma. He married MARGARET ENO KERIT; died in Jacksonville, FL.
11. SUSAN LAURA HALLMAN (D426B)
12. LENA IRENE HALLMAN, born 07 Sep 1900 in Lincoln Co., NC; died 20 Jul 1981 in Lincoln Co., NC. She married EDWARD WALTER RISQUE in Feb 1928 in Gaston Co., NC; born 26 Mar 1898 in Gastonia, Gaston Co., NC.
13. RUBY LOUISE HALLMAN (D426D)
14. CARRIE LUCILLE HALLMAN (D426E)
15. WILBUR PURVIE HALLMAN (D426F)

References: 6-Sarah Mae (Huss) Lantz, 29-Dist 110 Lincolnton Lincoln Co NC H25

D428 WILLIAM SIDNEY HALLMAN D42

WILLIAM SIDNEY HALLMAN was born 18 Sep 1858 in Lincoln Co., NC, and died 14 Jun 1933. He married EMMA SHERRILL. She was born 07 Sep 1857 in Caldwell Co., NC, and died 19 Dec 1940 in Hickory, Catawba Co., NC.

Children of WILLIAM HALLMAN and EMMA SHERRILL are:

1. UNKNOWN HALLMAN, born and died before 1900 in Caldwell Co., NC.
2. MARY A. HALLMAN, born in Dec 1882 in Caldwell Co., NC.
3. FANNIE L. HALLMAN, born in Jul 1884 in Caldwell Co., NC.
4. JOHN WESLEY HALLMAN, born 01 Aug 1888 in Caldwell Co., NC; died 30 Jun 1967 in NC.
5. GEORGE W. HALLMAN, born 01 Jun 1890 in Caldwell Co., NC; died Mar 1961 in NC.
6. LELA C. HALLMAN, born in Oct 1892 in Caldwell Co., NC.
7. CARRIE SUSIE HALLMAN, born in Dec 1898 in Caldwell Co., NC.
8. MABEL HALLMAN, born in 1900 in Caldwell Co., NC.

References: 29-Dist 28 Lovelady Caldwell Co NC H251, 30-Dist 0061 Lovelady Caldwell Co NC H63

D434 JOSEPH MANGRUM FISHER D43

JOSEPH MANGRUM. FISHER was born in 1849 in Lincoln Co., NC. He married JANE in

Caldwell Co., NC. She was born in 1849 in NC.

Children of JOSEPH FISHER and JANE are:

1. MARTHA S. FISHER, born in 1871 in Caldwell Co., NC.
2. IDA E. FISHER, born in 1876 in Caldwell Co., NC.
3. ALICE FISHER, born in 1878 in Caldwell Co., NC.

References: 27-Lovelady Twp Caldwell Co NC 053 H198

D441 SAMUEL JACOB HALLMAN D44

SAMUEL JACOB HALLMAN was born 09 Nov 1845 in Shelby, Cleveland Co., NC, and died 17 Sep 1905 in Johnson Co., TX. He married VIRGINIA MARGARET SANDERS 28 May 1871 in AL. She was born 13 Jul 1853, and died 08 Mar 1920.

Children of SAMUEL HALLMAN and VIRGINIA SANDERS are:

1. MARGARET HALLMAN, born on 28 Aug 1874; died 18 Feb 1876.
2. GEORGE RICHARD HALLMAN (D4412)
3. JOHN SANDERS HALLMAN, born on 16 Aug 1879 in Waldron, Scott Co., Arkansas; died 15 Aug 1951. He married GRACE TEAS on 05 Jun 1903 in Corsicana, Texas; died 15 Feb 1945.
4. ELIZABETH RUTH HALLMAN (D4414).
5. SAMUEL MARCELLUS HALLMAN, born on 20 Jul 1884 in Alvarado, Johnson Co., TX; died 03 Sep 1956. He married ALA MAY BAIN; born 31 Jul 1889.
6. JAMES ALFORD HALLMAN, born on 11 Dec 1886 in Alvarado, Johnson Co., TX; died 08 Aug 1959. He married (1) BERTHA MAE REES. He married (2) NETTIE LEE WIER.
7. ERNEST LEROY HALLMAN (D4417)
8. MATTIE EULALIE HALLMAN, born on 15 Jun 1895 in Johnson Co., TX. She married WILLIAM EDWARD MCLEROY in Johnson Co., TX; born on 11 Oct 1895; died 05 Feb 1959.

References: 6-Sarah Mae (Huss) Lantz, 30-Dist 0056 Alvardo Johnson Co TX H99, 30-Dist 0056 Alvardo Johnson Co TX H102, 29-Dist 60 Justice Precinct 4 Johnson Co TX H174, 27-Cedar Scott Co AR H139

D444 JOHN CALHOUN HALLMAN D44

JOHN CALHOUN HALLMAN was born 26 Sep 1853 in Shelby, Cleveland Co., NC, and died 06 Jun 1937 in Atlanta, GA. He married ISABELLA HENDERSON.

Children of JOHN HALLMAN and ISABELLA HENDERSON are:

1. UNKNOWN HALLMAN, born and died before 1900 in Atlanta, Fulton Co., GA.

2. HENDERSON HALLMAN, born in Apr 1870 in Atlanta, Fulton Co., GA.
3. RUTH HALLMAN, born in Oct 1873 in Atlanta, Fulton Co., GA.
4. ERNEST G. HALLMAN, born in Sep 1875 in Atlanta, Fulton Co., GA.
5. EARL HALLMAN, born in 1878 and died before 1900 in Atlanta, Fulton Co., GA.

References: 6-Sarah Mae (Huss) Lantz, 27-Atlanta Fulton Co GA H31, 29-Dist 80 Atlanta Ward 6 Fulton Co GA H437

D452 SARAH ANN SUMMEROUR D45

SARAH ANN SUMMEROUR was born in 1851 in Lincoln Co., NC. She married DAVID MULL in Lincoln Co., NC. He was born in 1853 in NC.

Child of SARAH SUMMEROUR and DAVID MULL is:

1. MAMIE MULL, born in 1879 in Lincolnton, Lincoln Co., NC.

References: 27-Lincolnton Lincoln Co NC H446

D514 JOHN WILLIAM PROPST D51

JOHN WILLIAM PROPST was born 25 May 1840 in Catawba Co., NC and died 18 Aug 1916 in Catawba Co., NC. He married (1) SARAH CATHERINE JARRETT on 10 Jan 1861 in Catawba Co., NC. She was born 21 Oct 1849 in NC and died 10 Aug 1886 in Catawba Co., NC. He married (2) MARGARET C. KISTLER in Catawba Co., NC. She married (1) _______ Robinson in Catawba Co., NC. She was born in 28 Jan 1837 in NC and died 22 Sep 1892 in Catawba Co., NC. He married (3) PANTHY LOUVINA GREENE on 09 May 1897 in Catawba Co., NC, daughter of OLIVER C. GREEN and PERCEDA. She married (1) PAUL HUNSUCKER on 17 Mar 1891 in Catawba Co., NC. She was born in 1850 in NC. He and his 1st and 2nd wives are buried in Grace Lutheran Cemetery in Newton, Catawba Co., NC.

Children of JOHN PROBST and SARAH JARRETT are:

1. MARY A. PROPST, born in 28 Dec 1861 in Catawba Co., NC; died 09 Jul 1948 in Catawba Co., NC; married HENRY F. SIGMON in Catawba Co., NC; born on 22 Jan 1854 in NC; died 19 Jul 1929 in Catawba Co., NC. Both are buried in Grace Lutheran Cemetery in Newton, Catawba Co., NC.
2. ALICE ISABELLE PROPST (D5142)
3. LAURA PROPST, born in 1866 in Catawba Co., NC.
4. CANDES PROPST, born in 1869 in Catawba Co., NC.
5. FRANCES EFFIE PROPST, born in Dec 1873 in Catawba Co., NC.
6. JAMES A. PROPST, born in 1875 in Catawba Co., NC.
7. BARTLETT PROPST, born in 1876 in Catawba Co., NC.
8. OLIVER M. PROPST, born in Jul 1878 in Catawba Co., NC.

Child of JOHN PROBST and MARGARET KISTLER is:

9. PEARL H. PROPST, born in 1892 in Catawba Co., NC.

Child of JOHN PROBST and PANTHY GREEN is:

10. EVA PROPST, born in 1901 in Catawba Co., NC.

References: 25-Catawba Co NC H575, 45, 65, 26-Jacobs Fork Twp Catawba Co NC H184, 27-Jacobs Fork Twp Catawba Co NC 046 H196, 29-Hickory Twp Catawba Co NC 0041 H66, 30-Hickory Twp Catawba Co NC 0025 H86

D612 LOGAN SAINE D61

LOGAN SAINE was born 1852 in Lincoln Co., NC. He married SARAH A. in Lincoln Co., NC. She was born in 1851 in NC.

Child of LOGAN SAINE and is:

1. GRICE B. SAINE, born in 1877 in Lincoln Co., NC.
2. ELLA M. SAINE, born in 1882 in Lincoln Co., NC.
3. MARY SAINE, born in 1890 in Lincoln Co., NC.

References: 27-Howsrds Creek Twp Lincoln Co NC 103 H320, 29-Beam Precinct Lincoln Co NC H19

D614 ADOLPHUS D. SAINE D61

ADOLPHUS D. SAINE was born 1855 in Lincoln Co., NC. He married SARAH E. in Lincoln Co., NC. She was born in Sep 1857 in NC.

Children of ADOLPHUS SAINE and SARAH are:

1. FANNIE L. SAINE, born in Aug 1881 in Lincoln Co., NC.
2. MOLIE SAINE, born in Jun 1884 in Lincoln Co., NC.
3. BURNICE F. SAINE, born in Jul 1888 in Lincoln Co., NC.
4. LLOYD A. SAINE, born in Jan 1892 in Lincoln Co., NC.

References: 29-Dist 0064 Paw Creek Twp Mecklenburg NC H93, 30-Paw Creek Twp Mecklenburg NC 0132 H44

D634 DANIEL A. SAINE D63

DANIEL A. SAINE was born on 20 Jun1858 in Lincoln Co., NC and died 23 Apr 1944 in Lincoln Co., NC. He married ISABELLE J. SUMMEROW in Lincoln Co., NC. She was born on 23 Sep 1860 in NC and died 07 Oct 1945 in Lincoln Co., NC. Both are buried in Hollybrook Cemetery, Lincolnton, Lincoln Co., NC.

Children of DANIEL SAINE and ISABELLE SUMMEROW are:

1. ELLA MARY SAINE, born in Oct 1891 in Lincoln Co., NC.
2. MYRA EMMA SAINE, born in Dec 1894 in Lincoln Co., NC.
3. GEORGE SOLOMON SAINE, born on 09 Nov 1895 in Lincoln Co., NC; buried in Hollybrook Cemetery, Lincolnton, Lincoln Co., NC.
4. CLIFFORD CALDWELL SAINE, born in Apr 1898 in Lincoln Co., NC.
5. GLADDUS SAINE (m), born in 1903 in Lincoln Co., NC.

References: 45, 29-Dist 0110 Lincolnton Lincoln Co NC H609, 30-Lincolnton Lincoln Co 0071 NC H188

D661 LUTHER ERNEST HOUSER D66

LUTHER ERNEST HOUSER, Sr. was born 30 Aug 1870 in Lincoln Co., NC, and died 15 Jul 1940. He married CANDACE SUSAN HUSS 22 Mar 1896, daughter of DAVID HUSS and MARY LEONHARDT. She was born 05 Sep 1878 in Lincoln Co., NC, and died 02 Jan 1957. Both are buried at Zion United Methodist Church Cemetery, Lincoln Co., NC.

Children of LUTHER HOUSER and CANDACE HUSS are:

1. JAMES MARSHALL HOUSER (D6611)
2. REUBEN ERVIN HOUSER, born 07 Mar 1902 in Lincoln Co., NC; died 05 Sep 1980 in Burke Co., NC. He married (1) ANNA PARKER. He married (2) OLLIE MAE YORK 09 Aug 1935; born 08 May 1911 in Lincoln Co., NC; died 09 May 1963 in Lincoln Co., NC. Reuben and Ollie are buried at Bethphage Lutheran Church Cemetery, Crouse, Lincoln Co., NC.
3. NORA STELLA HOUSER (D6613)
4. MARY PHYLECTOR HOUSER (D6614)
5. ALICE PEARL HOUSER (D6615)
6. LUTHER ERNEST HOUSER, Jr., born 18 Jul 1911 in Lincoln Co., NC; died 30 May 1984 in Shelby, Cleveland Co., NC.
7. EDNA ILESE HOUSER (D6617)
8. ROBERT LEE HOUSER (D6618)

References: 6-Sarah Mae (Huss) Lantz, 29-Dist 107 Howard Creek Lincoln Co NC H48

D662 REUBEN E. HOUSER D66

REUBEN E. HOUSER was born 19 Feb 1873, and died 24 Jun 1898. He married ALICE JANE SHULL 24 Jan 1895. She was born 01 Jan 1873.

Child of REUBEN HOUSER and ALICE SHULL is:

1. ETHEL PEARL HOUSER (D6621)

References: 6-Sarah Mae (Huss) Lantz, 29-Dist 113 Besses Chapple Lincoln Co NC H10

D1742 ALFORD CALVIN ROCKETT LANTZ D174

ALFORD CALVIN ROCKETT LANTZ was born 06 Nov 1882 in Shenandoah, Page Co., IA, and died 14 May 1961 in Buffalo Co., NE. He married MARY ROSE MORAN on 02 Sep 1911 at St. Mary's Church in Wayne, Wayne Co., NE. She was born 15 Dec 1886 in NE and died 18 Sep 1969 in Buffalo Co., NE. He was the owner and operator of Lantz Drug Store in Kearney, Buffalo Co., NE. Both are buried in Kearney Cemetery, Kearney, Buffalo Co., NE.

Children of ALFORD LANTZ and MARY MORAN are:

1. ALFORD LEWIS LANTZ, born on 05 Aug 1912 in Kearney, Buffalo Co., NE; died 15 Feb 1968 in Buffalo Co., NE. He married ALICE SCHLUND.
2. CLAIRE MARIE LANTZ, born 1914 in Kearney, Buffalo Co., NE; died 1981. She married ARTHUR EDWARD HABERLAN.
3. CATHERINE JANE LANTZ, born 1915 in Kearney, Buffalo Co., NE; died 1972. She married RONALD WILMER THOMPSON.
4. FRANCIS MORAN LANTZ (D17424)
5. MARCELLA MAE LANTZ, born 1919 in Kearney, Buffalo Co., NE. She married RAYMOND FRANCIS ROTH.
6. MILDRED ANN LANTZ, born 1921 in Kearney, Buffalo Co., NE.
7. MARY ROSE LANTZ (D17427)

References: 6-Sarah Mae (Huss) Lantz, 10-Dist 48 Kearney Buffalo Co NE H193, 31-Dist 48 Kearney Buffalo Co NE H184, 6-Francys Pattie Lantz Phillips, 45

ALFORD CALVIN ROCKETT LANTZ

D1743 FRED VERN LANTZ D174

FREDERICK VERN LANTZ was born Dec 1883 in IA, and died 1964. He married ELIZABETH M. WATTS. She was born 1890 in OH.

Children of FRED LANTZ and ELIZABETH WATTS are:

1. LESTER LANTZ, born 1915 in Johnson Co., NE.

2. ROBERT LEE LANTZ, born 1915 in Johnson Co., NE.
3. MARY ELIZABETH LANTZ, born 1926 in Johnson Co., NE.

References: 6-Sarah Mae (Huss) Lantz, 10-Dist 26 Nemaha Johnson Co NE H5, 31-Dist 4 Nemaha Johnson Co NE H61A, Tecumseh Johnson Co NE 49-9 H483

D1744 TWILLA MAY LANTZ D174

TWILLA MAY LANTZ was born Aug 1886 in NE, and died 07 Dec 1970 in Johnson Co., NE. She married WILLIAM PEEK in Johnson Co., NE. He was born in 1884 in NE and died 30 May 1964 in Johnson Co., NE. Both are buried in Tecumseh Cemetery, Tecumseh, Johnson Co., NE.

Children of TRELLA LANTZ and WILLIAM PEEK are:

1. IDA H. PEEK, born on 29 Jan 1916 in Johnson Co., NE; died 27 May 1992 in Johnson Co., NE; married BENJAMIN REIBER; died 04 Apr 1984 in Johnson Co., NE; Both are buried in Tecumseh Cemetery, Tecumseh, Johnson Co., NE.
2. LEO R. PEEK, born in 1921 in Johnson Co., NE.
3. LAVERNE PEEK, born in 1923 in Johnson Co., NE.

References: 10-Dist 24 Lincoln Johnson Co NE H47, 31-Dist 2 Lincoln Johnson Co NE H31, 45

D1745 ETHEL BLANCHE LANTZ D174

ETHEL BLANCHE LANTZ was born 26 Apr 1888 in NE, and died 23 Oct 1967 in Santa Barbara Co., CA. She married DANIEL JOSEPH MCCARTHY. He was born 08 Nov 1892 in KS and died 13 Jun 1971 in Santa Barbara Co., CA. Both are buried in Goleta Cemetery, Goleta, Santa Barbara Co., CA.

Child of ETHEL LANTZ and DANIEL MCCARTHY is:

1. JOE DELONE MCCARTHY, born on 18 Apr 1921 in Johnson Co., NE; died 04 Sep 1998; buried in Goleta Cemetery, Goleta, Santa Barbara Co., CA.
2. DANIEL JOSEPH MCCARTHY, born 1922 in Johnson Co., NE.

References: 6-Sarah Mae (Huss) Lantz, 31-Dist 9 Nemaha Johnson Co NE H42, 40-Tecumseh Johnson Co NE 49-9 H324, 45

D1746 DURWARD BELMONT LANTZ D174

DURWARD BELMONT LANTZ was born Dec 1890 in NE, and died 04 Nov 1977 in Johnson Co., NE. He married SARAH HELEN PLACE in Johnson Co., NE. She was born 1895 in NE and died 05 Mar 1983 in Johnson Co., NE. Both are buried in Tecumseh Cemetery, Tecumseh, Johnson Co., NE.

Child of DURWARD LANTZ and SARAH PLACE is:

1. KENNETH D. LANTZ, born 1924 in Johnson Co., NE.

References: 6-Sarah Mae (Huss) Lantz, 31-Dist 2 Lincoln Johnson Co NE H65, 40-Dist 2 Lincoln Johnson Co NE 49-2 H70, 45

D1747 IVAN WASHINGTON LANTZ D174

IVAN WASHINGTON LANTZ was born 21 Jul 1893 in NE, and died 02 Jun 1965 in Johnson Co., NE. He married GEORGIA A. PLACE. She was born 20 Jun 1901 in NE and died 20 May 1986 in Johnson Co., NE. Both are buried in Tecumseh Cemetery, Tecumseh, Johnson Co., NE.

Children of Ivan Lantz and Georgia Place are:

1. DONALD IVAN LANTZ, born 1918 in Johnson Co., NE.
2. CHESTER LEE LANTZ, born 1919 in Johnson Co., NE.
3. HARTFORD LANTZ, born 1922 in Johnson Co., NE.

References: 6-Sarah Mae (Huss) Lantz, 31-Dist 4 Nemaha Johnson Co NE H24, 45

D1751 RAY ELMER LANTZ D175

RAY ELMER LANTZ was born 26 Apr 1889 in Van Wert, Decatur Co., IA, and died 02 Sep 1961 in Leon, Decatur, IA. He married (1) FLORA COLE. He married (2) SARAH ALICE LEFFLER 26 Jan 1910, daughter of LUTHER LEFFLER and LAURA HAND. She was born 22 Feb 1891, and died 20 Jul 1924.

Children of RAY LANTZ and SARAH LEFFLER are:

1. MILDRED IRENE LANTZ, born 18 Jun 1911 in Van Wert, Decatur Co., IA; died 26 Jun 1911.
2. NADENE IRENE LANTZ, born 19 Jul 1913 in Van Wert, Decatur Co., IA. She married RAYMOND REDMAN 10 Feb 1931.
3. ESTHER OLIVE LANTZ (D17513)

References: 6-Sarah Mae (Huss) Lantz, 30-Dist 0045 Franklin Decatur Co IA H26

D1812 JAMES RALPH PARKER D181

JAMES RALPH PARKER was born in Mar 1885 in IA. He married AUGUSTA R. in Davis Co., IA. She was born in 1889 in KS.

Children of JAMES PARKER and AUGUSTA are:

1. FRANCES L. PARKER, born in 1906 in IA.
2. LLOYD A. PARKER, born in 1908 in IA.
3. EDWIN P. PARKER, born in 1909 in IA.

References: 30-Wyacondah Twp Davis Co IA H25

D1831 LEO CLIFFORD FOSTER D183

LEO CLIFFORD FOSTER was born on 09 Feb 1890 in IA and died in May 1968 in Davis Co., IA. He married LELIA G. LEYDA in Davis Co., IA. She was born on 08 Aug 1894 in IA and died in Oct 1984 in Davis Co., IA. Both are buried in Hopkins Cemetery, Davis Co., IA.

Children of LEO FOSTER and LELIA are:

1. RUTH F. FOSTER, born in 1922 in Davis Co., IA.
2. IRA C. FOSTER, born in 1926 in Davis Co., IA.
3. DONALD R. FOSTER, born in 1930 in Davis Co., IA.
4. ALICE L. FOSTER, born in 1934 in Davis Co., IA.

References: 31-Dist 2 Cleveland Twp Davis Co IA H26, 40-Cleveland Twp Davis Co IA 26-3 H12, 45

D1832 NOEL FERREE FOSTER D183

NOEL FERREE FOSTER was born on 21 Oct 1891 in IA and died 24 Oct 1934 in Davis Co., IA. He married IRENE WOODS in Davis Co., IA. She was born on 10 Jul 1902 in IA. He is buried in Hopkins Cemetery, Davis Co., IA.

Children of NOEL FOSTER and IRENE are:

1. IONE FOSTER, born in 1922 in Davis Co., IA.
2. IRIS FOSTER, born in 1927 in Davis Co., IA.

References: 31-Dist 18 West Grove Twp Davis Co IA H5, 40-West Grove Twp Davis Co IA 26-20 H65, 45

D1834 VERA MABEL FOSTER D183

VERA MABEL FOSTER was born on 28 Dec 1896 in IA and died 01 Jan 1993 in Davis Co., IA. She married ELVIN LUTHER MCCULLOUGH in Davis Co., IA. He was born in 15 Aug 1893 in IA and died 29 Jul 1990 in Davis Co., IA. Both are buried in Hopkins Cemetery, Davis Co., IA.

Children of VERA FOSTER and ELVIN MCCULLOUGH are:

1. S. IONE MCCULLOUGH, born in 1924 in Davis Co., IA.
2. S. IRENE MCCULLOUGH, born in 1925 in Davis Co., IA.
3. CLEO J. MCCULLOUGH, born in 1927 in Davis Co., IA.

4. LEOLA M. MCCULLOUGH, born in 1929 in Davis Co., IA.
5. VERA L. MCCULLOUGH, born in 1931 in Davis Co., IA.
6. GLENICE A. MCCULLOUGH, born in 1933 in Davis Co., IA.
7. MARYLIN J. MCCULLOUGH, born in 1935 in Davis Co., IA.
8. FRANKLIN F. MCCULLOUGH, born in 1939 in Davis Co., IA.

References: 31-Dist 5 Fabius Twp Davis Co IA H37, 40-Fabius Twp Davis Co IA 26-6 H2, 45

D1835 OSCAR JUDSON FOSTER D183

OSCAR JUDSON FOSTER was born in 04 Nov 1898 in IA and died 1930 in Davis Co., IA. He married GERTRUDE DABNEY in Davis Co., IA. She was born in 1903 in IA and died 1983 in Davis Co., IA. Both are buried in Hopkins Cemetery, Davis Co., IA.

Child of OSCAR FOSTER and GERTRUDE is:

1. VERA EMOGENE FOSTER, born on 26 Aug 1922 in Davis Co., IA; died 18 Jan 1985 in Gladstone, MO; married _______ MCELROY; She is buried in Hopkins Cemetery, Davis Co., IA.

References: 31-Dist 18 West Grove Twp Davis Co IA H90, 45

D3111 ALBERT LANTZ D311

ALBERT LANTZ was born 28 May 1875 in TX. He married GRACE E. HOYT in TX, daughter of JOSIAH L HOYT. She was born in 1882 in NE.

Children of ALBERT LANTZ and GRACE HOYT are:

1. ANONA GRACE LANTZ, born in 1905 in Tarrant Co., TX.
2. MARY EDNA LANTZ, born in 1907 in Tarrant Co., TX.

References: 5, 30-Dist 0119 Fort Worth Ward 6 Tarrant Co TX H116, 10-Dist 141 Fort Worth Ward 10 Tarrant Co TX H405

D3113 FANNIE LANTZ D311

FANNIE LANTZ was born 07 Jan 1879 in TX. She married EVERETT D. MARTIN. He was born in 1882 in MO.

Children of FANNIE LANTZ and EVERETT MARTIN are:

1. OPAL P. MARTIN, born in 1903 in MO.
2. WILLIAM BENTON MARTIN, born in 1905 in MO.
3. AILEEN MARTIN, born in 1907 in MO.

4. FRANCES PAULINE MARTIN, born in 1909 in MO.

References: 5, 10-Dist 2 Benton Adair Co MO H163, 31-Dist 0007 Kirksville Ward 4 Adair Co MO H219

D3114 MAUD LANTZ D311

MAUD LANTZ was born 15 Feb 1881 in TX. She married EDWARD E. DENTON. He was born in 1879 in TN

Children of Maud Lantz and EDWARD DENTON are:

1. INEZ DENTON, born in 1908 in Carter Co., OK.
2. OLIVER DENTON, born in 1918 in Carter Co., OK.

References: 5, 30-Dist 0041 Ardmore Ward 2 Carter Co OK H175, 10-Dist 0046 Ardmore Ward 4 Carter Co OK H449

D3117 JOHN LANTZ D311

JOHN LANTZ was born 16 Mar 1888 in TX. He married EVA KNIGHT. She was born in 1891 in MS.

Children of JOHN LANTZ and EVA KNIGHT are:

1. RAYMOND LEON LANTZ, born in 1914 in TX.
2. MARIE LANTZ, born in 1916 in TX.
3. EVELINE LANTZ, born in 1930 in OK.

References: 5, 31-Dist 16 Eldorado Jackson Co OK H77

D3118 GEORGE LANTZ D311

GEORGE LANTZ was born on 22 Feb 1890 in Parker Co., TX. He married BESSIE EVANS in TX. She was born in 1893 in TX.

Child of GEORGE LANTZ and BESSIE EVANS is:

1. GEORGE LANTZ, born in 1818 in TX.

References: 10-Fort Worth Ward 7 Tarrant Co TX H117

D3119 LEONIDAS LANTZ D311

LEONIDAS "LON" LANTZ was born on 19 Aug 1893 in Parker Co., TX. He married JEMIMA LOU in Parker Co., TX. She was born in 1899 in AL.

Children of LEONIDAS LANTZ and JEMIMA are:

1. JIMMIE LANTZ, born in 1924 in Parker Co., TX.

2. MARY LOU LANTZ, born in 1938 in Parker Co., TX.

References: 31-Precinct 2 Parker Co TX H199, 10-Justice Precinct 2 Parker Co TX H80, 40-Justice Precinct 2 Parker Co TX H46

D3134 MARY ELIZABETH MONROE D313

MARY "BETTIE" ELIZABETH MONROE was born in Dec 1868 in TX. She married GEORGE E. PATTERSON in TX. He was born in Sep 1867 in TX.

Children of BETTIE MONROE and GEORGE PATTERSON are:

1. MURRAY E. PATTERSON, born in Feb 1893 in TX.
2. WARREN W. PATTERSON, born in Feb 1895 in TX.
3. LORA PATTERSON, born in Oct 1896 in Indian Territory.
4. OLIVER BURMAN PATTERSON, born in Oct 1899 in OK.
5. MATTIE PATTERSON, born in 1902 in OK.

References: 5, 30-Dist 0036 Justice Precinct 6 Clay Co TX H37, 10-Dist 23 Justice Precinct 6 Clay Co TX H91, 29-Dist 29 Moore Cleveland Co OK H298

D3172 IRL HARRISON LANTZ D317

IRL HARRISON LANTZ was born 14 Jul 1889 in Springtown, Parker, TX, and died 15 Jun 1954. He married FRANCES SMEGNER 21 Oct 1911. She was born 08 Jan 1893 in Strajii, Austria-Hungary, and died 11 Mar 1976.

Children of IRL LANTZ and FRANCES SMEGNER are:

1. DEBS WOODROW LANTZ, born on 01 May 1913 in Mesquite, Texas. He married MACY FLINT on 06 May 1950 in St. Louis, MO.
2. ELAIN FRANCES LANTZ (D31722)
3. EDITH PEARL LANTZ, born on 12 Mar 1922 in Dallas, Dallas, TX; died 27 Dec 1922.
4. MILO DAVID LANTZ, born on 26 Sep 1923. He married (1) ROSALIE CHADWELL. He married (2) JIMMIE SMOOT on 18 Dec 1961 in Fredericksburg, TX.
5. JOHN ALTON LANTZ, born on 19 Dec 1925 in Dallas, Dallas, TX. He married BETTYE PETERS ALLISON in 1950.
6. JUNE LUCILLE LANTZ, born on 26 Jun 1931 in Dallas, Dallas, TX. She married FINZA REID BROOKS on 21 Oct 1950 in Abilene, Taylor, TX.

References: 6-Sarah Mae (Huss) Lantz, 5, 10-Dist 104 Western Heights Dallas Co TX H339, 31-Dist 36 Smackover Union Co AR H225, 40-Abilene Taylor Co TX 221-8B H19

D3191 WALTER L. COLEMAN D319

WALTER L. COLEMAN was born on 25 Dec 1881 in TX and died 09 Mar 1960 in Parker Co., TX. He married GENEVA L. in Parker Co., TX. She was born on 05 Dec 1880 and died 14 Sep 1976 in Parker Co., TX. Both are buried in Veal Station Cemetery, Springtown, Parker Co.,

TX.

1. JAMES HOWARD COLEMAN (D31911)
2. INA RUTH COLEMAN, born in 1916 in Parker Co., TX.

References: 30-Justice Precinct 2 Parker Co TX 0073 H27, 45, 10-Dist 68 Justice Precinct 2 Parker Co TX H106

D3195 ROY EDWARD SMILEY D319

ROY EDWARD COLEMAN was born on 06 Aug 1891 in TX and died 09 Nov 1958 in Parker Co., TX. He married ADA in Parker Co., TX. She was born on 16 Dec 1891 in TX and died 18 Oct 1954 in Parker Co., TX. Both are buried in Oakland Cemetery, Weatherford, Parker Co., TX.

Child of ROY COLEMAN and ADA is:

1. ROY EDWARD COLEMAN, born on 21 May 1917 in Parker Co., TX; died 27 Oct 1961 in Parker Co., TX; buried in Oakland Cemetery, Weatherford, Parker Co., TX.

References: 45, 10-Dist 63 Ward 3 Weatherford Parker Co TX H85

D3313 GRIER R. SMILEY D331

GRIER R. SMILEY was born in 1882 in VA. He married NORA KROME. She was born in 1888 in IL.

Child of GRIER SMILEY and NORA KROME is:

1. HELEN GILAM SMILEY, born in 1913 in KY.

References: 5, 10-Dist 81 Louisville Ward 3 Jefferson Co KY H326, 31-Dist 4 Louisville Jefferson Co KY H83

D3518 WILLIAM W. CALDWELL D351

WILLIAM W. CALDWELL was born in Jul 1871 in NC. He married EMMA in NC. She was born in Oct 1875 in NC.

Children of WILLIAM CALDWELL and EMMA are:

1. WILLIAM L. CALDWELL, born in Sep 1898 in NC.
2. WILMA M. CALDWELL, born in Jan 1900 in Lincolnton, Lincoln Co., NC.

References: 29-Lincolnton Lincoln Co NC H341

D3522 A. SHUFORD WILKINSON D352

A. SHUFORD "CASEY" WILKINSON was born in Nov 1873 in Lincoln Co., NC. He married ANNIE in NC. She was born in Feb 1875.

Child of SHUFORD WILKINSON and ANNIE is:

1. EVERETT S. WILKINSON, born in Jan 1899 in Scotland Co., NC.
2. ALBERT A. WILKINSON, born in Jan 1902 in NC.
3. DAVID WILKINSON, born in Jan 1908 in NC.

References: 29-Dist 0095 Stewartsville Scotland Co., NC, 30-Ward 3 Asheville Buncombe Co NC 0009 H152, 10-Dist 12 Ward 3 Asheville Buncombe Co NC H327

D3523 MARVIN ALEXANDER WILKINSON D352

MARVIN ALEXANDERWILKINSON was born on 13 Nov 1875 in Lincoln Co., NC and died 04 Feb 1962 in Mecklenburg Co., NC. He married GRACE RIGLER in NC. She was born on 29 Oct 1884 in NC and died 23 Nov 1964 in Mecklenburg Co., NC. Both are buried in Elmwood Cemetery, Charlotte, Mecklenburg Co., NC.

Children of MARVIN WILKENSON and GRACE RIGLER are:

1. IRMA R. WILKINSON, born in 1910 in Charlotte, Mecklenburg Co., NC.
2. MARVIN ALEXANDER WILKINSON, born in 16 May1916 in Charlotte, Mecklenburg Co., NC; died 20 Sep 1971 in Mecklenburg Co., NC; buried in Elmwood Cemetery, Charlotte, Mecklenburg Co., NC.

References: 30-Ward 6 Charlotte Mecklenburg Co NC 0108 H82

D3546 ALDOLPHUS STAMEY DRUM D354

ALDOLPHUS STAMEY DRUM was born in 15 Oct 1880 in Catawba Co., NC and died 26 Sep 1934 in Catawba Co., NC. He married BLANCHE MARTHA DRUM in Catawba Co., NC, daughter of PINKNEY D. DRUM and FANNIE E. She was born on 04 Jun 1887 in NC and died 13 Jul 1966 in Catawba Co., NC. Both are buried in Pisqah United Methodist Church Cemetery, Catawba, Catawba Co., NC.

Children of ALDOLPHUS DRUM and BLANCHE DRUM are:

1. LILLIAN DRUM, born in 1903 in Catawba Co., NC.
2. ELLIOTT DRUM, born in 1905 in Catawba Co., NC.
3. LOIS DRUM, born in 1907 in Catawba Co., NC.
4. AZALEA DRUM, born in 1909 in Catawba Co., NC.
5. STELLA DRUM, born in 1911 in Catawba Co., NC.
6. DOROTHY DRUM, born in 1913 in Catawba Co., NC.
7. LOLA DRUM, born in 1915 in Catawba Co., NC.
8. JASPER DRUM (D35468)
9. EULOLAH DRUM, born in 1919 in Catawba Co., NC.
10. VIRGINIA DRUM, born in 1922 in Catawba Co., NC, married PAUL R. ROGERS in

Catawba Co., NC; born 1919 in NC.
11. ALVIN W. DRUM, born in 1925 in Catawba Co., NC.

References: 45, 30-Caldwell Twp Catawba Co NC 0017 H98, 10-Dist 29 Caldwell Twp Catawba Co NC H80, 10-Dist 2 Caldwell Twp Catawba Co NC H350, 10-Caldwell Twp Catawba Co NC 18-3 H152

D3581 EVERETT R. WILKINSON D358

EVERETT R. WILKINSON was born in 1875 in NC. He married MARY E. in NC. She was born in 1876 in NC.

1. LEON WILKINSON, born in 1899 in Statesville, Iredell Co., NC.
2. HAZEL R. WILKINSON, born in 1902 in Statesville, Iredell Co., NC.
3. AMICE E. WILKINSON, born in 1904 in Statesville, Iredell Co., NC.
4. NANNIE BELL WILKINSON, born in 1906 in Statesville, Iredell Co., NC.
5. WESLEY L. WILKINSON, born in 1909 in Statesville, Iredell Co., NC.
6. WILLIAM W. WILKINSON, born in 1912 in Statesville, Iredell Co., NC.
7. ROBERT V. WILKINSON, born in 1915 in Statesville, Iredell Co., NC.
8. JAMES I. WILKINSON, born in 1919 in Statesville, Iredell Co., NC.

References: 30-Statesville Iredell Co NC H153, 10-Statesville Iredell Co NC H662, 31-Statesville Iredell Co NC H121

D35A1 J. FRANCIS M. DRUM D35A

J. FRANCIS M. DRUM was born 15 Dec 1854 in Catawba Co., NC, and died 12 Aug 1942. He married MARY F. LOFTIN. She was born 1856, and died 08 May 1936.

Child of J. DRUM and MARY LOFTIN is:

1. CHARLES HENRY DRUM (D35A11)
2. ERA M. DRUM (f), born in Apr 1880 in Catawba Co., NC.

References: 6-Sarah Mae (Huss) Lantz, 27-Catawba Catawba Co NC H227

D35A2 MARTHA JANE DRUM D35A

MARTHA JANE DRUM was born 24 Jun 1856 in Catawba Co., NC, and died 08 Oct 1925 in Catawba Co., NC. She married JAMES M. COOKE in Catawba Co., NC. He was born in Apr 1850 in NC.

Children of MARTHA DRUM and JAMES COOKE are:

1. UNKNOWN COOKE, born and died before 1900 in Catawba Co., NC.
2. NOVELLA F. COOKE, born in Oct 1879 in Catawba Co., NC.
3. GEORGE M. COOKE, born in Sep 1882 in Catawba Co., NC.

4. IVY MURL COOKE, born in Jul 1886 in Catawba Co., NC.
5. LILLIE S. COOKE, born in Sep 1888 in Catawba Co., NC.
6. GRACE E. COOKE, born in Sep 1893 in Catawba Co., NC.
7. JOHN L. COOKE, born in Aug 1895 in Catawba Co., NC.

References: 6-Sarah Mae (Huss) Lantz, 29-Dist 46 Newton Catawba Co NC H192

D35A4 GEORGE P. DRUM D35A

Rev. GEORGE P. DRUM was born on 29 Jul 1859 in Catawba Co., NC and died 12 Oct 1939 in Catawba Co., NC. He married CORA E. LINEBERGER in Catawba Co., NC. She was born on 05 Apr 1870 in NC and died 30 Oct 1953 in Catawba Co., NC. Both are buried in Eastview Cemetery, Newton, Catawba Co., NC.

Children of GEORGE DRUM and CORA LINEBERGER are:

1. FLOYD JAMES DRUM, born in May 1892 in Catawba Co., NC.
2. IVEY DRUM, born in Feb 1894 in Catawba Co., NC.
3. HOYLE DRUM, born in Jan 1897 in Catawba Co., NC.
4. VINCENT B. DRUM (D35A44)
5. BRIAN BRIGGS DRUM, born in 1908 in Catawba Co., NC.

References: 45, 29-Dist 0046 Newton Catawba Co NC H44, 30-Newton Catawba Co NC 0030 H183, 10-Dist 46 Newton Catawba Co NC H84

D35A5 THOMAS JEFFERSON DRUM D35A

THOMAS JEFFERSON DRUM was born on 29 Jul 1859 in Catawba Co., NC and died 08 Sep 1939 in Iredell Co., NC. He married MARTHA L. STINE in Catawba Co., NC. She was born on 23 Oct 1864 in NC and died 07 Sep 1937 in Iredell Co., NC. Both are buried in Oakwood Cemetery, Statesville, Iredell Co., NC.

Children of THOMAS DRUM and MARTHA STINE are:

1. RUFUS MONROE DRUM (D35A51)
2. CHARLES GENTRY DRUM (D35A52)
3. ROBY WESLEY DRUM, born in Nov 1893 in Catawba Co., NC.
4. CLARENCE FRANKLIN DRUM, born on 23 Apr 1899 in Catawba Co., NC; died 23 Jul 1963 in Iredell Co., NC; married MARY IONA ALLGOOD in NC; born on 14 Oct 1902 in NC; died 04 Jan 1989 in Iredell Co., NC. Both are buried in Oakwood Cemetery, Statesville, Iredell Co., NC.

References: 45, 29-Dist 0034 Caldwell Twp Catawba Co NC H175

D35B1 FANNIE JULIA ERA WILKINSON D35B

FANNIE JULIA ERA WILKINSON was born 18 Jan 1885 in Catawba Co., NC, and died 09 Apr 1970 in Charlotte, Mecklenburg Co., NC. She married TULLEROW R. DRUM in NC. He was born on 06 Oct 1875 in Catawba Co., NC, and died 23 Sep 1961 in Charlotte, Mecklenburg Co., NC. Both are buried in Elmwood Cemetery, Charlotte, Mecklenburg Co., NC

Children of FANNIE WILKINSON and TULLEROW DRUM are:

1. PRITTLE R. DRUM, born on 23 Jan 1907 in Charlotte, Mecklenburg Co., NC; died 20 Jul 1985. He married VELMA PROPST; born on 24 May 1911; died 10 May 1975.
2. LYNDELL VICTORIA DRUM, born in 1908 in Charlotte, Mecklenburg Co., NC.
3. JUANITA ELIZABETH DRUM, born on 05 Jun 1910 in Charlotte, Mecklenburg Co., NC; died 23 Mar 2001. She married ADOLPHUS LOWE KISTLER; born on 29 Aug 1906; died 25 Jul 1984 in Charlotte, Mecklenburg Co., NC.
4. EVELYN DRUM (D35B14)
5. VERNON BURGE DRUM, Sr. (D35B15)

References: 6-Sarah Mae (Huss) Lantz, 30-Dist 0112 Charlotte Ward 8 Mecklenburg Co NC H204, 10-Dist 152 Charlotte Ward 8 Mecklenburg Co NC H126, 10-Dist 29 Charlotte Mecklenburg Co NC H184, 45

D3612 SARAH ANN MOOSE D361

SARAH "SALLIE" ANN MOOSE was born 31 May 1864 in Newton, Catawba Co., NC. She married JOHN W. HARDISTER in 1886 in Catawba Co., NC. He was born in 1859 in NC.

Child of SARAH MOOSE and JOHN HARDISTER is:

1. MARY ELIZABETH HARDISTER, born in Jun 1891 in Catawba Co., NC.

References: 6-Sarah Mae (Huss) Lantz, 5, 29-Dist 47 Newton Catawba Co NC H250

D3613 DORA FRANCES MOOSE D361

DORA FRANCES MOOSE was born 31 Aug 1868 in Newton, Catawba Co., NC. She married CARROL CLAPP in 1892. He was born in Aug 1863 in TX.

Child of DORA MOOSE and CARROL CLAPP is:

1. SARAH LEWIS CLAPP, born in Oct 1893 in Bowie, Montaque Co., TX.

References: 6-Sarah Mae (Huss) Lantz, 5, 29-Dist 54 Bowie Montaque Co TX H56

D3614 GEORGE HOWARD MOOSE D361

GEORGE HOWARD MOOSE was born 08 Jul 1877 in Newton, Catawba Co., NC. He married PAULINE MILLER PAGE on 29 Jan 1908 in Newton, Catawba Co., NC. She was born in 1879 in NC.

Children of GEORGE MOOSE and PAULINE PAGE are:

1. PAULINE PAGE MOOSE, born on 14 Dec 1908 in Newton, Catawba Co., NC.
2. GEORGE HOWARD MOOSE, Jr., born on 03 Jul 1911 in Newton, Catawba Co., NC.
3. MARY KATHERINE MOOSE, born on 28 May 1915 in Newton, Catawba Co., NC.

References: 6-Sarah Mae (Huss) Lantz, 5, 30-Dist 0032 Newton Catawba Co NC H218, 10-Dist 0032 Newton Catawba Co NC H39

D3641 SARAH OLA ROBINSON D364

SARAH OLA ROBINSON was born on 06 Jul 1867 in Catawba Co., NC. She married FRANCIS LOCKMON BEALTY on 18 Dec 1884 in Catawba Co., NC. He was born in Apr 1865 in NC.

Children of SARAH ROBINSON and FRANCIS BEALTY are:

1. DOWD I. BEALTY (D35411)
2. FRANK G. BEALTY, born in Aug 1887 and died at age 22 in Catawba Co,. NC.
3. ERNEST L. BEALTY, born in May 1889 in Catawba Co,. NC.
4. OTHA L. BEALTY, born in Mar 1891 in Catawba Co,. NC.
5. AUGUSTUS H. BEALTY, born in Mar 1894 in Catawba Co,. NC.
6. NANCY M. BEALTY, born in May 1896 in Catawba Co,. NC.
7. EUNICE E. BEALTY, born in Sep 1898 in Catawba Co,. NC.
8. THOMAS BEALTY, born in 1903 in Catawba Co,. NC.
9. SUSAN V. BEALTY, born in 1904 in Catawba Co,. NC.
10. FRED L. BEALTY, born in 1907 in Catawba Co,. NC.

References: 5, 29-Dist 43 Sherrils Ford Catawba Co NC H153, 30-Dist 0027 Sherrils Ford Catawba Co NC H158

D3651 EVA CAROLINE POWELL D365

EVA CAROLINE POWELL was born 13 May 1870 in Catawba Co., NC. She married J. F. JOHNSON in 1892. She married Dr. KNOTT in 1904.

Child of EVA POWELL and J. JOHNSON is:

1. JOHANNA R. JOHNSON (D36511)

References: 5, 27-Ashville Ward 4 Buncombe Co NC H251

D3842 BESSIE ERA LANTZ D384

BESSIE ERA LANTZ was born on 13 May 1883 in Lincoln Co., NC and died 10 Dec 1970 in Lincoln Co., NC. She married DAVID COON KILLIAN on 21 Feb 1907 in Lincoln Co., NC, son of . He was born on 10 Feb 1884, and died 28 Jan 1976 in Lincoln Co. Schools.

Children of BESSIE LANTZ and DAVID KILLIAN are:

1. LAURA ELIZABETH KILLIAN (D38421)
2. FRANKLIN AMZIE KILLIAN (D38422)
3. ROBERT LANTZ KILLIAN (D38423)
4. WILLIAM DAVID KILLIAN (D38424)

References: 6-Sarah Mae (Huss) Lantz, 5, 10-Dist 103 Howards Creek Lincoln Co NC H195, 31-Dist 5 Howards Creek Lincoln Co NC H158

D3843 ADA CAROLINE LANTZ D384

ADA CAROLINE LANTZ was born on 10 Aug 1886 in Lincoln Co., NC and died 05 Dec 1973. She married JACOB LEVI QUICKEL in 1906 in Lincoln Co., NC at Daniels' Reformed Church. He was born on 14 Mar 1884 and died 01 Nov 1952 in NC.

Children of ADA LANTZ and JACOB QUICKEL are:

1. PAUL L. QUICKEL, Sr. (D38431)
2. RICHARD LEROY QUICKEL, Sr. (D38432)
3. JOHN HENRY QUICKEL, born in 1913 in Lincoln Co., NC.

References: 6-Sarah Mae (Huss) Lantz, 5, 30-Dist 0067 Howards Creek Lincoln Co NC H252, 10-Dist 0067 Howards Creek Lincoln Co NC H193, 40-Howards Creek Lincoln Co NC 55-5 H207

D3845 COY FRANKLIN LANTZ D384

COY FRANKLIN LANTZ was born on 15 Sep 1895 in Lincoln Co., NC and died 01 Aug 1969 in Lincoln Co., NC. He married DAISY BLANCHE YODER on 25 Jun 1924 in Lincolnton, Lincoln Co., NC, daughter of CHARLES YODER and CARRIE JARRETT. She was born 27 Oct 1899 in Catawba Co., NC, and died 20 Feb 1989 in Gaston Co., NC.

Children of COY LANTZ and DAISY YODER are:

1. LAURA MARGARET LANTZ (D38451)
2. MARY ANN LANTZ (D38452)
3. FRANCES CAROLYN LANTZ (D38453)
4. JOHN CHARLES LANTZ (D38454)

References: 6-Sarah Mae (Huss) Lantz, 5, 31-Dist 5 Howards Creek Lincoln Co NC H189, 40-Howards Creek Lincoln Co NC 55-5 H217, 68

L to R: COY FRANKLIN LANTZ; DAISY YODER LANTZ; MARGARET LANTZ BIRKE; ANN LANTZ REEP; FRANCES LANTZ BUTLER; JOHN CHARLES LANTZ (1962)

COY FRANKLIN LANTZ and his mother, LAURA ADELINE ROBINSON LANTZ (c 1915)

D4111 ARTHUR M. CARPENTER D411

ARTHUR M. CARPENTER was born in Jul 1852 in Lincoln Co., NC. He married MARTHA in NC. She was born in Jul 1859 in NC.

Children of ARTHUR CARPENTER and MARTHA are:

1. LAURA CARPENTER, born in Sep 1879 in Ironton, Lincoln Co., NC.
2. UNKNOWN CARPENTER, died young before 1880 in Ironton, Lincoln Co., NC.
3. UNKNOWN CARPENTER, died young before 1880 in Ironton, Lincoln Co., NC.
4. UNKNOWN CARPENTER, died young before 1880 in Ironton, Lincoln Co., NC.
5. UNKNOWN CARPENTER, died young before 1880 in Ironton, Lincoln Co., NC.

References: 27-Ironton Lincoln Co NC H79, 29-Gastonia Twp Gaston Co NC H230

D4112 JOHN C. CARPENTER D411

JOHN C. CARPENTER was born in 1854 in Lincoln Co., NC. He married NANCY in NC. She was born in 1860 in NC.

Children of JOHN CARPENTER and NANCY are:

1. LUTHER EDGAR CARPENTER, born in Sep 1879 in Ironton, Lincoln Co., NC.

2. CARL S. CARPENTER, born in Aug 1881 in Ironton, Lincoln Co., NC.
3. ADA C. CARPENTER, born in Feb 1883 in Ironton, Lincoln Co., NC.
4. WALTER P. CARPENTER (D41124)
5. JACOB W. CARPENTER, born in Jan 1893 in Ironton, Lincoln Co., NC.

References: 27-Ironton Lincoln Co NC H78, 29- Ironton Lincoln Co NC H332

D4114 ELAIN CATHARINE CARPENTER D411

ELAIN CATHARINE CARPENTER was born in Nov 1855 in Lincoln Co., NC. She married JONAS JENKINS in Gaston Co., NC. He was born in Jul 1827 in NC and died before 1910 in Gaston Co., NC..

Children of ELAIN CARPENTER and JONAS JENKINS are:

1. SLOAN JENKINS, born in Mar 1895 in Gaston Co., NC.
2. LUCINDA JENKINS, born in Jan 1897 in Gaston Co., NC.

References: 29- Gastonia Twp Gaston Co NC H11, 30- Gastonia Twp Gaston Co NC H459

D4116 ELVIN CLATON CARPENTER D411

ELVIN CLATON CARPENTER was born in Apr 1862 in Lincoln Co., NC and died before 1920 in Mecklenburg Co., NC. He married NANNIE B. SHERRILL in Gaston Co., NC. She was born in Sep 1867 in NC.

Children of ELVIN CARPENTER and NANNIE are:

1. FRANK T. CARPENTER, born in Jul 1891 in Gaston Co., NC.
2. CHARLIE CARPENTER, born in Sep 1899 in Gaston Co., NC; died before 1910 in NC.
3. LEWIS S. CARPENTER, born in 1903 in NC.
4. FRED C. CARPENTER, born in 1907 in NC
5. UNKNOWN CARPENTER, born and died before 1910 in NC.
6. UNKNOWN CARPENTER, born and died before 1910 in NC.
7. UNKNOWN CARPENTER, born and died before 1910 in NC.

References: 29- Gastonia Twp Gaston Co NC H202, 30-Charlotte Ward 6 Mecklenburg Co NC H268, 10-Charlotte Ward 6 Mecklenburg Co NC H182

D4117 WINNIE CARPENTER D411

WINNIE CARPENTER was born in Jun 1864 in Lincoln Co., NC. She married HENRY T. HOVIS in Gaston Co., NC. He was born in Jan 1867 in NC.

Children WINNIE CARPENTER and HENRY HOVIS are:

1. HUGH HOVIS, born in Dec 1889 in Gaston Co., NC.
2. LOY HOVIS, born in Jul 1891 in Gaston Co., NC.

3. CLARENCE HOVIS, born in Jun 1894 in Gaston Co., NC.
4. LELA HOVIS, born in May 1896 in Gaston Co., NC.
5. BLAIR HOVIS, born in May 1899 in Gaston Co., NC.
6. GARRET "GARY" HOVIS, born in May 1899 in Gaston Co., NC.
7. GUY HOVIS, born in 1902 in Gaston Co., NC.
8. GEORGE HOVIS, born in 1903 in Gaston Co., NC.

References: 29-Dallas Twp Gaston Co NC H90, 30-Dallas Twp Gaston Co NC H93, 10-Dallas Twp Gaston Co NC H166

D4119 WILLIAM B. CARPENTER D411

WILLIAM B. CARPENTER was born in Oct 1868 in Lincoln Co., NC. He married LUCY E. STUBBS in Gaston Co., NC. She was born in Jan 1868 in NC.

Children of WILLIAM CARPENTER and LUCY are:

1. EDITH M. CARPENTER, born in Jan 1892 in Gaston Co., NC.
2. FRED W. CARPENTER, born in May 1894 in Gaston Co., NC.
3. BESSIE G. CARPENTER, born in Jul 1896 in Gaston Co., NC.
4. NELLIE R CARPENTER, born in Jan 1899 in Gaston Co., NC.
5. BEULAH E. CARPENTER, born in 1902 in NC.
6. JOHN W. CARPENTER (D41196)
7. MINNIE LUCILE CARPENTER, born in 1907 in NC.
8. JAMES BEELAR CARPENTER, born in 1908 in NC - Grandson.
9. GEORGE F. CARPENTER, born in Jan 1912 in Charlotte, Mecklenburg Co., NC.

References: 29-Gastonia Twp Gaston Co NC H61, 30-Charlotte Ward 6 Mecklenburg Co NC H235, 10-Charlotte Ward 6 Mecklenburg Co NC H193, 31-Dist 16 Charlotte Mecklenburg Co NC H252

D411B ALICE CARPENTER D411

ALICE CARPENTER was born in Nov 1872 in Lincoln Co., NC. She married CHARLES EPLEY in Gaston Co., NC. He was born in Nov 1872 in NC.

Children of ALICE CARPENTER and CHARLES EPLEY are:

1. GERTIE EPLEY, born in Dec 1897 in Gaston Co., NC.
2. RALPH W. EPLEY, born in May 1899 in Gaston Co., NC
3. ORA EPLEY, born in May 1902 in Gaston Co., NC
4. STELLA EPLEY, born in 1907 in Gaston Co., NC
5. CORA EPLEY, born in 1910 in Gaston Co., NC
6. UNKNOWN EPLEY, born and died 1900-1910 in Gaston Co., NC.
7. JUANITA EPLEY, born in 1914 in Gaston Co., NC.

References: 29-Gastonia Twp Gaston Co NC H92, 30-Gastonia Twp Gaston Co NC H103, 10-

Charlotte Mecklenburg Co NC H264

D4262 MARY ETTA HALLMAN D426

MARY ETTA HALLMAN was born on 11 Nov 1881 in Lincoln Co., NC, and died 22 Dec 1972 in Lincoln Co., NC. She married MARTIN LUTHER FINGER, Sr. on 22 Dec 1903 in Catawba Co., NC, son of HENRY FINGER and SELENA ANTHONY. He was born on 02 Jul 1877, and died 22 Nov 1952 in Lincoln Co., NC.

Children of MARY HALLMAN and MARTIN FINGER are:

1. PAULINE HALLMAN FINGER (D42621)
2. SUE BETTY FINGER (D42622)
3. ANNIE LEE FINGER (D42623)
4. MARY ETTA FINGER (D42624)
5. MARTIN LUTHER FINGER, Jr. (D42625)
6. JAMES GALAIN FINGER, born 21 Dec 1906 in Lincoln Co., NC; died Jan 1972. He married ETHEL G. HOOVER; born 30 Apr 1905 in Lincoln Co., NC; died 19 May 1995 in Gaston Co., NC.

References: 6-Sarah Mae (Huss) Lantz, 30-Dist 0026 Jacobs Fork Catawba Co NC H33, 10-Dist 0026 Jacobs Fork Catawba Co NC H97, 31-Dist 15 Lincolnton Lincoln Co NC H132

D4264 JAMES LEVY HALLMAN D426

JAMES LEVY HALLMAN was born on 31 Jan 1885 in Lincoln Co., NC, and died 02 Mar 1960 in Lincoln Co., NC. He married LUCY LEE HOOVER on 24 Nov 1909 in Lincoln Co., NC. She was born on 28 Dec 1888, and died 20 Jun 1980 in Lincoln Co., NC.

Children of JAMES HALLMAN and LUCY HOOVER are:

1. HELEN ANGELINE HALLMAN (D42641)
2. MARGARET CARRA HALLMAN (D42642)
3. JAMES LEE HALLMAN, SR. (D42643)
4. HAROLD HOOVER HALLMAN, SR. (D42644)
5. ROBERT ANTHONY HALLMAN, SR. (D42645)

References: 6-Sarah Mae (Huss) Lantz, 10-Dist 106 Lincolnton Lincoln Co NC H121, 31-Dist 15 Lincolnton Lincoln Co NC H129

D4265 BESSIE HALLMAN D426

BESSIE HALLMAN was born on 27 May 1887 in Lincoln Co., NC, and died 23 Dec 1979 in Lincoln Co., NC. She married EDWARD LAWRENCE CARPENTER on 01 Jan 1908 in Lincoln Co., NC, son of WILLIAM CARPENTER and MARTHA HINSON. He was born on 02 Jun 1881, and died 04 Mar 1961 in Lincoln Co., NC.

Children of BESSIE HALLMAN and EDWARD CARPENTER are:

1. JAMES WILLIAM CARPENTER (D42651)
2. EDWARD HALLMAN CARPENTER (D42652)
3. MARY LOUISE CARPENTER, born on 23 Jan 1916 in Lincoln Co., NC. She married RICHARD LUTZ.

References: 6-Sarah Mae (Huss) Lantz, 10-Dist 106 Lincolnton Lincoln Co NC H112

D4268 FANNIE GEORGIANNA HALLMAN D426

FANNIE GEORGIANNA HALLMAN was born on 14 Nov 1893 in Lincoln Co., NC, and died 10 Jan 1981 in Ridgeville, SC. She married WILLIAM LUTHER ARMSTRONG on 03 Apr 1912 in Lincoln Co., NC. He was born on 16 Feb 1884 in Lincoln Co., NC, and died 10 Jul 1960 in Ridgeville, SC.

Children of FANNIE HALLMAN and WILLIAM ARMSTRONG are:

1. SUSAN BLANCHE ARMSTRONG, born on 25 Apr 1913 in Iron Station, Lincoln Co., NC. She married WILLIAM H. GRAYSON on 09 Oct 1959; born on 21 Jan 1914; died 27 Mar 1986.
2. JAMES WILLIAM ARMSTRONG, born on 26 Jun 1915 in Lincoln Co., NC; died 02 Aug 1920.
3. LUTHER VOIGHT ARMSTRONG (D42683)
4. RUBY ISABELLE ARMSTRONG (D42684)
5. ANNA CAROLYN ARMSTRONG (D42685)
6. VIRGINIA BLAIR ARMSTRONG (D42686)
7. BETTY RUTH ARMSTRONG (D42687)

References: 6-Sarah Mae (Huss) Lantz, 10-Dist 105 Ironton Lincoln Co NC H54, 31-Dist 10 Saint George Dorchester Co SC H112

D426B SUSAN LAURA HALLMAN D426

SUSAN LAURA HALLMAN was born on 08 Nov 1897 in Lincoln Co., NC, and died 02 Mar 1985 in Lincoln Co., NC. She married ODUS CLYDE CARPENTER, Sr. on 17 Nov 1920, son of WILLIAM CARPENTER and MARTHA HINSON. He was born on 15 Jan 1891, and died 09 Mar 1972 in Lincoln Co., NC.

Children of SUSAN HALLMAN and ODUS CARPENTER are:

1. MARTHA KATHLEEN CARPENTER (D426B1)
2. ODUS CLYDE CARPENTER, Jr. (D426B2)
3. FREDERICK HALLMAN CARPENTER, Sr. (D426B3)

References: 6-Sarah Mae (Huss) Lantz, 31-Dist 15 Lincolnton Lincoln Co NC H170

D426D RUBY LOUISE HALLMAN D426

RUBY LOUISE HALLMAN was born on 19 Oct 1902 in Lincoln Co., NC, and died 04 Jun

1991 in Wilmington, NC. She married JENNINGS BRYAN EDWARDS, Sr. on 19 Oct 1921 in Lincoln Co., NC, son of ROBERT EDWARDS and MARY SETZER. He was born on 15 Mar 1897 in Lincoln Co., NC, and died Jun 1968 in Wilmington, NC.

Children of RUBY HALLMAN and JENNINGS EDWARDS are:

1. JENNINGS BRYAN EDWARDS, Jr. (D426D1)
2. JAMES ROBERT EDWARDS, Sr. (D426D2)

References: 6-Sarah Mae (Huss) Lantz, 40-Wilmington New Hanover Co NC 65-38 H49

D426E CARRIE LUCILLE HALLMAN D426

CARRIE LUCILLE HALLMAN was born on 23 Nov 1904 in Lincoln Co., NC, and died 19 Dec 2000. She married CALVIN BANKS FINGER, Sr. on 06 May 1926 in Lincoln Co., NC, son of TOMAC FINGER and ELIZABETH KILLIAN. He was born on 01 Sep 1895, and died 05 Dec 1988 in Lincoln Co., NC.

Children of CARRIE HALLMAN and CALVIN FINGER are:

1. CALVIN BANKS FINGER, Jr. (D426E1)
2. MICHAEL NEIL FINGER (D426E1)
3. PATRICIA ANN FINGER (D426E1)
4. HOWARD LINN FINGER (D426E1)

References: 6-Sarah Mae (Huss) Lantz, 40-Jacobs Fork Catawba Co NC 18-24B H91

D426F WILBUR PURVIE HALLMAN D426

WILBUR PURVIE HALLMAN was born on 18 Jul 1907 in Lincoln Co., NC. He married BERTA EMILY NIX on 23 Jan 1932 in Durant, OK. She was born on 25 Jul 1908 in Roxton, TX.

Children of WILBUR HALLMAN and BERTA NIX are:

1. NANCY ANN HALLMAN (D426F1)
2. BETTY JEAN HALLMAN (D426F2)

References: 6-Sarah Mae (Huss) Lantz, 40-Other Places Dallas Co TX 57-9A H240

D4412 GEORGE RICHARD HALLMAN D441

GEORGE RICHARD HALLMAN was born on 15 Feb 1876 in Waldron, Scott Co., Arkansas, and died 15 Apr 1946. He married EUDORA FORRESTER on 25 Jan 1903 in Italy, Ellis Co., TX. She was born on 27 Mar 1881 in TX.

Children of GEORGE HALLMAN and EUDORA FORRESTER are:

1. WINNARD TEAGUE HALLMAN, born 12 Mar 1904 in Alvarado, Johnson Co., TX;

died 05 Mar 1949. He married MARY LOUISE CULVER 02 Sep 1931; born 05 Jul 1906; died 16 Mar 1946.

2. VIRGINIA HALLMAN (D44122)

References: 6-Sarah Mae (Huss) Lantz, 30-Dist 0056 Alvardo Johnson Co TX H101, 30-Dist 0056 Alvardo Johnson Co TX H101

D4414 ELIZABETH RUTH HALLMAN D441

ELIZABETH RUTH HALLMAN was born on 05 Aug 1881 in AR. She married CHARLES ALBERT KELLEY on 24 Dec 1900 in Alvarado, TX. He was born on 02 Jan 1878 in TX, and died 29 Mar 1953.

Children of ELIZABETH HALLMAN and CHARLES KELLEY are:

1. JAMES HALLMAN KELLEY, born on 30 Sep 1901 in Johnson Co., TX.
2. GRACE KELLEY, born on 26 Nov 1902 in Johnson Co., TX.
3. SAMUEL ALBERT KELLEY, born on 04 Jan 1906 in Johnson Co., TX.
4. J. QUENTIN KELLEY, born in 1908 in Johnson Co., TX

References: 6-Sarah Mae (Huss) Lantz, 30-Dist 0054 Alvardo Johnson Co TX H124

D4417 ERNEST LEROY HALLMAN D441

ERNEST LEROY HALLMAN, Sr. was born on 20 Oct 1890 in Waldron, Scott Co., Arkansas, and died 28 May 1973 in Cleburne, Johnson Co., TX. He married WILLA ILA PRESTRIDGE on 04 Nov 1914 in Alvarado, Johnson Co., TX. She was born on 25 Oct 1892 in Alvarado, Johnson Co., TX, and died 15 Apr 1947 in Grandview, Johnson Co., TX.

Children of ERNEST HALLMAN and WILLA PRESTRIDGE are:

1. ERNEST LEROY HALLMAN, Jr. (D44171)
2. WILLIAM PRESTRIDGE HALLMAN, Sr. (D44172)

References: 6-Sarah Mae (Huss) Lantz, 10-Dist 51 Grandview Johnson Co TX H65

D5142 ALICE ISABELLE PROPST D514

ALICE ISABELLE PROPST was born on 29 Mar 1863 in Catawba Co., NC and died 12 Dec 1945 in Catawba Co., NC. She married LOUIS NAPOLEON RUDISILL in NC. He was born on 05 Apr 1862 in Lincoln Co., NC and died 19 May 1940 Lincoln Co., NC. Both are buried in Grace Lutheran Cemetery in Newton, Catawba Co., NC.

Children of ALICE PROPST and LOUIS RUDISILL are:

1. GEORGIA W. RUDISILL, born in Feb 1890 in Catawba Co., NC
2. THOMAS HENRY RUDISILL, born in May 1891 in Catawba Co., NC; died in 1919.
3. PERCY LEE RUDISILL, born in Nov 1893 in Catawba Co., NC; died in 1952.

4. CLYDE SOLOMON RUDISILL, born Jun 1896 in Catawba Co., NC; died in 1971.
5. LOUIS C. RUDISILL, born in Apr 1898 in Catawba Co., NC.
6. SON RUDISILL, born in Feb 1900 in Catawba Co., NC.

References: 29-Dist 0042 Jacobs Fork Twp Catawba Co NC H188

D6611 JAMES MARSHALL HOUSER D661

JAMES MARSHALL HOUSER was born on 26 Nov 1899 in Lincoln Co., NC, and died 13 Jan 1975 in Concord, NC. He married MAUDE BIVENS CANIPE. She was born on 01 Apr 1911, and died 09 Apr 1956. Both are buried at Leonards Fork Baptist Church Cemetery, Lincoln Co., NC.

Children of JAMES HOUSER and MAUDE CANIPE are:

1. ROBERT LEE HOUSER, Sr. (D66111)
2. ILESE HOUSER
3. JUDY HOUSER
4. SARAH HOUSER
5. LINDA HOUSER

References: 6-Sarah Mae (Huss) Lantz

D6613 NORA STELLA HOUSER D661

NORA STELLA HOUSER was born on 07 Mar 1904 in Lincoln Co., NC, and died 09 Apr 1987 in Hickory, Catawba Co., NC. She married MAURICE PAUL SMITH on 19 Nov 1917. He was born on 06 Sep 1892, and died 05 Aug 1956.

Child of NORA HOUSER and MAURICE SMITH is:

1. BLAKE A. SMITH, born in 1918 in Lincoln Co., NC.
2. PAUL J. SMITH, born in 1921 in Lincoln Co., NC.
3. LYNN B. SMITH, born in 1923 in Lincoln Co., NC.
4. FAYE SMITH, born in 1940 in Lincoln Co., NC.

References: 6-Sarah Mae (Huss) Lantz, 31-Dist 6 Howards Creek Lincoln Co NC H335, 40-Longview Catawba Co NC 18-19 H15

D6614 MARY PHYLECTOR HOUSER D661

MARY PHYLECTOR HOUSER was born on 22 May 1906 in Lincoln Co., NC, and died 20 May 2005 in Cherryville, Gaston Co., NC. She married CLYDE WARLICK FORTENBERRY 11 Jan 1930. He was born on 03 Feb 1907 in Lincoln Co., NC and died 13 Feb 1978 in Lincoln Co., NC. Both are buried at New Home United Methodist Church Cemetery, Casar, NC.

Child of MARY HOUSER and CLYDE FORTENBERRY is:

1. ROBERT DWIGHT HOUSER (D66141)

References: 6-Sarah Mae (Huss) Lantz, 40-Howards Creek Lincoln Co NC 55-7 H140

D6615 ALICE PEARL HOUSER D661

ALICE PEARL HOUSER was born on 24 Dec 1908 in Lincoln Co., NC, and died 19 May 1997. She married DAVID CARR HOUSER on 08 Sep 1934 in Lincoln Co., NC.

Children of ALICE HOUSER and DAVID HOUSER are:

1. EDNA ALENE HOUSER (D66151)
2. PEGGY JANE HOUSER (D66152)

References: 6-Sarah Mae (Huss) Lantz, 40-North Brook Lincoln Co NC 55-23 H39

D6617 EDNA ILESE HOUSER D661

EDNA ILESE HOUSER was born on 12 Jan 1914 in Lincoln Co., NC, and died 30 Jun 1986 in Lincoln Co., NC. She married ROY ZEBULON NEILL, Sr. on 06 Apr 1951, son of DOCK NEILL and FLORENCE TUTHEROW. He was born on 18 May 1911 in Lincoln Co., NC, and died 10 Feb 1970 in Lincoln Co., NC. Both are buried at Zion United Methodist Church Cemetery, Lincoln Co., NC.

Children of EDNA HOUSER and ROY NEILL are:

1. LARRY DEAN NEILL
2. GALE NEILL (D66172)
3. ROY ZEBULON NEILL, Jr.
4. EMMA JEAN NEILL, born 24 Apr 1952 in Lincoln Co., NC; died 15 Apr 1992 in Gaston Co., NC.

References: 6-Sarah Mae (Huss) Lantz

D6618 ROBERT LEE HOUSER D661

ROBERT LEE HOUSER was born on 19 Feb 1916 in Lincoln Co., NC, and died 03 Aug 1939 in Lincoln Co., NC. He married LUCY MAE WEAVER on 09 Nov 1935 in Lincoln Co., NC.

Children of ROBERT HOUSER and LUCY WEAVER are:

1. BOBBIE SUE HOUSER, born in 1938 in Lincoln Co., NC
2. BARBARA HOUSER (D66182)

References: 6-Sarah Mae (Huss) Lantz, 40-Ironton Lincoln Co NC 55-12 H3

D6621 ETHEL PEARL HOUSER D661

ETHEL PEARL HOUSER was born in 1897 in NC. She married JESSE LLOYD BEAM in NC. He was born 30 Mar 1893, and died 07 Jun 1935.

Children of ETHEL HOUSER and JESSE BEAM are:

1. HARRIET ANN BEAM
2. CAROL LEE BEAM
3. SARAH JANE BEAM

References: 6-Sarah Mae (Huss) Lantz

D17424 FRANCIS MORAN LANTZ D1742

FRANCIS MORAN LANTZ was born 11 Jan 1917 in Kearney, Buffalo Co., NE and died 24 Feb 1979 in Shawnee, Pottawatomie Co., OK. He married MARJORIE LEE SULLIVAN. She was born on 20 Apr 1925 and died 15 Apr 1992 in Shawnee, Pottawatomie Co., OK. Both are buried in Calvary Cemetery, Shawnee, Pottawatomie Co., OK

Children of FRANCIS LANTZ and MARJORIE SULLIVAN are:

1. LAWRENCE "LARRY" THOMAS LANTZ
2. FRANCYS PATTIE LANTZ, born 1952; married ROBBIN K. PHILLIPS 22 May 1975 in Nueces Co., TX; born 1954

References: 6-Francys Pattie Lantz Phillips, 63, 45

D17427 MILDRED ANN LANTZ D1742

MILDRED ANN LANTZ was born in 1921 in Kearney, Buffalo Co., NE. She married DONALD MACDONALD in Kearney, Buffalo Co., NE. He was born in 1921, and died 1955.

Children of MILDRED LANTZ and DONALD MACDONALD are:

1. MARY ROSE MACDONALD, born 1949; died 1977.
2. CATHERINE HARRIET MACDONALD, born 1950. She married GIOVANNI MARTINO GROPPO.
3. DONALD LANTZ MACDONALD, born 1951; died 1974.
4. MARK ALAN MACDONALD, born 1952. He married BRENDA SUE KELLER.

References: 6-Sarah Mae (Huss) Lantz

D17513 ESTHER OLIVE LANTZ D1751

ESTHER OLIVE LANTZ was born on 05 Dec 1915 in Decatur Co., IA, and died 08 Feb 1999 in Leon, Decatur, IA. She married (1) ORLAND WATSON. She married (2) CHESTER L. HEDLUND on 05 Jan 1935 in Leon, Decatur Co., IA, son of E. HEDLUND and MINNIE BRIDGES. He was born on 20 Apr 1915 in IA.

Child of ESTHER LANTZ and CHESTER HEDLUND is:

1. ESTHER ELAINE HEDLUND (D175131)

References: 6-Sarah Mae (Huss) Lantz, 40-Franklin Decatur Co IA 27-11 H20

D31722 ELAIN FRANCES LANTZ D3172

ELAIN FRANCES LANTZ was born 20 Feb 1917 in Dallas, Dallas, TX. She married JESSE BARNETT WHITEHEAD on 16 Feb 1941 in Brownwood, Brown, TX. He was born 03 Jul 1913 in Brownwood, Brown, TX.

Children of ELAIN LANTZ and JESSE WHITEHEAD are:

1. BARBARA JEAN WHITEHEAD (D317221)
2. CAROLE ANN WHITEHEAD, born 22 Jul 1949 in Brownwood, Brown, TX. She married JOHN VICTOR FOWLER 11 Jan 1970 in Brownwood, Brown, TX.

References: 6-Sarah Mae (Huss) Lantz

D31911 JAMES HOWARD COLEMAN D3191

JAMES HOWARD COLEMAN was born in 17 Sep 1907 in Parker Co., TX and died 16 Nov 1991 in Parker Co., TX. He married GLADYS MORROW in Parker Co., TX. She was born on 10 Jun 1912 in TX and died 26 May 2001 in Parker Co., TX. Both are buried in Springtown Cemetery, Springtown, Parker Co., TX.

Child of JAMES COLEMAN and GLADYS MORROW is:

1. WILBURN HOWARD COLEMAN, born on 14 Aug 1934 in Parker Co., TX; died 02 Sep 2010 in Parker Co., TX; buried Springtown Cemetery, Springtown, Parker Co., TX.

References: Other Places Parker Co TX 184-11 H18

D35468 JASPER PINKNEY DRUM D3546

JASPER PINKNEY DRUM was born on 08 Jan 1917 in Catawba Co., NC and died 17 Aug 2003 in Burke Co., NC. He married FLORENCE in Catawba Co., NC. She was born in 1915 in NC. He is buried in Spruce Pine Memorial Cemetery, Spruce Pine, Mitchell Co., NC.

Children of JASPER DRUM and FLORENCE are:

1. KENNETH DRUM, born in 1937 in Catawba Co., NC.
2. MARTHA DRUM, born in 1938 in Catawba Co., NC.

References: 40-Newton Catawba Co NC 18-30 H97

D35A11 CHARLES HENRY DRUM D35A1

CHARLES HENRY DRUM was born on 03 Aug 1877 in Catawba Co., NC and died 02 Jul

1956 in Catawba Co., NC. He married EDITH VIRGINIA ABERNETHY in Catawba Co., NC. She was born on 08 Jun 1879 in NC and died in Dec 1966 in Catawba Co., NC. Both are buried in Catawba United Methodist Church Cemetery, Catawba, Catawba Co., NC.

Children of CHARLES DRUM and EDITH ABERNETHY are:

1. ANNIE V. DRUM, born in 1908 in Catawba Co., NC.
2. MARY E. DRUM, born in 1909 in Catawba Co., NC.
3. HENRY O. DRUM, born in 1912 in Catawba Co., NC.
4. FLOYE DRUM, born in 1914 in Catawba Co., NC.
5. EUNICE M. DRUM, born in 1916 in Catawba Co., NC.
6. CHARLES M. DRUM, born in 1918 in Catawba Co., NC.
7. LEWIS F. DRUM, born in 1920 in Catawba Co., NC. He married EVELYN BARRINGER.

References: 6-Sarah Mae (Huss) Lantz, 30-Dist 0018 Catawba Catawba Co NC H51, 31-Dist 0018 Catawba Catawba Co NC H47, 45

D35A44 VINCENT BOYD DRUM D35A4

VINCENT BOYD DRUM was born on 20 Apr 1906 in Catawba Co., NC and died 29 Jul 1932 in Catawba Co., NC. He married HELEN CLARA MARTIN in Catawba Co., NC. She was born on 03 Aug 1907 in NC and died in Feb 1976 in Catawba Co., NC. Both are buried in Eastview Cemetery, Newton, Catawba Co., NC.

Child of VINCENT DRUM and HELEN MARTIN is:

1. CAROLYN E. DRUM, born in 1928 in Catawba Co., NC.

References: 45, 31-Dist 23 Newton Catawba Co NC H51

D35A51 RUFUS MONROE DRUM D35A5

RUFUS MONROE DRUM was born on 29 Jul 1883 in Catawba Co., NC; died 27 Jun 1966 in Catawba Co., NC. He married NANCY ALICE WITHERS in Catawba Co., NC. She was born on 29 Feb 1884 in NC and died 17 Aug 1965 in Catawba Co., NC. Both are buried in Oakwood Cemetery, Statesville, Iredell Co., NC.

Children of RUFUS DRUM and NANCY WITHERS are:

1. MAY DRUM, born in 1902 in Catawba Co., NC.
2. BOYD DRUM, born in 1906 in Catawba Co., NC.
3. BRYAN DRUM, born in 1909 in Catawba Co., NC.
4. BROTHER DRUM, born in 1912 in Catawba Co., NC.
5. LORENE DRUM, born in 1915 in Catawba Co., NC.

References: 45, 30-Caldwell Twp Catawba Co NC 0017 H142, 10-Dist 29 Caldwell Twp

D35A52 CHARLES GENTRY DRUM D35A5

CHARLES GENTRY DRUM was born on 19 Mar 1889 in Catawba Co., NC and died 24 Feb 1969 in Lincoln Co., NC. He married MINNIE DORA in Catawba Co., NC. She was born on 11 Mar 1884 in NC and died 13 May 1930 in Lincoln Co., NC. Both are buried in Ivey Memorial United Methodist Church Cemetery, Pumpkin Center, Lincoln Co., NC.

Children of CHARLES DRUM and MINNIE are:

1. WESLEY VANCE DRUM, born on 13 Oct 1907 in Catawba Co., NC; died 06 Jun 1991 in Lincoln Co., NC; married ESTHER EDNA C. in NC; born on 13 Feb 1913 in NC; died 12 Apr 1988 in Lincoln Co., NC. He is buried in Ivey Memorial United Methodist Church Cemetery, Pumpkin Center, Lincoln Co., NC.
2. THOMAS ALVIE DRUM, born on 21 May1909 in Catawba Co., NC; died 31 Oct 2003 in Lincoln Co., NC; married LOIS ETHEL HAGER in NC; born on 14 Aug 1912 in NC; died 04 Feb 2003 in Lincoln Co., NC. Both are buried in Ivey Memorial United Methodist Church Cemetery, Pumpkin Center, Lincoln Co., NC.
3. CHARLES WOODROW DRUM, born on 14 Sep1914 in NC; died 23 Nov 1935 in Lincoln Co., NC. He is buried in Ivey Memorial United Methodist Church Cemetery, Pumpkin Center, Lincoln Co., NC.
4. PEELER ROBERT DRUM, born on 12 Nov 1916 in NC; died 31 Aug 1988 in Lincoln Co., NC; married BETTY RUTH BRYANT in NC; born on 26 Jul 1930 in NC; died 19 Mar 2008 in Lincoln Co., NC. Both are buried in Ivey Memorial United Methodist Church Cemetery, Pumpkin Center, Lincoln Co., NC.
5. GAITHER MONROE DRUM, born on 14 Oct 1921 in NC; died 30 Sep 1981 in Lincoln Co., NC; married DORA LOUELLA DRUM in NC; born on 27 Feb 1923 in NC; died 30 Jun1995 in Lincoln Co., NC. Both are buried in Ivey Memorial United Methodist Church Cemetery, Pumpkin Center, Lincoln Co., NC.

References: 45, 30-Caldwell Twp Catawba Co NC 0017 H144, 10-Dist 104 Ironton Lincoln Co NC H171, 31-Dist 9 Ironton Lincoln Co NC H144

D35B14 EVELYN DRUM D35B1

EVELYN DRUM was born on 10 Nov 1913 in Charlotte, Mecklenburg Co., NC. She married CHARLIE LEVI ROBINSON. He was born on 11 Feb 1901 in Lincoln Co., NC, and died 21 Jun 1979 in Charlotte, Mecklenburg Co., NC.

Child of EVELYN DRUM and CHARLIE ROBINSON is:

1. SHIRLEY ANNE ROBINSON (D35B141)

References: 6-Sarah Mae (Huss) Lantz, 40-Charlotte Mecklenburg Co NC 60-61B H146

D35B15 VERNON BURGE DRUM D35B1

VERNON BURGE DRUM, Sr. was born on 15 May 1921 in Charlotte, Mecklenburg Co., NC. He married (1) ELIZABETH HAMRICK. He married (2) MAXINE RAGGS. She was born 14 Jan 1924.

Children of VERNON DRUM and ELIZABETH HAMRICK are:

1. LYNDELL DRUM (D35B151)
2. VERNON BURGE DRUM, Jr., born on 20 Jul 1956.

References: 6-Sarah Mae (Huss) Lantz

D35411 DOWD I. BEALTY D3541

DOWD I. BEALTY was born in Nov 1885 in Catawba Co,. NC. He married MATTIE L. in Catawba Co., NC. She was born in 1890 in NC.

Child of DOWD BEALTY and MATTIE is:

1. NATHAN H. BEALTY, born in 1910 in Catawba Co., NC.

References: 30-Dist 0027 Sherrils Ford Catawba Co NC H191

D36511 JOHANNA R. JOHNSON D3651

JOHANNA R. JOHNSON was born in Feb 1893 in Ashville, Buncombe Co., NC. She married GLADSTONE WILLIAMS in Oct 1912 in Ashville, Buncombe Co., NC. He was born in 1891 in AR.

Child of JOHANNA JOHNSON and GLADSTONE WILLIAMS is:

1. POWELL G. WILLIAMS (D365111)
2. EUGENE F. WILLIAMS, born 1921 in AR.
3. JOHN F. WILLIAMS, born 1926 in AR.

References: 5, 31-Dist 7 Crawfordsville Crittenden Co AR H12

D38421 LAURA ELIZABETH KILLIAN D3842

LAURA ELIZABETH KILLIAN was born on 02 May 1912 in Lincoln Co., NC. She married DANIEL FRANKLIN MOSTELLER. He was born on 25 Mar 1903 in Lincoln Co., NC, and died 23 Nov 1979 in Lincoln Co., NC.

Children of LAURA KILLIAN and DANIEL MOSTELLER are:

1. ALICE LAVADA MOSTELLER (D384211)
2. DAVID ELIAS MOSTELLER (D384212)
3. ROBERT PAUL MOSTELLER (D384213)

4. ANN ELIZABETH MOSTELLER (D384214)
5. HELEN SUE MOSTELLER (D384215)

References: 6-Sarah Mae (Huss) Lantz, 40-Howards Creek Lincoln Co NC 55-6H96

D38422 FRANKLIN AMZIE KILLIAN D3842

FRANKLIN AMZIE KILLIAN was born on 01 Feb 1915 in Lincoln Co., N.C., and died 18 Oct 1999. He married LUCY MAUDE PEARSON. She was born on 22 Jun 1915 in North Wilkesboro, NC.

Children of FRANKLIN KILLIAN and LUCY PEARSON are:

1. NANCY JANE KILLIAN (D384221)
2. JAMES FRANKLIN KILLIAN (D384222)
3. CHARLES FREDERICK KILLIAN (D384223)

References: 6-Sarah Mae (Huss) Lantz

D38423 ROBERT LANTZ KILLIAN D3842

ROBERT LANTZ KILLIAN was born on 27 Aug 1916 in Lincoln Co., N.C. He married ESTHER FINGER. She was born on 25 Apr 1914 and died 17 Jul 1989 in Charlotte, NC.

Children of ROBERT KILLIAN and ESTHER FINGER are:

1. ELIZABETH ANN KILLIAN, born 05 Feb 1950. She married (1) SHERMAN HONEYCUTT. She married (2) LELAND TARVER CLARKE, Jr.; born 09 Mar 1948; died 10 Oct 1982.
2. ESTHER ROBERTA KILLIAN (D384232)

References: 6-Sarah Mae (Huss) Lantz

D38424 WILLIAM DAVID KILLIAN D3842

WILLIAM DAVID KILLIAN was born 12 May 1922 in Lincoln Co., NC. He married HELEN SHUFORD HOUSER. She was born 24 Jan 1924.

Children of WILLIAM KILLIAN and HELEN HOUSER are:

1. WILLIAM JEFFREY KILLIAN (D384241)
2. MICHAEL DAVID KILLIAN, born on 20 Feb 1951. He married JOELLA MARIE CHAMBERS; born on 11 Sep 1954 in Winston-Salem, NC.
3. STEVEN CHARLES KILLIAN, born on 11 Jul 1955 in Lincoln Co., NC. He married NORA ANN ROBINSON.
4. SUSAN ELIZABETH KILLIAN (D384244)

References: 6-Sarah Mae (Huss) Lantz

D38431 PAUL QUICKEL D3843

PAUL QUICKEL, Sr.

Child of PAUL QUICKEL, Sr. is:

1. PAUL QUICKEL, Jr.

References: 6-Sarah Mae (Huss) Lantz

D38432 RICHARD LEROY QUICKEL D3843

RICHARD LEROY QUICKEL, Sr. was born on 23 Feb 1908 in Lincoln Co., N.C., and died 06 Jun 1993 in Mecklenburg Co., NC. He married MYRTLE LOUISE COULTER. She was born on 03 Dec 1907 in Catawba Co., NC, and died 14 Dec 1998.

Children of RICHARD QUICKEL and MYRTLE COULTER are:

1. DOROTHY JEAN QUICKEL (D384321)
2. RICHARD LEROY QUICKEL, Jr. (D384322)
3. ANN ELIZA QUICKEL (D384323)
4. JACOB CRAIG QUICKEL (D384324)
5. CARROLL COULTER QUICKEL, born and died in 1935 in Lincoln Co., NC.

References: 6-Sarah Mae (Huss) Lantz

D38451 LAURA MARGARET LANTZ D3845

LAURA MARGARET LANTZ was born on 12 Oct 1927 in Lincoln Co., NC. She married ROBERT MANESSE BIRKE on 05 Aug 1950 in Daniels Reformed Church, Lincoln Co., NC. He was born on 15 Dec 1925.

Children of LAURA LANTZ and ROBERT BIRKE are:

1. KATHRYN ELAINE BIRKE, born on 30 Nov 1952. She married WILLIAM L. GRAY on 28 Dec 1985 in Fayetteville, NC at Haywood United Methodist Church.
2. AMY LAURA BIRKE (D384512)

References: 6-Sarah Mae (Huss) Lantz

D38452 MARY ANN LANTZ D3845

MARY ANN LANTZ was born on 23 Oct 1932 in Howards Creek, Lincoln Co., NC. She married MILTON HUITT REEP on 14 Jun 1958 in Daniels's Reformed Church, Lincoln Co., NC, son of LUTHER REEP and MINNIE RHYNE. He was born on 30 Apr 1933 in Lincoln Co., NC.

Children of MARY LANTZ and MILTON REEP are:

1. MICHAEL HUITT REEP (D384521)
2. MARK LANTZ REEP (D384522)

References: 6-Sarah Mae (Huss) Lantz, 68

D38453 FRANCES CAROLYN LANTZ D3845

FRANCES CAROLYN LANTZ was born on 17 Sep 1936 in Howards Creek, Lincoln Co., NC. She married BILL ROY BUTLER 16 Dec 1956 in Daniel's Reformed Church, Lincolnton, Lincoln Co., NC. He was born on 24 Feb 1937.

Children of FRANCES LANTZ and BILL BUTLER are:

1. JOAN CAROL BUTLER (D384531)
2. DAVID BRUCE BUTLER (D384532)
3. ELIZABETH ANN BUTLER, born on 14 Jun 1962. She married GREGORY MICHAEL SMITH on 18 Apr 1997.
4. ERIC WILLIAM BUTLER, born on 24 Mar 1964. He married BON MORRIS 18 Jan 1987.
5. BARRY DOUGLAS BUTLER, born on 19 Jul 1966.
6. SUZANNE CAROLINE BUTLER, born on 16 Jun 1969. She married JON PAUL CHURCH on 13 Dec 2003 in Birmingham, AL.

References: 6-Sarah Mae (Huss) Lantz, 68

D38454 JOHN CHARLES LANTZ D3845

JOHN CHARLES LANTZ was born on 03 Jul 1939 in Lincoln Co., NC. He married SARAH MAE HUSS 02 Jun 1962 in Lincolnton, Lincoln Co., NC, daughter of ERVIN HUSS and INA HOVIS. She was born on 20 Jan 1942 in Iron Station, Lincoln Co., NC.

"SARAH graduated from Appalachian State Teacher's College (now Appalachian State University), Boone, NC, in 1963 with a double-major in Health & PE and Social Studies. She met JOHN CHARLES LANTZ, also from Lincoln County, NC, while there. She began her career in the Lincoln County Schools as a history, health and P.E. teacher. In 1980, Sarah received her Master's Degree in Library Science from Winthrop University, SC, and spent the last twenty years as a Media Specialist, retiring in 2000 after 35 years in the Lincoln County Schools system."

"JOHN also graduated from Appalachian with a BS degree, then later a Masters Degree in Science. He retired from the Lincoln County Schools System in 1996 after 35 years as a science teacher."

Child of JOHN LANTZ and SARAH HUSS is:

1. KIMBERLY LEE LANTZ (D384541)

References: 6-Sarah Mae (Huss) Lantz

L to R: (front) SAMUEL LANTZ BOWERS; (center) CALEB LEE BOWERS
(back) JOHN CHARLES LANTZ; KIMBERLY LEE (LANTZ) BOWERS; BRIAN WARD BOWERS; JACOB BRIAN BOWERS; SARAH MAE (HUSS) LANTZ (2012)

JOHN CHARLES & SARAH MAE (HUSS) LANTZ
50th Wedding Anniversary – Alaska Cruise

D41124 WALTER P. CARPENTER D4112

WALTER P. CARPENTER was born in Mar 1890 in Ironton, Lincoln Co., NC. He married ADDIE S. in Gaston Co., NC. She was born in 1889 in NC.

Children of WALTER CARPENTER and ADDIE are:

1. FRED W. CARPENTER (D411241)
2. IRENE W. CARPENTER, born in 1911 in Gaston Co., NC; married PLEASANT R. BEANE; born 1901 in NC.
3. MILDRED E. CARPENTER, born in 1921 in NC.

References: 30-Gastonia Twp Gaston Co NC H424, 10-Dallas Twp Gaston Co NC H56, 31-Charlotte Mecklenburg Co NC H119

D41196 JOHN W. CARPENTER D4119

JOHN W. CARPENTER was born in 1904 in NC. He married CHRISTINE in Charlotte, Mecklenburg Co., NC. She was born in 1904 in NC.

Child of JOHN CARPENTER and CHRISTINE is:

1. BILLIE CARPENTER, born in 1925 in Charlotte, Mecklenburg Co., NC.

References: 31-Dist 16 Charlotte Mecklenburg Co NC H251

D42621 PAULINE HALLMAN FINGER D4262

PAULINE HALLMAN FINGER was born on 30 Nov 1904 in Lincoln Co., NC, and died 01 Dec 1999 in Lincoln Co., NC. She married HOLLY LOUIS BEATTY, Sr. on 24 Jan 1931. He was born on 21 Jan 1893, and died 13 Jan 1954.

Children of PAULINE FINGER and HOLLY BEATTY are:

1. HOLLY LOUIS BEATTY, Jr., born on 20 Mar 1932 in Lincoln Co., NC. He married HELEN GREEN.
2. DAVID LEE BEATTY, Sr. (D426212)

References: 6-Sarah Mae (Huss) Lantz

D42622 SUE BETTY FINGER D4262

SUE BETTY FINGER was born on 12 Dec 1909 in Lincoln Co., NC, and died Jan 1999. She married ROBERT RUDISILL RHYNE, Sr. on 01 Jun 1934 in Lincoln Co., NC. He was born on 29 Oct 1908.

Children of SUE FINGER and ROBERT RHYNE are:

1. ROBERT RUDISILL RHYNE, Jr. (D426221)
2. RICHARD WAKEFIELD RHYNE, born 13 Jun 1942 in Charlotte, Mecklenburg Co., NC. He married MARY RUTH MAUNEY 30 Jan 1965 in Roanoke, VA; born 30 Oct 1941.

References: 6-Sarah Mae (Huss) Lantz

D42623 ANNIE LEE FINGER D4262

ANNIE LEE FINGER was born on 04 Jul 1912 in Lincoln Co., NC. She married (1) POWELL. She married (2) JOHN VICTOR HAWN 02 Oct 1934 in Lincoln Co., NC. He was born on 01 Jun 1910 in NC.

Children of ANNIE FINGER and JOHN HAWN are:

1. JOHN MARTIN HAWN (D426231)
2. KENNETH LEE HAWN, born on 23 Jan 1939 in Lincoln Co., NC. He married PATRICIA STELL on 11 Jan 1964; born on 10 Jul 1942.

References: 6-Sarah Mae (Huss) Lantz, 40-Staunton Staunton City Co VA 121-12 H288

D42624 MARY ETTA FINGER D4262

MARY ETTA FINGER was born on 14 Apr 1918 in Lincoln Co., NC. She married ROBERT R. BATTEY. He was born on 06 Sep 1919 in Springfield, MA, and died 06 Dec 2002 in Indian Trail, NC.

Children of MARY FINGER and ROBERT BATTEY are:

1. JANICE BATTEY (D426241)
2. ED BATTEY
3. MIKE BATTEY

References: 6-Sarah Mae (Huss) Lantz

D42625 MARTIN LUTHER FINGER D4262

MARTIN LUTHER FINGER, Jr. was born on 05 Dec 1920 in Lincoln Co., NC. He married HELEN FRANCES FRIDAY on 24 Dec 1940 in York, SC. She was born on 12 Oct 1924.

Children of MARTIN FINGER and HELEN FRIDAY are:

1. LARRY MARTIN FINGER (D426251)
2. JAMES ALFRED FINGER (D426252)
3. JERRY DANIEL FINGER (D426253)

References: 6-Sarah Mae (Huss) Lantz

D42641 HELEN ANGELINE HALLMAN D4264

HELEN ANGELINE HALLMAN was born on 09 Nov 1911 in Lincoln Co., NC. She married HAROLD PAUL RUDISILL, Sr. on 13 Sep 1933 in Gaffney, Cherokee Co., SC. He was born on 27 Feb 1911, and died 08 Dec 1945 in Lincoln Co., NC.

Children of HELEN HALLMAN and HAROLD RUDISILL are:

1. HELEN PATRICIA RUDISILL, born 25 Jul 1934. She married ROBERT HENRY INGRAM on 14 Apr 1965 in Charlotte, Mecklenburg Co., NC; born 01 Sep 1927 in Stanley Co., NC.
2. HAROLD PAUL RUDISILL, Jr., born on 14 Sep 1935 in Lincoln Co., NC; died 12 Feb 1939 in NC.
3. CHARLES EDWARD RUDISILL, Sr. (D426413)
4. CORA LEE RUDISILL (D426414)
5. JUDITH ANN RUDISILL (D426415)
6. HARRY HALLMAN RUDISILL, born 03 Sep 1942 in Lincoln Co., NC; died 27 Feb 1980 in Lincoln Co., NC.

References: 6-Sarah Mae (Huss) Lantz, 40-Statesville Iredell Co NC 49-39 H150

D42642 MARGARET CARRA HALLMAN D4264

MARGARET CARRA HALLMAN was born on 12 Jul 1915 in Lincoln Co., NC, and died 05 Oct 2003 in Raleigh, NC. She married HAROLD FREDERICK RUDISILL on 05 Oct 1934 in Lincoln Co., NC. He was born on 17 Mar 1914, and died 20 Aug 1978 in Lincoln Co., NC.

Children of MARGARET HALLMAN and HAROLD RUDISILL are:

1. THOMAS ALLAN RUDISILL (D426421)
2. DORIS JEAN RUDISILL (D426422)
3. LINDA MARGARET RUDISILL (D426423)

References: 6-Sarah Mae (Huss) Lantz, 40-Lincolnton Lincoln Co NC 55-15 H33

D42643 JAMES LEE HALLMAN D4264

JAMES LEE HALLMAN, Sr. was born on 02 Oct 1917 in Lincoln Co., NC. He married MARY MCARVER on 14 Sep 1940 in Gaston Co., NC. She was born on 19 May 1919.

Children of JAMES HALLMAN and MARY MCARVER are:

1. JOYCE ANN HALLMAN (D426431)
2. JAMES LEE HALLMAN, Jr., born 01 Mar 1948 in Gastonia, Gaston Co., NC.

References: 6-Sarah Mae (Huss) Lantz

D42644 HAROLD HOOVER HALLMAN D4264

HAROLD HOOVER HALLMAN, Sr. was born on 13 Feb 1922 in Lincoln Co., NC, and died 12 Apr 1973. He married (1) HELEN SELLERS, daughter of PHILLIP SELLERS and CARA DELLINGER. She was born on 20 Apr 1926 in Lincoln Co., NC. He married (2) ELIZABETH CHRISTINE GRAYSON on 20 Jul 1944.

Child of HAROLD HALLMAN and HELEN SELLERS is:

1. HAROLD HOOVER HALLMAN, Jr. (D426443)

Children of HAROLD HALLMAN and ELIZABETH GRAYSON are:

2. HELEN EUGENIA HALLMAN (D426441)
3. SHARON LUANN HALLMAN, born 06 Sep 1961 in Lincoln Co., NC. She married Richard Blair Keener 22 May 1993.

References: 6-Sarah Mae (Huss) Lantz

D42645 ROBERT ANTHONY HALLMAN D4264

ROBERT ANTHONY HALLMAN, Sr. was born on 18 Sep 1926 in Lincoln Co., NC. He married HAZEL BESSIE EUREY on 02 Feb 1945 in York, SC, daughter of JOHN EUREY and HATTIE SAUNDERS. She was born on 07 Nov 1926, and died 1999.

Children of ROBERT HALLMAN and HAZEL EUREY are:

1. ROBERT ANTHONY HALLMAN, Jr. (D426451)
2. RICHARD EUREY HALLMAN (D426452)

References: 6-Sarah Mae (Huss) Lantz

D42651 JAMES WILLIAM CARPENTER D4265

JAMES WILLIAM CARPENTER was born on 11 Oct 1908 in Lincoln Co., NC, and died 17 Sep 1993 in Salisbury, Rowan Co., NC. He met INEZ CLEO CAGLE on 07 Jul 1934 in Salisbury, NC. She was born on 15 Jun 1910.

Child of JAMES CARPENTER and INEZ CAGLE is:

1. BETTIE RAYE CARPENTER (D426511)

References: 6-Sarah Mae (Huss) Lantz

D42652 EDWARD HALLMAN CARPENTER D4265

EDWARD HALLMAN CARPENTER was born on 07 Jun 1912 in Lincoln Co., NC, and died Jul 1997. He married MAUDE EVA HERMAN on 18 Aug 1940 in York, SC. She was born on 16 May 1919 in Catawba Co., NC.

Children of EDWARD CARPENTER and MAUDE HERMAN are:

1. SANDRA KAY CARPENTER (D426521)
2. PHYLLIS MARLENE CARPENTER, born 02 Jan 1951 in Hickory, Catawba Co., NC. She married ROBERT ALFRED SCHRAGE; born 13 Sep 1948 in Chicago, IL.

References: 6-Sarah Mae (Huss) Lantz

D42683 LUTHER VOIGHT ARMSTRONG D4268

LUTHER VOIGHT ARMSTRONG was born on 18 Sep 1918 in Iron Station, Lincoln Co., NC, and died in Asheville, NC. He married MARY FRANCES PATRIC.

Child of Luther Armstrong and Mary Patric is:

1. WILLIAM LUTHER ARMSTRONG

References: 6-Sarah Mae (Huss) Lantz

D42684 RUBY ISABELLE ARMSTRONG D4268

RUBY ISABELLE ARMSTRONG was born on 30 Mar 1921 in Gastonia, Gaston Co., NC. She married (1) WILLIAM MCKINLEY WILLIAMS on 07 Nov 1940. She married (2) ROBERT ASBURY SMITH 05 Feb 1949. He was born on 04 Apr 1920 in Berkley Co., SC, and died 11 Aug 1991 in Ridgeville, SC.

Children OF RUBY ARMSTRONG and WILLIAM WILLIAMS are:

1. LINDA SUE SMITH (D426841)
2. JAMES MCKINLEY SMITH (D426842)

References: 6-Sarah Mae (Huss) Lantz

D42685 ANNA CAROLYN ARMSTRONG D4268

ANNA CAROLYN ARMSTRONG was born on 27 Aug 1923 in Gastonia, Gaston Co., NC, and died 27 Dec 1985 in Ridgeville, SC. She married GEORGE JAMES SMITH, Jr. on 16 Jan 1944 in Harleyville, SC. He was born on 16 Feb 1921 in Florence, SC, and died 16 Sep 1977 in Charleston, Charleston Co., SC.

Children of ANNA ARMSTRONG and GEORGE SMITH are:

1. BETTY ANN SMITH (D426851)
2. GEORGE WILLIAM SMITH, born 09 May 1948 in Summerville, Dorchester Co., SC.
3. JANE IRENE SMITH, born 04 Jun 1952 in Summerville, Dorchester Co., SC; died 17 Apr 1987 in Ridgeville, SC.
4. JACK LUTHER SMITH, SR. (D426854)

References: 6-Sarah Mae (Huss) Lantz

D42686 VIRGINIA BLAIR ARMSTRONG D4268

VIRGINIA BLAIR ARMSTRONG was born on 05 May 1927 in Gastonia, Gaston Co., NC. She married DAVID SEYMOUR QUARTERMAN on 06 Sep 1946 in Ridgeville, Dorchester Co., SC. He was born on 29 Jul 1924.

Children of VIRGINIA ARMSTRONG and DAVID QUARTERMAN are:

1. JANICE BLAIR QUARTERMAN, born 10 May 1951 in Charleston, Charleston Co., SC. She married LEONARD PAUL GOLDMAN 22 Jun 1975 in Charleston, SC; born 22 Jun 1946 in Charleston, Charleston Co., SC.
2. ANNE MARIE QUARTERMAN (D426862)
3. SHARON LYNN QUARTERMAN (D426863)
4. VIRGINIA CLEO QUARTERMAN (D426864)

References: 6-Sarah Mae (Huss) Lantz

D42687 BETTY RUTH ARMSTRONG D4268

BETTY RUTH ARMSTRONG was born on 18 Mar 1930 in St. George, SC. She married WILLIAM LEWIS BEHIE 18 Sep 1949 in Ridgeville, Dorchester Co., SC. He was born on 20 Oct 1923, and died on 03 Apr 1983 in Harleyville, SC.

Children of BETTY ARMSTRONG and WILLIAM BEHIE are:

1. SHIRLEY GEORGANN BEHIE (D426871)
2. WILLIAM LEWIS BEHIE (D426872)
3. ELIZABETH RUBY BEHIE (D426873)
4. LINDA KAREN BEHIE (D426874)

References: 6-Sarah Mae (Huss) Lantz

D426B1 MARTHA KATHLEEN CARPENTER D426B

MARTHA KATHLEEN CARPENTER was born on 13 Oct 1921 in Lincoln Co., NC. She married CARL FINGER TURBYFILL on 21 Jul 1940 in Lincoln Co., NC, son of ROY TURBYFILL and DOLLY FISHER. He was born on 03 May 1919.

Children of MARTHA CARPENTER and CARL TURBYFILL are:

1. HAROLD CARPENTER TURBYFILL (D426B11)
2. DONALD RAY TURBYFILL (D426B12)
3. BARBARA ANN TURBYFILL (D426B13)
4. KENNETH DEAN TURBYFILL, born on 03 Mar 1964 in Burlington, Alamance Co., NC.

References: 6-Sarah Mae (Huss) Lantz

D426B2 ODUS CLYDE CARPENTER D426B

ODUS CLYDE CARPENTER, Jr. was born on 26 Nov 1922 in Lincoln Co., NC. He married VERA DARE MCGINNIS on 27 Jan 1944 in Lincoln Co., NC. She was born on 03 Dec 1925.

Child of ODUS CARPENTER and VERA MCGINNIS is:

1. ROBERT GLENN CARPENTER (D426B21)

References: 6-Sarah Mae (Huss) Lantz

D426B3 FRED HALLMAN CARPENTER D426B

FRED HALLMAN CARPENTER, Sr. was born on 21 Nov 1927 in Lincoln Co., NC. He married AUDREY VIRGINIA SIMS on 03 Jul 1952 in Newton, Catawba Co., NC. She was born on 17 Nov 1929 in Newton, Catawba Co., NC.

Children of FRED CARPENTER and AUDREY SIMS are:

1. SUSAN GLYNIS CARPENTER, born on 01 Feb 1954 in Lincoln Co., NC. She married LADDIE CHARLES WUCHAE on 22 May 1977 in Lincoln Co., NC at Salem Lutheran Church; born on 10 Dec 1941.
2. FRED HALLMAN CARPENTER (D426B32)

References: 6-Sarah Mae (Huss) Lantz

D426D1 JENNINGS BRYAN EDWARDS D426D

JENNINGS BRYAN EDWARDS, Jr. was born on 14 Jul 1922 in Lincoln Co., NC. He married ODESSA EDITH WILLIAMS on 05 Jun 1954 in Raleigh, NC. She was born on 21 Jun 1921 in Hemp-Robins.

Child of JENNINGS EDWARDS and ODESSA WILLIAMS is:

1. ELIZABETH ABIGAIL EDWARDS, born 28 Oct 1957 in Ware Co., NC.

References: 6-Sarah Mae (Huss) Lantz

D426D2 JAMES ROBERT EDWARDS D426D

JAMES ROBERT EDWARDS, Sr. was born on 04 Oct 1923 in Dallas, Gaston Co., NC. He married RUTH HELEN BARGAR on 08 Nov 1952 in Fries, VA. She was born on 02 Aug 1931 in Carbondale, PA.

Children of James Edwards and Ruth Bargar are:

1. JAMES ROBERT EDWARDS (D426D21)
2. CAROL ANN EDWARDS (D426D22)

3. FRANK BRYAN EDWARDS (D426D23)

References: 6-Sarah Mae (Huss) Lantz

D426E1 CALVIN BANKS FINGER D426E

CALVIN BANKS FINGER, Jr. was born on 25 Apr 1927 in Lincoln Co., NC. He married BEATRICE DOUGLAS on 23 Mar 1952 in Sanford, NC. She was born on 10 Nov 1927.

Children of CALVIN FINGER and BEATRICE DOUGLAS are:

1. CALVIN BANKS FINGER III, born on 15 Apr 1954 in Franklin, Macon Co., NC.
2. STEPHEN DOUGLAS FINGER, born on 14 Nov 1957 in Waynesville, Macon Co., NC.
3. CARRIE LEE FINGER, born on 21 Jun 1959 in Charlotte, Mecklenburg Co., NC.
4. JAMES EDWARD FINGER, born on 06 Apr 1963 in Winston-Salem, Forsyth Co., NC.

References: 6-Sarah Mae (Huss) Lantz

D426E2 MICHAEL NEIL FINGER D426E

MICHAEL NEIL FINGER was born on 17 May 1930 in Lincoln Co., NC. He married SARAH NELL MATHIS on 20 Jun 1953 in Jonesville, NC. She was born on 30 Oct 1930.

Children of MICHAEL FINGER and SARAH MATHIS are:

1. JAN ELIZABETH FINGER, born on 07 Aug 1955 in Elkin, Surry Co., NC.
2. KATHRYN JEAN FINGER, born on 20 Apr 1958 in Columbia, Richland Co., SC.

References: 6-Sarah Mae (Huss) Lantz

D426E3 PATRICIA ANN FINGER D426E

PATRICIA ANN FINGER was born on 07 Feb 1933 in Lincoln Co., NC. She married GABRIEL ANDREW AVRAM on 23 Sep 1955 in Riverdale, NY. He was born on 08 May 1932 in Bucharest, Romania.

Children of PATRICIA FINGER and GABRIEL AVRAM are:

1. RANDALL DAVID AVRAM (D426E31)
2. MICHAEL ANDREW AVRAM (D426E32)

References: 6-Sarah Mae (Huss) Lantz

D426E4 HOWARD LINN FINGER D426E

HOWARD LINN FINGER was born on 10 Aug 1938 in Lincoln Co., NC. He married MARY LOU SCHULZ on 09 May 1964 in Lancaster, PA. She was born on 04 Sep 1940 in Lancaster, PA.

Children of HOWARD FINGER and MARY SCHULZ are:

1. JENNIFER LYNN FINGER, born on 17 Jun 1966 in Lancaster, PA.
2. MICHAEL EMORY FINGER, born on 21 Jul 1971 in Williamsburg, PA.

References: 6-Sarah Mae (Huss) Lantz

D426F1 NANCY ANN HALLMAN D426F

NANCY ANN HALLMAN was born on 09 Dec 1933 in Dallas, Dallas Co., TX. She married ROBERT FRELAND CASON on 06 Mar 1952 in Dallas, TX, son of LONNIE CASON and GOLDA CUMMINS. He was born on 14 Oct 1931 in Dallas, Dallas Co., TX.

Children of NANCY HALLMAN and ROBERT CASON are:

1. SHERYL ANN CASON (D426F11)
2. DAVID GREGORY CASON (D426F12)
3. INFANT CASON, born on 26 Jan 1961 and died 26 Jan 1961 in Dallas, Dallas Co., TX.

References: 6-Sarah Mae (Huss) Lantz

D426F2 BETTY JEAN HALLMAN D426F

BETTY JEAN HALLMAN was born on 24 Sep 1936 in Dallas, Dallas Co., TX. She married (1) BILLY RAY MCCOMMAS 01 Mar 1954 in Garland, TX. He was born on 22 Nov 1931, and died 30 Mar 1980. She married (2) PHILLIP LEON HOOVER on 26 Dec 1980 in Dallas, TX. He was born on 31 Aug 1941 in Dallas, Dallas Co., TX.

Children of BETTY HALLMAN and BILLY MCCOMMAS are:

1. TERRY GLEN MCCOMMAS (D426F21)
2. GARY LYNN MCCOMMAS (D426F22)
3. SHERI KIM MCCOMMAS (D426F23)

References: 6-Sarah Mae (Huss) Lantz

D44122 VIRGINIA HALLMAN D4412

VIRGINIA HALLMAN was born on 20 Jul 1908 in Alvarado, Johnson Co., TX. She married WILLIAM RILEY HALE on 11 Nov 1927 in Dallas, TX. He was born on 22 Sep 1899.

Children of Virginia Hallman and William Hale are:

1. MARILYN HALE.
2. DIANE HALE, born on 26 Aug 1929.

References: 6-Sarah Mae (Huss) Lantz

D44171 ERNEST LEROY HALLMAN D4417

ERNEST LEROY HALLMAN, Jr. was born on 16 Jul 1915 in Grandview, Johnson Co., TX.

He married MARTHA ELIZABETH BOOKER on 12 Nov 1944 in Macon, Bibb Co., GA. She was born on 09 Jun 1924 in Macon, Bibb Co., GA, and died 06 Oct 1994 in Dallas, Dallas Co., TX.

Children of ERNEST HALLMAN and MARTHA BOOKER are:

1. MARTHA BOOKER HALLMAN (D441711)
2. WILLA ANNE HALLMAN (D441712)
3. SAMUEL JOHN HALLMAN (D441713)

References: 6-Sarah Mae (Huss) Lantz

D44172 WILLIAM PRESTRIDGE HALLMAN D4417

WILLIAM PRESTRIDGE HALLMAN, Sr. was born on 24 May 1917 in Grandview, Johnson Co., TX. He married IDA RUTH JAMES on 22 Nov 1941 in Cleburne, Johnson Co., TX. She was born on 09 Mar 1920 in Cleburne, Johnson Co., TX.

Children of WILLIAM HALLMAN and IDA JAMES are:

1. WILLIAM PRESTRIDGE HALLMAN, JR. (D441721)
2. JAMES ERNEST HALLMAN, SR. (D441722)
3. WILLA RUTH HALLMAN (D441723)

References: 6-Sarah Mae (Huss) Lantz

D66111 ROBERT LEE HOUSER D6611

ROBERT LEE HOUSER, Sr. married RUBY GAIL WILLIS.

Children of ROBERT HOUSER and RUBY WILLIS are:

1. ROBERT LEE HOUSER, Jr., born on 11 Feb 1963.
2. TOMMY WAYNE HOUSER, born on 06 Aug 1964.
3. BOBBY JAMES HOUSER, born on 29 Dec 1965.
4. TERESA GAIL HOUSER, born on 23 Sep 1967.

References: 6-Sarah Mae (Huss) Lantz

D66141 ROBERT DWIGHT HOUSER D6614

ROBERT DWIGHT HOUSER was born on 24 Sep 1931. He married JOANN BEAM WEHUNT.

Child of ROBERT HOUSER and JOANN WEHUNT is:

1. SHERRY HOUSER

References: 6-Sarah Mae (Huss) Lantz

D66151 EDNA ALENE HOUSER D6615

EDNA ALENE HOUSER was born on 18 Jun 1935. She married KEN JONES.

Child of EDNA HOUSER and KEN JONES is:

1. MARCUS JONES

References: 6-Sarah Mae (Huss) Lantz

D66152 PEGGY JANE HOUSER D6615

PEGGY JANE HOUSER was born on 24 Aug 1936. She married (1) EARL DAY. She married (2) JOE WISE.

Child of PEGGY HOUSER and EARL DAY is:

1. CANDY DAY

References: 6-Sarah Mae (Huss) Lantz

D66172 GALE NEILL D6617

GALE NEILL She married LARRY TOWERY.

Children of GALE NEILL and LARRY TOWERY are:

1. KELLY TOWERY
2. TAMMY TOWERY
3. TINA TOWERY

References: 6-Sarah Mae (Huss) Lantz

D66182 BARBARA HOUSER D6618

BARBARA HOUSER was born on 14 Mar 1938. She married FRANK D. HEAVNER.

Children of BARBARA HOUSER and FRANK HEAVNER are:

1. DEBORAH KAY HEAVNER, born on 10 Nov 1956; died 11 Nov 1956.
2. MELISSA ANN HEAVNER, born on 21 Feb 1959.
3. ANITA SUE HEAVNER, born on 04 Aug 1964.

References: 6-Sarah Mae (Huss) Lantz

D175131 ESTHER ELAINE HEDLUND D17513

ESTHER ELAINE HEDLUND was born on 17 Sep 1935 in Leon, Decatur Co., IA. She married (1) JOHN FISHER. She married (2) JAMES R. CANNEY. She married (3) WENDELL H. WEST on 20 Apr 1957 in Leon, Decatur Co., IA, son of GERALD WEST and EULA HALL. He was born on 01 Mar 1935 in IA.

Children of ESTHER HEDLUND and WENDELL WEST are:

1. REBECCA LYNN WEST, born on 04 Nov 1959 in Tacoma (Army Hosp.), Washington. She married MARK THEDENS on 12 Oct 1985 in Osceola, IA (Mother's Home).
2. RONAL RAY WEST, born on 04 Jul 1961 in Leon, Decatur Co., IA. He married LAURIE LOCKHART on 12 Apr 1996 in Lake Tahoe, CA.

References: 6-Sarah Mae (Huss) Lantz

D317221 BARBARA JEAN WHITEHEAD D31722

BARBARA JEAN WHITEHEAD was born on 20 Oct 1944 in Los Angeles, CA. She married ORAN HARPER LOGAN on 02 Feb 1962 in Abilene, Taylor, TX.

Children of BARBARA WHITEHEAD and ORAN LOGAN are:

1. DEANDRA LOGAN, born 1962.
2. SHAY LOGAN, born in 1973.

References: 6-Sarah Mae (Huss) Lantz

D35B141 SHIRLEY ANNE ROBINSON D35B14

SHIRLEY ANNE ROBINSON was born on 31 Aug 1937 in Charlotte, Mecklenburg Co., NC. She married JOE BILLY DELLINGER. He was born on 05 Sep 1936 in Lincoln Co., NC, and died 24 Sep 1999 in Cherryville, Gaston Co., NC.

Children of SHIRLEY ROBINSON and JOE DELLINGER are:

1. MICHAEL DAVID DELLINGER, born on 10 Mar 1958 in Charlotte, Mecklenburg Co., NC. He married KATHERINE SUSAN WILSON; born on 29 Oct 1958.
2. KAREN LYNN DELLINGER, born on 14 Jun 1963. She married DAVID ANDREW BAIRD; born on 15 Dec 1969.

References: 6-Sarah Mae (Huss) Lantz

D35B151 LYNDELL DRUM D35B1

LYNDELL DRUM was born on 27 Dec 1944. She married (1) NORMAN EDDIE YOUNGBLOOD III. He was born on 12 Nov 1942. She married (2) HOWARD D. SOLOMON, Md.

Child of LYNDELL DRUM and NORMAN YOUNGBLOOD is:

1. NORMAN EDDIE YOUNGBLOOD IV, born on 16 Nov 1965.

Child of LYNDELL DRUM and HOWARD SOLOMON is:

2. DAVID COURTNEY YOUNGBLOOD SOLOMON, born on 02 Oct 1973.

References: 6-Sarah Mae (Huss) Lantz

D365111 POWELL G. WILLIAMS D36511

POWELL G. WILLIAMS was born 1913 in AR. He married MARGARET in TN. She was born in 1919 in AR.

Child of POWELL WILLIAMS and MARGARET is:

1. THOMAS WILLIAMS, born in 1939 in TN.

References: Hughes St Francis Co AR 62-5 H80

D384211 ALICE LAVADA MOSTELLER D38421

ALICE LAVADA MOSTELLER was born on 07 Jul 1941 in Lincoln Co., NC. She married CHARLES ALEXANDER CHILDERS. He was born on 20 Jun 1939.

Children of ALICE MOSTELLER and CHARLES CHILDERS are:

1. DEBORAH ANN CHILDERS, born on 06 Dec 1957. She married TONY JOSEPH BRYANT; born on 11 May 1958.
2. ELISA PAULETTE CHILDERS, born on 28 Jun 1963.

References: 6-Sarah Mae (Huss) Lantz

D384212 DAVID ELIAS MOSTELLER D38421

DAVID ELIAS MOSTELLER was born on 21 Jun 1944 in Lincoln Co., NC. He married MARIANNE BORCHERT. She was born on 09 Sep 1943.

Children of DAVID MOSTELLER and MARIANNE BORCHERT are:

1. KAREN MICHELE MOSTELLER, born on 07 May 1969.
2. KEVIN DAVID MOSTELLER, born on 13 Nov 1972.

References: 6-Sarah Mae (Huss) Lantz

D384213 ROBERT PAUL MOSTELLER D38421

ROBERT PAUL MOSTELLER was born on 25 May 1948 in Lincoln Co., NC. He married SARAH ELIZABETH GIBSON. She was born on 07 Nov 1950.

Children of ROBERT MOSTELLER and SARAH GIBSON are:

1. BENJAMIN GIBSON MOSTELLER
2. DANIEL PAUL MOSTELLER, born on 09 Feb 1981.

References: 6-Sarah Mae (Huss) Lantz

D384214 ANN ELIZABETH MOSTELLER D38421

ANN ELIZABETH MOSTELLER was born on 25 Nov 1949 in Lincoln Co., NC. She married JAMES SUMNER. He was born on 07 May 1950.

Children of ANN MOSTELLER and JAMES SUMNER are:

1. MARK DAVID SUMNER.
2. LAUREN ELIZABETH MOSTELLER SUMNER, born on 21 May 1980.

References: 6-Sarah Mae (Huss) Lantz

D384215 HELEN SUE MOSTELLER D38421

HELEN SUE MOSTELLER was born on 04 Dec 1952 in Lincoln Co., NC. She married EDGER LEWIS RUTLEDGE. He was born on 08 Nov 1952.

Children of HELEN MOSTELLER and EDGER RUTLEDGE are:

1. TYSON ANDREW RUTLEDGE, born on 12 Oct 1973.
2. TALIA ANN RUTLEDGE, born on 03 Aug 1977.

References: 6-Sarah Mae (Huss) Lantz

D384221 NANCY JANE KILLIAN D38422

NANCY JANE KILLIAN was born on 17 Jan 1942 in Lincoln Co., NC. She married GARY WAYNE CONNER. He was born on 29 Aug 1938 in Lincoln Co., N.C., and died 12 Jan 1998.

Children of NANCY KILLIAN and GARY CONNER are:

1. LISA MARIE CONNER, born on 10 Oct 1964. She married JERRY KENNETH SAINE, Jr. on 28 Feb 1987; born 28 May 1963.
2. ERIC WAYNE CONNER, born on 04 Mar 1975.

References: 6-Sarah Mae (Huss) Lantz

D384222 JAMES FRANKLIN KILLIAN D38422

JAMES FRANKLIN KILLIAN was born on 11 Apr 1945. He married (1) LINDA HALL ROMEYN. He married (2) FRANCES ELIZABETH TAYLOR. She was born on 31 Oct 1943.

Child of JAMES KILLIAN and FRANCES TAYLOR is:

1. ALEXANDRA TAYLOR KILLIAN, born on 07 Aug 1980.

References: 6-Sarah Mae (Huss) Lantz

D384223 CHARLES FREDERICK KILLIAN D38422

CHARLES FREDERICK KILLIAN was born on 01 Jan 1948 in Lincoln Co., N.C. He married PATRICIA YVONNE HARTSOE. She was born on 21 Dec 1947 in Lincoln Co., N.C.

Child of CHARLES KILLIAN and PATRICIA HARTSOE is:

1. PATRICE NOEL KILLIAN, born on 10 Dec 1981.

References: 6-Sarah Mae (Huss) Lantz

D384232 ESTHER ROBERTA KILLIAN D38423

ESTHER ROBERTA KILLIAN was born on 17 Oct 1951. She married JOHN LEROY HIPP. He was born on 09 Nov 1948.

Children of ESTHER KILLIAN and JOHN HIPP are:

1. JENNA ELIZABETH HIPP, born on 17 Feb 1979.
2. KEELY REBECCA HIPP, born on 15 Nov 1980.
3. ROBERT KENTON HIPP, born on 11 Jan 1987.

References: 6-Sarah Mae (Huss) Lantz

D384241 WILLIAM JEFFREY KILLIAN D38424

WILLIAM JEFFREY KILLIAN was born on 12 Jan 1950. He married SUSAN MATT BOWMAN. She was born 05 Jul 1950.

Child of WILLIAM KILLIAN and SUSAN BOWMAN is:

1. MATT BOWMAN KILLIAN, born on 17 May 1978.

References: 6-Sarah Mae (Huss) Lantz

D384244 SUSAN ELIZABETH KILLIAN D38424

SUSAN ELIZABETH KILLIAN was born on 04 Sep 1957. She married JOHN MARK SUTTON.

Children of SUSAN KILLIAN and JOHN SUTTON are:

1. KATHRYN ELIZABETH SUTTON
2. AMY LYNNE SUTTON

References: 6-Sarah Mae (Huss) Lantz

D384321 DOROTHY JEAN QUICKEL D38432

DOROTHY JEAN QUICKEL She married WILLIAM B. YEAGER, Jr., son of JOHN YEAGER and CARRIE CRITES.

Children of DOROTHY QUICKEL and WILLIAM YEAGER are:

1. ANNE CARTER YEAGER, born on 04 Nov 1959.
2. CATHERINE LEE YEAGER, born on 04 Apr 1962.

References: 6-Sarah Mae (Huss) Lantz

D384322 RICHARD LEROY QUICKEL D38432

RICHARD LEROY QUICKEL, Jr. married MARGARET VILLAH HOOVER.

Children of RICHARD QUICKEL and MARGARET HOOVER are:

1. LINDA LEE QUICKEL.
2. BARRY CRAIG QUICKEL.
3. ROBERT LEE QUICKEL.

References: 6-Sarah Mae (Huss) Lantz

D384323 ANN ELIZA QUICKEL D38432

ANN ELIZA QUICKEL married RICHARD FRANK MCNABB.

Children of ANN QUICKEL and RICHARD MCNABB are:

1. RICHARD KENT MCNABB, born in 1963.
2. DEBRA JEAN MCNABB, born in 1968.

References: 6-Sarah Mae (Huss) Lantz

D384324 JACOB CRAIG QUICKEL D38432

JACOB CRAIG QUICKEL married Faye Harden.

Child of JACOB QUICKEL and FAYE HARDEN is:

1. SHARON LYNNE QUICKEL.

References: 6-Sarah Mae (Huss) Lantz

D384512 AMY LAURA BIRKE D38451

AMY LAURA BIRKE was born on 07 Dec 1958. She married GERALD CURTIS DEAN on 21 Apr 1984 in Fayetteville, NC at Haywood United Methodist Church.

Children of AMY BIRKE and GERALD DEAN are:

1. CURTIS CHARLES DEAN, born on 30 Mar 1991.
2. ELIZABETH BIRKE DEAN, born on 18 May 1996.

References: 6-Sarah Mae (Huss) Lantz

D384521 MICHAEL HUITT REEP D38452

MICHAEL HUITT REEP was born on 23 Oct 1962 in Sanford, NC. He married SHARON STARK JOHNSON on 20 Jun 1987 in Raleigh, NC.

Child of MICHAEL REEP and SHARON JOHNSON is:

1. EMILY WYATT REEP, born 27 Dec 1990.

References: 6-Sarah Mae (Huss) Lantz

D384522 MARK LANTZ REEP D38453

MARK LANTZ REEP was born on 11 Oct 1966. He married KELLEY SUZETTE HUGHES on 15 Feb 1992.

Children of MARK REEP and KELLEY HUGHES are:

1. CASEY ANN REEP, born on 24 Nov 1992.
2. JOHN PRESTON REEP, born on 19 Dec 1994.
3. JOANNA ELIZABETH REEP, born on 19 Aug 1997.

References: 6-Sarah Mae (Huss) Lantz

D384531 JOAN CAROL BUTLER D38453

JOAN CAROL BUTLER was born on 12 Oct 1957. She married ANTHONY PAUL UNDERWOOD on 27 May 1978 in Florence, Alabama.

Children of JOAN BUTLER and ANTHONY UNDERWOOD are:

1. ANDREW RYAN UNDERWOOD, born on 16 Dec 1992.
2. ELIZABETH KAITLIN UNDERWOOD, born on 13 Jan 1996.
3. CAROLINE MACKENZIE UNDERWOOD, born on 13 Jan 1996.

References: 6-Sarah Mae (Huss) Lantz

D384532 DAVID BRUCE BUTLER D38453

DAVID BRUCE BUTLER was born on 27 Apr 1960. He married SHANNA THORSON.

Children of DAVID BUTLER and SHANNA THORSON are:

1. DILLON BLAKE BUTLER, born on 22 Mar 1993.
2. BETHANY NICOLE BUTLER, born on 15 Jul 1994.

References: 6-Sarah Mae (Huss) Lantz

D384541 KIMBERLY LEE LANTZ D38454

KIMBERLY LEE LANTZ was born on 24 Jun 1968 in Shelby, Cleveland Co., NC,

Cleveland Memorial Hospital. She married BRIAN WARD BOWERS on 23 Sep 1995 in Lincolnton, Lincoln Co., NC, son of GENE BOWERS and BARBARA WARD. He was born on 30 Apr 1968 in Soperton, Georgia.

Children of KIMBERLY LANTZ and BRIAN BOWERS are:

1. JACOB BRIAN BOWERS, born on 17 Nov 2000 in Durham, Durham Co., NC.
2. CALEB LEE BOWERS, born on 09 Sep 2002 in Durham, Durham Co., NC.
3. SAMUEL LANTZ BOWERS, born on 08 Aug 2007 in Durham, Durham Co., NC.

References: 6-Sarah Mae (Huss) Lantz

D411241 FRED W. CARPENTER D41124

FRED W. CARPENTER was born in 1908 in Ironton, Lincoln Co., NC. He married NELL E. in NC. She was born in 1909 in NC.

Child of FRED CARPENTER and NELL is:

1. FRED W. CARPENTER, born in 1927 in NC.

References: 31-Charlotte Mecklenburg Co NC H120

D426212 DAVID LEE BEATTY D42621

DAVID LEE BEATTY, Sr. was born on 27 Nov 1936 in Lincoln Co., NC. He married JANICE METTS on 28 May 1960. She was born on 20 Sep 1939.

Child of DAVID BEATTY and JANICE METTS is:

1. DAVID LEE BEATTY, Jr., born on 08 Aug 1963 in Ft. Bragg, Cumberland Co., NC.

References: 6-Sarah Mae (Huss) Lantz

D426221 ROBERT RUDISILL RHYNE D42622

ROBERT RUDISILL RHYNE, Jr. was born on 06 May 1937 in Lincoln Co., NC. He married LINDA RUTH CONRAD on 14 Sep 1960 in Hickory, Catawba Co., NC. She was born on 07 Mar 1941.

Children of ROBERT RHYNE and LINDA CONRAD are:

1. ROBERT RUDISILL RHYNE III, born on 26 May 1963 in Charlotte, Mecklenburg Co., NC.
2. KIMBERLY ANNETTE RHYNE, born on 27 Jul 1964 in Charlotte, Mecklenburg Co., NC.

References: 6-Sarah Mae (Huss) Lantz

D426231 JOHN MARTIN HAWN D42623

JOHN MARTIN HAWN was born on 14 Mar 1937 in Lincoln Co., NC. He married LETA LYNN KENDALL on 24 Jun 1961 in Charlotte, Mecklenburg Co., NC. She was born on 28 May 1939.

Child of JOHN HAWN and LETA KENDALL is:

1. MARK KENDALL HAWN, born on 08 Feb 1963 in Hendersonville, Henderson Co., NC.

References: 6-Sarah Mae (Huss) Lantz

D426241 JANICE BATTEY D42624

JANICE BATTEY married GARY WILLIAMS.

Child of JANICE BATTEY and GARY WILLIAMS is:

1. MELANIE WILLIAMS.

References: 6-Sarah Mae (Huss) Lantz

D426251 LARRY MARTIN FINGER D42625

LARRY MARTIN FINGER was born on 03 Oct 1941 in Lincoln Co., NC. He married (1) ANN TUNEY. He married (2) RAY FRANCES GILBERT in Apr 1959 in York, SC, daughter of AUSTIN GILBERT and NELLIE HOUSER. She was born on 03 Apr 1942.

Children of LARRY FINGER and RAY GILBERT are:

1. TIMOTHY PAUL FINGER, born on 06 Jan 1960 in Lincoln Co., NC. He married TINA LEONHARDT 1979.
2. RICHARD TODD FINGER, born on 15 May 1964 in Lincoln Co., NC.

References: 6-Sarah Mae (Huss) Lantz

D426252 JAMES ALFRED FINGER D42625

JAMES ALFRED FINGER was born 16 Aug 1943 in Lincoln Co., NC. He married (1) JUDY PARKER. He married (2) CATHY GRIGG 20 Dec 1964.

Children of JAMES FINGER and CATHY GRIGG are:

1. TOMMY FINGER, born 12 Mar 1965 in Shelby, Cleveland Co., NC. He married TREVIE GANTT 06 May 1989.
2. JASON MARTIN FINGER, born 19 Jul 1975 in Gastonia, Gaston Co., NC.

References: 6-Sarah Mae (Huss) Lantz

D426253 JERRY DANIEL FINGER D42625

JERRY DANIEL FINGER was born on 10 Aug 1945 in Lincoln Co., NC. He married (1) ANN MILLER. She was born on 24 Feb 1952. He married (2) SHARON STARR.

Children of JERRY FINGER and ANN MILLER are:

1. DARRICK FINGER, born on 28 Jul 1967 in Lincoln Co., NC.
2. TRACI FINGER, born on 09 Jun 1974 in Hickory, Catawba Co., NC.
3. CHRISTOPHER FINGER, born on 04 Feb 1977 in Hickory, Catawba Co., NC.

References: 6-Sarah Mae (Huss) Lantz

D426413 CHARLES EDWARD RUDISILL D42641

CHARLES EDWARD RUDISILL, Sr. was born on 20 Mar 1937 in Lincoln Co., NC. He married (1) Paulette Stroup Byrd. He married (2) SHIRLEY LAMBETH POLHILL on 17 Aug 1957 in Gaffney, Cherokee Co., SC, daughter of JOSEPH POLHILL and MARTHA LAMBETH. She was born on 30 Sep 1940.

Children of CHARLES RUDISILL and PAULETTE BYRD are:

1. DAVID RUDISILL, born on 18 Jan 1969.
2. PAUL RUDISILL, born on 04 Apr 1972.

Children of CHARLES RUDISILL and SHIRLEY POLHILL are:

3. JOEL WARREN RUDISILL, born on 04 May 1958 in Lincoln Co., NC.
4. JANET LEAH RUDISILL, born on 04 May 1959 in Lincoln Co., NC. She married TIMOTHY DEAN BARTLETT on 31 Jan 1982; born on 10 Oct 1954.
5. DEBRA DENISE RUDISILL, born on 28 Aug 1960 in Lincoln Co., NC. She married TIMOTHY DALE POPE on 14 Nov 1987; born on 15 Mar 1960.
6. CHARLES EDWARD RUDISILL, Jr., born on 10 Mar 1964.

References: 6-Sarah Mae (Huss) Lantz

D426414 CORA LEE RUDISILL D42641

CORA LEE RUDISILL was born on 30 May 1939 in Lexington, NC. She married (1) MAX G. JARVIS on 24 Sep 1961 in Lincoln Co., NC. He was born on 01 Feb 1938, and died 18 Mar 1975 in Hanover, MASS. She married (2) DAN HENRY GOOD on 24 May 1991. He was born on 08 Jan 1935 in McDowell Co., NC.

Children of CORA RUDISILL and MAX JARVIS are:

1. VERA LYNN JARVIS, born on 09 Nov 1962 in New Iberia, Iberia Co., LA. She married STEVEN TODD LANIER on 20 Apr 1985 in Lincoln Co., NC; born on 11 Mar 1963 in Lincoln Co., NC.

2. MELANIE SUE JARVIS, born on 06 Aug 1964 in Patuxent River, MD. She married MICHAEL ALFRED MARRIOTT on 23 Jul 1994 in Washington, D.C.; born on 22 Dec 1953.

References: 6-Sarah Mae (Huss) Lantz

D426415 JUDITH ANN RUDISILL D42641

JUDITH ANN RUDISILL was born on 05 Nov 1940 in Statesville, NC, and died 29 Dec 1998. She married KENNETH EDWARD HARRISON on 07 Nov 1958 in York, SC. He was born on 20 Mar 1937.

Children of JUDITH RUDISILL and KENNETH HARRISON are:

1. CYNTHIA ANNETTE HARRISON, born on 23 Mar 1961 in Newton, Catawba Co., NC.
2. KENNETH CHRISTOPHER HARRISON, born on 05 Dec 1962 in Lincoln Co., NC. He married SUSAN ANNETTE CARPENTER on 04 Jan 1992 in Denver, Lincoln Co., NC; born on 13 Oct 1965 in Iredell Co., NC.

References: 6-Sarah Mae (Huss) Lantz

D426421 THOMAS ALLAN RUDISILL D42642

THOMAS ALLAN RUDISILL was born on 20 Aug 1935 in Lincoln Co., NC. He married BARBARA ANN DAVES on 19 Dec 1954 in Burlington, NC. She was born on 31 Mar 1934.

Children of THOMAS RUDISILL and BARBARA DAVES are:

1. CAROL MARIE RUDISILL, born on 11 Nov 1955 in Ft. Hood, Bell Co., TX.
2. ALLAN DAVES RUDISILL, born on 13 Aug 1957 in Wilson, Wilson Co., NC.
3. SANDRA LYNN RUDISILL, born on 06 Jan 1959 in Wilson, Wilson Co., NC. She married (1) RODERICK STEWART GRIFFITH. She married (2) SCOTT EUGENE CROCKETT on 06 Jan 1979.

References: 6-Sarah Mae (Huss) Lantz

D426422 DORIS JEAN RUDISILL D42642

DORIS JEAN RUDISILL was born on 20 Aug 1938 in Lincoln Co., NC. She married CHARLES FRANK SIMRIL on 22 May 1960 in Lincoln Co., NC. He was born on 31 Jan 1934.

Children of DORIS RUDISILL and CHARLES SIMRIL are:

1. CARLA JO SIMRIL, born on 13 Mar 1961 in Charlotte, Mecklenburg Co., NC. She married DONALD WAYNE WREATH on 01 Sep 1984; born on 31 Dec 1962 in Orion, IL.
2. DAN MCLANE SIMRIL, born on 03 Jun 1963 in Charlotte, Mecklenburg Co., NC. He married KELLY ANN ROSSI; born on 01 Sep 1966 in Pequannock, NJ.

References: 6-Sarah Mae (Huss) Lantz

D426423 LINDA MARGARET RUDISILL D42642

LINDA MARGARET RUDISILL was born on 23 Feb 1947 in Lincoln Co., NC. She married STEVE MONROE PAIGE on 02 Jun 1968 in Lincoln Co., NC, son of C. PAIGE and POLLY CHILDERS. He was born on 19 Mar 1947 in Kannapolis, NC.

Children of LINDA RUDISILL and STEVE PAIGE are:

1. DOUGLAS PAIGE, born on 10 Sep 1971 in Hickory, Catawba Co., NC.
2. EMILY MARGARET PAIGE, born on 08 Aug 1976 in Hickory, Catawba Co., NC.

References: 6-Sarah Mae (Huss) Lantz

D426431 JOYCE ANN HALLMAN D42643

JOYCE ANN HALLMAN was born on 18 Mar 1942 in Gastonia, Gaston Co., NC. She married JOHN CLARENCE PLAXCO on 25 Jun 1960. He was born on 11 Sep 1938.

Child of JOYCE HALLMAN and JOHN PLAXCO is:

1. JOHN MARTIN PLAXCO, born on 06 Oct 1961 in Huntsville, Madison Co., AL.

References: 6-Sarah Mae (Huss) Lantz

D426441 HELEN EUGENIA HALLMAN D42644

HELEN EUGENIA HALLMAN was born on 23 Aug 1952 in Lincoln Co., NC. She married (1) ROBERT LEMUEL DYSON, Jr. She married (2) JOSEPH HALL AVERY on 02 Jun 1976.

Child of HELEN HALLMAN and ROBERT DYSON is:

1. ROBERT BRENT DYSON, born on 30 Jul 1972.

References: 6-Sarah Mae (Huss) Lantz

D426443 HAROLD HOOVER HALLMAN D42644

HAROLD HOOVER HALLMAN, Jr. was born on 14 Dec 1942. He married ANN NANCY K.

Children of HAROLD HALLMAN and ANN K are:

1. MELISA HALLMAN, born in 1973 in Wilmington, NC.
2. DAN LEVY HALLMAN, born in 1975 in Wilmington, NC.

References: 6-Sarah Mae (Huss) Lantz

D426451 ROBERT ANTHONY HALLMAN D42645

ROBERT ANTHONY HALLMAN, Jr. was born 25 Jul 1947 in Lincoln Co., NC, and died 14 Jul 1993. He married FREDA GRACE EAKER 24 Jun 1967 in Lincoln Co., NC. She was born 23 Dec 1947 in Lincoln Co., NC.

Children of ROBERT HALLMAN and FREDA EAKER are:

1. ROBERT ANTHONY HALLMAN III, born on 17 Jul 1969 in Charlotte, Mecklenburg Co., NC. He married DIANE LYNN EMANUELSON on 29 May 1994 in Boger City, Lincoln Co., NC.
2. AMY ELIZABETH HALLMAN, born on 29 May 1971 in Lincoln Co., NC. She married RODNEY WALTER GRAGG on 17 Oct 1993 in Lincoln Co., NC.

References: 6-Sarah Mae (Huss) Lantz

D426452 RICHARD EUREY HALLMAN D42645

RICHARD EUREY HALLMAN was born on 05 Apr 1954 in Lincoln Co., NC. He married LINDA MARIE MCLEOD on 10 Oct 1976 in Lincoln Co., NC. She was born on 08 May 1955 in Lincoln Co., NC.

Children of RICHARD HALLMAN and LINDA MCLEOD are:

1. RICHARD LEE HALLMAN, born on 07 Aug 1981 in Hickory, Catawba Co., NC.
2. KEITH RYAN HALLMAN, born on 22 May 1987 in Hickory, Catawba Co., NC.

References: 6-Sarah Mae (Huss) Lantz

D426511 BETTIE RAYE CARPENTER D42651

BETTIE RAYE CARPENTER was born on 18 Sep 1940 in Salisbury, Rowan Co., NC. She married JAMES EDWARD LYERLY on 22 Nov 1962 in Salisbury, Rowan Co., NC. He was born on 21 Feb 1939 in Salisbury, Rowan Co., NC.

Children of BETTIE CARPENTER and JAMES LYERLY are:

1. LAURA CAROLINE LYERLY, born on 15 Jun 1969 in Salisbury, Rowan Co., NC.
2. WILLIAM JOSEPH LYERLY, born on 29 Apr 1975 in Charlotte, Mecklenburg Co., NC.

References: 6-Sarah Mae (Huss) Lantz

D426521 SANDRA KAY CARPENTER D42652

SANDRA KAY CARPENTER was born on 16 Jul 1941 in Lincoln Co., NC. She married LARRY LEROY BAKER on 07 Jun 1959 in Catawba Co., NC. He was born on 05 May 1937.

Child of SANDRA CARPENTER and LARRY BAKER is:

1. JEFFREY HALLMAN BAKER, born on 13 Sep 1960 in Hickory, Catawba Co., NC.

References: 6-Sarah Mae (Huss) Lantz

D426841 LINDA SUE SMITH D42684

LINDA SUE SMITH was born on 01 Mar 1943 in Summerville, Dorchester Co., SC. She married MICHAEL HARLEY PATE on 05 Jun 1965 in Ridgeville, Dorchester Co., SC at Mount Tabor Methodist Church. He was born on 30 Jan 1943 in Summerville, Dorchester Co., SC.

Children of LINDA SMITH and MICHAEL PATE are:

1. KAREN MICHELLE PATE, born on 03 Sep 1966 in Summerville, Dorchester Co., SC. She married MICHAEL ANTHONY SCHWENDINGER on 30 Oct 1988 in Dorchester, SC Married in home of bride's parents; born on 30 Jan 1965 in Bellflower, CA.
2. LYNN SUZANNE PATE, born on 24 Sep 1968 in Summerville, Dorchester Co., SC. She married KENT MCCRAY JUDY on 18 May 1991 in Summerville, SC at Salem United Methodist Church; born on 06 Nov 1967 in Orangeburg, SC.

References: 6-Sarah Mae (Huss) Lantz

D426842 JAMES MCKINLEY SMITH D42684

JAMES MCKINLEY SMITH was born on 01 Jan 1945 in Summerville, Dorchester Co., SC. He married (1) DOROTHY MAXINE KNIGHT on 02 Feb 1963 in Ridgeville, Dorchester Co., SC. She was born on 07 Feb 1945. He married (2) CAREY KIGER on 14 May 1988.

Children of JAMES SMITH and DOROTHY KNIGHT are:

1. PENNY LEIGH SMITH, born on 11 Oct 1963 in Summerville, Dorchester Co., SC. She married MICHAEL PATRICK BUCKLEY on 25 Aug 1984 in Columbia, SC; born on 28 Aug 1962 in New York, NY.
2. MARY PATRICIA SMITH, born on 06 Sep 1964 in Summerville, Dorchester Co., SC. She married WILLIAM THOMAS MULLEN, Sr.; born on 27 Dec 1963 in Middleboro, MASS.

References: 6-Sarah Mae (Huss) Lantz

D426851 BETTY ANN SMITH D42685

BETTY ANN SMITH was born on 04 Jul 1946 in Charleston, Charleston Co., SC. She married ROBERT NATHAN HUGHES, Sr. on 23 Nov 1965 in Walterboro, SC. He was born on 24 Mar 1945 in Charleston, Charleston Co., SC.

Children of BETTY SMITH and ROBERT HUGHES are:

1. ROBERT NATHAN HUGHES, Jr. born on 10 Nov 1966 in Summerville, Dorchester Co., SC. He married MARTINA HUGO.

2. SHELLEY LYNN HUGHES, born on 14 Feb 1968 in Summerville, Dorchester Co., SC. She married BRYON GUIDRY on 27 Mar 1993.
3. ANNI MELLARD HUGHES, born on 18 Mar 1970 in Charleston, Charleston Co., SC. She married LEVI MARTIN on 26 Jul 1988.

References: 6-Sarah Mae (Huss) Lantz

D426854 JACK LUTHER SMITH D42685

JACK LUTHER SMITH, Sr. was born on 06 Feb 1954 in Summerville, Dorchester Co., SC. He married (1) MARY JEANETTE BUSCH on 16 Dec 1976. She died 25 Nov 1990 in Charleston, Charleston Co., SC. He married (2) JENNIFER MARIE BRAZIER 26 Jul 1988 in Monks Corner, SC. She was born on 27 Feb 1962.

Children of JACK SMITH and MARY BUSCH are:

1. JACK LUTHER SMITH, Jr., born on 02 Nov 1977 in Charleston, Charleston Co., SC.
2. JAMIE LEIGH SMITH, born on 08 Aug 1982 in Charleston, Charleston Co., SC.

Children of Jack Smith and Jennifer Brazier are:

3. JEREMY WAYNE SMITH, born on 28 Nov 1987 in Charleston, Charleston Co., SC; died 08 Dec 1987 in Lebanon, SC.
4. JERICA MARIE SMITH, born on 31 Oct 1988 in Charleston, Charleston Co., SC.
5. CRYSTAL MARGARET SMITH, born on 09 Jun 1990 in Charleston, Charleston Co., SC.

References: 6-Sarah Mae (Huss) Lantz

D426862 ANNE MARIE QUARTERMAN D42686

ANNE MARIE QUARTERMAN was born 30 Jul 1954 in Charleston, Charleston Co., SC. She married AUBREY ALLEN PATRICK 04 Oct 1974. He was born 19 Feb 1948 in St. George, SC.

Children of ANNE QUARTERMAN and AUBREY PATRICK are:

1. COURTNEY ANNE PATRICK, born 20 Oct 1983 in Charleston, Charleston Co., SC.
2. DANIEL ALLEN PATRICK, born 21 Dec 1988 in Charleston, Charleston Co., SC.

References: 6-Sarah Mae (Huss) Lantz

D426863 SHARON LYNN QUARTERMAN D426863

SHARON LYNN QUARTERMAN was born 16 Jul 1957 in Charleston, Charleston Co., SC. She married JAMES FREDERICK WALDROP. He was born 26 Nov 1955 in Charleston, Charleston Co., SC.

Children of SHARON QUARTERMAN and JAMES WALDROP are:

1. DAVID WALDROP, born 04 May 1988 in Charleston, Charleston Co., SC.
2. MADISON LYNN WALDROP, born 13 Mar 1994 in Mt. Pleasant, Charleston Co., SC.

References: 6-Sarah Mae (Huss) Lantz

D426864 VIRGINIA CLEO QUARTERMAN D42686

VIRGINIA CLEO QUARTERMAN was born on 29 Jul 1959 in Charleston, Charleston Co., SC. She married PERRY GENE PATRICK, Jr. on 25 Jun 1983 in Charleston, SC. He was born on 03 Sep 1958 in Charleston, Charleston Co., SC.

Children of VIRGINIA QUARTERMAN and PERRY PATRICK are:

1. RACHEL LYNN PATRICK, born on 20 Nov 1986 in Mt. Pleasant, Charleston Co., SC.
2. MEGAN ELIZABETH PATRICK, born on 15 May 1990 in Mt. Pleasant, Charleston Co., SC.
3. ASHLEY GRACE PATRICK, born on 19 Dec 1994 in Charleston, Charleston Co., SC.

References: 6-Sarah Mae (Huss) Lantz

D426871 SHIRLEY GEORGANN BEHIE D42687

SHIRLEY GEORGANN BEHIE was born on 11 Jul 1950 in Ridgeville, SC. She married JOHN DANIEL KEIGANS, Sr.. He was born on 17 Apr 1953.

Children of SHIRLEY BEHIE and JOHN KEIGANS are:

1. CARMEN RUTH KEIGANS, born on 24 Mar 1982 in Orangeburg, SC.
2. JOHN DANIEL KEIGANS, Jr., born on 11 Apr 1984 in Orangeburg, SC.

References: 6-Sarah Mae (Huss) Lantz

D426872 WILLIAM LEWIS BEHIE D42687

WILLIAM LEWIS BEHIE was born on 24 Mar 1954 in Ridgeville, SC. He married DEBORAH JEAN HILTON. She was born on 24 Oct 1953.

Children of WILLIAM BEHIE and DEBORAH HILTON are:

1. WILLIAM NATHANIEL BEHIE, born on 04 Apr 1973 in Dorchester, Dorchester Co., SC.
2. JAMES JOSEPH BEHIE, born on 14 Nov 1974 in Dorchester, Dorchester Co., SC.

References: 6-Sarah Mae (Huss) Lantz

D426873 ELIZABETH RUBY BEHIE D42687

ELIZABETH RUBY BEHIE was born 27 Nov 1957 in Harleyville, Dorchester Co., SC. She married JOSEPH DONALD ANDERSON 06 Aug 1983 in Harleyville, SC. He was born 01 Oct

1957 in Orangeburg, SC.

Children of ELIZABETH BEHIE and JOSEPH ANDERSON are:

1. KYLE WHITNEY ANDERSON, born on 05 Sep 1986 in Charlotte, Mecklenburg Co., NC.
2. ANDREW JOSEPH ANDERSON, born on 09 Feb 1988 in Charlotte, Mecklenburg Co., NC.

References: 6-Sarah Mae (Huss) Lantz

D426874 LINDA KAREN BEHIE D42687

LINDA KAREN BEHIE was born on 21 Jun 1961 in Harleyville, Dorchester Co., SC. She married SHANNON WAYNE MIXON on 06 Aug 1983 in Harleyville, SC. He was born on 21 Aug 1962.

Child of LINDA BEHIE and SHANNON MIXON is:

1. TROY WAYNE MIXON, born on 21 May 1986 in Harleyville, Dorchester Co., SC.

References: 6-Sarah Mae (Huss) Lantz

D426B11 HAROLD CARPENTER TURBYFILL D426B1

HAROLD CARPENTER TURBYFILL was born on 04 Oct 1941 in Kinston, Lenoir Co., NC. He married FRANCES SUSAN PENDER on 06 Aug 1966. She was born on 17 May 1944 in Durham, NC.

Child of HAROLD TURBYFILL and FRANCES PENDER is:

1. DAWN ALLISON TURBYFILL, born on 30 Jan 1971 in Morehead City, Cateret Co., NC.

References: 6-Sarah Mae (Huss) Lantz

D426B12 DONALD RAY TURBYFILL D426B1

DONALD RAY TURBYFILL was born on 19 Jan 1943 in Winston-Salem, Forsyth Co., NC. He married BARBARA LAWS HIBBERTS on 14 Feb 1970. She was born on 08 Feb 1942 in Kannapolis, NC.

Child of DONALD TURBYFILL and BARBARA HIBBERTS is:

1. BRETT MASON TURBYFILL, born on 19 May 1975 in Gastonia, Gaston Co., NC.

References: 6-Sarah Mae (Huss) Lantz

D426B13 BARBARA ANN TURBYFILL D426B1

BARBARA ANN TURBYFILL was born on 03 Dec 1950 in Burlington, Alamance Co., NC. She married (1) DENNIS JAMES WORKMAN on 22 Feb 1969. He was born on 21 Mar 1951. She married (2) WILLIAM C. BAKER on 04 Jun 1983. He was born on 06 Jan 1933 in Kinston, Lenoir Co., NC.

Children of BARBARA TURBYFILL and DENNIS WORKMAN are:

1. RONNIE WADE WORKMAN, born on 21 Sep 1969 in Burlington, Alamance Co., NC.
2. LAURA ANN WORKMAN, born on 26 May 1976 in Burlington, Alamance Co., NC.

References: 6-Sarah Mae (Huss) Lantz

D426B21 ROBERT GLENN CARPENTER D426B2

ROBERT GLENN CARPENTER, Sr. was born on 07 Jul 1945 in Lincoln Co., NC. He married SARAH EMILY POOLE on 04 May 1974 in Columbia, SC. She was born on 19 Nov 1949 in Anderson, SC.

Child of ROBERT CARPENTER and SARAH POOLE is:

1. ROBERT GLENN CARPENTER, Jr., born on 01 Apr 1977 in Columbia, Richland Co., SC.

References: 6-Sarah Mae (Huss) Lantz

D426B32 FRED HALLMAN CARPENTER D426B3

FRED HALLMAN CARPENTER, Jr. was born on 21 Dec 1954 in Lincoln Co., NC. He married SUSAN PATRICIA PAYSEUR on 19 Aug 1975, daughter of ROBERT PAYSEUR and MARTHA GATES. She was born on 28 Mar 1957.

Children of FRED CARPENTER and SUSAN PAYSEUR are:

1. CARRIE ALLISON CARPENTER, born on 13 Jun 1982 in Gastonia, Gaston Co., NC.
2. SADIE MARIE CARPENTER, born on 18 Aug 1985 in Gastonia, Gaston Co., NC.
3. JAMIE ALYSSA CARPENTER, born on 02 Mar 1989 in Gastonia, Gaston Co., NC.

References: 6-Sarah Mae (Huss) Lantz

D426D21 JAMES ROBERT EDWARDS D426D2

JAMES ROBERT EDWARDS, Jr. was born on 19 Dec 1953 in Wilmington, New Hanover Co., NC. He married REGINA LEIGH JACKSON on 18 Nov 1978 in Sanford, NC. She was born on 31 Mar 1957 in Roxboro, NC.

Children of JAMES EDWARDS and REGINA JACKSON are:

1. CYNTHIA JEANETTE EDWARDS, born on 27 Apr 1981 in Sanford, Lee Co., NC.
2. PRISCILLA ANNE EDWARDS, born on 28 Mar 1983 in Sanford, Lee Co., NC.

3. ROXANNE LEIGH EDWARDS, born on 27 Jul 1987 in Sanford, Lee Co., NC.
4. DIANNA LYNN EDWARDS, born on 27 Jul 1987 in Sanford, Lee Co., NC.

References: 6-Sarah Mae (Huss) Lantz

D426D22 CAROL ANN EDWARDS D426D2

CAROL ANN EDWARDS was born on 11 Sep 1955. She married (1) NORMAN E. WARD III. She married (2) EDWARD BRANTLEY BURNS.

Child of CAROL EDWARDS and NORMAN WARD is:

1. AMANDA GAIL WARD, born on 04 Sep 1982 in Stuttgart, Germany.

Children of CAROL EDWARDS and EDWARD BURNS are:

2. KELLY LELANI BURNS, born on 05 Dec 1985 in Honolulu, Hawaii.
3. PATRICK EDWARD BURNS, born on 01 Feb 1989 in Anniston, AL.

References: 6-Sarah Mae (Huss) Lantz

D426D23 FRANK BRYAN EDWARDS D426D2

FRANK BRYAN EDWARDS was born on 14 Sep 1956 in Wilmington, NC. He married MARIE KELLY on 03 Nov 1990 in Greenville, SC.

Child of FRANK EDWARDS and MARIE KELLY is:

1. KRISTA EDWARDS, born on 09 Nov 1992 in Greenville, SC.

References: 6-Sarah Mae (Huss) Lantz

D426E31 RANDALL DAVID AVRAM D426E3

RANDALL DAVID AVRAM, Sr. was born on 14 Jan 1958 in Ithaca, Tompkins Co., NY. He married AMY CRAFT on 06 Aug 1984 in Wilson, NC. She was born on 28 Oct 1959 in Saratoga, NC.

Children of RANDALL AVRAM and AMY CRAFT are:

1. RANDALL DAVID AVRAM, Jr., born on 09 Feb 1986 in Winston-Salem, Forsyth Co., NC.
2. ANDREW CRAFT AVRAM, born on 26 Oct 1988 in Raleigh, Wake Co., NC.

References: 6-Sarah Mae (Huss) Lantz

D426E32 MICHAEL ANDREW AVRAM D426E3

MICHAEL ANDREW AVRAM was born on 03 Apr 1960 in Bronxville, NY. He married SARAH TUFLI on 10 Aug 1987 in Blowing Rock, Watauga Co., NC. She was born on 26 Apr

1965 in Grand Rapids, Michigan.

Child of MICHAEL AVRAM and SARAH TUFLI is:

1. TUCKER LEIGHTON AVRAM, born on 21 Oct 1988.

References: 6-Sarah Mae (Huss) Lantz

D426F11 SHERYL ANN CASON D426F1

SHERYL ANN CASON was born on 04 Apr 1955 in Dallas, Dallas Co., TX. She married (1) MICHAEL DAVID MCDOWELL on 25 Jun 1977 in Dallas, Dallas Co., TX, son of ROBERT MCDOWELL and LOIS MARTIN. He was born on 21 Jul 1953 in Kennett, MO. She married (2) ROGER WAYNE GILLIAM on 21 Nov 1999 in Mesquite, Dallas Co., TX, son of FLOYD GILLIAM and IOLA NYE. He was born on 22 Nov 1948 in Rangeley, Rio Glanco Co., CO.

Children of SHERYL CASON and MICHAEL MCDOWELL are:

1. JOANNA LEIGH MCDOWELL, born on 12 Jan 1981 in Garland, Dallas Co., TX. She married STEVEN SCOTT DANIEL born on 14 Jun 2003 in Rockwall Co., TX.
2. STEPHEN MICHAEL MCDOWELL, born on 29 Jul 1985 in Dallas, Dallas Co., TX.
3. JAMES ROBERT MCDOWELL, born on 20 Jan 1987 in Dallas, Dallas Co., TX.
4. KATHLEEN SOPHIA MCDOWELL, born on 02 Mar 1990 in Dallas, Dallas Co., TX.

References: 6-Sarah Mae (Huss) Lantz

D426F12 DAVID GREGORY CASON D426F1

DAVID GREGORY CASON was born on 06 Feb 1957 in Dallas, Dallas Co., TX. He married DONNA ELAINE CARTER on 07 Aug 1982 in Dallas, Dallas Co., TX, daughter of CHARLES CARTER and PAT. She was born on 02 Nov 1960.

Children of DAVID CASON and DONNA CARTER are:

1. SAMUEL DAVID CASON, born on 24 Apr 1989 in Dallas, Dallas Co., TX.
2. TIMOTHY PAUL CASON, born on 12 Sep 1990 in Garland, Dallas Co., TX.

References: 6-Sarah Mae (Huss) Lantz

D426F21 TERRY GLEN MCCOMMAS D426F2

TERRY GLEN MCCOMMAS was born on 11 Dec 1954 in Bayou La Batre, Mobile Co., AL. He married (1) MARY MILLER. He married (2) DORCAS PETERS 1973.

Child of TERRY MCCOMMAS and MARY MILLER is:

1. TERRANCE NICHOLAS MCCOMMAS, born in Jan 1985.

Child of TERRY MCCOMMAS and DORCAS PETERS is:

2. JOSHUA LYNN MCCOMMAS, born on 10 Oct 1973.

References: 6-Sarah Mae (Huss) Lantz

D426F22 GARY LYNN MCCOMMAS D426F2

GARY LYNN MCCOMMAS was born on 14 Feb 1956 in Dallas, Dallas Co., TX. He married (1) SHERRY STURGER. He married (2) RITA ANN ROYSE on 22 Dec 1974. He married (3) DONNA THOMPSON in 1985.

Child of GARY MCCOMMAS and SHERRY STURGER is:

1. TAYLOR LYNN MCCOMMAS, born on 28 Feb 1994.

References: 6-Sarah Mae (Huss) Lantz

D426F23 SHERI KIM MCCOMMAS D426F2

SHERI KIM MCCOMMAS was born on 24 May 1957 in Dallas, Dallas Co., TX. She married (1) RONNY LEE CHAPMAN on 25 Jan 1974. He was born 24 Apr 1950. She married (2) EMMETT SIMPSON, Sr. in 1990.

Children of SHERI MCCOMMAS and RONNY CHAPMAN are:

1. CHRISTINA LYNN CHAPMAN, born on 12 Aug 1974. She married (1) ROBERT SPENCER. She married (2) MIKE NIELF after 1992.
2. RONNY LEE CHAPMAN, born on 20 Dec 1975.
3. BILLY JACK CHAPMAN, born on 30 Mar 1979. He married MISTY RENEAU.

Children of Sheri McCommas and Emmett Simpson are:

4. EMMETT SIMPSON, Jr., born on 18 Jan 1990.
5. JAMIE LEE SIMPSON, born on 13 Nov 1991.
6. AMY CHERIE SIMPSON, born on 13 Nov 1991.

References: 6-Sarah Mae (Huss) Lantz

D441711 MARTHA BOOKER HALLMAN D44171

MARTHA BOOKER HALLMAN was born on 03 May 1946 in Dallas, Dallas Co., TX. She married ROBERT COLE GRABLE on 29 Jun 1968 in Dallas, Dallas Co., TX. He was born on 21 Apr 1946 in San Antonia, Bexar Co., TX.

Children of MARTHA HALLMAN and ROBERT GRABLE are:

1. JEFFREY ROBERT GRABLE, born on 19 Jun 1971.
2. LAURA MARTHA GRABLE, born on 08 Jan 1974.

References: 6-Sarah Mae (Huss) Lantz

D441712 WILLA ANNE HALLMAN D44171

WILLA ANNE HALLMAN was born 18 Apr 1949 in Dallas, Dallas Co., TX. She married ROBERT KEYS FOWLER 09 Jun 1973 in Dallas, Dallas Co., TX. He was born 12 Nov 1944 in Oklahoma City, OK.

Children of WILLA HALLMAN and ROBERT FOWLER are:

1. LESLIE ANNE FOWLER
2. BRIAN LEE FOWLER, born on 05 Oct 1974.

References: 6-Sarah Mae (Huss) Lantz

D441713 SAMUEL JOHN HALLMAN D44171

SAMUEL JOHN HALLMAN was born on 08 Apr 1952 in Dallas, Dallas Co., TX. He married JUDY DIANA CLOUD on 24 Apr 1982 in Dallas, Dallas Co., TX. She was born on 14 Apr 1952 in Mesa, Maricopa, AZ.

Children of SAMUEL HALLMAN and JUDY CLOUD are:

1. MONTE TODD PACE, born on 21 Mar 1973.
2. JOHN ANDREW HALLMAN, born on 04 Aug 1986.

References: 6-Sarah Mae (Huss) Lantz

D441721 WILLIAM PRESTRIDGE HALLMAN D44172

WILLIAM PRESTRIDGE HALLMAN, Jr. was born on 05 Sep 1942 in Cleburne, Johnson Co., TX. He married NANCY LAW on 18 Nov 1978 in Albany, Throckmorton Co., TX. She was born on 05 May 1952 in Albany, Throckmorton Co., TX.

Children of WILLIAM HALLMAN and NANCY LAW are:

1. LEE CAROLINE HALLMAN, born on 22 Feb 1980.
2. WILLIAM PRESTRIDGE HALLMAN III, born on 20 Jan 1983.
3. MARY SUSANNE HALLMAN, born on 14 Jul 1985.

References: 6-Sarah Mae (Huss) Lantz

D441722 JAMES ERNEST HALLMAN D44172

JAMES ERNEST HALLMAN, Sr. was born on 18 Aug 1948 in Cleburne, Johnson Co., TX. He married KATHY BOLIN on 18 Dec 1971 in McKinney, Collin Co., TX.

Children of JAMES HALLMAN and KATHY BOLIN are:

1. KATHRYN RUTH HALLMAN, born on 27 Dec 1973.

2. JAMES ERNEST HALLMAN, Jr., born on 14 Dec 1977.
3. LAURA BETTY HALLMAN, born on 10 Mar 1990.

References: 6-Sarah Mae (Huss) Lantz

D441723 WILLA RUTH HALLMAN D44172

WILLA RUTH HALLMAN was born on 29 Apr 1954 in Cleburne, Johnson Co., TX. She married JAMES ROBERT SCOGIN, Sr. on 05 Mar 1978 in Cleburne, Johnson Co., TX. He was born on 28 Aug 1954 in Sweetwater, TX.

Children of WILLA HALLMAN and JAMES SCOGIN are:

1. JAMES ROBERT SCOGIN, Jr., born on 20 Apr 1982.
2. CARA NAN SCOGIN, born on 13 Dec 1985.

References: 6-Sarah Mae (Huss) Lantz

CHAPTER VI

E MAGDALENA LANTZ I

MAGDALENA LANTZ, born in Albany Twp., Berks Co., PA; died in Albany Twp., Berks Co, PA. To date no further information has been discovered and it is not certain whether or not that she was ever married or had any children.

References: 6-Sarah Mae (Huss) Lantz

REFERENCES

1. Michael Wuskrow. *Hutchinson Cemetery Altoona Pennsylvania.* (Altoona, PA: Michael Wuskrow 1978).
2. Waterman, Watkins & Co. *History of Bedford, Somerset and Fulton Counties Pennsylvania.* (Chicago, IL: Waterman, Watkins & Co. 1884).
3. J. Simpson Africa. *History of Huntingdon and Blair Counties Pennsylvania.* (Philadelphia, PA: Louis H. Everts 1883).
4. National Archives and Records Administration. *Civil War Service and Pension Records.* (Washington, DC).
5. Jacob W. Lantz. *The Lantz Family Record.* (Cedar Springs, VA: Jacob W. Lantz 1931).
6. Named descendant and/or researcher provided data and/or remarks.
7. J. F. Richard. *History of Franklin County Pennsylvania.* (City, ST: Pub Year).
8. Hoenstine Genealogical Rental Library. *Your Family Tree.* (Hollidaysburg, PA: Hoenstine Genealogical Rental Library 1969-1983).
9. Floyd G. Hoenstine. *Soldiers of Blair County Pennsylvania.* (Harrisburg, PA: The Telegraph Press 1940).
10. Ancestry.com. *1920 United States Federal Census* [database on-line]. (Provo, UT, USA: Ancestry.com Operations Inc, 2010). Images reproduced by FamilySearch.
11. Blair County Genealogical Society. *Blair County Tax records 1846.* (Altoona, PA: Blair County Genealogical Society 1981).
12. Blair County Genealogical Society, *The Stevens Mortuary Altoona, Pennsylvania.* (Altoona, PA: Blair County Genealogical Society 1983).
13. Altoona Tribune. *Newspaper Marriages and Deaths.* (Altoona, PA: Altoona Tribune).

14. Register and Recorder. *Blair County Marriage and Death Records.* (Hollidaysburg, PA).

15. Hollidaysburg Register. *Newspaper Marriages and Deaths.* (Hollidaysburg, PA: Hollidaysburg Register).

16. Altoona Mirror. *Newspaper Marriages and Deaths.* (Altoona, PA: Altoona Mirror).

17. Blair County Genealogical Society. *Zion Evangelical Lutheran Church Records Hollidaysburg Frankstown, PA 1824 – 1914.* (Altoona, PA: Blair County Genealogical Society 1985).

18. Blair County Genealogical Society. *Hickey – O'Neill Funeral Home Records Altoona, PA 1887 – 1911 from Funeral Home Records.* (Altoona, PA: Blair County Genealogical Society).

19. John T. Humphrey. *Pennsylvania Births Berks County 1710-1780.* (Washington, DC: Humphrey Publications 1997).

20. Ancestry.com. *1810 United States Federal Census* [database on-line]. (Provo, UT, USA: Ancestry.com Operations, Inc., 2010). Images reproduced by FamilySearch.

21. Ancestry.com. *1820 United States Federal Census* [database on-line]. (Provo, UT, USA: Ancestry.com Operations, Inc., 2010). Images reproduced by FamilySearch.

22. Ancestry.com. *1830 United States Federal Census* [database on-line]. (Provo, UT, USA: Ancestry.com Operations, Inc., 2010). Images reproduced by FamilySearch.

23. Ancestry.com. *1840 United States Federal Census* [database on-line]. (Provo, UT, USA: Ancestry.com Operations, Inc., 2010). Images reproduced by FamilySearch.

24. Ancestry.com. *1850 United States Federal Census* [database on-line]. (Provo, UT, USA: Ancestry.com Operations, Inc., 2009). Images reproduced by FamilySearch.

25. Ancestry.com. *1860 United States Federal Census* [database on-line]. (Provo, UT, USA: Ancestry.com Operations, Inc., 2009). Images reproduced by FamilySearch.

26. Ancestry.com. *1870 United States Federal Census* [database on-line]. (Provo, UT, USA: Ancestry.com Operations, Inc., 2009). Images reproduced by FamilySearch.

27. Ancestry.com and The Church of Jesus Christ of Latter-day Saints. *1880 United States Federal Census* [database on-line]. (Provo, UT, USA: Ancestry.com Operations Inc, 2010).

28. Ancestry.com. *1890 Veterans Schedules* [database on-line]. (Provo, UT, USA: Ancestry.com Operations Inc, 2005).

29. Ancestry.com. *1900 United States Federal Census* [database on-line]. (Provo, UT, USA: Ancestry.com Operations Inc, 2004).

30. Ancestry.com. *1910 United States Federal Census* [database on-line]. (Provo, UT, USA: Ancestry.com Operations Inc, 2006).

31. Familysearch.org. *International Genealogical Index/Ancestral File*. (Salt Lake, UT: Intellectual Reserve, Inc., 1999-2012).

32. Ancestry.com. *1930 United States Federal Census* [database on-line]. Provo, UT, USA: Ancestry.com Operations Inc, 2002.

33. Chas. B. Clark. *Clark's Directory of the City of Altoona, Pa., for the Year 1890.* (Altoona, PA: N. C. Barclay & Sons, Steam Power Press Printers, 1890).

34. Blair County Genealogical Society. *McFarland Funeral Home Hollidaysburg 1837-1932.* (Altoona, PA: Blair County Genealogical Society 1986).

35. Hugh F. Gingrich and Rachel W. Kreider. *Amish and Amish Mennonite Genealogies.* (Morgantown, PA: Masthof Press 2007).

36. Herbert C. Bell. *History of Northumberland County Pennsylvania.* (Chicago, Il: Brown, Runk & Co., Publishers 1891).

37. John T. Humphrey. *Pennsylvania Births Berks County 1781-1800.* (Washington, DC: Humphrey Publications 1998).

38. Ancestry.com. *1790 United States Federal Census* [database on-line]. (Provo, UT, USA: Ancestry.com Operations Inc, 2010). Images reproduced by FamilySearch.

39. Ancestry.com. *1800 United States Federal Census* [database on-line]. (Provo, UT, USA: Ancestry.com Operations Inc, 2010). Images reproduced by FamilySearch.

40. Ancestry.com. *1940 United States Federal Census* [database on-line]. (Provo, UT, USA: Ancestry.com Operations, Inc., 2012).

41. Ancestry.com. *U.S. Federal Census Mortality Schedules, 1850-1885* [database on-line]. (Provo, UT, USA: Ancestry.com Operations, Inc., 2010).

42. Register of Deeds. *Lincoln County Deeds.* (Lincolnton, NC).

43. Raymond C. Lantz. *Lantz-Crossley an Experience in Genealogy: Volume I, A-E, 2nd Edition* (Westminster, MD: Heritage Books, Inc. 2009).

44. Raymond C. Lantz. *Lantz-Crossley an Experience in Genealogy: Supplement I to Volumes I-IV, 2nd Edition* (Westminster, MD: Heritage Books, Inc. 2011).

45. Find A Grave, Inc. *Find A Grave.* (Databases. http://www.findagrave.com: 2012).

46. Vital Records. *Birth (B), Death (D) or Marriage (M) records.* Type record/name(s) or initials of individual(s)/file, certificate number or book and page/location of record office in which filed, or repository in which copy was found - e.g. archives.

47. John T. Humphrey. *Pennsylvania Births Lehigh County 1734-1800.* (Washington, DC: Humphrey Publications 1992).

48. John T. Humphrey. *Pennsylvania Births Carbon, Monroe, Schuylkill Counties*. (Washington, DC: Humphrey Publications 2006).

49. Morton Montgomery. *Biographies from Historical and Biographical Annals of Berks County Pennsylvania.* (Chicago, IL: Beers Publishing Company 1909).

50. Ancestry.com. *Iowa, State Census Collection, 1836-1925.* [database on-line]. (Provo, UT, USA: Ancestry.com Operations Inc, 2007).

51. Frederick S. Weiser. *Records of St. John's Evangelical Lutheran Church, Hagerstown, Washington County, Maryland 1770-1819.* Maryland German Church Records Vol. 13 (Westminster, MD: Historical Society of Carroll County 1999).

52. Dale Walton Morrow and Deborah Jensen Morrow. *Washington County, Maryland Marriages an Index: 1799-1860.* (Westminster, MD: Willow Bend Books 2000).

53. John L. Kistler. *Baptismal Records of Jerusalem Lutheran and Reformed Church Berks County, Pennsylvania.* Special Publications Number 23. (Arlington, VA: National Genealogical Society 1987).

54. H. Z. Williams & Bro: Homer Everett. *History of Sandusky County, Ohio.* (Cleveland, OH: H.Z. Williams & Bro. 1882).

55. Sarah E. Wilson. *Follmers in Pennsylvania Descendants of Hans Jakob Vollmar 1698-1762.* (Baltimore, MD: Gateway Press 1976).

56. Curtis Bynum. *Marriage Bonds of Tryon and Lincoln Counties, North Carolina.* (Baltimore, MD: Genealogical Publishing Company 1996).

57. Familysearch.org. *Illinois, Cook County Deaths, 1878-1922.* (https://familysearch.org/pal:/MM9.1.1/N7VK-NVG).

58. Familysearch.org. *Michigan, Deaths and Burials, 1800-1995.* (https://familysearch.org/pal:/MM9.1.1/FH57-SQ7).

59. Familysearch.org. *Michigan, Marriages, 1822-1995.* (https://familysearch.org/pal:/MM9.1.1/FCL2-91V).

60. Familysearch.org. *North Carolina, Estate Files, 1663-1979.* (https://familysearch.org/pal:/MM9.1.1/VH6X-TD5).

61. Russell D. and Corinne P. Earnest. *Papers for Birth Dayes: Guide to the Fraktur Artists and Scriveners* (East Berlin, Pa.: Russell D. Earnest Associates, 1997).

62. Familysearch.org. *Pennsylvania, Births and Christenings, 1709-1950.* (https://familysearch.org/pal:/MM9.1.1/V2N6-BQS).

63. Familysearch.org. *Texas, Marriages, 1966-2010.* (https://familysearch.org/pal:/MM9.1.1/VTGT-JHS).

64. Blair County Genealogical Society. *Altoona City Hall Birth Records 1886 – 1905.* (Altoona, PA: Blair County Genealogical Society 1994).

65. Familysearch.org. *North Carolina, Marriages, 1759-1979.* (https://familysearch.org/pal:/MM9.1.1/F832-VY5).

66. Biographical Publishing Company. *Book of Biographies. This Volume Contains Biographical Sketches of Leading Citizens of the Seventh Congressional District Pennsylvania.* (Buffalo, NY & Chicago, IL: Biographical Publishing Company, 1899)

67. J. L. Floyd & Co. *Genealogical and Biographical Annals of Northumberland County Pennsylvania.* (Chicago, IL: J. L. Floyd & Co., 1911)

68. Familysearch.org. *North Carolina, Birth Index, 1800-2000.* (https://familysearch.org/pal:/MM9.1.1/VH5F-7HC)

www.ingramcontent.com/pod-product-compliance
Lightning Source LLC
Chambersburg PA
CBHW080224270326
41926CB00020B/4135